FOR THE COMMON GOOD?

FOR THE COMMON GOOD?

◆ ◆

American Civic Life and the Golden Age of Fraternity

JASON KAUFMAN

OXFORD

UNIVERSITY PRESS

2002

OXFORD
UNIVERSITY PRESS

Oxford   New York
Auckland   Bangkok   Buenos Aires   Cape Town   Chennai
Dar es Salaam   Delhi   Hong Kong   Istanbul   Karachi   Kolkata
Kuala Lumpur   Madrid   Melbourne   Mexico City   Mumbai   Nairobi
São Paulo   Shanghai   Singapore   Taipei   Tokyo   Toronto

and an associated company in Berlin

Copyright © 2002 by Oxford University Press, Inc.

Published by Oxford University Press, Inc.,
198 Madison Avenue, New York, New York 10016

www.oup.com

Oxford is a registered trademark of Oxford University Press

Library of Congress Cataloging-in-Publication Data
Kaufman, Jason Andrew, 1970–
For the common good? : American Civic life and the Golden age of fraternity / by
Jason Kaufman.
p. cm.
Includes bibliographical references and index.
ISBN 0-19-514857-6
1. Voluntarism—United States—History.   2. Pressure groups—United States—History.
3. Associations, institutions, etc.—United States—History.   I. Title.

HN49.V64 K375 2002
361.3'7'0973—dc21   2002020118

1 3 5 7 9 8 6 4 2

Printed in the United States of America
on acid-free paper

This book is fondly dedicated to my

MOTHER AND FATHER

and to the memory of

AAGE B. SORENSEN

a cherished friend and mentor

◆ ◆ ◆ ◆ ◆ ◆ ◆ ◆ ◆ ◆ ◆ ◆ ◆ ◆ ◆ ◆

ACKNOWLEDGMENTS

Two nights ago, I was talking with some local artists about things that used to be cool
and weren't anymore—things that we missed. . . . I told them that I missed "standing
alone"—the whole idea that "standing alone" was an okay thing to do in a democracy.
"Like *High Noon*," I explained, and one of them said, "Oh, you could do that today . . .
(pause for effect) . . . But first you'd have to form a Stand-Alone Support Group!"
Everyone laughed at this, and I did too, because she was probably right, but I didn't
laugh that hard, because, at the time, I was proofing this book, which constitutes my
own last, tiny fling at standing alone. —DAVE HICKEY, *Air Guitar*

Most scholars argue on behalf of one or another conception of society because
it jibes with some element of their personal experience. There is some truth to
this in my case—I am definitely not a "joiner," nor am I particularly fond of the
racial, ethnic, gender, and religious boundaries that divide our world today.
Nonetheless, despite my biases, this particular project stems almost wholly from
serendipity: As a confused and hapless doctoral student, I unwittingly happened
upon a panel discussion at the 1996 Social Science History Association conference that would change my life. Theda Skocpol and Robert Putnam were speaking about something called "American associationalism," and although I had
read Tocqueville as an undergraduate and toyed with various topics in American
political development as a graduate student, this particular subject was completely
foreign to me. Bowling alone? The golden age of fraternity? Why hadn't the history books ever mentioned this? Had there really been such an enormous proliferation of voluntary organizations in the United States between the Civil War
and World War I? Whatever for?

Eagerly sensing a topic worthy of dissertations galore, I leapt on the Tocqueville
debate as a fruitful place to put two competing theories of democracy to the test:
Putnam and Skocpol's endorsement of associationalism as a fount of collective
engagement versus my parents' insistence that voluntarism and political protest
were both big wastes of time. Fortuitously, Putnam and Skocpol both referred

in their talks to something called "city directories" as a miraculous source of information on the associational life of cities and towns in late nineteenth-century America. So, I started looking at some city directories, photocopying them in droves, and scribbling notes whenever an entry struck me as strange, surprising, or simply incomprehensible. Ethnic and religious groups were far more prevalent than I had ever imagined, for example. There were quasi-Masonic fraternal organizations of every shape, size, and character imaginable. And I was shocked to see how many nativist organizations and so-called independent militias had once existed in these United States.

Time and ambition being what they may, my dissertation only provided tentative answers to these many questions. I had unsuccessfully tried to divide my time between the study of associationalism in the postbellum United States and the relative homogeneity of municipal political institutions during that same period. At my dissertation defense, it became painfully clear that I had failed in both respects, and though my dissertation advisor suggested that the civil society angle was trendy claptrap, I immediately launched into the "civic" half of my project, leaving the other parts for later. No matter how much he might disagree with my choice of topic, I owe my former advisor at Princeton, Frank Dobbin, much gratitude, nonetheless; for it was he, and none other, who urged me, cajoled me, but never forced me to reconsider the rather postmodern epistemology I had adopted as a cocky undergraduate. Through his infinite patience and goodwill, Frank finally won me over to the side of empiricism. He taught me that careful methods, and even more careful logic, really do matter, if only because they raise the stakes of argument beyond mere hearsay. Although he may or may not approve of certain aspects of this work, I am eternally grateful for his many years of guidance, as well as his steadfast insistence that I make my own decisions and thus my own mistakes.

A whole host of other folks served admirably as cheerleaders, critics, colleagues, and friends along the way, including: Kenneth "Andy" Andrews, Irene Bloemraad, Walter Dean Burnham, Heather Caldwell, Bayliss Camp, Anne Carman, Naomi Cassirer, Mariko Chang, Mary Ann Clawson, Julian Dierkes, Paul DiMaggio, Gwen Dordick, John Evans, Claude Fischer, David Frank, Gerald Gamm, Marshall Ganz, Joe Gerteis, William Gienapp, John Giggie, Jeff Goodwin, Kristin Goss, Roger Gould, Liah Greenfeld, Hendrik Hartog, Kieran Healy, Miriam Jaffe, Stan Katz, Erin Kelly, Michele Lamont, Stan Lieberson, Peter Marsden, Doug McAdam, David Meyer, Cheri Minton, Ziad Munson, Susan Olzak, Orlando Patterson, Chick Perrow, Bob Putnam, Barbara Reskin, Dan Rodgers, William Rorabaugh, Libby Schweber, Richard Sennett, Theda Skocpol, Stephen Skowronek, John Skrentny, Neil Smelser, Aage Sørensen, Mette Sørensen, Paul Starr, Brian Steensland, John Stilgoe, Sid Tarrow, Stephan Thernstrom, Alexander Von Hoffman, Mary Waters, Bruce Western, Chris Winship, Diane Winston, Bob Wuthnow, Marty Whyte, Viviana Zelizer, and many, many others. John Skrentny, in particular, has been a great friend and mentor since my earliest days as an undergraduate. Dedi Felman was, and is, all the things a young writer could ever hope for in an editor. She has been kind, attentive, watchful, and wary in good measure, participating as a not-so-silent partner in the long and sometimes scary publishing process. She and all the staff at Oxford University Press, plus the half dozen or so readers who agreed to serve as outside referees, are all duly thanked for their generous support.

Along the way, I also had the good fortune to spend an entire summer working among (and playing much volleyball with) a cohort of young historians, geographers, political scientists, and sociologists convened at the Center for Advanced Study in the Behavior Sciences (CASBS) to discuss the finer points of contentious politics under the tutelage of Doug McAdam and Chuck Tilly. If I had to name one person to whom I am most indebted for help during every stage of this project, it would have to be Chuck Tilly. Big-hearted, sober-minded, wickedly insightful, and somehow never too busy for students (even visiting students from other doctoral programs), Chuck is a model for us all in the mensch department.

In addition, I have to thank the members of Chuck's Columbia–New School workshops on contentious politics; the Princeton Religion and Culture workshop and Wilson Society of Fellows; the graduate workshop on social movements, politics, and religion by the Harvard's Sociology Department; the Murray Research Center at the Radcliffe Institute for Advanced Study; and all the fine scholars at CASBS for hearing me out, questioning me at every turn, and pushing me in directions I had not previously considered. Faculty and students at the Universities of Washington and Minnesota, Yale, Cornell, and New York University also provided much-needed feedback at a critical stage, just before I began this manuscript in earnest. Katsch Belash, Evelina Fedorenko, Miriam Jaffe, Cheri Minton, Gian Pangaro, David Weintraub, and the members of my 1999–2000 Harvard junior tutorial on civil society and participatory democracy provided invaluable research assistance. Heather Caldwell served ably as my chief librarian and life partner, and if this book didn't already have three "dedicatees," it would be surely be dedicated to her.

Several sections of this book initially saw light of day as research articles in scholarly journals. I owe the editors and reviewers at the *American Journal of Sociology, Studies in American Political History, Voluntas, Journal of Interdisciplinary History,* and *Journal of Urban History (JUH)* great thanks for their commentary and advice, particularly Diane Davis, Ed Freedman, John Giggie, Roger Gould, Hank Johnston, Stephen Skowronek, and Diane Winston, each of whom lent me an ear as we wrangled mightily over matters of content and form. (Diane and John played an especially big role in getting this book off the ground by recruiting me to write an essay on the associational dimension of interdenominational competition in late nineteenth-century American cities for a special issue of *JUH* on religious identity and urban history.) I also owe great thanks to the National Science Foundation, the Center for Advanced Study in the Behavioral Sciences, the Mellon Foundation (for funding the 2000 summer institute at CASBS), the Woodrow Wilson Society of Fellows at Princeton University, the Sociology Departments at Harvard and Princeton, and Harvard's and Princeton's Faculties of Arts and Sciences for looking after me at various stages of the project, both socially and financially. If there is one form of (moderately exclusive) voluntary organization that I wholeheartedly endorse, it is the American research university.

Above all, I'd like to thank my mom and dad, whose endless hours of discussion, debate, and high-brow skepticism have always kept me questioning, thinking, speculating, and learning. This volume is thus devoted to returning the civil society debate to the place where it all begins: the family table.

CONTENTS

FOR THE COMMON GOOD?

INTRODUCTION

The Tocqueville Debate—What's at Stake?

Nothing is more annoying in the ordinary intercourse of life

than this irritable patriotism of the Americans.

—ALEXIS DE TOCQUEVILLE, Democracy in America

Isn't it ironic, Arthur M. Schlesinger once noted, that "a country famed for being individualistic should provide the world's greatest example of joiners?" Indeed, Americans formed and joined thousands of voluntary organizations in the late nineteenth and early twentieth centuries, thus creating a landscape of social and economic associations without precedent on our shores and, I cautiously assert, without equal anywhere in the world. By 1944, however, when Schlesinger wrote his now-famous "Biography of a Nation of Joiners," American associationalism was fast reaching its peak, initiating a long decline that numerous pundits and scholars have since come to lament as the end of an era of greatness in American history.[1]

So pronounced was the associational boom of the late nineteenth century that historians and social scientists sometimes refer to it as the golden age of fraternity, a term coined by W. S. Harwood in his 1897 *North American Review* article, "Secret Societies in America." Of course, most American secret societies were only "secret" in name—they proudly advertised their presence in parades and publications. So visible were they, in fact, that Harwood's actual description reads, "So *numerous,* so *powerful,* have these orders become that these closing years of the century might well be called the Golden Age of fraternity."[2]

That fraternities were "numerous" and "powerful" at the end of the nineteenth century is not worth disputing—they clearly were. The issue at stake here is what impact, if any, the fraternal boom might have had on the shape and character of American institutions and mores, as well as how and why the boom occurred in the first place.

Rather than engaging the new *civisme* from a presentist perspective, I have elected to tackle this problem at its roots, the period in American history most often cited by scholars as the exemplar of civic virtue in America—the late nineteenth and early twentieth centuries. Robert Putnam, Theda Skocpol, and David T. Beito, among others, have targeted the post–Civil War period as the locus of Americans' first meaningful experiment with voluntarism.[3] Says Putnam, for example, "During the years from 1870 to 1920 civic inventiveness reached a crescendo unmatched in American history, not merely in terms of numbers of clubs, but in the range and durability of the newly founded organizations," and "the foundation stone of twentieth-century civil society was set in place by the generation of 1870–1900."[4] Nonetheless, the question remains, How do we rectify Americans' impressive record as joiners and organizers with their reputation as rugged individualists?

Schlesinger himself tackled the individualism-voluntarism question by declaring, "To Americans individualism has meant, not the individual's independence on other individuals, but his and their *freedom from governmental restraint.*"[5] French sociologist Alexis de Tocqueville is commonly cited as the progenitor of this view, and indeed, he writes in *Democracy in America*, "The more government takes the place of associations, the more will individuals lose the idea of forming associations and need the government to come to their help. That is a vicious cycle of cause and effect."[6] Today, any number of pundits and scholars have followed Tocqueville's lead in decrying the destructive influence of state growth on America's once vibrant civic sector.[7]

Likewise, Tocqueville has been taken up by another group of scholars similarly concerned with the state of American *civisme*, though driven by somewhat different ideological currents. Led most notably by political scientist Robert Putnam, this group has taken to heart Tocqueville's assertion that "feelings and ideas are renewed, the heart enlarged, and the understanding developed only by the reciprocal action of men one upon another."[8] Neo-Tocquevillians like Putnam take associationalism to be a vital force in the creation of what he calls social capital, or "trust, norms, and networks that can improve the efficiency of society by facilitating coordinated action."[9] Though social capital might be seen to encompass many different aspects of social life, from voter participation to family cohesion to mental health, Putnam focuses on one particular variant of social capital—participation in voluntary organizations—as the key to the personal and political health of nations. Above and beyond the pluralist role associations play in articulating the wants and needs of specific groups in society, social capital theorists cite associationalism as a fount of civility, decency, and trust vital to the functioning of democratic societies. Or, as Tocqueville himself says, "If men are to remain civilized or to become civilized, the art of association must develop and improve among them at the same speed as equality of conditions spreads."[10]

In contrast, Tocqueville's contemporary James Madison is the intellectual founder of a rival intellectual tradition, the "associations as interest groups" school. Though both Tocqueville and Madison saw associationalism as a powerful obstacle to tyranny, they did so for very different reasons—Tocqueville because he viewed associations as extensions of the commonweal, Madison because he saw them as powerful instruments of self-seeking.[11] "The latent causes of faction are . . . sown in the nature of man; and we see them everywhere brought into different degrees of activity, according to the different circumstances of civil society," writes Madison in the *Federalist Papers*:

> A zeal for different opinions concerning religion, concerning government, and many other points, as well of speculation as of practice; an attachment to different leaders ambitiously contending for pre-eminence and power; or to persons of other descriptions who have been interesting to the human passions, have, in turn, *divided mankind into parties,* inflamed them with mutual animosity, and *rendered them much more disposed to vex and oppress each other than to co-operate for their common good.*[12]

Only by encouraging such factionalism, argues Madison, can any one faction be blocked from dominating society to deleterious effect.

Debate about the value of associationalism reflects a political quandary at least as old as democracy itself. In ancient Athens, a series of elite coups in the fifth century B.C.E. left the populace deeply suspicious of secret societies (*synomosiai*) and political clubs (*hetaireias*). Classical authors connect such clubs with bribery, electoral fraud, intimidation of juries and witnesses, and even homicide. Thucydides and Plato, among others, talk of *hetaeries* with fear, disdain, and regret. Nonetheless, participation in such clubs was popular among the Athenian upper classes, particularly as a "necessary and usual means of defense against the attacks of enemies."[13] Many statesmen in nineteenth-century Europe shared the Athenians' negative opinion of associationalism, indiscriminately banning clubs and associations for fear that they might lead to treason or conspiracy. In the contemporary United States, however, associations are often viewed in a more positive light. Communitarians, pluralists, and social capital theorists alike extol the social benefits of associationalism and lament its decline in recent decades. Rising crime rates, declining voter turnout, and the deterioration of the American social fabric have all been related to the decline in associational participation.[14] At the same time, others complain that large corporate philanthropies and advocacy groups have replaced fraternal orders and neighborhood associations as primary means of participation in civil society.[15]

In the midst of all this debate lurks one central question: Do people form associations because they aspire to community and cooperation or because they accept the challenges of intrasocial competition? Group membership is a valuable asset in both cases, though each has different implications for our understanding of humanity. Arthur M. Schlesinger (and Tocqueville before him) argues that individuals are more than capable of amicable social relations if government will only keep out of their way. Pluralists (and Madison before them) seem more dubious about associationalism's potential for building consensus. They advocate associational competition as an indirect means of obstructing the prospects of any single faction. In either case, one is left wondering why it is that Americans of yore founded so many various and sundry voluntary organizations and why their enthusiasm for associationalism has lingered in more recent years.

It is the aim of this book to demonstrate how Schlesinger's paradox—"that a country famed for being individualistic should provide the world's greatest example of joiners"—is not a question of national values or state structure or ideological faith. It is a question of historical development, a question most readily solved with a little deductive reasoning and a lot of historical research, none of which requires any a priori assumptions about government, association, or humanity sui generis.

Although Madison, Tocqueville, and their avatars focus much attention on the desired ends of voluntarism, they generally fail to consider what is unique about voluntary organizations as such, as well as the specific ways in which their organizational structure can affect political development over time. Sociology is a discipline uniquely suited to such questions, and it is thus my aim to reframe what was an age-old question in political philosophy—how best to manage diversity in democratic societies—as a new set of questions in the sociology of organizations: How did the organizational form of the secret society come to dominate American voluntarism in the nineteenth century, and what impact did it have on the social and political development of the American people in the years thereafter?

Madison and Tocqueville take group interests to be somehow primordial—things to be dealt with in the construction of an ideal republic—and they thus look to voluntarism as the single best means of assuring the representation of those interests in the public sphere. I argue, in contrast, that the creation of an organizational form based around secrecy and exclusivity—the fraternal order—helped give rise to, or at least shape the development of, those interests as such. Organization building became an end in itself during the golden age, in other words, and the struggle to create exclusive voluntary organizations prompted many disparate social groups to "find themselves" through organizing. Recruitment, retention, and rivalry promoted a system of social differentiation in America in which voluntarism, brotherhood, and mutual aid became bywords for segregation, not integration. If I am correct, and I muster dozens of charts, graphs, and primary sources in the hope of convincing you that I am, we will both soon believe that there is good cause to reconsider contemporary aspirations for civil society and civic reengagement. All voluntary organizations are not of a piece, and the competitive dynamics of widespread voluntarism can have quite unexpected effects, as you will soon see.

Consider, for example, what sociologists know about the social dynamics of organization building: Two necessities for any organization to survive, let alone flourish, are the presence of members and the availability of relevant resources. But because individuals have limited time, money, and energy, there is a natural limit to the number and diversity of organizations likely to flourish simultaneously. Sociologists refer to this as organizational ecology, or the way in which organizations interact with one another in competition for finite resources and opportunities.[16]

Naturally, exogenous factors like government endorsements, employer incentives, and raw population size may alter the supply and demand for organizational opportunities in a given social space. Net of such factors, however, organizational ecology has internal dynamics of its own. The scope and size of earlier organizations will have a powerful influence on the shape of later organizations, for example.[17] The way in which social spaces come to be filled by rival organizations will determine, furthermore, which organizations flourish and thrive or starve and vanish in that environment over time.[18]

In the case of American associationalism, for example, the religious orientation of many early to mid-nineteenth-century voluntary organizations tended to foster similar efforts among rival ethnoreligious groups. The Knights of Luther, a Protestant secret society formed in Des Moines, Iowa, in 1912, gave the following as their reason for forming: "Fighting the Romanist Church with weapons like those with which it fights."[19] Social clubs, secret societies, and charitable organizations were all organizational venues used by evangelists to entice newcomers to the fold. The fear that coreligionists might be tempted to convert led many congregations to create comparable organizations in the hope of retaining members. And the more success such groups had with a specific organizational form, the more likely it was to be imitated by others, thus spurring a period of competitive emulation, which helped catalyze the associational boom of the post–Civil War era.[20]

I refer to this phenomenon as "competitive voluntarism," a general social process whereby the number of voluntary, or nonprofit, organizations in a given society rapidly increases, thus fueling competition among them for members, money, institutional legitimacy, and political power. One unanticipated outcome of such a process is the increasing differentiation of society, largely because of these factors:

1. Recruitment practices tend to bring in new members who share the preferences, backgrounds, and social networks of existing members.
2. Participation tends to reinforce these similarities as members share information and social network ties over time.
3. Those members who do not fit in are more likely to quit the group than those who do, further reinforcing the selection pressures incumbent on the membership-attainment process.[21]

Thus, regardless of the aims and motivations of a group's founders, the membership of such groups will tend to become more and more homogeneous over time, a stark challenge to the argument that associationalism can help bridge gaps in the social fabric, joining disparate populations together in fellowship and solidarity.[22]

The primary thesis of this book is that the huge wave of organization building between the Civil War and World War I was motivated by the desire for exclusive social outlets that would allow individuals of different genders, races, ethnicities, and birthplaces to socialize in private, self-segregated groups. Some such organizations were explicitly designed to help their members acquire sickness and burial insurance. A few also served more instrumental ends, helping members coordinate group-related political activities. In concert and in competition, the presence of these groups gave rise to an associational boom that would shape American society for decades to come.

Explaining how, exactly, all this happened will be the task of the first third of this book. Here, I explain how demand for and the cost of affordable sickness and burial insurance increased in the decades after the Civil War. Because fraternal orders were generally exempt from government taxation and regulation, they proved particularly amenable to such pursuits. In addition, the fraternal organizational form lent itself to easy adoption, transformation, and imitation, thus making it an easily replicable form of social insurance agency. This led to the flowering of competitive voluntarism as described above. Though similar organizations existed in Europe during this period, Europeans were generally beginning to replace their guilds, lodges, and *compagnonnages* with trade unions and state-run social service collectives by the mid-nineteenth century, the very beginning of the associational boom in the United States. Thus, associationalism takes its place alongside other classical explanations of American exceptionalism—the absence of feudalism in the colonial United States,[23] sectional competition among the different regions of the country,[24] the weakness of America's federalist political system,[25] the strength of America's courts and parties,[26] the influence of America's wide-open spaces and unsettled frontier,[27] and the unusually middle-class outlook of the American people as a whole.[28] More specifically, *For The Common Good?* sheds new light on an old topic in the study of American political development—the causes and consequences of American voters' fragmentation along ethnic and religious, as opposed to strictly economic, lines.[29]

But why the desire to use associations as a means of self-segregation? Why, in other words, were so many fraternal orders and voluntary organizations segregated by race, religion, and gender? The answer, I believe, lies in the confluence of two factors: On the one hand, immigration helped fuel the desire for self-segregation among immigrants and native-born Americans alike. The period of America's associational boom was, not surprisingly, a period of enormous immigration to this country. During the late nineteenth and early twentieth centuries, many ethnonational and ethnoreligious groups fostered separatism by recruiting newcomers into sectarian voluntary organizations. At the same time, so-called native Americans—those born in the United States to parents of Anglo-Saxon lineage—formed similar groups of their own and expressly kept out blacks, Catholics, and Jews.[30]

On the other hand, the associational boom was fueled by a momentum all its own—competitive voluntarism. The emerging success of existing fraternal groups, coupled with their constant need to recruit new dues-paying members, spurred the formation of ever more fraternal organizations, thus creating a period of exponential growth that peaked around 1910. Given the ease with which such groups could be founded, furthermore, minor disagreements among members often resulted in the formation of yet more organizations. In the words of Arthur M. Schlesinger, "A process of splitting and splintering, or what sociologists like to call 'schismatic differentiation,' has marked the course of practically every sort of [American voluntary] association."[31] Although Catholics and Protestants sometimes tried to form fraternal organizations together, for example, religious differences were just as likely to drive them apart, resulting in the foundation of parallel organizations identical in all but name. Similar disputes arose over the participation of women in traditionally male organizations, blacks in white ones, Jews in Christian ones, and so on. Even minor matters of lodge ritual and policy could be grounds for schism. The 1900 Boston city directory lists at least 56 different fraternal and sororal organizations, for example, including 6 separate branches of the Odd Fellows—2 for blacks (1 integrated; 1 for blacks only), 2 for women, and 2 for white men.[32]

Sociologists refer to such groups as "high-exit organizations," meaning that it is relatively easy for members to quit and to form new organizations, as opposed to sticking around and resolving their differences.[33] The fact that American fraternal and voluntary organizations were so susceptible to imitation and duplication helps explain why the United States—one among many multiethnic, multiracial, and multireligious nations—has historically engendered more ethnic, racial, and religious separatism than most.[34] American associationalism exacerbated existing differences by enfranchising them in exclusive organizations. And by encouraging Americans to bond together along gender, ethnonational, and ethnoreligious lines, associationalism further disposed them to fear one another and thus to fear government itself—particularly any government program that might require the redistribution of income or collectivization of risk.[35] The result was a nation with a rather bizarre sense of self, one rooted not in the benefits of citizenry or in the value of inclusion but in libertarian paranoia and mutual distrust.

That so many pundits should herald this American tradition as a model for the future I find deeply troubling. At the expense of sounding dogmatic, I think the costs of the "golden age" greatly outweigh the benefits. Its most lasting legacies have been those very problems most lamented in America today: a long-standing tradition of racial prejudice and interethnic hostility; a pernicious political system dominated by special-interest groups; an ominous love for guns, accompanied by a menacing fear of government; a weak and subservient labor movement; and a half-hearted tradition of public social service provision, capped by the repeated failure to pass even the most rudimentary universal health insurance legislation.[36]

In documenting this argument, I rely on a number of different sources, most important among them the extensive collections of nineteenth-century city directories currently available on microfilm in research libraries throughout the country. These directories afford historical sociologists a unique opportunity in that they include comprehensive social, political, and economic information about American cities in a form that is easily concatenated both longitudinally and cross-sectionally.

My own work in this vein began with an investigation of voluntary organizations listed in the city directories of 53 major American cities as of 1880. By matching cross-sectional associational density with dependent variables such as voter participation and a raft of variables that reflect different domains of municipal social spending, I was able to show that cities with higher numbers of civic associations (per capita) neither spent less on municipal social services, such as poor relief and education, nor had significantly higher rates of voter turnout.[37] Associationally rich cities did, however, demonstrate interesting patterns whereby the presence of large aggregations of associations devoted to specific sectors of the economy were strongly correlated with higher municipal appropriations in exactly those same areas. Though such conclusions are based on statistical correlation and not observed fact, countless historical monographs have confirmed my hunch that many so-called civic associations of this era were actively engaged in the pursuit of segmental self-interest. Such self-seeking is not irreconcilable with neo-Tocquevillian and communitarian theories of associationalism, but my findings did at least convince me that there was a lot that had yet to be learned about this unique period in American history, the so-called golden age of fraternity.

Excited at the prospect of making a real contribution to a debate of contemporary significance, I soon planned two additional data-collection endeavors: a second, 1890, wave of city directory data to add to my 1880 span, and annual time-series data on a subset of these cities for the years 1880 through 1890. Having completed both of these tasks and published papers reporting the results, I then sought the help of several enterprising young students in collecting longitudinal data on four of these cities for the period 1850–1940 at 20-year intervals.[38] (See the appendix for a complete list of all city directories examined here.) As one last step, I personally recoded all the Boston city directories we collected in order to double-check our analyses and examine the trends in detail.[39]

At this point, armed with thousands of pages of photocopied microfilm and several preliminary hypotheses, I was finally ready to visit libraries and archives to satisfy my curiosity about several foundational questions:

1. What was the original impetus for founding fraternal organizations?
2. How and why did ethnic militias form in American cities in the nineteenth century?
3. What role did fraternal, benevolent, and commercial organizations play in the political life of American cities?
4. Was there notable variation in the way different ethnic, racial, and religious groups utilized the basic form of fraternal organizations?
5. How did associational practice vary in the United States and various western European countries during this period, and how might these differences help add to our knowledge of cross-national variation in political development?

Naturally, many historians and social scientists have already documented bits and pieces of these stories. The primary contribution of this book is, I believe, the attempt to synthesize so many disparate areas of historical scholarship into a single, somewhat counterintuitive account of a particularly important period in American history. Though it proved impossible to read everything or cite every source that contributed to my research, I sincerely hope that all the relevant parties recognize their contributions to my work and take its challenges as collegial invitations to further dialogue rather than adversarial snubs.

Undoubtedly, the thrust of my account of the golden age is biased toward the urban end of the spectrum, and following my initial hunches about these data, my subsequent analyses have tended to focus more on the mutual aid and self-help end of the associational web than the charitable and/or political ends explored in other accounts. Moreover, the American South does not receive the particular attention it deserves, especially the interesting rise of "colored" fraternal orders and militia groups in the Jim Crow era. There is a cost and a benefit to such choices: On the plus side, my purview brings new nooks and crannies of late nineteenth-century associationalism to light; on the minus side, there are discrepancies between my account and others' that reflect our individual biases more than the facts might merit.

Several caveats remain: First, the data at hand say much more about the number and type of associations listed in city directories than they do about the members. Though I was able to track down several sources of information on members, the bulk of data presented here reflects only the number of organizations, not the size or scope of their membership. Group mergers and membership growth are two sources of organizational change that we were unable to track with any accuracy, though they are clearly relevant to the topic at hand. Furthermore, this study pays far less attention to the various organizational hierarchies of American fraternal organizations than some specialists might want. In sorting through so much information on so many organizations, I chose to over-look the subtle distinctions among lodges, encampments, cantons, and other groups embedded in the hierarchies of these organizations. For my purposes, these distinctions were less important than the overall presence and number of organized entities.

Second, the bulk of my data is focused around a relatively short period of time, 1880–1900, though one firmly in the midst of the associational bubble. Because these data come from city directories and not archives or newspapers, they are probably also biased toward those organizations with the good standing and reputation to merit inclusion, thus relegating many lesser but equally impor-tant associations uncounted. Negro associations in Southern cities are probably the biggest lacuna in my data, though many underground political, labor, ethnic, and women's groups were probably overlooked as well.

In addition, few city directories of the period actually offer detailed informa-tion about the organizations listed. Club names are often ambiguous, mislead-ing, or downright indecipherable. (Misspellings are also common, particularly for clubs with non-English names; when presented with such dilemmas, I use the spelling given in the text rather than what I believe to be the proper one.) Many of the listings either say nothing about the organizations' primary func-tions, encompass an usually broad range of functions, or make potentially mis-leading claims about the functions of the group. A prime example of this last phenomenon is the frequent use of the term "benevolent society" to refer to groups that were actually mutual aid societies. When I consulted the 1880 and 1890 San Francisco directories, which give unusually detailed information about the goals of such organizations, I found descriptions like the following: "Nether-lands' Benevolent Association—Organized 1873. . . . Number of members twenty-six. . . . Object: Relief of its *members* in sickness, want, and distress."[40] What one might have taken as an ordinary eleemosynary organization was actually just a members-only insurance collective for people of Dutch ancestry.

With so many cases at hand, it was impossible to research the specifics of each organization. Such uncertainties are an inevitable shortcoming of quantitative history, one exacerbated by the high stakes such accounts have come to bear in current political debate. Fortunately, I found much valuable help along the way. Theda Skocpol and her assistants working on the Civic Engagement Project (CEP) were enormously helpful in clarifying questions, offering advice, and sharing with me the spectacular resources accumulated in their group office, just two floors down from mine. Several key associational encyclopedias and reference volumes also filled some gaps.[41] And most fortuitously, the 1880 and 1890 San Francisco city directories (just mentioned) proved a godsend, as they include detailed in-formation about the self-proclaimed "object" of many of the listed organizations. Using the San Francisco directories as a sort of dictionary of late nineteenth-century American organizational forms and titles, I was able to extrapolate much about the organizations listed in other cities' directories.

Suffice it so say, I read many thousands of entries, raised more questions than answers, and improved my vocabulary significantly as a result of this endeavor. If there is a lesson to be learned here, and I think there is a good one, it is that the application of simple quantitative methods to real historical data is not only instructive in plying statistical trends but also essential in uncovering nooks and crannies overlooked by historians (who tend to shy away from the systematic codification of such materials). Though most of the analysis presented here does not rely explicitly on the quantitative data over which I and several research assistants so assiduously labored, the basic exercise of reading and coding so many thousands of entries opened my eyes to nearly all of the avenues explored here. Whenever the opportunity exists, this is one of the best ways for sociologists to make distinctive contributions to the field of history. Although I do not suspect that you will agree with every observation or interpretation made here, I do stand by the methods by which they were derived. Extensive city directory collections exist in the holdings of most university and public libraries, and I invite you to look for yourself. City directories are a rich and regrettably underexploited source of information about America's past.

Part One

ASSOCIATIONAL GROWTH AND DECLINE, 1870–1920

This first section is intended as a general introduction to the golden age of fraternity. In chapter 1, I outline the basic parameters of the debate and offer a brief tour of American associationalism writ large. Chapter 2 delves more deeply into one of the primary, and oft overlooked, features underlying the associational boom—the drive to offer affordable life and health insurance to working families through fraternal lodges and mutual benefit societies. It also fleshes out some of the inherent weaknesses of the fraternal beneficiary system as such and relates them to the decline of associationalism after World War I. Chapter 3 then turns to a discussion of the sociocultural dynamics underlying this trend, namely, the impact of immigration, religious recruitment, racial and gender segregation, and ethnic separatism on American notions of collective identity in the late nineteenth and early twentieth centuries. The section that follows considers several popular variants of the fraternal organizational form—special-interest group lobbies, labor fraternities, and civilian military organizations—as well as their impact on American political development more generally.

RISE AND FALL OF A NATION OF JOINERS

On January 3, 1831, three leading citizens of Frankford, Pennsylvania, held a meeting to discuss the creation of the Oxford Provident Building Association, the first ever building and loan association established in the United States. Two of Oxford's founding members, Samuel Pilling and Jeremiah Horrocks, were prominent textile manufacturers in town, a small Philadelphia suburb of 2,000. And, having both emigrated from England, they (apparently) agreed on "the beneficial results which had been achieved by the English building societies in encouraging workingmen to save systematically."[1] Their partner, Henry Taylor, was also Anglo-American, a Frankford physician who, according to record, "had at heart the welfare of the working people among whom he had a large practice."[2]

Pilling, Horrocks, and Taylor aimed to create what we would now call a rotating credit association—a mutual, nonprofit bank that would help workers save money to build or buy homes. As planned, the association would sell shares in itself at the price of $5, plus a monthly payment of $3 that would entitle the bearer to bid for a loan of $500 (per share). It was also agreed that "the association shall continue until every member shall have opportunity of building or purchasing a dwelling house for each share of stock he may hold in the same, after which the balance of the treasury shall be equally divided among the members according to their respective shares."[3] Some pains were also taken to ensure that the operation would run smoothly: Fines would be issued for failure to pay monthly dues and for coming to meetings drunk, and all houses built with Oxford money would have to be no more than 5 miles from Frankford township.

On May 9, 1831, two Frenchmen, Alexis de Tocqueville and Gustave de Beaumont, touched ground in Newport, Rhode Island, their first stop on one of the most famous American tours ever, one that would indelibly stamp the United States as home to the world's greatest proliferation of civic associations. Describing his impressions of the new republic, Tocqueville confided, "I have come across several types of association in America of which, I confess, I had not previously the slightest conception, and I have often admired the extreme skill they show in proposing a common object for the exertions of very many and in inducing them voluntarily to pursue it."[4] Later, in an oft-quoted passage from *Democracy in America*, Tocqueville adds, "Better use has been made of association and this powerful instrument of action has been applied to more varied aims in America than anywhere else in the world."[5]

The Oxford Provident Building Association typifies exactly the type of civic association that so captivated Tocqueville—a voluntary, nonprofit group organized to pursue some common goal at the behest of its members. And somewhat ironically, the very same day Tocqueville and Beaumont arrived in Newport, the members of the Oxford Provident voted to approve a new membership statute: "Any person who shall hereafter wish to become a member of the association shall be proposed at a stated meeting by a member and balloted for and if a majority of the members present shall be in favor of his becoming a member he shall be admitted into the association."[6] In other words, the only way to join the Oxford Provident would henceforth be by assent of its members, based on whatever criteria they deemed fit. [7]

Such exclusivity would become a cornerstone of American associational practice over the next 100 years and beyond. As recently as the late 1980s, blacks, women, and Jews have protested their systematic exclusion from many of the nation's most reputed civic societies, including the Elks, Moose, Kiwanis, Rotary International, and Jaycees. Nonetheless, the associational right of exclusion has been defended time and time again by the American judiciary.[8] In one 1972 case, *Moose Lodge No. 107 v. Irvis*, the Supreme Court even defended a Harrisburg, Pennsylvania, lodge's right to deny service to the black guest of a white member, stating that the "Moose Lodge is a private club in the ordinary meaning of that term. It is a local chapter of a national fraternal organization having well-defined requirements for membership," one of which was that all members must be "male persons of the Caucasian or White race above the age of twenty-one years, and not married to someone of any other than the Caucasian or White race, who are of good moral character, physically and mentally normal, who shall profess a belief in a Supreme Being."[9]

Private clubs in the United States can discriminate against anyone, on any grounds, for any reason, as long as such discrimination does not interfere with the general right to public expression and/or pursuit of economic ends. Though Tocqueville left the United States infatuated with the glamour of its civic institutions, he scarcely noticed that self-segregation was one of their chief features. But as one member of the Elks professed during formal debates over repeal of their all-white membership requirement (in 1972), "It cannot be said, I think, that there is any [Elks] Lodge in the country where there are not at least three members who would blackball any non-white put up."[10]

American fraternal lodges and voluntary organizations have historically been segregated along lines of race, gender, religion, and ethnicity. Groups sometimes formed within specific occupations and classes, but for the most part class standing was less a basis for membership than a common aspiration of members.[11] Unfortunately, information about the members of specific clubs, their race, class, and ethnicity, is exceedingly difficult to come by. We turn later to analyses of the membership rolls of at least two prominent fraternal organizations—the Knights of Pythias and the International Order of Odd Fellows—but for now let it be recognized that many such organizations actually had criteria that explicitly prohibited members of certain groups from even seeking membership therein.

The following charts summarize the membership policies of all 56 fraternal organizations listed in the 1900 *Boston City Directory* (see Figures 1.1 and 1.2).[12] Each fraternal order is categorized according to its membership policies on race and gender and then multiplied by the number of lodges active in that order.[13] Religion and ethnicity were also important categories of associational identity at this time, though it is far more difficult to document this through the examination of membership policies alone. For now, suffice it to say that there were many, many voluntary organizations during this period (relative to other times and places) and that the majority of these groups helped to enfranchise "difference" along organizational lines. Obviously, such differences existed before the formation of the organizations in question; that such differences were exacerbated by them is the case I aim to make here.

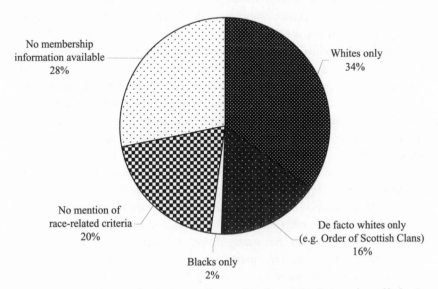

FIGURE 1.1 Race Segregation in Boston Fraternal Lodges, 1900 (by number of lodges)

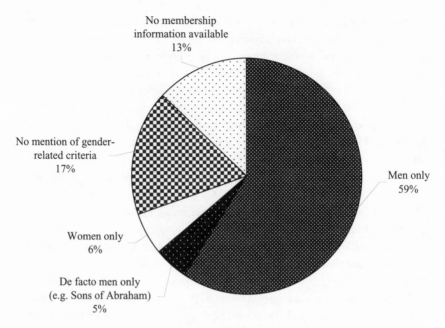

FIGURE 1.2 Sex Segregation in Boston Fraternal Lodges, 1900 (by number of lodges)

When Tocqueville returned to France, he began a long treatise on the differences in political climate between the United States and France, the inestimable two-volume *Democracy in America.* The respective leaders of both countries, Andrew Jackson and King Louis Philippe, were commonly thought of as "men of the people," though France was noticeably different than the country that Tocqueville had just visited.

One of the principal aims of the French Revolution had been freedom of association. The revolution's successor, Napoleon Bonaparte, clamped down hard on such freedoms, nonetheless, stating the insurrectionary power of association as his cause for action. By 1834, King Louis Philippe had further tightened the French *Loi sur les Associations,* closing an earlier loophole that had permitted groups smaller than 20 persons to associate freely. France did not amend its strict antiassociational laws until 1901.[14]

This was the norm throughout western Europe: "Virtually every European country placed severe restrictions on freedom of assembly and association during part or all of the 1815–1914 era," writes political scientist Robert J. Goldstein. With the exception of Great Britain, and later Belgium and Switzerland, most European nation-states viewed associationalism as an invitation to political insurrection, particularly during the stormy years around 1848, when revolutionary ferment swept most of the continent.[15] Thus, in order to pool their capital, nineteenth-century European workers generally relied on trade unions and state-run social service agencies instead of mutual savings groups and fraternal orders.[16]

In America, on the other hand, the civic sphere was just beginning to flourish around 1830. The United States Tocqueville saw was a nation in the throes of passion for voluntary organization. New evangelical Christian sects spread like wildfire across the mid-Atlantic states. At the same time, the first ever business corporations were forming to legally indemnify shareholders from debts and damages accrued in new canal- and railroad-building schemes. Even an anti-Masonic movement flourished for a time, mounting enough public support to front its own candidate in the presidential election of 1832.[17]

But this was only the beginning. In the years just before and after the Civil War, the American social landscape filled with voluntary organizations of every shape, size, and function imaginable. The city directories of the 1880s and 1890s are literally exploding with them: The Alibi Club of Washington, D.C.; the German Bakers' Singing Society of Paterson, New Jersey; even the Excelsior Lodge No. 3 of Deaf Mutes in Albany, New York.[18] To the best of my knowledge, no country in Western history has ever been so blessed (or cursed) by voluntary organizations of this size, scope, or diversity. One might call it a private, nonprofit organizational craze. (Figure 1.3 offers a quick glance at the growth of different types of nonprofit organizations listed in the Boston city directories, 1861–1940.[19])

For 30 or 40 years—roughly 1870–1910—up to half of all Americans participated in fraternal lodges, service clubs, and leisure organizations of one kind or another.[20] Wearing fancy uniforms was undoubtedly a big attraction, as was the

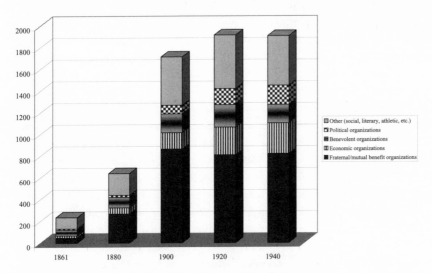

FIGURE 1.3 Associations by Function, Boston, 1861–1940

convenience of having cheap, well-organized clubhouses where only you and your buddies could fraternize. By the late nineteenth century, enthusiasm for "clubbing" was so great that journalist W. S. Harwood had to coin the term *jiners* as an archetypal, if not slightly hilarious, kind of American stereotype. Dolts, followers, and goodtime boys, jiners were "men found in every community who are more eager to be initiated into some new [fraternal] order than to be strengthened in business standing."[21]

For many jiners, drinking was a major feature of club life, and the lodge meeting could, by all accounts, turn into quite a raucous affair. One of the nation's oldest surviving fraternal organizations, the Benevolent Protective Order of Elks, was actually founded by "the Jolly Corks," a band of happy-go-lucky actors looking for a place to enjoy "refreshments" on Sundays. Though several apocryphal stories about the Corks' name survive, including one that refers to the fact that many of the original members worked in the theater (cork was commonly used to put on black face), an official biography of the Elks explains that the origin of the name actually derives from the fact that "when a party of them met at a saloon at any time, each one was required to place his cork upon the bar before ordering, and to *keep it there* until leaving; if he could not produce his cork he was 'fined' to 'buy the drink.'"[22] The Corks evolved into a full-blown fraternal order only when they began collecting donations for sick and unemployed members. Thus was born one of the nation's prototypical fraternal organizations—less a model of civic virtue than bacchanalian excess, though one rarely hears of this from contemporary advocates of fraternalism.

In fact, there was a major shift in American alcohol consumption patterns at just about the same moment that the associational bubble began to bloom. Over the period in question, historical statistics show that per capita consumption of beer rose from 3.5 gallons per person in 1865 to 20.2 gallons per person in 1915, with the largest single jump in consumption occurring between 1880 and 1885 (6.9 gallons to 11.4 gallons per capita). Calculating for the average absolute alcohol content of beer and spirits of various kinds, actual consumption of alcohol quadrupled between 1880 and 1915.[23]

There were many places to drink beside the fraternal lodge, of course, but few that could offer such privacy or social status. Furthermore, brewing companies were in the practice of subsidizing meeting halls located above saloons because, in the words of one observer, "Some [fraternities] hold lodge meetings above the saloon and after-meetings in the saloon below."[24] The lodge hall was, more or less, a private bar for friends and "brothers," a secret, special place, isolated from the chaos of modernity and the diversity of its new citizenry.

But, of course, not all jiners were so interested in alcohol. A good many detested it, in fact. For those of more sober persuasions, temperance fraternities, total abstinence societies, and moral reform clubs provided alternative fraternal opportunities centered exactly around their members' contempt for drink.[25] One mainstream fraternal order, the Knights of Pythias, even considered prohibiting bartenders, liquor dealers, and brewers from joining its ranks.[26] Thus, whether for or against, consumption of alcoholic beverages was undoubtedly central to the rise of American fraternalism.

It is hard to know what participation in the fraternals of the period was really like—they called themselves secret societies, after all[27]—but eyewitness accounts support several generalizations about temperate and intemperate lodges alike: Regardless of the means or motivation for associating, the normal course of events featured much fancy dress, elaborate ritual, and a modicum of self-governance. So bizarre (yet so predictable) was the club mania that Harwood quipped,

> It would all but revolutionize a large section of American Society if the wives and growing-up daughters of the households of the men who belong to these organizations should insist on their right to spend for their own adornment or their own personal pleasure dollar for dollar spent by husband or brother for dues and initiations, for regalia and uniforms and swords, for plumes and banners and banquets.[28]

Naturally, not all jiners joined for the regalia, the good times, or the fraternal bonding. Many civic associations were actually founded to serve highly instrumental purposes, such as lobbying for lower taxes, greater municipal appropriations, personally advantageous legislation, and so on. In fact, late nineteenth-century Americans left a lasting legacy of economic associations sorely underappreciated by scholars of the age (and pundits of our own).

Economic associations were voluntary organizations in the strict sense of the term, but they hardly served to advance communal interests, let alone "self-interest properly understood" (Tocqueville's rationale for the self-seeking motives behind every communal act).[29] The fraternal mode of organizing proved useful for those interested in money and power, as well as rites and rituals. Professional organizations helped give rise to modern monopolies of doctors, lawyers, pilots, pharmacists, podiatrists and so forth.[30] Employers' associations functioned like guilds for capitalists. Free to muster troops under the Second Amendment's militia clause, employers' associations built mercenary armies to crush the earliest flickers of trade unionism in this country.[31] Mercantile and commercial associations provided businessmen valuable private forums to share information, negotiate deals, lobby legislatures, and form illicit cartels.[32] I describe all of these quasi-fraternal organizations in detail in chapter 4.

On another front, the fraternal-club template was a driving idea behind the amazing spread of early American life insurance. Following the Civil War, American funeral directors made great strides toward the commodification of death. Fancy caskets and embalming of the deceased were commercial innovations of this period. Finding and paying for an appropriate, legal burial plot could also prove an increasingly difficult affair, particularly in the swollen cities of the age.[33]

Thus, nearly every fraternal society listed in the city directories of the late nineteenth century ran some form of burial insurance program for members. (A quick pass through any cemetery with burial plots circa 1870–1940 will bear me out. Often, entire sections of cemeteries are cordoned off for members of a particular fraternal order, burial society, or church guild.) Many fraternal organizations were founded expressly for this purpose, expanding into other avenues only after establishing a viable burial fund. After all, most fraternals were unregulated and tax-exempt, and they did sometimes grow large enough to embrace thousands of members, all comparative advantages in the market for risk management. On the other hand, fraternal insurance schemes were almost never professionally managed, and stories of fiscal collapse, corruption, and catastrophe fill the annals of American fraternal history, as you will soon see.[34]

Another stimulus to the rise of fraternalism was the increased demand for professional health care. Though historians often dispute the efficacy of most nineteenth-century innovations in medical practice, the rising perception that disease could be combated, if not prevented, through professional care that put new and increasingly costly demands on family budgets.[35] Enterprising physicians, usually not of the top caliber, began contracting out their services to fraternal orders on a capitation basis—the first American HMOs (health maintenance organizations), so to speak.[36] Like their avatars today, one persistent problem with fraternal health care was inconsistency of coverage. Women, the elderly, and those already sick were routinely excluded from lodge coverage, for example, and membership for eligible (i.e., young and healthy) men was limited to those who could afford the fees, as well as pass muster with enough existing members to gain admission.[37]

Not surprisingly, fraternals played a big hand in opposing the passage of national health care legislation in the early twentieth century. Their reasons were twofold: First, and most obviously, any new government program to provide health benefits to Americans would draw members away from fraternal benefit plans, if it did not do away with them altogether. Arguably, the proposed collectivization of health care also threatened another mainstay of American life: self-segregation. The fraternalization of American society split Americans into many ethnonational, racial, and religious boxes, and for all intents and purposes, it split their financial assets into these boxes as well. Collectivizing insurance dollars into state-run plans, then, would represent something that was inimical to the fraternal ideal: pooling resources without regard to race, creed, and gender, not to mention moral orientation.

Political scientists and sociologists often note that the specific way in which a polity is divided into distinct cleavages has important repercussions for its political development.[38] Understanding American political development thus requires careful consideration of the role voluntary organizations played in the construction of such cleavages. The case of religiously grounded associations deserves special consideration, for unlike race, gender, or birthplace, religious affiliation is one thing a person can escape, change, or adopt with relative ease. According to historian Timothy L. Smith, nineteenth-century American immigrants most commonly grouped themselves along ethnoreligious, as opposed to ethnonational, lines.[39] Tensions ran high among Protestants, Catholics, and Jews as a result of the immigrant boom of the postbellum period. Protestant missionary activity also increased at the time. State subsidies to faith-based relief organizations were also common, thus bringing interdenominational competition to bear in the realm of municipal politics, as well as actual social work. In response, the organizational trappings of religious communities became extremely important appendages of community life, erecting, as well as maintaining, boundaries between rival groups.[40]

Fraternalism also played a role in religious life through the advent of hybrid organizations such as congregationally oriented social clubs, sodalities, and ethnoreligious fraternal lodges. Because the rise of commercial culture and mass media provided ever new and titillating temptations for citizens of the late nineteenth century, churches and synagogues decided that one way to protect their constituents from these temptations was to offer rival diversions within the congregation. Two of the era's most prominent fraternities, the Knights of Columbus and B'nai B'rith, were founded expressly by and for Catholics and Jews, respectively. The many thousands of temperance and total abstinence societies of the period offered similar diversions for Protestants and Catholics. Individual churches and denominations also frequently established young men's and women's clubs, reading rooms, and fancy clubhouses for members. In the face of ever-escalating ethnoreligious competition, such organizations became crucial to community well-being, both as a fortification against rival groups and as a disincentive to membership defection. Though Catholics and Jews did not generally seek to proselytize members of other faiths, they still needed to guard against the efforts of Protestant missionaries who were trying to convert would-be congregants. A further problem was the persistent fear about the reputation of Catholic and Jewish people among the Protestant majority. Seeing to the needs of the Jewish and Catholic poor and needy thus became an exercise in image building, as well as in community maintenance.[41]

Over time, people in immigrant communities came to identify heavily with the predominant group identity, particularly in communities where there was a high concentration of coethnics and where members had little contact with those outside the community, or "ethnic niche." "These interactions make them feel that they belong to a group," writes sociologist Roger Waldinger. Furthermore, notes Waldinger, "If the niche is one of the salient traits that group members share," as it is when race, ethnicity, or religion become central criteria for participation in local voluntary organizations, "it also helps define who they are. As a result, members pay greater attention to the boundaries of the niche and the characteristics of those who can and cannot cross those boundaries. As the niche strengthens group identity, it sharpens the distinctions between insiders and outsiders."[42] Though residential and occupational segregation invariably play a part in this process, the seminal feature of the golden age was the role voluntary organizations played in inculcating a sense of difference among Americans of different backgrounds.

The emergence of so-called national identity groups, such as Italian Americans or Greek Americans, is an especially important (and often overlooked) feature of this process. Most European immigrants to America viewed themselves as (former) members of a given province, region, or town, rather than as citizens of a given country. As newcomers to America, many immigrants thus resisted the idea that they were part of some larger, national identity group. (Remember that many western European nation-states were still being born during this period, Germany and Italy among them.) Private mutual benefit societies for Walloons, Alsatians, Serbs, Slovaks, Swiss Germans, and Scots are just some of the ethno-regional groups prevalent in the city directories of the period.

Furthermore, common language was often not enough to cement bonds between immigrants from different regions. In the case of the Italian-American community, business leaders looked to create loyalty among Italian workers and consumers by creating overreaching, national fraternal and mutual benefit societies. They also received help from the new Italian national government, which sponsored voluntary organizations for Italian Americans in the hope of forging a single national identity among Italian migrant workers living abroad, as well as ensuring their eventual return to the motherland.[43] In this way, along with many others, competitive voluntarism contributed to the differentiation of the American public. Whole new social groups were founded and reinforced by the organizational boxes created to contain them.

But not all immigrant groups had the same experience with fraternal organizations. Chinese and Japanese immigrants practiced a distinctive form of voluntary organization during the golden age, for example. Though they eschewed the ritualistic aspects of Masonic-style fraternalism, Chinese and Japanese workers relied heavily on clan-based economic associations to provide jobs, markets, and credit to member-owned businesses. Arguably, such organizations were vital to the early success of Asian migrant communities in the western United States, though they were not without their own price, namely, rigid confirmity to clan-based codes of conduct. Refusal to play by clan rules could result in alienation, punishment, or even death. Thus, one can say that Chinese and Japanese Americans used a variant of the fraternal form as a bootstrap into the American economy, though this one-size-fits-all formula surely alienated many in their midst.[44]

Mexican Americans also seem to have had some success with mutualism, though the dynamics of competitive voluntarism are clearly evident in at least one account:

The emphasis on self-reliance caused the proliferation of Chicano fraternal orders and benefit organizations on a vast scale as hundreds of protective clubs appeared in *barrios* throughout the country. These associations offered a multitude of services to members and their families as well as to their communities, often competing with each other in the services offered as they strove for popularity in the Chicano community.[45]

African Americans, in contrast, had few if any successes with fraternalism. Blocked almost completely from joining white fraternal organizations, African Americans sporadically formed quasi-Masonic spinoffs for themselves. (As shown in Figure 1.1, 34% of the fraternal lodges listed in the 1900 Boston city directory formally excluded blacks from membership, and at least another 16% had de facto barriers to racial integration.) Prince Hall Masonry was one variant of fraternalism for middle-class black men, and Marcus Garvey's United Negro Improvement Association was another, though both organizations proved to be sources of division rather than unification within the African-American community as a whole.[46]

Black-owned mutual savings banks and loan collectives were another common form of black voluntarism, though very few took root and thrived. By the late 1920s, most had failed or been bought out by whites.[47] Arguably, even the thriving tradition of church-based associations failed African Americans in some respects: "Despite the grouping of most black Protestants into four or five major denominations, black church organizations were more splintered than their white counterparts; their individual churches more independent from one another; their sects and cults more short-lived."[48] As I argue time and time again in this volume, organizational proliferation can prove to be too much of a good thing in communities where unity, not division, is needed. Black fraternalism may have provided symbolic encouragement for members of the black community, but it also fomented controversy and mistrust that were counterproductive to the cause of black unity and political empowerment.

White women made up another group that was decidedly marginalized from the world of fraternalism. Some mainstream fraternal organizations, most notably the Masons and the Odd Fellows, created auxiliary orders for women, though they were strictly supervised by their male counterparts, and all female initiates had to be relatives of male members to qualify. According to historian Mary Ann Clawson, the Knights of Pythias, another prominent order, patently refused to recognize "their women's auxiliary, the Order of Pythian Sisters, as an official Pythian organization, until 1904, twenty-seven years after it was initially proposed."[49] It can be argued that organization in the face of such entrenched discrimination helped foster the spirit of resistance among American women of the late nineteenth century. Despite men's best efforts to deny them the privilege of membership, religious clubs, ancillary fraternal lodges, and relief societies provided valuable opportunities for women to organize by and for themselves.[50]

The majority of women's associations in this period were only vaguely political, however. The results of an 1899 survey of women's clubs and associations published in the *Bulletin of the Department of Labor* found, for example, that of the 1,283 clubs that responded, only 33% said that they carried out "practical" political or philanthropic work, and only 6% said that this work was their club's principal occupation.[51] But regardless of their purpose or motivation, such groups did form national membership federations, publish journals, send delegations to meetings, erect statutes and bylaws, and thus form the organizational backbone of the suffrage movement. Whether members actually pursued political goals or not, their participation in such groups may have helped disseminate information about the social goals and achievements of their counterparts in other parts of the country, thus bolstering civil society in the form of a transcontinental communications network.[52]

If there is one area of American fraternalism about which significant mystery still remains, it is the activities of the implicit majority—white, Protestant, native-born males. Besides the few openly nativist fraternities of the golden age, systematic exclusion based on race, gender, and creed generally kept a low profile. Bigotry sometimes took the high-brow form of hereditary societies, patriotic clubs, and fraternities for ancestors of the Pilgrims and such, but these groups most likely discriminated against their poor Protestant brethren, as well as Catholics, blacks, Asians, and Jews.[53] Extant rulebooks from several mainstream (i.e., nonsectarian) fraternal organizations indicate that membership was commonly closed to women and nonwhites (see figures 1.1 and 1.2), but it is exceedingly difficult to judge how open they were to white, male Catholics and Jews. It is possible that some of the larger fraternal organizations admitted ethnics but segregated them into distinct orders and lodges. City directories list lodges with names like Germania, Hermann, St. John's, and the like, indirect evidence that there may have been ethnic and religious segmentation within organizations. In general, however, it will take some doing to uncover the ethnic and religious diversity of specific lodges and orders of the period. This, I believe, is the next great task for historians of the golden age. Nonetheless, although most, but not all, of my argument rests on the assumption that non-WASP (white Anglo-Saxon Protestants) looked to the fraternal form as a means of social organization in response to systematic discrimination in American society, the case for minority self-segregation can stand just as well on its own. Whether organizational segregation stemmed from supply- or demand-side concerns seems rather beside the point (though it would be a valuable thing to know, if such distinctions can be made with any certainty).

The thesis of this book is actually quite simple: The fraternal model of self-organizing had a tremendous impact on the way in which Americans came to see (and act on) their political interests. Fraternalism taught Americans to seek financial services from private, rather than public, intermediaries. It taught them that self-segregation was acceptable, if not preferable to cooperation and collec-tivization. And it provided them with a venue for social and political action notable for its modest demands and ease of exit.

Political scientists often argue that political experience helps shape and frame the activities of competing interest groups; I differ only in pointing to a case in which experience outside the normal domain of politics actually constrained the way in which interest groups came to view themselves vis-à-vis the state. The American voluntarist tradition evolved before the American government ever got involved in domains such as social insurance or health care, for example, and the subsequent trajectory of American state growth bears its stamp to this day.[54]

I have adopted the metaphor of *competitive voluntarism* to clarify some of the mechanisms that lie behind the unusual proliferation of voluntary organiza-tions in the United States between the Civil War and World War I. Competitive voluntarism helps explain why the founding of a few mutual savings societies like the Oxford Provident gave rise to a full-blown associational boom. Suc-cess with mutualism in one community gave rise to similar experiments in others, and given the financial underpinning of most such endeavors, as well as the inexorable need to recruit and retain new members, American cities and towns soon found themselves filling with rival groups, particularly those in the fraternal or quasi-fraternal mode. This is not to say that all future organizational innovations will give rise to similar moments of competitive emulation, nor does it serve as some invariant means of predicting exactly where and how such pat-terns will evolve (and dissolve); it is merely a social scientific way of describing the mechanisms that underlie a complex but not uncommon social process that once dominated the American social scene. Given the primacy of assertions about American civil society in current political debates about democracy and mod-ernization in the late twentieth (and twenty-first) centuries, an accurate assess-ment of democracy and local governance in American history seems both timely and important. The civil society perspective is helpful in pointing out the role local grassroots organization might have played in fostering political participa-tion and community mindedness, but it also has the potential to obscure the intense social divisions that so often dwelled beneath their surface.

The foundations of the fraternal movement began seriously eroding when commercial insurers started actively competing with fraternities for the life in-surance business of America's less affluent citizens. Commercial underwriters had, until the early 1900s, neglected to see the immense profit that could be gained by selling inexpensive life insurance policies. Soon thereafter, they launched a full-out assault on America's working families, employing veritable armies of door-to-door salesmen trained in the latest "scientific" marketing techniques. Commercial health insurance cooperatives like Blue Cross and professionally run ethnoreligious hospitals (your St. Mary's and Mt. Sinai's) eventually began com-peting with fraternal health care programs as well. By the end of the Great Depression, even mutual banking cooperatives like the Oxford Provident became rare in all but the most agrarian communities. The mutuals were swept away by mergers, acquisitions, and foreclosures. Those organizations that were able to weather the mass defaults of the 1930s were only shells of their former selves.[55] This, too, is a known feature of competitive voluntarism: As a given social space becomes more and more saturated with similar organizations offering compa-rable benefits, demand for such opportunities begins to decline—thus, the ten-dency for boom-bust cycles in organization building, as well as a pronounced inclination for hybrid organizational forms to emerge along the way.[56] The rise of new financial intermediaries left the fraternals little ground to call their own.

But, arguably, the real end of American associationalism and the beginning of "bowling alone," if you will, was World War I, not the Great Depression or the Vietnam era. Mobilization for World War I was not nearly as intense as that for the Civil War or World War II, but it had important ideological implica-tions for the perceived meaning of American citizenship. Not only were many thousands of men from diverse backgrounds forced into the trenches to fight alongside one another, but also the pride and paranoia of wartime patriotism required ethnics to wear their patriotism on their sleeves. Reaffirming one's "Americanness" thus became a matter of paramount importance, as many Ger-man Americans realized in the face of increasingly shrill anti-German protests and disturbances. Almost immediately, one of America's largest, proudest, and most politically active ethnic groups began shedding the external trappings of its ethnic distinctiveness. German-language newspapers were closed, German-named voluntary organizations were renamed, and every effort was made to put an American face on what had previously been a solidly separatist commu-nity. Just after the war, furthermore, Congress virtually shut the doors on for-eign immigration. Lacking new replacements from abroad, the assimilation of America's white ethnic communities continued apace. Intermarriage, already prevalent, accelerated appreciably, and ethnonational social organizations, as well as foreign-language presses and schools, all began to wane as a final generation of foreign-born ethnics gave way to their native-born children.[57]

Only a sparse few remnants of the lodge system remain in place today. Active members in the nation's surviving fraternal orders are largely those men whose primary attachment to the lodge is the social comfort it offers—a small, rapidly dwindling, rather elderly subset of Americans, to say the least. In fact, a recent New York Times investigation of the subject implied that most current mem-bers' participation stems primarily from an attachment to old friends, cheap li-quor, and an exclusive environment, where one need never deal with strangers (read: blacks, women, Hispanics, liberals, youngsters, etc.). "The last few years the rule changed to say you have to allow blacks and women in the door," says Rod Palma, age 60, a member of the Mount Holly, New Jersey, Elks for 35 years. "It's all for the better," he adds, "but a lot of members don't see it that way. They'd rather have the lodge die with them than pass it on to the next generation with all these changes." Mr. Palma's wife adds that the lodge helped keep a lot of marriages together, because, she says, "I didn't have to worry that he [her husband] was off at some public bar where there were other women around." Mr. Palma sums up the lure of the lodge hall perfectly: "At the lodge, you're safe. You always know what to expect. No matter how much changes, you always have that little place you can turn to."[58]

One could argue that the golden age of fraternity lent American politics three characteristics that have overdetermined its political development in the years since: First, associationalism hindered the development of political organizations for American workers. The associational system drained American workers of the motivation to forge the kinds of coalitions necessary for lasting national political mobilization. And by recasting ordinary citizens as Catholics, whites, Germans, and so on, American associations heightened the various ethnic, religious, and racial lines that divide the country. Such is the story of the ill-fated Knights of Labor (discussed in chapter 6). What was once one of the nation's most viable opportunities for national working-class mobilization collapsed under a welter of rival interests and associational alternatives, a fine opportunity for coalition building lost to factional infighting and competitive voluntarism.

Another peculiarity of American politics is the American people's unusual tolerance for and love affair with guns. This, too, has its origins in American associationalism, as I argue in chapter 7. Until the early twentieth century, the U.S. national defense was built largely around civilian militias instead of a professional standing army. Following the War of 1812, even the compulsory state militias began a long, slow period of decline, giving way to a rash of private, "volunteer" militias, many of which were explicitly organized around ethnic and religious lines. Technically, these private militias served at the behest of their respective mayors and governors, though they could prove recalcitrant at times. Most served more beer than boot camp, furthermore, thus forcing the Union army to hastily reorganize at the outset of the Civil War. For the remainder of the century, federal officials looked to bolster the nation's military preparedness not by increasing the size of the professional army but by sponsoring private, voluntary organizations designed to foster military readiness among the male population at large. The National Rifle Association (NRA), founded in 1871, subsequently sponsored shooting competitions, gun clubs, and anything else that would encourage interest in marksmanship among the general American population. By the beginning of the twentieth century, just before the outbreak of World War I, the NRA, with federal assistance, actually started giving away firearms to civilians, as well as promoting the formation of gun clubs in high schools throughout the nation. By the time federal law enforcement officials thought to begin clamping down on gun ownership in the 1920s and 1930s, there were already far too many guns (and gun-loving voters) to do much about the situation. In this respect, nineteenth-century Americans' faith in civic, voluntary military organizations primed the pump for twentieth- and twenty-first-century America's nearly unstoppable demand for pistols, rifles, and automatic weapons.[59]

Related to these last two characteristics, is another of America's greatest or worst features (again, depending on your political preferences)—its extensive tradition of antistatism, or distrust of government institutions. Though some argue that this disposition dates as far back as the American Revolution, I believe that the most telling and crucial step in this political trajectory actually came in the decades after the Civil War, when, not coincidentally, Americans also made their greatest efforts in establishing voluntary, nonprofit organizations. Because postbellum fraternal social services were governed by Catholic Knights of America for Catholic Knights of America, Sons of Hermann for Sons of Hermann, Moose for Moose, and so on, prominent members of each group were hostile to the idea of turning such functions over to a government that represented all citizens, not just Catholics or Germans or Moose or Masons. Even nonsectarian fraternal lodges like the Odd Fellows had something to lose by granting government a role formerly dominated by their own "relief" organizations. Thus, when the opportunity came to consider collectivizing key social services under the government's umbrella, most Americans clung to the comforts of sectarianism and private self-insurance, as I describe in detail in chapter 8.

Surely, the founders of the Oxford Provident Building Association had no idea that what they were up to would have such an enormous impact on American political development. Nor did Tocqueville, though his sunny observations about American civic life have since fueled an entire political movement. Nonetheless, Tocqueville was right about one thing—for a good long spell, Americans really were enamoured with the practice of associationalism. The subsequent decline of American civic activism may not have been inevitable and it may be a genuine cause for concern, but I think it is important that we at least explore the belly of the beast before mounting it for a ride.

Before continuing, let me first reassert that my goal here is not to run down Tocqueville or to browbeat his avatars but to cast new light on the historical currency of their ideas. As the great William James once said,

> It always leads to a better understanding of a thing's significance to consider its exaggerations and perversions, its equivalents and substitutes and nearest relatives elsewhere. Not that we may thereby swamp the thing in the wholesale condemnation which we pass on its inferior congeners, but rather that we may by contrast ascertain the more precisely in what its merits consist, by learning at the same time to what particular dangers of corruption it may also be exposed.[60]

METHOD AND INQUIRY

Some Socioeconomic Factors

Underlying the Associational Boom

Several Common (Mis-)Conceptions of the Golden Age

Hindsight is not always so perfect, and contemporary studies of nineteenth-century American associationalism are no exception. Whether it be the need for community, relief from work and gender roles, or political empowerment, most of the leading explanations of the associational boom rely on untenable assumptions about the emotional equilibrium of the American people. Though convincing in the abstract, such explanations rely on post hoc imputations of individually aggregated sentiments, the justification for which is usually based on the claim that there is some connection between changing macrosocial conditions, such as industrialization, and the universal needs of individuals, such as the desire to maintain connection to the mores of a bygone era.

One such body of literature, that produced largely by historians, describes America's late nineteenth-century civic boom as a response to the rapid, and presumably disconcerting, social transformations of the era. Industrialization, urbanization, secularization, and the feminization of the household shocked antebellum Americans, it is argued, and fraternal-sororal organizations were a logical response—a "search for order" in the words of historian Robert Wiebe.[1] Although such psychosocial explanations are fruitful to the extent that they provide mechanisms with which to explain macrosocial change, sociologists generally reject such modes of explanation as fanciful extrapolation. Sociologist Arthur Stinchcombe argues, for example,

> Telling a just-so story about how individuals might possibly have been acting so as to produce the aggregate pattern does not improve the theory unless there are new predictions implied. If the individual-level theory is not solid enough so that the opposite results could have been predicted with a minor change (a change which might be true of individuals), for example, then the mechanism adds nothing but philosophical satisfaction. . . . In such

cases, rather than inventing fictional individuals who might have behaved so as to create the pattern, one is well advised to continue to work on the evidence that can be collected at the collective level.[2]

Though many social historians prefer to work in the psychosocial vein, their analyses achieve more in describing society as it views itself than they do in empirically explaining social change.

Depictions of the rise and fall of the American associational boom tend to stand on firmer ground where sociologists and political scientists have entered the fray, thus replacing psychosocial interpretation with bread-and-butter analysis. Nonetheless, conjecture and wishful thinking are as common here as in the domain of social history proper. Rather than portraying the associational boom as a response to latent social-psychological pressures, this school argues mightily for fraternalism's power as an expressive vehicle of pluralist politics. Adopting the Madisonian mode of analysis, scholars in this tradition focus on the role fraternal orders played in providing a template for political mobilization among farmers, workers, and women, all of whom had been denied access to the pernicious "courts and parties" system in the later nineteenth century.[3] The Populists, the Grangers, and the Knights of Labor epitomize such groups—grassroots movements that, in the end, failed to accomplish much for their members. Though such accounts attribute much significance to the rise of politically motivated, voluntary organizations in the late nineteenth-century United States, they generally focus on movements that failed to achieve their goals (like the Populists[4]), failed to clearly articulate their goals (like the Knights of Labor[5]), or succeeded in inflicting questionable policies on the nation at large (like the Women's Christian Temperance Union and its partners in the temperance movement[6]).

Pluralists and liberal social theorists consent to this adversarial portrayal of associations and counter that democracy hinges on the articulation of difference in just such ways.[7] In contrast, communitarians look to the golden age as an example of American cooperation at its finest. Scholars like David Beito and Marvin Olasky take to heart Tocqueville's observations of American associationalism and the "habits of the heart" it supposedly generates through "the reciprocal action of men upon one another."[8]

In sum, modern-day conservatives tend to treat associationalism as a response to modernization and an attempt to rediscover the republican ideals of the founding fathers, whereas liberals tend to describe late nineteenth-century associationalism as a light that failed, a once spirited attempt to democratize American politics by enfranchising the disenfranchised. Although neither perspective is wholly incorrect, neither should we take them at face value. It is my aim to leave the hindsighting aside and focus on the predominant factors underlying the rise and fall of American associationalism.

To do so, I must fulfill several obligations: First, the phenomenon under examination must be clearly and unambiguously described, thus making it clear what exactly we are trying to explain, as well as when and where we should expect to find it. Second I must offer an explanation of the phenomenon's rise that is unique to its time and place of origin. In the preceding chapters I have argued that it was the rising demand for affordable burial and sickness insurance that was primarily responsible for motivating the creation of the nation's many fraternal orders and mutual benefit societies. This, coupled with the internal dynamics of organizational competition and the increasing diversity of the American population, provided a catalyst for organization building that would continue through the early decades of the twentieth century. This explanation has the additional feature of positing causes that are analytically distinct from the phenomenon being explained; that is, they do not explain the rise of associationalism as a result of an increased desire to associate. The validity of this argument is bolstered, furthermore, by its ability to account for the decline, as well as the rise, of the associational movement. Though many fraternal organizations persisted after the rise of commercial life insurance, the cooptation of their primary reason for existence (i.e., providing low-cost life insurance to working families), coupled with the declining significance of ethnonational identity, spelled the beginning of the end for the fraternal tradition in the United States. Thus, we achieve a symmetry of sorts in explaining both the rise and fall of American associationalism.

A third criterion of explanation in comparative-historical sociology, the one that makes our job both so difficult and so stimulating, is the need to posit an explanatory framework that has cross-national validity. Whatever gave rise to the associational boom in the United States after the Civil War should be absent in countries that lack such traditions. Naturally, this aim is complicated by the fact that national developments do not occur in vacuums; innovations and events in one country at one time may (and often are) adopted by residents of other countries. Nonetheless, the pursuit of cross-nationally valid explanations offers a powerful tool in the search for root causes. Given the historical lag between American and western European development in the eighteenth and nineteenth centuries, early incarnations of associationalism in countries like France and England may provide clues about its diffusion in the United States.

In sum, I aim to satisfy four criteria in order to provide an epistemologically sound account of the golden age: First, I define the phenomenon's component parts—what makes it unique and how it can be differentiated from other, related phenomena. Second, I identify one spatiotemporally distinct set of causes that explain both the rise and fall of the phenomenon in question (and also account for its absence in other times and places). Third, I assess the salience of other possible explanations in light of my own. Fourth, I examine the generalizability of this argument by seeing how well it works in explaining similar trends in other times and places. This four-step process is, I believe, the only way to satisfactorily advance a reliable account of social change.

What Was American Associationalism All About?

Many macrohistorical debates devolve from one simple issue: the definition of the phenomenon in question. All too often, scholars disagree simply because they are not talking about the same thing, which then leads to confusion, evasion, and perpetual redefinition of the problem at hand. Sometimes this is a good, if not downright necessary, thing, especially in areas where the phenomenon in question lacks objective markers of its own—the true nature of the working class, for example, or the exact timing of the Industrial Revolution. I applaud such efforts, and indeed, much of this book is devoted to similar definitional issues, namely, the ideal–typical character of American associationalism in the face of contemporary disagreement.

Nonetheless, if this were the extent of historical scholarship, all we would have is a perpetually shifting hill of beans. Historians generally do a better, if no less enjoyable, job explaining social phenomena with clearly defined parameters, areas where they can put semantics aside and debate the root causes of social change, as well as the ramifications thereof. Slavery is a good example: Though the forms and functions of slavery have varied dramatically over space and time, it does have a concrete set of features that allow one to differentiate instances of slavery from those that are not. Wage laborers and domestic partners may sometimes feel as if they are bound in slavelike relationships, but their physical independence and lack of fungible property value clearly distinguishes them from slaves sui generis. Such distinctions may seem petty or inconsequential, but the creation of generalizable categories of difference is a vital tool in the pursuit of macrohistorical knowledge. Much detail is set aside in the process, but it is not lost, only recast in the light of larger differences.

This strategy of intentional overgeneralization draws directly on Max Weber's notion of ideal-types, or "generalized uniformities of empirical process." Weber's method is the gold standard of historical inquiry in the social sciences, "the causal explanation of some historically and culturally important phenomenon." Weber writes, "As in the case of every generalizing science, the abstract character of the concepts of sociology is responsible for the fact that, compared with actual historical reality, they are relatively lacking in fullness of concrete content. To compensate for this disadvantage, sociological analysis can offer a greater precision of concepts."[9] Such precision is one of the ways in which historical sociologists contribute to the study of history as such. Though generally less devoted to detail than professional historians, historical sociologists specialize in the arts of typification, causal interpretation, and the systematic investigation of social change.

In this particular case we are unusually fortunate because Weber not only outlined a method custom-tailored to our purposes but also was quite interested in American associationalism, a phenomenon to which, after traveling in the United States for several months, he devoted most of a scholarly article entitled "The Protestant Sects and the Spirit of Capitalism."[10] In 1904, Weber delivered his first public lecture in over 6 years before the Congress of Arts and Sciences at the Universal Exposition in St. Louis, Missouri. Though he lectured primarily on the social structure of contemporary Germany, it was America that seemed to hold Weber's attention throughout most of his trip. According to one biographer, Weber "was fascinated by the rush hour in lower Manhattan, which he liked to view from the middle of the Brooklyn Bridge as a panorama of mass transportation and noisy motion. The skyscrapers, which he saw as 'fortresses of capital,' reminded him of 'the old pictures of the towers in Bologna and Florence.'"[11] More trenchant are Weber's comments on the nature of American associationalism:

> If one paid some attention it was striking to observe . . . that surprisingly many men among the American middle classes (always outside of the quite modern metropolitan areas and the immigration centers) were wearing a little badge (of varying color) in the buttonhole, which reminded one very closely of the rosette of the French Legion of Honor.
>
> When asked what it meant, people regularly mentioned an association with a sometimes adventurous and fantastic name. And it became obvious that its significance and purpose consisted in the following: Almost always the association functioned as a burial insurance, besides offering greatly varied services. . . . Furthermore—and this is the main point in this instance—membership was again acquired through balloting after investigation and a determination of moral worth. And hence the badge in the buttonhole meant, "I am a gentleman patented after investigation and probation and guaranteed by my membership."[12]

Although one might approach Weber's observations about the geographical variance of associational activity with some caution—he had neither much data nor more than a few months' experience in America to back this up[13]—his comments about the economic nature of associational activity confirm my own sense of the ideal-type American association. Leaving questions of membership and geography aside, the prototypical association in the late nineteenth-century United States would have had the following features: (1) exclusive membership criteria, which required the assent of all (or at least most) existing members for admission of new entrants; (2) a formal organizational structure, which laid out meeting times and procedures, eligibility, dues, and rules and regulations, as well as fines and punishments for their violation; and (3) some not-for-profit levy scheme whereby members' monetary resources could be gathered for redistribution to other members in need (usually only under very carefully specified sets of circumstances). Certainly all associations did not fit these criteria—a second ideal-type of association, the political association, or party, is outlined shortly—but for now, my attention is turned to convincing you that Weber had it right about American lodge-based fraternities, inexperienced though he was in the American context.

The Rise of Fraternal Self-Insurance

Though it is commonly argued that fraternal life insurance was born in response to Christian doctrine forbidding "gambling" on human lives, a more parsimonious, and valid, explanation can be found in the changing economics of burial in the years just after the Civil War.[14] On the one hand, the requisites of "proper" burial were becoming ever more expensive; on the other hand, commercial insurance policies were not yet available to modest working families. Fraternal orders were a logical response to this new situation. Through formal, tax-exempt, voluntary organizations, the fraternal form presented a perfect apparatus for the collection and redistribution of death benefits.

Without going into too much detail on the history of the American funeral business, allow me to establish the (causally quite important) fact that the general cost of burial, and the scope of goods and services associated with it, increased dramatically in the years just after the Civil War. The enormous death toll of the war stimulated formation of a new industry, or rather several new industries, in the United States, from casket manufacturing to embalming and even the orchestration of funeral services. In the early 1870s, the Stein Manufacturing Company began to mass-produce caskets in Rochester, New York, and in 1876, it sponsored a lavish display at the Philadelphia Centennial Exhibition. Stein even financed publication of *The Casket*, a new trade journal devoted to the funeral service industry. "Funeral costs increased as much as 250 percent between 1880 and 1920," writes historian James J. Farrell.[15]

In the early 1880s, undertakers around the country began forming professional organizations (they also adopted the formal title of "funeral directors" at this time). According to Farrell, the National Funeral Directors' Association (NFDA) was founded in 1882 in response to the formation of the National Burial Case Association (NBCA), a coffin manufacturers' group determined to raise industry prices for caskets and coffins. In seeking a way to keep coffin prices down, funeral directors realized the benefits of "combination," or special-interest group organization (something I discuss in more detail in chapter 4). At the first NFDA convention, secretary S. R. Lippincott exclaimed, "We have met . . . to lay the cornerstone to a new structure to art and science . . . to unfurl our bright new banner to the breeze, and to plant our standard in the army of science."[16] Embalming was one such "scientific," and expensive, practice. By the 1880s, it also became common for funeral homes to offer floral bouquets and lavish ceremonies as part of burial. The day of the unadorned pine coffin and do-it-yourself wake were quickly coming to a close for all but the poorest Americans: "To a great extent, funeral directors created the demand for funeral homes because they would profit from their complete control of the corpse and ceremony."[17]

In turn, many Americans looked to the eighteenth-century tradition of English friendly societies for relief, adapting them to the American social climate by forging life insurance collectives with fraternal trappings. Developed in the late eighteenth century, English friendly societies melded mutual assurance with convivial lodge gatherings. They pooled members' capital in the form of regular dues, which were then stockpiled to pay sickness, burial, and/or unemployment insurance to members.[18] In retrospect, it is somewhat hard to differentiate British fraternal orders from British friendly societies since the two tended to converge on the same model by the early nineteenth century, but the fact remains that the growth of mutual benefit societies parallels that of industrialization in Britain, which itself precedes both industrialization and fraternalization in the United States by some 50 years.[19]

Many, if not most, American fraternal organizations were organized by, or at least modeled after, the English friendly society, and the connection thus bears mention in establishing a basis for understanding the American case (as well as establishing an ideal-type that is applicable in both cases). The first American fraternal beneficiary society was the Ancient Order of United Workmen (AOUW), founded in 1868 in Meadville, Pennsylvania. Benefits and expenses varied greatly from lodge to lodge—some even paid doctors an annual capitation fee for agreeing to attend to sick members—but all held the maintenance and protection of such funds as a primary reason for their existence.

The chief difference between the British and American mutual benefit systems lies in their timing, a feature that is centrally important in the following chapters. (A second feature is the general lack of ethnic, racial, or religious distinctions in the British system, another subject to which I shortly return.) The British mutual benefit movement peaked in the early nineteenth century, and by the 1880s it was on the decline, having been supplanted by the many benefit plans being offered by commercial firms, state agencies, and trade unions.[20] The American self-help movement, on the other hand, was just gaining steam during the 1880s and would continue to dominate the American market until at least 1910. As I discuss in detail later, this time differential had a huge impact on the diverging structure of American and British social policies: Whereas the British (and French and Germans) gradually replaced mutual benefit plans with state-run pension, sickness, and unemployment insurance plans, the Americans, enamoured with fraternalism, clung to the remnants of an increasingly lackluster system of private benefit provision. I explain this process in much greater detail in chapters 7 and 8, but for now, consider only the way in which the British system came to America and was adopted and expanded by working men (and sometimes women) across the country.

Freemasonry, once the domain of a select core of American elites, had long been a source of fascination, and sometimes contempt, for middle-class Americans, and by the mid-nineteenth century, following the violent anti-Masonic movement of the 1820s and 1830s, American Masonry was quickly transformed into a popular social organization for middle-class men. In Great Britain, Masonry had been a close cousin of the British friendly society system, and soon hybrid organizations, combining features of both, were enthusiastically adopted by Americans.[21] The editor of one fraternal compendium, Albert C. Stevens, concludes:

> The transplanted English friendly society finds congenial soil here, but is outnumbered by the assessment beneficiary fraternities, many of which admit both men and women [women were rarely extended the same insurance benefits as men]. The latter variety of the modern secret society has commercialized the mechanism of older fraternities by carrying on a system of coöperative insurance in brotherhoods designed, in some instances, to advance social or political objects, total abstinence, coöperative buying and selling, the cultivation of patriotism, the protection of the interests of labor, and the propagation of partisan political views. On the whole, it has encouraged the development of practical coöperation more, perhaps, than any other one influence.[22]

Though other fraternal organizations predate the AOUW in America, it was the first to offer low-cost life (or burial, as it was then called) insurance, and this innovation single-handedly ignited the fraternal movement in this country. By 1890, according to historian Morton Keller, more life insurance was held in the United States than in the entire British Empire, and soon thereafter American life insurance holdings surpassed the aggregate total of the entire world. It remains a (largely unanswered) mystery why Americans became so infatuated with the life insurance enterprise—the absence of publicly supervised, antiquarian burial grounds may have been a significant factor—but it does seem clear at least that the rise of American fraternalism was intimately related to the desire to find new means of providing working families with affordable sickness and burial insurance.[23]

It should be noted, however, that the average death benefit offered by most American fraternal orders greatly exceeded the cost of even a fairly showy funeral service. According to sociologist Mary Ann Clawson, the AOUW paid the families of deceased members $2,000, whereas the average annual income of a moderately skilled worker was a mere $500. Thus, it would appear that members were truly seeking the equivalent of modern-day life insurance, as opposed to simple burial insurance, the distinction being that the former is generally designed to pay out a benefit large enough to support the benefactor's family in comfort for several years or more.[24]

Arguably, the desire for such policies was also related to the growth of wage labor in the American economy at about that same time (though not for psychosocial reasons, like the declining social status of artisans and workers). Industrialization increased workers' reliance on cash income and also increased the immediate dangers incumbent upon them. Under the edict of "contributory negligence," late nineteenth-century courts rarely, if ever, held employers liable for even the most egregious industrial accidents, a factor that must have contributed to workers' fears for their families in the event of untimely death. Crippling injury or death could strike a worker on the job at any moment, and many presumably turned to fraternal benefit policies as an early form of protection for their families.[25]

How Prevalent Were Fraternal Benefit Plans?

In his 1897 account, "Secret Societies in America," W. S. Harwood makes the following estimate of fraternal participation in the United States:

> The membership of the secret fraternal orders of the United States in the month of December, 1896, was, in round numbers, 5,400,000. Taking the adult male population of the nation at the present time to be nineteen millions, and allowing that some men belong to more than one order, it will be seen that, broadly speaking, every fifth, or possibly every eighth, man you meet is identified with some fraternal organization.[26]

It is exceedingly difficult to confirm Harwood's figures. Though fraternal records indicate how many members were active in an order at a given time, they do not allow us to know how many members were active in all the orders or how many participants actually held memberships in more than one order at a time.

My own best effort to estimate average participation in American mutual benefit plans are based on *Langley's San Francisco Directory for 1890*, which is a unique source of information about American associationalism in that it offers fairly comprehensive descriptions of the societies and associations listed, including membership tallies in many cases.[27] Even *Langley's* requires some guesswork, however. Forty-eight fraternal and/or mutual benefit societies listed give the exact size of each participating lodge. This amounts to some 14,300 members in all, primarily white men of at least 18 years of age, with actual lodge sizes ranging from 18 to 850 members.[28] Two additional organizations reveal the size of their membership in the city as a whole but give no specific figures for each lodge: The Ancient Order of United Workmen had 18,000 members distributed across 252 lodges, and the Knights of Honor had 4,300 members in 58 separate lodges, which gives estimated average lodge sizes of 71.4 and 74.1 members, respectively. However, another 68 fraternal and/or mutual benefit societies (and their 430 affiliated lodges, councils, parlors, groves, and encampments) give no information whatsoever about their membership size. Given the similarity of my two previous estimates, plus one independent estimate, we might thus use the figure of 73 members per lodge to estimate how many members belonged to these 430 affiliated lodges.[29]

Multiplying 73 times the total number of unenumerated lodges listed in *Langley's San Francisco Directory for 1890* gives a figure of 31,390 additional members, which when combined with those that do provide membership information (36,600 members) gives a net total of 67,990 members in all. Given that the total population of San Francisco for the year 1890 was 298,997 (according to census figures[30]), this estimate shows that about 23% of the city population participated in mutual benefit societies of one form or another—a figure remarkably close to the 20% participation rate given by Harwood.[31]

But first, we need to account for several additional factors that might influence our final estimate. Several monographs on fraternal benefit plans assert that it was common for participants to carry policies in more than one such society at a time.[32] If we assume an average of 1.5 memberships per policyholder, we need to reduce our original membership estimate to approximately 45,327 distinct individuals who are holding at least 1 mutual benefit policy (67,990 total policies divided by 1.5). Furthermore, since life insurance was purchased largely to protect families in the event of death of the wage earner, we might use the 1890 census estimate of the total number of eligible families instead of the city population as a whole. There were 52,535 families reported in San Francisco for this year, which would imply that 86% percent of all families in the city held some type of mutual benefit insurance policy. On the other hand, this figure fails to account for those policyholders who were single, widowed, divorced, estranged, or merely childless.

Another, more conservative estimate would use the number of white males of voting age (21 years and older) in the city at that time: 93,759 by the census estimates, which would give a membership rate of about 48% among this category of eligible candidates. Alternatively, if we keep this denominator but assume that the average person held not 1.5 but 2 policies (or 33,995 policies in all), our final estimate comes to 36% of the adult, white, male population holding at least 1 such policy.[33]

Unfortunately, these are only wild guesses of the actual prevalence of such policies, and they fail to account for the fact that participation in fraternal orders and mutual benefit societies was generally higher in small towns and villages than in big cities like San Francisco.[34] Interurban differences are also likely, as we shall soon see. Presumably, participation rates would have varied with the age, gender, race, and ethnicity of the population in question. And as I show in chapter 8, the average lodge size in at least one prominent fraternal order, the

International Order of Odd Fellows, changed over time, increasing from about 70 members per lodge in 1890 to a peak of approximately 113 members per lodge in 1920. Nonetheless, although none of these estimates is as precise as one would like, they do seem to indicate that participation in fraternities and mutual benefit societies was quite widespread, somewhere between one-fifth and one-half of the adult, white, male population.

When Did the Fraternal Boom Begin and End?

Whereas *Langley's San Francisco Directory* affords the opportunity to estimate overall membership levels in that city's fraternal orders and mutual benefit societies circa 1890, we are not nearly so lucky in other places and times. I was able to measure the number of lodges and mutual benefit societies per capita in each city over a long period of time, but the actual size of each lodge remains somewhat of a mystery (see above). Nonetheless, we can use city directory listings of various types of voluntary organizations to estimate organizational density over a decent span of time.

Relying on city directory information from a more or less random sample of American cities and small towns, Gerald Gamm and Robert Putnam have estimated that the organizational density of fraternal orders began a rapid period of growth around 1880 and reached its peak between 1900 and 1910, after which it began a long decline (through at least 1940, when their data series ends).[35] My own sample of medium-sized cities produces more or less comparable results. As seen in the following figures, illustrating results from four such cities—Boston, Milwaukee, New Orleans, and San Francisco—the raw number of organizations in 1860 was quite small in each case and grew in the decades thereafter (see figures 2.1–2.4).[36] New Orleans displays the most pronounced rise and fall, peaking in 1920, only to fall back again. Fraternal lodges in Boston and San Francisco appear to grow in number between 1860 and 1900 and then remain at about the same levels thereafter. Milwaukee displays a similar trend, except that the density of fraternal lodges peaks earlier there, in 1880, and only rises again between 1930 and 1940, after 50 years of decline. It is not immediately clear why these disparities exist, though it is a question well worth further inquiry. Moreover, although the overall number of lodges stays about the same as a percentage of population in three of the four sample cities, it is hard to know whether average lodge sizes remained constant. At least three qualitative accounts of fraternalism in the 1920s and 1930s indicate that many lodges soldiered on in the face of dwindling membership.[37] Most of the remaining organizations abandoned the idea of providing sickness and death benefits, however, because members were increasingly turning to commercial insurers to purchase such services (again, see chapter 8). In response, many fraternal orders folded, merged, or started aggressive campaigns to revamp their public image.

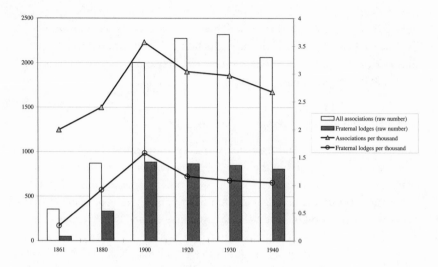

FIGURE 2.1 Associational Growth in Boston, 1861–1940

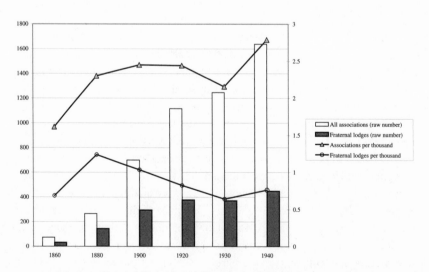

FIGURE 2.2 Associational Growth in Milwaukee, 1860–1940

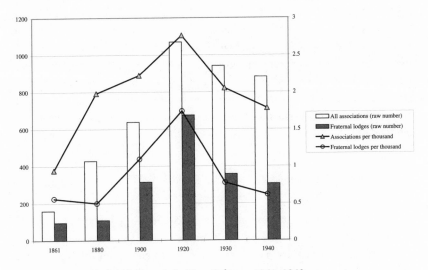

FIGURE 2.3 Associational Growth in New Orleans, 1861–1940

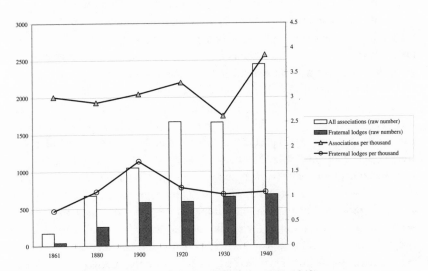

FIGURE 2.4 Associational Growth in San Francisco, 1861–1940

45

Yet another issue that this and other studies tend to overlook is the question of organizational founding rates. In all likelihood, many voluntary organizations failed to survive more than a few years, though their members may well have gone on to found new organizations in their stead. If this is true, as I believe it is, there is good cause to reassess the nostalgic view of the golden age as one of earnest stability built on dedication to specific community organizations. As I argue repeatedly in the pages to come, the world of late nineteenth- and early twentieth-century American voluntarism appears to have been far more competitive and chaotic than previously imagined.[38]

What Explains Fraternalism's Unique Appeal to Late Nineteenth-Century Americans?

As I have argued and supported with evidence regarding the social origins of American fraternalism in the English friendly society movement, the primary lure of nineteenth-century fraternalism appears to have been the fact that fraternities offered low- and middle-income families access to much-needed financial security currently unavailable by other means. But why, then, all the rites and rituals?

Once again, some historians have proffered that the quasi-religious atmosphere of fraternal practice stemmed from workers' desire to escape the psychosocial pressures of work and family. I, for one, find Max Weber's explanation far more convincing: Fraternal groups made good business sense for working- and middle-class men. Not only did they provide an affordable source of life insurance for members; lodge meetings could be an important source of business contacts. Lodge affiliation helped ensure the credit worthiness of members. Rites and rituals were not only amusing and fun but also provided an organizational structure that certified members' loyalty and bonded individuals to the organization in such a way as to solidify their financial commitment to the group.

The late Georg Simmel addressed this issue specifically in his work on the sociological functions of secrecy: "The first internal relation typical of the secret society is the reciprocal *confidence* [*Vertrauen*] among its members," writes Simmel. "It is required to a particularly great extent, because the purpose of secrecy is, above all, *protection*."[39] Simmel's description of the latent functions of secrecy conforms perfectly with the social conditions under which the fraternals operated—shaky, rather uncertain fiduciary arrangements in which members have little recourse but to trust one another in the adequate contribution, supervision, and distribution of their collective monies. The trappings of secrecy and ritual helped reinforce group solidarity, trust, and confidence: "The striking feature in the treatment of [secret] ritual is not only the rigor of its observance but, above all, the anxiousness with which it is guarded as a secret."[40] The vow of secrecy thus served as an intrinsic promise to pay one's dues faithfully and to execute the fiscal affairs of the order in an upright, honest fashion. This does not mean that such promises were always kept, but it does help make sense of the fraternalists' intense devotion to ritual secrecy.

Still one might ask, Why fraternal organizations and not some other form of social insurance? If there were inherent drawbacks to the financial structure of fraternal benefit plans, as I describe shortly, why did they become popular in the first place? The answer is actually quite simple: (1) because other means of affordable insurance were not yet available on the open market, nor was commercial banking itself a well-developed enterprise in the United States; and (2) because the English friendly society and fraternal movements provided valuable and widely accessible precedents for action.

Why, then, the enormous jump in the total number of fraternal organizations? Why did fraternal self-insurance spread so quickly? As mentioned before, there is an internal logic to the exponential growth of organizations, that is, the legitimacy of success. Once a new model of collective organization proves its ability to create and satisfy demand, imitators soon follow. This is the fundamental dynamic of competitive voluntarism. But this in itself is not a very satisfying explanation for a phenomenon as complex as the fraternal movement. A closer look at the economics of fraternal benefit insurance is needed to understand why exactly the fraternal movement grew so quickly in the decades after the Civil War.

The Economics of Fraternal Self-Insurance

In essence, most fraternities and mutual benefit societies relied on what we now call Ponzi schemes, a type of investment scheme named after Charles Ponzi, a notorious American con man indicted in 1920 for selling investors promissory notes that were to pay an impossible 50% profit in 45 days. Ponzi made good on his promises by continually recruiting new investors, whose premiums then supplied the capital necessary to pay their predecessors. Fraternal insurance operated much like a classic Ponzi scheme, minus the false pretenses: Current benefit payments were financed by the dues of new members, who in turn relied on successive waves of yet newer members to pay their returns in kind.[41] The key to the success of such schemes is the recruitment of successively larger cohorts of investors, which is exactly the shortfall of contemporary pay-as-you-go schemes like the social security system.

Originally, friendly societies and fraternal orders paid death benefits to the families of deceased members by merely collecting an assessment from all the remaining members. As one might imagine, this often proved unreliable and difficult to administer: when a member died, his or her death benefit was paid by the remaining members, a condition that kept lodges in perpetual search of new recruits. Thus the practice of requiring annual (or monthly) dues from members came into practice. Unlike contemporary life insurance plans, however, most fraternal lodges resisted the idea of adjusting dues to match the age of the member. In effect, then, younger members were being asked to subsidize life insurance for their older counterparts.[42]

More problematic still was the fact that few if any fraternal comptrollers thought it necessary to invest members' premiums in order to accumulate a reserve fund, thus insuring against unexpected emergencies, such as the simultaneous death of several members. Despite frequent warnings from actuaries and social scientists, many fraternal orders simply ignored the call for better financial planning.[43] The Modern Woodmen of America, for example, voted down an 1897 proposal to create an emergency reserve fund by a vote of four to one. "The society kept defeating a similar resolution for more than twenty years," comments one historian. "Many fraternal societies felt that reserve funds were necessary only for commercial insurance firms. Apparently most felt that the fraternal spirit would compensate for actuarial weakness."[44]

Instead of investing premiums in stable financial instruments, as is common practice today, most lodges relied on the fact that demand for fraternal benefit insurance was strong. As long as demand outpaced supply, competitive voluntarism continued apace. Many fraternal orders even took to employing professional agents, or "lodge organizers," to scour the countryside in search of new members. One edition of the *Fraternal Monitor*, a national fraternal periodical founded in 1890, included ads such as "WANTED—Good live wires with experience in the fraternal field can secure liberal contracts and real opportunities in one of America's societies by writing to E. M. Butterfield, Box 197, Hutchinson, Kas. [*sic*]." The *Monitor* also contains advice columns for fraternal salesmen with titles like "Some Arguments That I Have Used" and "Separate Argument for Each Prospect."[45] One column sternly chided organizers: "Just pack this into your inner consciousness and hammer it in hard—that every report of membership which shows no gain shows a loss. If you are no further ahead than you were when the last report was rendered you are not standing still—you are sliding back."[46]

So popular, so sought after were fraternal memberships that any ambitious swindler could invent an order and start selling policies in it, and pricey paraphernalia to boot. One lodge organizer in the employ of the Ancient Order of United Workmen, Dr. James M. Bunn, was fired for plagiarizing Masonic rituals and passing them off as the AOUW's own. Bunn was also reputedly "not averse to reaping the financial gain that might result."[47] Furthermore, competitive voluntarism had another downside for lodge organizers, for while it was exceedingly easy to form a lodge and start collecting dues, it was just as easy for members to quit, defect, or simply stop contributing. One study of the International Order of Odd Fellows found that young people were particularly susceptible to membership defection, presumably because they were at more of a financial disadvantage than to their older counterparts (see above).[48] According to another study, over 85 percent of the white fraternal organizations founded between 1870 and 1910 failed after an average life span of 15 years.[49]

Abandoning an insolvent lodge and forming new ones was easily done; all it took was a mite of entrepreneurship and a touch of knowhow. As one (1911) study notes,

> Societies of this nature [i.e., mutual assessment societies] commence usually with young people who have seceded from older lodges or societies, on account of high assessments, and at the outset the rates are very low and many years are often required before an increasing average age makes additional assessments necessary, with the ultimate result that failure becomes imminent unless additional dues or assessments are raised to extraordinary proportions. This has practically been the history of the rise and fall of assessment fraternal insurance in America, as well as the earlier friendly societies in England.[50]

Thus, throughout its early decades, the fraternal system was characterized both by many start-ups and almost as many failures. The competitiveness of this system helped foster a rapid buildup in the number of fraternal benefit organizations, as well as a great many hybrids. Nonetheless, as with all market booms, the fraternal insurance market was extremely vulnerable to dramatic changes of fortune.

Factors Related to the Declining Popularity of Fraternalism

One might well ask why fraternal organizations were so popular in the late nineteenth century, given their financial liabilities and sometimes shady origins. This is not an easy question to answer with any certainty. Although fraternal benefit plans had their fair share of drawbacks, they were for many one of the only affordable means of purchasing sickness and burial insurance at all. On the other hand, it could be argued that the intense publicity and recruitment surrounding postbellum fraternalism created an atmosphere in which it was simply a popular thing to do. Either way, the movement lost much of its steam once better alternatives became widely available.

Several features of fraternal insurance likely contributed to its declining popularity in the early twentieth century. It is surprising, for example, that given the general importance of providing for one's wife and children in the event of untimely death, women were actively discouraged from founding their own beneficiary societies. The first fraternal insurance organization for women incorporated in the United States, the Ladies Catholic Benevolent Association, was not founded until 1890, and a circular distributed by the Archdiocese of Boston makes this claim: "It was the general opinion among the other fraternal organizations that an association of women for such a purpose would prove a failure."[51] Similarly, members of the Catholic Ladies of Ohio comment (in the same publication), "Many people do not approve of these women's fraternal societies, and argue that they do not really need Life Insurance."[52] The realization that women might need insurance of their own does not help explain why fraternalism fell out of favor with men in the early twentieth century, but it may explain why public policy in the United States traditionally tends to look upon women as dependents and men as their providers: American fraternalism reached out to men but kept women at arm's length, thus denying them the opportunity to purchase sickness and burial insurance of their own.[53]

Nonetheless, two additional liabilities of the fraternal beneficiary model would later come back to haunt the fraternal system in the 1920s and 1930s, when it began to decline in both popularity and influence. The first and most often cited deficiency of fraternal self-insurance was the simple problem of trying to finance life and sickness benefits with little or no professional actuarial guidance. In the years leading up to the commercial insurance boom, countless social scientists, actuaries, insurance agents, and civil servants spoke out against fraternalism, arguing that mutual assessment organizations were poorly managed, inefficient, risky, and subject to virtually no government oversight whatsoever. Toward the end of the nineteenth century, national organizations such as the National Fraternal Congress and the American Fraternal Congress were created to provide some oversight, if not regulation, of the fast-growing fraternal beneficiary industry. The National Fraternal Congress even passed a (nonbinding) "model bill" in 1910 that required all fraternal insurers to maintain a reserve fund, and by 1911, these measures had been enacted in 13 states.[54] But many other fraternal groups continued to rely on current income to pay claims.

A second, though perhaps less serious, liability was the perception of foul play and mischief in the industry. One 1902 study of fraternal beneficiary corporations in Massachusetts noted, for example, that there were enormous disparities in the percentage of income absorbed by expenses among various groups. The Massachusetts Catholic Order of Foresters had management expenses totaling 27.3% of their gross income, it was reported, and another, called simply the Catholic Association, was somehow spending 78.2% of its income on management.[55] State regulators had little or no power to control such abuses in the industry:

> The legislatures of various States have recognized the importance of these questions in different degrees, and, in Massachusetts, several laws have been passed for the regulation of Fraternal Beneficiary Corporations. . . . To the impartial student, however, all these measures bear marks of having been framed more in accordance with a vigilant regard for the protection of the public. For, although our most recent legislation has been a distinct step in

advance, the Insurance Commissioner is still left without adequate powers of supervision, and there remains ample chance for certain people to trade upon the credulity of the ignorant poor for their own selfish ends, and in this way to bring the really philanthropic societies into disrepute.[56]

A third, lesser known shortcoming previously alluded to is the fact that many fraternal orders did not offer sickness or life insurance benefits to all of their members. The Knights of Columbus, a national Catholic fraternity founded expressly for the "rendering of pecuniary aid to its members, and beneficiaries of members," relegated those applicants "unable to pass the medical examination required for admission as insurance members and for those who are beyond the insurable age" to a special category of "associate membership." Associate members could participate in all the regular social activities of the Knights but were not given insurance coverage, nor were they eligible to run as officers of the fraternity: "The associate member is simply a social member," comments one Knights circular, "with no voice in the conduct of the affairs of the Order."[57] The nonchalance of this statement is quite striking. It plainly states that policy-holders alone would be allowed to participate in decisions concerning lodge business. "Every member of the Massachusetts Catholic Order of Foresters is eligible to membership in the Social Division," comments another circular. But only "members of the Social Division under fifty years of age, who pass the medical examination, are eligible to membership in the Insurance Division."[58]

Special funds and services were often maintained specifically for the aged and infirm; for example, the Massachusetts Catholic Order of Foresters was in the process of erecting a Home for Aged Foresters at the time the above-mentioned report was published in 1908, but one still wonders how completely such "associate" or "social" members were able to participate in the functions of these organizations, as well as how such vociferously "benevolent" organizations could turn away those members most in need of assistance. Herein lies the question of the ancillary benefits of fraternalism: If some members insisted on participating despite their lack of benefits or voice in the affairs of the order, then what was their motivation? Why bother at all?

The Ancillary Benefits of Fraternal Participation

Consider the cultural climate of the United States following the Civil War: Though most Americans had probably had their fill of blood and guts by 1865, the presence of massive armies traveling across the country must surely have bolstered enthusiasm for brotherhood, honor, loyalty, and men in uniform, particularly among those young enough to remember the war but not old enough to have served in it (exactly the generation that would spearhead the fraternal movement in the years to come). Consider, too, the morbid preoccupation with death that was cultivated during the war years. Is it any surprise that life insurance became a primary concern of millions of Americans in the subsequent decades? Finally, consider the vast commercial enterprise mobilized to outfit the soldiers of the great war and the huge profits to be had selling uniforms, badges, and ribbons to fraternalists in the years thereafter. If one were to assume that individuals learn to like the fads and fashions offered by marketers and retailers, the urge to join a fraternal lodge must have been almost irresistible. Newspapers from the era are filled with accounts of the latest lodge banquet, picnic, or parade. City directories from the period also contain dozens of advertisements for purveyors of lodge-related paraphernalia. Public expenditure on such goods was so great that journalist W. S. Harwood was moved to joke, "There are many elevating and ennobling elements in these fraternities, but the broad, rich acres of man's selfishness are nowhere more carefully fertilized, tended, tilled, and reaped than in the lodge-room." In fact, Harwood continues:

> It is probable that, for mere personal gratification, aside from any real or imaginary benefits, the members of the various secret organizations in the United States will spend annually in banquets, railroad and travelling expenses, costly gifts to retiring officers, testimonials, elaborate uniforms, and rare swords not less than two hundred and fifty millions of dollars, and this is allowing but fifty dollars a year as an average for the delightful, but probably wholly unnecessary, expenses connected with the fraternities.[59]

In a more general sense, fraternalism was surely fun, and given the alternatives, it was probably a welcome opportunity for many working men to get out of the house and drink their worries away in a climate of exclusive collegiality. But still, why do so in the fraternal format, as opposed to merely patronizing a local beer hall or saloon? Again, consider the stigma attached to saloons, the vociferous condemnation of such places by temperance advocates, wives, and religious leaders.[60] Lodge participation also satisfied the yen for militarism and military garb prevalent at the time. Personally, I would like to think that fraternalists had a sense of humor about it all, that lodge meetings were more like a Marx Brothers movie than a march to the scaffold, but as former soldiers, Scouts, and athletes can attest, there is something special about same-sex bonding in uniform that is scarcely equaled elsewhere.[61]

Can We Generalize from the American Example?

Alexis de Tocqueville certainly found the American example a useful basis for comparison with his native France. The French brand of associationalism, like the American, revolved around the provision of mutual aid (*sociétés de secours mutuels*), though its membership base was markedly different. According to historical sociologist William Sewell, Jr., one distinctive characteristic of early nineteenth-century French workers' associations was "their constant use of the term 'fraternity' and its cognates 'fraternal' and 'brother.' . . . It gave a revolutionary respectability to the corporate trades' traditional sense of moral solidarity, and at the same time it gave a more specific content to the abstract revolutionary term 'Fraternity.'"[62] Contemporary French historians argue about the extent to which workers' associations actually fostered a unique working-class consciousness, but in the bigger picture, the contrast with the American system seems clear: French associations, though articulated around the same financial concerns as American associations, were incorporated into a preexisting system of class stratification, whereas American associations, lacking such a preexisting system, tended to form around the ethnonational and ethnoreligious identity of their members (to the detriment, I might add, of American working-class consciousness, as I detail in chapter 5). In other words, French associations evolved out of a centuries' old tradition of occupational guilds, or *compagnonnages*, whereas their American counterparts were founded on a rather more ad hoc basis, incorporating members by race, ethnicity, and religion, as well as occupation.[63] In addition, the French state regulated associations in a manner unfamiliar in the United States, which may help explain Tocqueville's enthusiasm for their nascent popularity in America.[64] Given the close connection between the political organization of French workers and the networks that provided their social insurance, it is not surprising that trade unions and worker-labor parties became their primary brokers of governmental support for social insurance later in the 19th century.[65]

In Germany, by contrast, social insurance was never totally private, though, as in France, mutual aid societies (*freie Hilfskassen*) were largely organized around occupational lines. Beginning with the 1794 General Law Code (*Allgemeines Landrecht*) in Prussia, "local and regional authorities had been granted increasing powers to compel different categories of workers to join sickness-insurance funds."[66] Though many German laborers still tried to use mutual aid societies as loci for political activism, the Bismarck administration passed a succession of laws in the 1870s that prohibited political associations and permitted government surveillance of all remaining mutual aid funds. By the late nineteenth century, state supervision of these funds was almost tantamount to state-supported social insurance, which may explain why Germany was at the forefront of welfare-state formation throughout the period before World War I.

Great Britain provided the organizational model on which the American fraternal beneficiary society was molded, but as I have noted, the prevalence of fraternities and friendly societies was in deep decline in Britain by the dawning of the golden age in the United States. According to sociologist Neil Smelser, savings banks, trade unions, and cooperative stores took the place of mutual aid societies in different respects, each because they were better suited to the demands of a rapidly industrializing society. Some friendly societies continued apace, but even these came more and more to resemble professional, highly bureaucratized banks and insurance companies.[67] "It was becoming a commercial proposition to provide for both the working man's insurance and his relaxation, thus the friendly societies gradually came to be in competition with outsiders in respect of both of their main forms of activity," writes historian P. H. J. H. Gosden.[68] "There were good reasons for the structural segregation of 'savings' from the more diffuse aspects of the friendly society," adds Smelser, "just as there were good reasons for segregating the 'trade union' from the friendly society."[69] Over time, government regulation increased and consumer demand diminished, culminating in the creation of state-run sickness and unemployment insurance programs, as well as old-age relief, in the early decades of the twentieth century.

These comparisons support the argument (made throughout this text) that cross-national variation in the size and scope of quasi-market fiduciary organizations played a significant role in national political development in these countries, particularly with regard to the formation of their social welfare institutions. But since I have now raised the issue of the political ramifications of fraternities and mutual aid associations, I must append my original ideal-typical description with a second form of association, the *political association*, or in the parlance of Max Weber, the "party":

> Parties may represent interests determined through "class situation" or "status situation" and they may recruit their following respectively from one or the other. But they need be neither purely "class" nor purely "status" parties. In most cases they are partly class parties and partly status parties, but sometimes they are neither. They may represent ephemeral or enduring structures. Their means of attaining power may be quite varied, ranging from naked violence of any sort to canvassing for votes with coarse or subtle means: money, social influence, the force of speech, suggestion, clumsy hoax, and so on.[70]

In the chapters to come, we shall see examples of nearly all these different kinds of party action, but for now it is enough to say that where and when ideal-typical nineteenth-century American associations dedicated themselves to lobbying, they were not acting "typically." They were manifesting a new kind of political action in the American social landscape: special-interest group organizing. But this is a subject for later in this volume, and in parts two and three, I turn to the ramifications of associationalism on American political development before World War II. For now, let it be said that I have offered, in a single, ideal-typical nutshell, an analytic description of American associationalism that appears to conform with the empirical record thereof.

In the next chapter I turn to a discussion of some sociodemographic factors underlying the associational boom, focusing in particular on the tensions that evolved between the competing forces of community building and self-segregation. This requires consideration of popular associations outside of the fraternal realm, namely, charitable and missionary organizations, as well social and literary clubs. One can argue that enthusiasm for these quasi-fraternal organizations was part of the larger "club mania" of the period, though they did not offer the same economic benefits to members that fraternal lodges did. Nonetheless, although these nonfraternal clubs differ from the ideal-type fraternal associations just described, there is one basic similarity—their voluntary, nonprofit status. They, too, embody many of the features of American associationalism essential to understanding the legacy of the golden age of fraternity.

"COMMUNITAS," OR

SOME SOCIOCULTURAL FACTORS BEHIND THE BOOM

According to the *Oxford English Dictionary*, second edition, the modern term *community* actually conflates two antecedent words: the ancient Latin word *communis*, which refers to the quality of fellowship, or a "community of relations or feelings," and the medieval Latin word *commonty*, which reflects a much different and I suspect more historically relevant meaning.[1] A *commonty* is "a body of fellows or fellow-townsmen," and it bears an exclusionary rather than inclusionary connotation, as in "The thynges of the comunete."[2] Thus, in contrast, a *commonty* is a jurisdiction or realm of privilege specific to a certain group of people, whereas *communis* denotes the touchy-feely way communitarians and associational enthusiasts would like us to feel about one another.[3]

This naturally raises a question relevant to the topic at hand: What, besides economic need, brought individuals together under the fraternal system of the postbellum era? Why was it such a popular form of social organization (if not simply because it provided a convenient means of collectively distributing risk)? Surely many men (and some women) grew to meet and like one another through the social activities of their respective organizations, as communitarians and neo-Tocquevillians claim; but does the need for sociability provide a satisfactory explanation of the rise and fall of American associationalism? This chapter re-examines the actual role that sociability and social networks played in the enormous proliferation of fraternal lodges and associations in the late nineteenth century, as well as the many related voluntary clubs, groups, and societies that emerged in their wake.

Organization Building and the Political Economy of Sociodemographic Competition in Late Nineteenth-Century American Cities

The period between about 1840 and World War I is known for the huge influx of immigrants that arrived from Europe and Asia to settle in the United States.

The massive immigration wave had two important ramifications for our under-standing of late nineteenth-century voluntarism: First, in bringing with them the personal and cultural trappings of their native lands, immigrants forged many new communities based explicitly on ethnonational identity. Some of these com-munities resembled artificial constructions reassembled out of previously un-connected groups, such as German speakers from across central Europe, while other communities were built around identities forced on them by other Ameri-cans, as happened to blacks and Chinese in their struggles to find a place in American society.[4] Nevertheless, the salience of in-group boundaries was argu-ably at an all time high in American history in the decades just after the Civil War. Never before, and arguably never since (until now), have so many indi-viduals laid claim to distinct ethnic identities, nor has American social life or labor force participation been so heavily stratified by birthplace.[5]

Equally important, however, were preexisting religious differences. The nineteenth-century immigration wave brought huge numbers of Catholics and Jews to the United States, and a clear religious divide soon developed, especially between Catholics and Protestants.[6] Because neither the state nor the market pro-vided much-needed resources for native-born and immigrant city dwellers, re-ligious congregations adopted the successful strategy of their secular counterparts in fashioning clubs and societies to provide such benefits for existing and would-be parishioners. Furthermore, because the religious atmosphere of late nine-teenth-century city life placed congregations in competition with one another for members, organizational innovations in one denomination were often duplicated, if not bested, by their rivals.[7] In turn, Catholic, Protestant, and Jewish denominations adopted a common organizational strategy for provid-ing benefits to members and would-be members. Finally, because religious dif-ferences were often coterminous with ethnonational differences, these two factors, religion and place of origin, came to be vitally important factors in the division of the American population.

Members of these various communities worked hard to build voluntary orga-nizations that would represent and retain members, and in so doing they rein-forced these dividing lines through organizational differentiation. In some cases, organizations even contributed to the construction of new identities: Both the Italian-American and Jewish-American communities were forged from previously disparate populations with little sense of collective identity, for example. In pro-viding the organizational apparatus for social segregation, associationalism thus contributed to the division of American society along ethnic and religious, as well as racial and gender-based lines. Exclusive associations helped each group foster a unique sense of identity, as well as customs, rituals, and nomenclature to match.

Ethnoreligious and ethnonational identity were related to the associational boom in at least five different ways, each of which can help inform our under-standing of the rise and fall of this tradition in American political life:

1. Given the scant economic and cultural capital of many newcomers, immigrants formed fraternal organizations endowed with the specific purpose of pooling resources within their community, for example, ethnonational fraternal organizations like the Sons of Hermann (for Germans), Ancient Order of Hibernians (for Irish Catholics), and Kesher Shel Barzel (for Jews of eastern European, particularly Polish, origin).[8]

2. In response to the immigrant influx, many native-born Americans, particularly those of Protestant origin, founded their own fraternal organizations designed to represent the interests of "native" Americans, both politically and socially, while providing the economic benefits common to all fraternal groups; the Patriotic Order Sons of America, Brotherhood of the Union, and Order of United American Mechanics are prominent examples.[9]

3. Moral differences (often related to religious and ethnic differences) also spurred the formation of morally tinged fraternal organizations, particularly around the issue of the potential prohibition of alcohol; for example, the Sons of Temperance, Independent Order of Good Templars, and Royal Templars of Temperance were all fraternal orders dedicated explicitly to temperance and implicitly to the prohibitionist cause.[10]

4. Religious differences among Protestants, Catholics, and Jews were also manifested through the formation of competing fraternal organizations as means of recruiting and retaining members; for example, the Knights of Columbus was founded as an effort to keep Catholics connected to the Catholic community.[11]

5. Though American history is not without its fair share of class conflict, the emergence of class consciousness in the United States after the Civil War was decidedly altered by the prevalence of cross-cutting ethnoreligious and ethnonational associational ties. Class conflict in the United States has traditionally been expressed in racial, ethnic, and religious terms, whereas Europeans tend to think of class as more of an all-encompassing category of social differentiation.[12]

Whether such social closure benefited Americans and American society as a whole is debatable, though matters such as this can never be answered in a truly objective fashion. Although it is clear that ethnic rivalry and chain migration both contributed to tight, cohesive ethnoreligious communities, it is worth asking whether this was a result of forced segregation or of communal self-segregation. A quick survey of the extant literature on the history of American immigration affirms the notion of a middle road to ethnoreligious segregation. Though many white Protestants may have tried to avoid social contact with ethnoreligious minorities during this period—the exclusivity of fraternal lodges was one way of securing such isolation—many also actively pursued "service" contact with minorities through volunteer work in missionary groups, settlement houses, and social service organizations. The city directories of the era are full of examples, from Penitent Female Refuges to Evangelical Baptist Benevolent and Missionary Societies and the Sons and Adopted Sons of Washington (presumably, a quasi-patriotic order for native-born and immigrant alike).[13] At the same time, many immigrants appear to have sought out their own self-segregation, preferring communal isolation to assimilation into the mainstream. Immigrant entrepreneurs, and even the home governments of immigrants from some parts of Europe, also actively tried to erect and maintain boundaries, real and imagined, that would preserve the ethnic distinctiveness of these communities.[14] Thus, we must be fair in allocating responsibility for the failures of the melting pot in the United States.

Several features of this process (often called *ethnicization* by immigration scholars) deserve further consideration here: *first*, the drive to found voluntary organizations for immigrants was not merely a product of the isolation and alienation of a downtrodden ethnic underclass. Surely, one could tell as many different stories of organizational life as there were (and are) ethnic and ethnoreligious organizations, though the historical literature on their nineteenth-century incarnations seem to support the observation that many if not most immigrant organizations were founded by rather well-to-do individuals with the time, resources, and inclination to organize their brethren. In the words of historian John Bodnar,

> Inevitably, competition for members among local lodges intensified over time as various leaders sought to expand and sustain their base of influence and power. Since these associations represented one of the few institutions which could mobilize large segments of the immigrant community, they were used by ambitious newcomers to embellish their financial and social standing within the group and promote political agendas.[15]

In other words, immigrant organizers could gain both clout and credibility for their efforts. In some cases, local organizers even received support from their home governments in Europe: "The Hungarian government supported an extensive program of 'American Action,'" writes Bodnar, "which used financial inducements to gain control over immigrant churches and newspapers in America in order to maintain a desire on the part of emigrants to return with their earnings and to blunt disaffection from the cause of Hungarian nationalism."[16]

Founding clubs could be lucrative as well. Since many immigrants did not speak (or desire to learn to speak) English, immigrant entrepreneurs could effectively count on a captive audience for well-organized social clubs, cultural events, and financial services. Of course, this does not discount the possibility that some if not much of the community organizing of the period was done in the spirit of pure and simple altruism. On the other hand, even altruists some-times benefit financially from their efforts. By the beginning decades of the twen-tieth century, in fact, ethnoreligious fraternal organizing had become something of a business:

> While most local lodges had been formed by artisans and small merchants with limited goals of mutual assistance, the drive toward the national con-solidation of fraternals was fueled by ambitious leaders who viewed these larger organizations as outlets for their entrepreneurial energies and drives for personal gain and status. Emanating largely from those with more for-mal education, these career-oriented fraternalists had strong idealogical positions and gradually adopted modern American business and invest-ment procedures to increase the stability and efficiency of their growing ventures.[17]

Elsewhere, Bodnar offers the instructive example of community-building ef-forts among Italian immigrants in San Francisco, where a number of Italian entrepreneurs

> struggled to reduce the influence of regionalism among fellow immigrants, which hindered the plans to build efficient manufacturing and commer-cial enterprises. Marco Fontana needed a large, efficient work force to ex-pand the productive capacity of the Del Monte Corporation. He hired Italians from diverse regions but worked to get them to overcome their differences in order to promote efficiency. Fellow Italian A. P. Giannini weaned immigrants away from regionally based mutual-aid societies so they would all save in his bank.[18]

Similarly, historian Josef Barton finds saloonkeepers and petty merchants be-hind the birth of many Italian, Rumanian, Czech, and Polish mutual benefit soci-eties in Cleveland, Ohio, though other immigrant enclaves, such as Cleveland's Slovak community, deferred to their clergymen for organizational impetus.[19]

Thus, regardless of their founders' motivations, ethnic voluntary organizations were not merely weapons of the weak, as some might believe. Nor should they be seen to represent a reactionary effort to recreate the pastoral affairs of European village life in the big cities of America. Historian Kathleen Neils Conzen writes here about the immigrant German community in antebellum Milwaukee:

> Such associational activity among immigrants is often interpreted as a way of coping with the trauma of adjustment in the face of exclusion from na-tive American society. . . . But it is difficult to view the rich associational life of Milwaukee's *Deutschtum* as an innovative response to the immigrant situation. Theirs was not the culture of the village. They counted in their ranks representatives of Germany's urbanized and educated "general es-

tate"; their numbers encompassed also the lower middle class world of the urban artisan and shopkeeper and the petty bourgeoisie. . . . Whether bourgeois or *kleinbürgerlich*, the divorce of their kind from the traditional life of the countryside had occurred before their move to America.[20]

Moreover, it would not be correct to assume that all or even most immigrants arrived in America with a self-conscious notion of their own ethnonational identity. Writes historian Victor Greene:

> The overwhelming bulk of East European, German, and Italian immigrants . . . both possessed and practiced certain cultural characteristics of their group—for example, a common national language—but they had little or no feeling of membership in an ethnic nation. Whether in Europe or America, they may have sensed that they were different from other nationalities, but when asked for their own group identification, they probably would have responded by naming their regional or local origins—their village or more likely their province. Very few would have replied "Polish," "Lithuanian," or "Italian."[21]

In sum, the modern map of Europe was still just taking shape in the late nineteenth century, and many immigrants came to America with little or no sense of having left a homeland or nation of any kind. If they carried any sense of identity with them from Europe or Asia to America, it was that of their village or region, a factor that only complicated the efforts of immigrant entrepreneurs to found ethnonational communal organizations.

The preexisting structure of many American churches exacerbated such questions, particularly for Catholics, who faced clerical opposition to the expression of ethnonational concerns in the religious arena. The Irish naturally dominated American Catholic affairs, being the first Catholic group to establish itself in any number in the United States. But when new communities of non-Irish Catholics began to form in American cities, Irish clergymen tended to try to maintain control of church institutions. In the subsequent struggle to create ethnic parishes for non-Irish Catholics, many immigrant communities began constructing ethnonational religious organizations and identity narratives devoted to their perceived heritage. This issue sometimes divided entire communities between those loyal to their church and those angry about their lack of representation therein:

> The disagreement produced an impasse that affected every parishioner. Eventually the tense atmosphere exploded into violence and disorder as parishioners took sides. It was in the crisis of having to choose which faction to support that ordinary Polish and Lithuanian immigrants became educated to their ethnic identity, and thereby raised their ethnic consciousness.[22]

Similar conflicts arose in other non-Irish Catholic communities. Among the Protestant denominations, conflict and schism over issues of ritual observance were common. Ethnonational churches, parishes, and whole denominations were formed by immigrant groups that were looking to find ways to preserve the religious experience of their homeland, both culturally and linguistically. Church entries in the city directories of the period often list numerous German, Swedish, Dutch, and Norwegian Lutheran congregations, for example.[23]

Such episodes of intracommunal conflict were not found only in religious affairs. Some ethnonational communities encompassed more than one dominant religious tradition, which often led to intracommunal divisions. One such dispute involved two of the nation's largest Polish-American fraternities, the Polish Roman Catholic Union, which remained closely tied to the Catholic Church, and the Polish National Alliance, which admitted members regardless of their religion. Slovaks experienced a similar rift between the First Catholic Slovak Union and the National Slovak Society.[24] Historian Kathleen Neils Conzen elicits a similar distinction between "church" and "club" Germans, the former being "pious Protestants and Catholics, often former peasants and small craftsmen, who focused their lives around their church and took relatively little interest in the broader affairs of the community," the latter being artisans and skilled craftsmen with little or no interest in organized religion. Jewish rabbis are also said to have "complained that lodges, clubs, societies, and other 'community' institutions undermined their authority, drained membership from congregations, and encouraged American Jewish indifference to religion."[25]

Cultural differences between overlapping generations of immigrants was another source of tension, as well as a great spate of organization building in late nineteenth- and early twentieth-century America. As immigrant communities became comfortable and established in American cities and towns, older immigrants and their children not infrequently developed a sense of stewardship for newer arrivals. They also expressed fear that new immigrants would ruin their communities' hard-won reputation for respectability and patriotism. Indeed, many clubs and societies appear to have been exclusively devoted to the successful assimilation of their brethren into the American fold, as shown by the foundation of B'nai B'rith, a German-Jewish mutual assistance society created in the American fraternal mold. Toward the turn of the century, as more and more Jews of eastern European descent arrived in the United States, the German-Jewish leaders of B'nai B'rith became increasingly aggressive in their efforts to assimilate immigrants and thus preserve the good reputation of the Jewish people in America. Members helped found the Jewish Alliance of California, for example, "a cooperative effort of several San Francisco Jewish organizations designed to Americanize and educate Jewish immigrants in the city and make them self-supporting."[26]

At the same time, ethnic newspapers like the *Hebrew American* (founded in 1894) self-consciously printed news for Jews in English, along with footnotes translating and transliterating difficult words and idioms into Yiddish. The editors of the *Hebrew American* proudly declared their mission to be "the promotion of the knowledge of English and education among the great masses of Hebrew settlers in America."[27] In addition to providing general news for Jews, the *Hebrew American* also aimed to "educate and initiate its readers in the duties of American citizenship, to acquaint them with the institutions and form of government of the United States, our adopted country."[28] The paper included news of Jewish affairs in Europe and America (including such stories as "The Jewish Conference in St. Petersburg"), success stories about Jews in America ("Rich Hebrew Club"), and a great deal of crime reporting ("Riot at Synagogue"; "A Drunk Mother with Child in a Gutter").[29] The editors of the *Hebrew American* elaborate on their organizational goals in the following published dispute with a rival paper, the *American Hebrew*:

> We are very thankful to *The American Hebrew* for its commendation of *The Hebrew American* in its last week's issue; but we object to its unwarranted warning to change the title of our journal on account of its similarity with *American Hebrew*. . . . Our journal is intended for a class of readers entirely different from his, and that our aims and purposes are just the reverse of those of the *American Hebrew*; for while it is the object of the former to convert Americans into Hebrews it is our task to convert Hebrews into Americans; *The Hebrew American* is cosmopolitan while *The American Hebrew* is national. Our journal is solely devoted to instruct the Hebrew masses in the English language, its contents being of interest to Hebrew and gentile alike, and there is nothing Hebrew about it, save for the definitions of words in the Judeo-German language spoken by a considerable portion of our race.[30]

Such disjunctures were increasingly common as established immigrants faced the arrival of coethnic newcomers: "In many cases . . . a social distance began to surface between foreign-born entrepreneurs and workers who were often responsible for their early success." Nonetheless, adds historian John Bodnar, "As the social distance between the classes in each group widened, those moving into higher social categories did not simply abandon those left behind. Frequently they made vigorous attempts to preach the advantages of hard work and efficiency that they now believed explained their own success and the value of ethnic identity."[31] This exemplifies one of the ways in which American class conflict has historically been inflected inward, as an issue of ethnic and racial group membership, rather than outward, as a society-wide conflict between rival classes.

My point here is not to deride the trials and tribulations of individual ethnic communities. I mention all of these sordid details only to point out several features of ethnonational and ethnoreligious voluntary organizations not commonly seen in contemporary accounts of the golden age. It is natural, though perhaps not inevitable, that ethnics would seek out friends, relatives, and kinfolk from their homeland upon arrival in a new country; that they would ply these networks for access to jobs, housing, and social opportunities (including the all-important search for a mate); and that they might form and join voluntary organizations to supplement these quests. In the American context, furthermore, immigrants were encouraged to do this by a legal climate favorable to nonprofit organizations; a political environment hostile to class-based organization; and a social environment generally hostile to foreigners, non-Christians, and nonwhites. But it is less well known that many such organizations were founded for profit and political influence and that they were often instrumental in fomenting intrareligious and intraethnic conflict in those very same immigrant communities.

Clearly, the quest for ethnic self-organization worked better in some communities than in others. Religious diversity proved an obstacle for Poles, for example; excessive provincialism made organizing Italian Americans a challenge; and controversy over the proper ritual observance of Judaism, coupled with the various cultures of diaspora Jews, spurred the formation of multiple, competing Jewish organizations. Historian John Bodnar, who has studied this issue in depth, offers a useful overview of immigrant participation in fraternal orders, though I disagree with the "glass is half empty" manner in which he presents it:

> A study of Germans in Cincinnati determined that about 52 percent of adult German males joined ethnic fraternals and similar organizations. The majority of Romanians probably never affiliated with any cultural or beneficial group. Only about one-half of the potential members joined the United Slavonian Benefit Association in Louisiana. . . . Among Poles, statistics suggest that fraternal membership rates were below 50 to 60 percent.[32]

Why Bodnar views 50 percent participation rates as low is not at all clear—remember, these rates include members of the community too poor to afford fraternal insurance—but they do nevertheless confirm the fact that ethnic voluntary organizations did have a significant impact on the American immigrant experience, particularly in the formation of distinct neighborhoods and communities.

Political scientist Gerald Gamm's book *Urban Exodus: Why the Jews Left Boston and the Catholics Stayed* provides an excellent summary of the costs and benefits of ethnoreligious community organization.[33] Using extensive quantitative and qualitative data from two ethnic communities in Boston over more than five decades, Gamm shows how the traditional parish organizations of

Boston Catholics kept working-class Irish families firmly rooted in the neighborhoods surrounding their local church. Boston Jews, on the other hand, were free to move away while still remaining active in their local synagogue. Gamm relates these differences to the subsequent settlement patterns of Boston's Irish and Jews—the Jews' flight from the now-blighted Roxbury section of Boston versus the decision of the Irish to entrench themselves in nearby Dorchester, where they have not only stayed but have also actively (and sometimes violently) resisted the encroachment of new ethnic groups looking for inexpensive housing and access to public transit. The Irish faced much higher exit costs than the Jews, argues Gamm. Jewish congregations remained in Roxbury until the majority of their constituents had already moved elsewhere, at which time they simply sold their synagogue building and built a new one in the suburbs.[34] Membership in Catholic parishes is determined by geography, not preference, however. Moving out of the neighborhood would mean leaving one's parish and joining a new and probably less distinctively Irish one. In response, the Irish circled their wagons in South Boston, cultivating over time a community ethos of paranoia, prejudice, and parochialism. (It is ironic how well the word *parochial* speaks to the connection between parish-based religious communities and their centripetal social outlook.) Thus, whereas there are clearly benefits in building strong ties between neighborhoods and religious communities, as the Irish did in Dorchester, there are also deep, long-term costs. Nor is this phenomenon specific to Boston's Irish and Jewish communities: In Gamm's own words,

> Any set of people—Catholics or Jews, whites or blacks, villagers or urban residents—bound to an institution characterized by the membership rules, rootedness rules, and authority rules of the territorial parish will demonstrate a tenacious commitment to their local area. And any set of people tied to autonomous, mobile institutions that set no boundaries to membership will be more loosely tied to a given district.[35]

In fact, one might well extend the principles of Gamm's analysis beyond that of geographical tenacity. The specific character of community organizations, particularly the incentives and disincentives to membership, as well as the barriers to entry and exit, plays an inordinate role in the development and outlook of the members of those communities. Those organizations that offer strong incentives to join and high barriers to exit tend to exert a centripetal effect on their members' sense of self. This helps build strong, rooted communities, but it can also create insurmountable obstacles to adaptation and integration with other communities. These competing dynamics deserve far more serious attention from those who suggest a return to the golden age, a revitalizing of civic associationalism in the United States today. I focus on four such dynamics in the section that follows, as well as in chapters 8 and 9.

Toward a Typology of Associational Communities

In table 3.1, I describe four categories of "difference" along four axes germane to the formation of distinct types of identity association or fraternity. The first two, entrance and exit, reflect the mechanisms by which individuals are socially designated to any of those four categories of difference; *exit*, more specifically, refers to potential barriers and opportunities for resisting or relinquishing such identification, whereas *entry* reflects the factors responsible for an individual's allocation to any of these categories. The other two columns detail two related features of identity-group organization building: recruitment and retention. These two mechanisms represent the ways in which social organizations are erected to lure and retain prospective members.[36] Merely qualifying for group membership does not ensure that one will choose to participate in it. Recruitment and retention refer to those mechanisms whereby pertinent individuals

TABLE 3.1: Factors Shaping the Ascription and Adoption of Sectarian Social Identities in Late Nineteenth-Century American Cities

	Entrance	Exit	Recruitment	Retention
Race	Forced at birth	No exit (except passing)	Weak efforts (voluntary organizations)	Weak incentives (cartels; voluntary organizations)
Ethnicity	Given at birth	Assimilation	Modest efforts (voluntary organizations; language-based opportunities)	Modest incentives (cartels; marriage markets; voluntary organizations)
Religion	Given at birth	Conversion or inattention	Strong efforts (proselytization; voluntary organizations)	Strong incentives (salvation; cartels; marriage markets; voluntary organizations)
Gender	Forced at birth	No exit (except passing)	Weak efforts (voluntary organizations)	Weak incentives (voluntary organizations)
Native "Majority" (WASP)	Birth; intermarriage; assimilation; passing	Temporary (slumming; ethnicization)	Weak efforts (voluntary organizations)	Strong incentives (opportunity hoarding; social status; voluntary organizations; marriage markets)

are induced to join, and stay involved in, the organizational life of their respective communities.

Though somewhat obvious in the abstract, I outline these four parameters of sectarian social organization in order to highlight some of the ways in which groups of individuals among each category adopted the fraternal model of social organization in creating lodge systems in late nineteenth-century America. Given the fluidity of religious boundaries, for example, a vast system of fraternal organizations built around religious distinctions arose, particularly for Catholics and Jews, who faced the dual threat of prejudice and evangelism. Though ethnicity was a less fluid category than religion, ethnic groups did commonly mobilize behind one of two agendas: assimilationist lodges oriented around Americanizing new ethnics, and Old World ethnic lodges aimed at cultivating and perpetuating customs and traditions of the ethnic past. Because both religion and ethnicity encompassed flexible (i.e., avoidable) social boundaries, furthermore, ethnoreligious and ethnonational associations were a particularly important venue for members of each community to attract and retain prospective members while collectivizing risk through in-group collaboration.

To understand the sectarian basis of American associationalism, one needs to examine in detail these four basic categories of "difference" along the four axes of identity formation, identity exit, membership recruitment, and membership retention. These four categories are race, ethnicity, religion, and gender, plus a fifth quasi category of those who might consider themselves unsullied by such distinctions—native-born white men, or the so-called white Anglo-Saxon Protestant (WASP) male.[37] Class, as you may note, is omitted here, self-consciously so, because, as discussed earlier (and in chapter 5), Americans have generally failed to coalesce around their common class interests in the same manner as their European counterparts. Another form of social identity omitted here, albeit one with far greater salience in the American context, is that of veterans and soldiers. Following the Civil War, this social category proved to be of lasting importance in American politics. Hundreds of lodges and fraternal orders were formed by and for veterans, including the Grand Army of the Republic, the American Legion, the Sons of Union Veterans, and the Military Order of the Loyal Legion of the United States. I have elected to save the issue of veterans' associations for later, however, because the social category of veteran differs from race, class, gender, ethnicity, and religion in being a mark of service, not social position. As mentioned, politics was not a direct goal of most *ideal-typical* fraternal organizations in the late nineteenth century. I consider veterans groups part of the ancillary associational tradition of special-interest group formation, as opposed to a part of the larger enterprise of community-building and self-identification per se (see chapter 4).

Competition between rival identity groups puts pressure on individuals to choose between competing identity-group affiliations (or to choose no such affiliations at all). Strong incentives for defection, in turn, raise the stakes of membership, thus affording members a strong sense of attachment, if not loyalty, to their chosen group. In the late nineteenth-century American context, nonwhites and women faced little or no recruitment from groups other than their own, whereas Catholics, Jews, and European ethnics faced enormous pressure to assimilate, convert, or rejuvenate commitment to their group of origin. Arguably, this had important consequences for the development of race and gender as social categories of difference in America. It is my contention that such social competition for group affiliation helps build and unify group identity. Clearly, conversion pressure is not the only source of group identity, but it can be one such source of stratification.

To understand the dynamics of conversion pressure, however, it might help to first consider two groups that did not face such pressures in the postbellum American social landscape: blacks and women. The Civil War may have freed the slaves, but it was at least another hundred years before the barriers to full social integration for blacks would even begin to falter. White Americans responded to the emancipation of blacks by circling their wagons, erecting ever more effective means of excluding blacks from white society. One way they did this was by forming fraternal organizations with whites-only membership criteria. Blacks had no say in their own social differentiation, in other words. One could not simply decide not to be black, though some especially light-skinned blacks did occasionally pass for white. Of course, other American ethnic groups were sometimes disparaged along racial lines—Italians, Jews, Greeks, and Slavs have all been characterized as European Negroes in one way or another[38]—but this only highlights the importance of racialized identity: To be categorized racially is to be excluded entirely from mainstream society.

In contrast, ethnic categorization holds the promise of future assimilation and thus the potential for conversion pressure (either to maintain ethnicity-based identities or to abandon them in favor of assimilation). In the words of sociologist Mary Waters, the "belief that ethnicity is biologically based acts as a constraint on the ethnic choices of some Americans, but there is nonetheless a range of latitude available in deciding how to identify oneself and whether to do so in ethnic terms. Whites enjoy a great deal of freedom in these choices; those defined in 'racial' terms as non-whites much less."[39]

Like race, gender played an unusual role in late nineteenth-century identity politics. Gender, like race, is not something someone generally gets to choose for oneself. It is an ascribed social category imputed to individuals at birth, though there are, of course, cases of women passing as men and vice versa. Like black Americans, furthermore, American women were largely excluded from the fraternal movement of the period. White men wanted little or nothing to do with blacks and women when it came to lodge meetings and fraternal social gatherings. And as with blacks, women were largely reduced to second-class status in the fraternal arena, participating in auxiliary lodges at the behest of their all-male counterparts. I have already documented the small number of clubs and lodges devoted to the interests of women (and blacks) in Boston in 1900 (see figures 1.1 and 1.2). However, in other domains, particularly those of religious and charitable organizations, women managed to create vital associational niches by and for themselves.[40]

Thus, we see a parallel between the situation for women and that for black Americans throughout this period. Both involve ascription at birth and little or no choice in the matter thereafter. Both are relatively inescapable social categories and thus not subject to the same kind of recruitment and retention efforts common to ethnoreligious communities. White males, furthermore, showed little desire to recruit blacks or women into their own organizations. In fact, they have historically worked quite hard to exclude them. In the face of such opposition, blacks and women faced an uphill battle to define themselves as privileged social groups, groups that one would aspire to join (see figures 3.1 and 3.2). Blacks and women were not as active in the fraternal movement as ethnic and religious groups of comparable size. The absence of competition for would-be black and female participants seems related to the subsequent difficulties they have faced organizing themselves as unified national interest groups. Presumably, this owes much to the fact that one cannot generally choose to join or leave a race or gender, at least not with the same fluidity as ethnicity and religion. Blacks and women have managed to forge distinct organizational niches for themselves, though even today neither group appears to have gained full equality or political representation in American society. On the other hand, the current vitality of race- and gender-based identity politics may be a reaction to this legacy of under-representation.

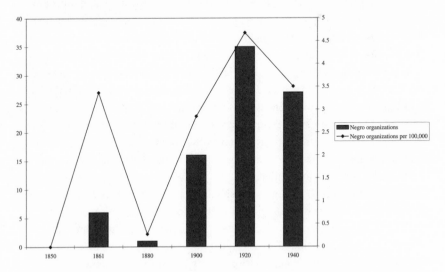

FIGURE 3.1 Negro/Colored Organizations (Excluding Churches) in Boston, 1850–1940

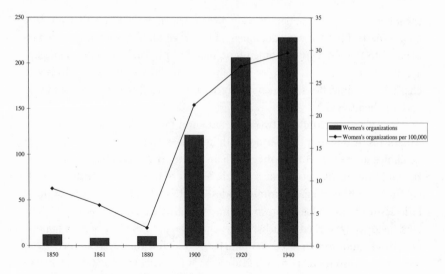

FIGURE 3.2 Organizations by and for Women in Boston, 1850–1940

Religious groups faced a much different scenario in the late 19th century, and the comparison helps elucidate the impact of conversion pressure of group-identity formation relative to groups facing no such pressures. As mentioned earlier, few religions (except possibly Judaism[41]) regard religious identity as a matter of birthright. One can be born into one religion, initiated into another, and buried in a third (as Americans increasingly are today). The United States has always sought to protect the religious freedom of its people, and thus it has become home to people of many religious persuasions. Competition for members, furthermore, has generally been an important component of American religious life. This competition, in concert with the rise of secular, nonsectarian fraternal orders and social clubs, created a climate in which organization building became central to the success or failure of religious communities in the late nineteenth-century United States.[42] As a result of the fluidity of religious identification and the persistent competition for members, those who did choose to participate in any given religious community tended to identify quite strongly with it, sometimes so strongly that they were willing to break with their coethnic community over religious differences.

Figure 3.3 shows the presence of such religiously identified groups, clubs, and fraternities in Boston over the period in question. Their absolute and relative number peaks in 1900, after which there is a rather rapid decline. There may be a number of contributing factors to this trend, but for our purposes consider the fact that Protestant evangelization efforts began to wane somewhat in the early decades of the twentieth century. Historian Yaakov Ariel states that,

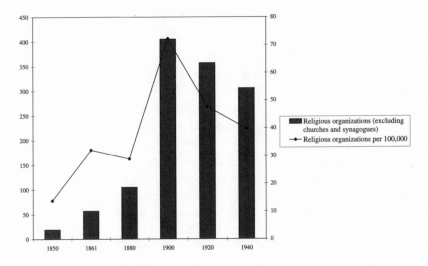

FIGURE 3.3 Religious Associations in Boston, 1850–1940

missions began directing their attention to the second generation, the sons and daughters of immigrants [around 1920]. Those young Jews had attended American schools and were much more at home in American society and culture than their parents were. Many missionary agencies moved from storefront missions in the immigrant quarters to the middle-class Jewish neighborhoods to which many Jews had moved.[43]

Though Ariel does not document a decline in the number of such missionary organizations over time, the Boston data seem to confirm the fact that the high stakes of late nineteenth-century religious competition had tempered somewhat by the early twentieth century. Absent the "immigrant menace" and given the gradual assimilation of Catholics and Jews into mainstream society, American religious life turned inward, diminishing the need for extracongregational organizations devoted to recruiting and retaining members.

But to fully understand this pattern, we also need to consider a closely related form of social identity, that of ethnicity, for as previously mentioned the lines between the two were often fuzzy at best. Ethnicity, unlike religion, is generally less a matter of choice than a matter of birth. One is born into an ethnic group based on the birthplace of his or her parents or grandparents. Nonetheless, like religion (and unlike race), most ethnicities are easily eschewed. One can simply stop attending ethnic events, speaking an ethnic dialect, or associating with coethnics. Like race and unlike religion, ex-ethnics may sometimes find it hard to convince outsiders of their change of heart, particularly in cases in which language and physical appearance are commonly associated with a particular ethnicity; but the general feature of ethnicity holds—it is a fairly fluid source of identity. On the other hand, ethnicity differs from religion in that it is uncommon for an ethnic group to recruit outsiders into the ethnic fold. Ethnic groups often seek respect and recognition from outsiders, and they are equally likely to create incentives for coethnics to openly identify with and participate in the ethnic community as such, but they do not generally try to add to their numbers through exogenous recruitment.

Nonetheless, ethnic clubs, newspapers, gatherings, festivals, militia groups, and mutual benefit organizations were common features of social life in late nineteenth-century America. (Figure 3.4 demonstrates their presence in Boston over the period 1850–1940.) On the whole, ethnicity seems to have evoked a weaker sense of identification from its bearers than religion, presumably because of the relative absence of organized competition for members. However, in cases in which an ethnic identity is attached to a religious identity, as with Irish Catholics and Irish Protestants, group identification can prove quite strong as a result of the tensions fomented by the presence of similar and dissimilar sources of identity in concert with one another (e.g., the relative proximity of Irish nationals, coupled with their religious differences, helps explain the ensuing rivalry between the two).

The majority of associational-fraternal organizations had no specific ethnoreligious or ethnonational markers; or at least their title and membership requirements carried no specific reference to any ascribed racial, ethnic, or religious group. The nation's largest fraternal organizations, the Odd Fellows, Elks, and

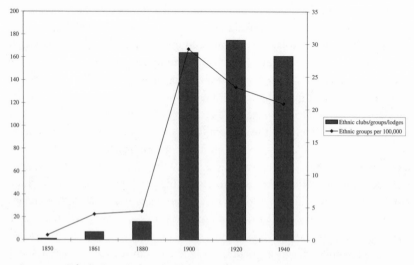

FIGURE 3.4 Ethnic Associations in Boston, 1850–1940

Masons, presented themselves as universalist, open organizations, for example. On the other hand, such universalist claims may only have been covers for implicit exclusion and segregation. Within the orders, lodges may have remained segregated, and we already know that the Masons and Odd Fellows limited participation by blacks and women to auxiliary orders kept at arm's distance from the central body. No other research on American associationalism has, to my knowledge, confirmed (or disproven) the presence of systematic segregation within so-called universalist orders, nor is it generally known to what extent such groups informally excluded blacks, Jews, Catholics, and so on from membership. (The presence of a select few minority members might only indicate token aberrations from an exclusionary mean.) One study of the Odd Fellows' membership between 1860 and 1929 supports the idea that even "universalist" fraternities were implicit sources of self-segregation in their communities:

> An IOOF lodge was an exclusive society, one that sorted people out, not an inclusive society that brought all people in a community together. It embraced adult white men from Anglo-Protestant backgrounds who had the incomes to become breadwinners and excluded non-whites, men with poor-health, and men whose occupations and behaviour violated IOOF moral codes. It relegated women and minors to an auxiliary role. It had low appeal for Roman Catholics, Jews, and immigrants from continental Europe. It was beyond the reach of men in low-income families.[44]

One might also hypothesize that within such "universalist" orders (i.e. those that did not officially discriminate), there was also some self-segregation—German speakers in one lodge, Irish Catholics in another, and so on. The 1894 *Buffalo Street Guide and Knights of Pythias Lodge Directory* provides a reasonable and unique opportunity to examine the ethnic diversity of one of the nineteenth century's largest universalist fraternal orders, the Knights of Pythias.[45] This directory lists the names of the members of the various Buffalo Pythian lodges as of 1894. By carefully comparing members' surnames, one can roughly extrapolate the ethnic origin of their names and thus the ethnic heterogeneity of their lodge.[46] To give but one brief example (see table 3.2), the Buffalo Pythian directory for the Triangle Lodge No. 92 lists members and their occupations, all or nearly all of whom have strongly German-sounding names (few of which appear to be obviously German Jewish, though such matters surely entail a strong dose of guesswork).

Naturally, it would be unfair to take this as evidence that all Pythian lodges were similarly homogeneous. It is worth noting, however, that in this same year, 1894, a proposal was made at the Pythians' national convention to "forbid the use of any other language than the English in the [Pythian] ritual."[47] Clearly, the English-only proposal was an assault on immigrant members of the organization; an article in the *New York Times* describing the proceedings at the 1894

TABLE 3.2 Membership of the Triangle Lodge No. 92, Knights of Pythias, Buffalo, New York, 1894

Backhause, Alfred (Laborer)	Holler, Gust. (Huckster)
Barnd, Fred (B. & Geiger Steam Heating)	Horn, Fred [no occup. listed]
Benz, Andrew (Bartender)	Hornung, John C. (Barber)
Bingel, Conrad (Contractor and Building)	Hugenschmidt, Anthony [no occup. listed]
Bogenshutz, Wm. A (Painter Foreman)	Joehrling, Herman (Machinist)
Bogenshutz, J. A. (Painter)	Kiefer, Emil [no occup. listed]
Braun, Chas. (Carpenter and Builder)	Knoll, John W. (Physician)
Demerly, Wm. J. [no occup. listed]	Krueger, John [no occup. listed]
Doerflein, Conrad (Barber)	Landraedel [no first name; no occup. listed]
Droegmiller, J. H. (Driver)	Leison, Chas. (Saloon and Restaurant)
Ebinger, Richard (Saloon)	Machwirth, A. (Mfg Cornice and Roofs)
Ernst, John P. (Cooper)	Ney, Frank (Marble Cutter)
Ewig, John B. (Shiping [sic] Clerk)	Nickel, Adam (Bartender)
Frank, Julius (Shipping Clerk)	Niebauer, Ed. (With Giese & Co.)
Frenz, John (Weighmaster Beals & Brown)	Pfender, Christ. [no occup. listed]
Glassmann, H. C. (Buffalo Fish Co.)	Randel, Geo. M. (Barber and Truss Mfg.)
Glassmann, Wm. J. [no occup. listed]	Riemer, Joe (Machinist)
Greenfield, Bernhard [no occup. listed]	Schlickenrieder, Aug. (Malster [sic])
Gritmacher, Chas. (Carpenter)	Schmidt, Peter [no occup. listed]
Grotka, John (Butcher)	Schnabel, Peter (Brewer)
Hachten, Fred (Meat Market)	Schumann, Wm. (Baker)
Harter, Christ. (Bartender)	Smith, Henry [no occup. listed]
Haug, Fred (Shoemaker)	Stauch, Ph. (Real Estate)
Haug, Herman [no occup. listed]	Vanderlau, Peter [no occup. listed]
Hefnagel, John [no occup. listed]	Voetch, Wm. Jr. (Edgewater Hotel)
Herboldt, Ph. M. (Bakery)	Warnecke, C. F. (Saloon)
Hilburger, John (Saloon and Restaurant)	Williams, J. B. (Saloon and Restaurant)
Hoffman, Chas. (Grocer and Saloon)	Wolf, J. R. [no occup. listed]
Hoffman, Christ. [no occup. listed]	Zacher, Chas. F. (Mason)
Hoffman, Peter (Millinery)	Zimmerman, Jacob (Butcher)
Hoffman, Val. (Oyster Dealer and Saloon)	Zuegle, Chas. (Bakery)

Pythian convention in Washington, D.C., went so far as to say, "A serious question to be decided is whether the ritual shall be translated into German. Some German lodges are disposed to be mutinous because this has not been done. The policy of America for Americans has been set up in opposition to this, and Supreme Chancellor Blackwell says it may come to the point of saying to the German members: 'Either become citizens of this country or get out of the order.'"[48]

In response, several German-speaking lodges in Baltimore resigned their charters and organized the alternative Independent Order Knights of Pythias, yet another example of competitive voluntarism in action.[49]

On the other hand, if our theory of fraternal self-segregation is to be deemed truly satisfactory, it must first confront the fact that fraternalism is generally believed to have been most popular in small towns and villages—places without much ethnonational or ethnoreligious diversity to speak of. Relying on their own study of city directories from a nationally representative sample of 26 cities and towns, Gerald Gamm and Robert Putnam find, for example, that "the wave of association building that swept the country in the second half of the nineteenth century was concentrated precisely in cities with low numbers of foreign-born residents."[50] Consulting my own collection of city directories from the nation's 55 largest cities as of 1890, I also find a weak, negative relationship between the size of a city's foreign-born population and its aggregate associational density (see figure 3.5), though I find no such relationship between foreign-born and fraternal lodge density per se (see figure 3.6). Furthermore, I do, find evidence for a fairly robust positive relationship between the size of a city's foreign-born population and the presence of ethnonational clubs and societies (see figure 3.7).[51]

We must take this objection seriously if the arguments made thus far are to be at all convincing. At least three factors help explain the observation that fraternalism was generally most popular in small towns without much ethnic diversity: First, it is quite likely that the type of xenophobia that might motivate

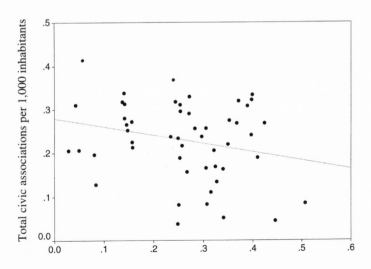

Percentage of residents who are foreign-born

FIGURE 3.5 Immigration and Associationalism, 1890

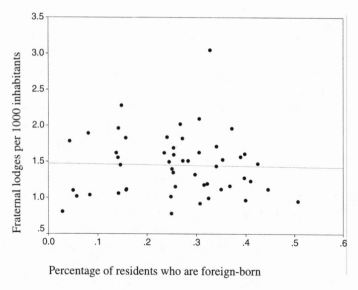

FIGURE 3.6 Immigrants and Fraternal Lodges, 1890

native-born Americans to flock to fraternal lodges would be most prevalent in places where there are few, if any, "foreigners" to fear. My own data show, in fact, that there was a statistically significant, negative relationship between the number of "nativist" fraternities (i.e., those expressly dedicated to the racial purification of the country) in a city and the percentage of foreign-born inhabitants there (see figure 3.8).[52] Second, small villages and towns offer far fewer

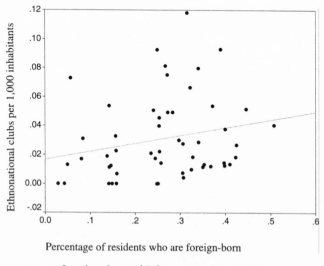

FIGURE 3.7 Immigration and Ethnonationalism, 1890

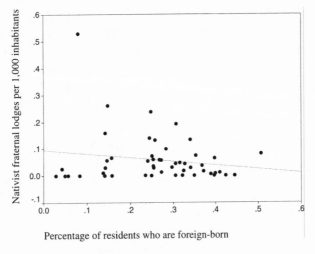

Percentage of residents who are foreign-born

FIGURE 3.8 Immigration and Nativism, 1890

social and financial opportunities for residents than do cities, thus making the appeal of fraternalism that much stronger. According to the Odd Fellows study mentioned earlier:

> The IOOF's below-average popularity in large cities arose partly from stiffer competition for its sick benefit. Compared to small urban places, cities also offered more social alternatives to lodge night. Finally, 46 per cent of the population of the nineteen largest American cities in 1910 were immigrants from continental Europe who tended to have below-average incomes and were largely Roman Catholic or Jewish. They had little prospect of becoming Odd Fellows.[53]

Though many such immigrants formed ethnonational and ethnoreligious fraternal organizations of their own, the difficulties and distractions of big-city life seem to account for the fact that big cities generally had fewer lodges and associations per capita than smaller cities and towns.

Third, one must not discount the fact that residents of even the smallest, least diverse villages and towns would find reasons and ways to self-segregate among themselves—the pious versus the secular, for example, or those from rival clans. Louis Atherton, a historian of midwestern country towns from 1865 to 1950, makes the following observation about the effect of associationalism on small-town America:

> Most devastating of all to small-town "togetherness" has been the advent of organizational life, especially the club movement. Clubs thrive on a sense of exclusiveness or of superiority, which injures community-wide unity.

Lions and Kiwanis, Camp Fire Girls and Girl Scouts, Laff-a-Lot bridge club and Twentieth Century bridge club, Professional Women's club and Mother's club—belonging even to one or more such clubs as these can help to create divisive activities in any town still small enough for people to be generally acquainted. In larger places, where a sense of unity is no longer possible, organizations may unite the individual with a larger whole but they encourage fragmentation and competition elsewhere.[54]

Atherton also cites a 1915 University of Minnesota study of the social and economic life of Ada, Minnesota, a small town north of Fargo: "While the people of the village formerly got together for general good times, to-day they are split up into groups or cliques, each group having its own social activities. . . . The splitting-up into groups within the village has been developed to such an extent as to be unfortunate."[55]

Deciphering the Social Impact of Associationalism on Its Members

Before moving to a discussion of the various probable effects that associational participation may have had on its members, let me first reiterate who exactly I'm referring to, the ideal-typical fraternal lodge goer, shall we say. This person would more likely be a he than a she, white more often than black, and not so rich as to scoff at the idea of fraternal beneficiary insurance but rich enough to make monthly dues payments.[56]

That native-born American males were loath to share benefit plans with blacks, foreigners, and women only complicates this picture. Because of their small but not insignificant size, fraternal lodges held all the promise but none of the power of social organizations founded for community uplift and empowerment. They were neither small enough to engage everyone in the collective negotiations of group process nor large enough to bear the financial or organizational resources to mobilize for meaningful collective action.

On the other hand, most lodges were not islands but archipelagos of risk. The ideal-typical form of fraternal lodge was an extralocal network of affiliated lodges connected by common ritual, aegis, and organization. In some cases, such networks were used to distribute life insurance risks across members in widely disparate locations, thus mitigating the risks implicit in specific occupational, regional, or demographic shortfalls. More important, however, was the political leverage such networks could exert, particularly in the federalist system of American states, where concerted action could muster national results if pursued correctly. Scholars such as Elisabeth Clemens, Theda Skocpol, and Robert Putnam have argued that the fraternal system provided a vital political tool for underrepresented women, workers, and reformers during the Progressive Era.[57]

Nonetheless, the easy replicability of the lodge model also had certain short-comings in the creation and maintenance of strong interpersonal networks among members. Consider, for example, the ease with which a subset of disgruntled or merely dissatisfied members might adopt a preexisting lodge structure under a new name. The frequency with which this took place in the late nineteenth-century United States is simply astonishing, and as I argue in chapter 5, it was a common impediment to concerted collective action on the part of American workers. Rather than settle their differences, members could simply create a splinter group more to their liking. Ultimately, this created an all-too-easy alternative to conflict resolution and compromise.

Furthermore, though independent orders could bar undesirable individuals from membership, they were generally unable to prevent such undesirables from imitating them in content and form. Copycat orders by and for blacks and women are common examples of such unflattering imitation: Comments one (1944) account of "Negro Secret Societies," for example: "Despite every effort of the white secret societies to discourage Negro imitation, Negro facsimiles flourish. The Negro Elks spent thousands of dollars to establish their legal right to use the name and paraphernalia of the Elks. Negro Masonic literature deals almost entirely with arguments against the white Mason's charge that Prince Hall Masonry is clandestine."[58]

It would appear by this account that the leaders of the Negro Elks and Masons were somewhat obsessed with proving their legitimacy. Moreover, by encouraging, indeed imitating, white, middle-class, Protestant respectability, these copycat fraternals created new rifts within their own communities. Sometimes, such efforts were actually counterproductive to their own people's cause, as with the Prince Hall Masons, who are reputed to have favored only those applicants light-skinned enough to distinguish themselves from the stereotypically dark African-American masses. It was not until after the turn of the century (the twentieth, that is), that darker blacks were routinely admitted into the Prince Hall Masons, though they still had to be respectably middle class to join. Until then, says historian William Muraskin, "Intraracial 'blackballing' by light-skinned blacks against darker ones was probably fairly widespread in the Order."[59]

In the longer run, fraternals had (normatively) mixed effects on the social, political, and economic development of the United States. It is hard to know whether German or Irish or Jewish Americans would have done as well without their fraternal networks, though existing records do indicate some ambivalence about the cultural implications of sectarian self-organization:

German immigrants in the United States found themselves in a peculiar situation. *Vereine* seemed more necessary than ever in a society that provided no ready-made avenues for social organization and cultural and political expression, yet the ultimate effect and direction of the *Vereine* were often diffuse and uncertain to their members. . . . Out of this pattern of organizational affiliation according to demographic criteria grew different layers of cultural ideals and political preferences. In the end, the *Vereine* would provide a rich soil for the often clashing views of German-Americans of different classes, whose presumed ethnic solidarity dissolved amid the conflicts of interest between the better-off and the poor, between the upwardly mobile and the working class.[60]

Associations helped accentuate such divisions within communities by providing members with readily available tools for self-segregation.

Nonetheless, as the American economy gradually moved away from the prevailing modes of ethnic stratification in the 1920s and 1930s, hyphenated Americans faced a perplexing dilemma: whether to maintain allegiance to their identity group or to assimilate into the American mainstream. Most chose the latter, at least those who found themselves eligible for better positions on the pecking order. Assimilation was especially prevalent among second- and third-generation members of white ethnic groups, many of whom abandoned their old networks to attend college, intermarry, and move to new, more diverse neighborhoods.[61]

There is no more striking example of twentieth-century assimilation (or deethnicization) than the virtual disappearance of German Americans from the American ethnic landscape. Once one of the most active and vociferous ethnic groups in the United States, German identity virtually disappeared during World War I and has made only minor gains since. Despite their best efforts to deflect anti-German sentiment on the home front, German Americans became the victims of often vicious attacks and condemnations during the war years.[62] In response to a 1918 congressional appeal to repeal the charter of the *Deutsch-Amerikanischer Nationalbund*, Teddy Roosevelt proudly proclaimed, "Organizations like the German-American Alliance have served Germany in America. Hereafter we must see that the melting pot really does melt. There should be but one language in this country—the English."[63]

In turn, ethnic identity among Americans of German ancestry quickly withered on the vine. German-American associations anglicized their titles. German-language newspapers and schools were closed. Traditional German foods were given American names. And young German-American men volunteered in droves for military service to prove their patriotism:

> Among the descendants of the 9 million or so German-speakers who lived on American soil in 1910, observed one historian (in 1966), at most 50,000 of those under eighteen years of age still speak German natively. . . . This is a development whose epic proportions should not be underestimated. The linguistic assimilation of 9 million German Americans—a group, be it remembered, which in 1916 was sufficiently influential to prevent

Theodore Roosevelt's renomination—is the most striking event of its kind in the annals of modern history. No other nationality group of equal numerical strength and living in one country has ever been so wellnigh completely assimilated.[64]

Nonetheless, as another historian comments, "While the First World War was the catalyst for total assimilation of the Germans in America, the amalgamating process was well underway before the American declaration of war in 1917. . . . Centrifugal forces would have caused the German element to disappear as swiftly and less noticeably if the martyr mentality of 1914–1918 had not provided a rallying issue."[65]

White ethnicity did not disappear entirely, of course, but it changed dramatically in relation to the economic and political lives of Americans. After World War I, few new immigrants were allowed into the country, thus drying up the supply of new ethnics needing foreign-language newspapers, clubs, and churches. White Christians increasingly began marrying across ethnic lines, and as more and more of them left the inner city and moved to the suburbs, the geographical basis for ethnic identification began to deteriorate as well.[66] Ironically, this generation of mid-twentieth-century postethnics also left many unanswered questions about the meaning of identity and ancestry for their progeny—the very students now flocking to ethnic studies programs in colleges and universities across the country.

But even before these landmark changes, ethnic communities began experiencing tension between the aspirations of the original immigrant leaders and their children and grandchildren. Historian Josef Barton quotes a real estate agent who observed, in 1909, "The young leaders are as interested in cultural organization as in mutual benefit societies, while the older men tend to be more interested in mutual benefit and religion."[67] Over time, these younger generations came to locate the source of their ethnicity in the holidays they celebrated, the foods they ate, and the ritual trappings of religious observation, passive tokens to something called tradition. They no longer expected to live and work with members of their own ethnicity, as did their forebears. Gradually, ethnicity was reduced to the St. Patrick's and Columbus Day parades, polka bands, and Hanukah celebrations by which we now know it. And as the political salience of ethnicity decreased, so did the presence of ethnonational voluntary organizations (see figure 3.4), though this alone does not explain the decline of associationalism in America.

I turn to this issue in chapter 8, after first exploring several ramifications of the associational tradition on American political development before World War II. As these are an important, if not the most important, part of the story I have to tell about the golden age, I hope that you will bear with me as I take several short detours in American political history: first, an exploration of the associational origins of special-interest group politics in America; second, a short look at the rise and fall of one of the nation's largest ever trade unions, the Knights of Labor; third, an exploration of the various connections between America's tradition of voluntarism and its love affair with guns; and, fourth, a look at the role of fraternal organizations in the rise of the "maternalist" American welfare state. Only after evaluating the perverse and unintended legacies of the golden age will we be ready to turn to the factors underlying its decline.

Part Two

COMPETITIVE VOLUNTARISM AND AMERICAN
POLITICAL DEVELOPMENT

Pundits and scholars often refer to three features of American political culture that distinguish it from its counterparts: the preponderant influence of special-interest groups and lobbies in American politics, the relative absence of class consciousness among American workers, and Americans' unusual love affair with guns. I argue here that all three can be traced back to the golden age of fraternity, its legacies of organization building and interest-group formation, more specifically.

On the one hand, fraternalism created avenues by which Americans could express their political interests outside the traditional party system. Fraternal orders, as well as their close cousins, ethnonational and ethnoreligious clubs, competed with political parties and labor unions for the time and interest of golden age Americans. Because fraternities also helped channel American identity-group formation along ethnic, racial, religious, and gender lines, they undercut the parties and the unions in their efforts to from broad political coalitions mobilized behind common goals.

On the other hand, competitive voluntarism itself gave spawn to a number of related (i.e., quasi-fraternal) organizations which had lasting ramifications of their own. Because fraternalism was an organizational model easily replicated and transformed, it lent itself to the formation of hybrid organizations that adapted its features for alternative purposes. One product of such malleability was the formation of several types of quasi-fraternal organization that entered the fray during this period, namely trade organizations, labor fraternities, elite social clubs, and civilian militias. Cause and effect is somewhat tricky here, as some forms of quasi fraternity predate the golden age as such. Thus, it might be more accurate to say that the spirit of competitive voluntarism in the early United States gave rise to several types of voluntary organization related to, but not necessarily descended from, the fraternal beneficiary society (as described in chapters 2 and 3). The point here, as before, is not that fraternalism alone is responsible for all of the particularities of American political culture but that fraternalism was part of a process I call competitive voluntarism, or the formation of a highly competitive market in which rival voluntary organizations strove to offer ever more attractive goods and benefits to recruit and retain members.

In chapter 4, I discuss the connections between the rise of the fraternal system and the rise of so-called special-interest groups in the late nineteenth century. Here, the primary concern is the rising power of specialized voluntary organizations devoted to pursuing their members' interests through political action outside of the traditional party system. In contrast, chapter 5 focuses on an example of organizational failure—the rise and fall of the Knights of Labor, a hybrid form of labor fraternity—to support the claim that the overheated associational climate of the postbellum years stunted the evolution of working-class politics in the United States. Chapter 6 focuses on another hybrid form of nineteenth-century voluntary organization, the independent civilian militia, which contributed both to the weakness of the American labor movement and to the strength of Americans' affinity for guns. Finally, chapter 7 discusses the role of the nation's many fraternal organizations in blocking efforts to pass universal health insurance legislation in the 1910s. All four chapters aim to elucidate the associational origins of contemporary American political culture.

In making these arguments, I often rely on a unique but not fail-safe line of reasoning: *counterfactual history.* This method entails speculation about the alternate paths history might have taken had some key feature of the social system not existed. Though highly suspect to some, particularly mainstream historians, the counterfactual method is a crucial tool for social scientists interested in the causal import of specific sociological phenomena.[1] Counterfactual history is not a perfect method for identifying causal relationships, but it does help one to imagine where significant forks in the road may have occurred, as well as the alternative outcomes that might have occurred otherwise.

In the argument that follows, the counterfactual goal is to imagine postbellum America without the abundant associationalism documented heretofore. The real question is this: How might American politics have developed differently in the absence of its extensive history of associationalism? Holding other factors constant—namely America's federalist system, its checks and balances, its legal system, its immigrant roots, and its ethnoreligious diversity—what impact did the associational system have on the nation's political development? The following four chapters provide some preliminary answers cobbled together with a dash of punditry here and there.

COMPETITIVE COLLUSION

The Associational Origins of Special-Interest

Group Politics in the United States

When Alexis de Tocqueville visited the United States, the formal business corporation barely existed. There were few if any formal means of protecting capital through legal charter. (As you might recall from chapter 1, the nation's first ever mutual building and loan association was founded in 1831, the very same year Tocqueville and Beaumont toured the country.) By the end of the nineteenth century, however, legal writs of incorporation were absolutely vital to collective enterprise; for-profit firms looked to corporate law as a means of protection from creditors and competitors, and voluntary, nonprofit organizations incorporated as a means of protection from unwanted government interference.[1]

American politics, too, changed dramatically over this same period. America's burgeoning cities and towns created new demand for government-sponsored goods and services, like turnpikes, sewers, and canals.[2] At the same time, the rise of national political parties and the appearance of full-blown electoral campaigning lent a new tenor of professionalism to politics.[3]

Seen in tandem, these forces created a world of opportunity for business leaders and politicians alike. On the one hand, there was work for engineers, contractors, planners, and administrators; on the other hand, there was a clear and present need for reliable means of state revenue collection and redistribution. The costs and benefits of lobbying for favorable treatment were thus enormous. Fortunes could be made building America's new cities, and fortunes could be lost paying the tax bill to finance them.[4]

Like the modern business corporation, born in the mid-nineteenth century, the modern special interest-group organization was a nineteenth-century organizational innovation designed to protect its members by creating a common front behind which they might operate. A well-funded interest group could lobby for special dispensation, holding the threat of electoral reprisal and lost campaign funds over the heads of legislators and executives alike. At the same time, the organization's common front would also allow members to participate in such efforts without exposing themselves to the costs and consequences of influence peddling.[5]

Competition with rival business interests was another pressing problem addressed by this new form of nonprofit organization. Given that small changes in state and municipal policy could have dramatic effects on the business climate for competing concerns, any effort to unify interests behind a common agenda could have huge payoffs over time. Using the voluntary organizational model, doctors and lawyers created professional groups to represent and regulate themselves, manufacturers and railroad owners created employers' associations to share in the fight against labor, and retailers and salesmen formed neighborhood associations and trade groups to support business-friendly urban development.[6]

Seen from a different light, the innovation of the modern special-interest group appears that much more impressive. Consider the dramatic changes that occurred midcentury in the size and scope of American business enterprise: The railroad and steamship had created a commercial revolution of unprecedented proportions, manufacturing had reached unheard of new levels in productivity and product range, and American consumers were just beginning to discover the wonders of retail merchandising.[7] Not only did this create great competition across sectors of the economy; it also created enormous competition within economic sectors for local market dominance. This presented American entrepreneurs with an enormous collective action problem: how to make rival firms cooperate in order to pursue public policies that would benefit them all.

Not surprisingly, the then-popular fraternal lodge model offered a brilliant solution to this and other problems. Since fraternal orders and mutual benefit societies were formally recognized as nonprofit institutions, they were generally unencumbered by either corporate taxation or state oversight (as opposed to for-profit corporations, who were subject to both). Since they were private clubs, they could keep their activities secret and exclude members on any basis they saw fit. And since the early fraternalists had already perfected techniques for founding and coordinating branch lodges, these organizations' sphere of influence could be expanded both quickly and easily.

The basic model of the fraternal lodge thus became the basis for any number of organizational innovations in late nineteenth-century politics, from the formation of professional organizations to the creation of employers' associations. The fraternal form also became useful for the many farmers, factory workers, and female suffragettes then pursuing political influence of their own.[8] In the long run, however, business and professional interests appear to have gotten the better end of the bargain. By using the voluntary organizational model developed and popularized by the early fraternalists, American capitalists gained a tool that would come to dominate American politics of the present day: the special–interest group lobby. Surprisingly few accounts of the golden age of fraternity ever make this connection, choosing instead to adopt James Madison's belief that a proliferation of interests would merely level the playing field.[9]

Political Associations and U.S. History

Much of the debate about American associationalism implicitly, if not self-consciously, revolves around Alexis de Tocqueville's distinction among the "three types of political association," a progression in size and scope from small to large. In its most basic form, asserts Tocqueville, "an association simply consists in the public and formal support of specific doctrines by a certain number of individuals who have undertaken to cooperate in a stated way in order to make these doctrines prevail. . . . An association unites the energies of divergent minds and vigorously directs them toward a clearly indicated goal."[10]

While this might seem an elegant description of all types of political association, this is only the first step in Tocqueville's trichotomy. The tie that binds the members of this first type of association is only an intellectual one:

> Freedom of assembly marks the second stage in the use made of the right of association. When a political association is allowed to form centers of action at certain important places in the country, its activity becomes greater and its influence more widespread. There men meet, active measures are planned, and opinions are expressed with that strength and warmth which the written word can never attain.[11]

So, meeting face to face is a natural step in the progression from mere intellectual coteries to actual political associations. That is, in Tocqueville's words, "in the first of these cases, men sharing one opinion are held together by a purely intellectual tie; in the second case, they meet together in small assemblies representing only a fraction of the party; finally, in the third case, they form something like a separate nation within the nation and a government within the government."[12] In other words, as he states elsewhere, "if the association is to have any power, the associates must be very numerous."[13]

Much recent work on American political development has been oriented around this last conception of associations.[14] By dredging the historical record in search of evidence consistent with Tocqueville's observations on "political association in the United States" (Chap. 4, Part II), historical sociologists have reconstructed a story about their probable impact on American politics. This story, in short, draws on two exceptional features of the sociopolitical landscape in late nineteenth-century America: the system of "courts and parties," in which the party machines supposedly dominated politics at the expense of popular participation,[15] and the unusual number of fraternal organizations founded during this same period.[16]

These two features fit together into a cogent story of American popular mobilization in the following manner: After decades of political domination by the corrupt marshals of state and local party organizations, a broad swathe of Americans came to realize that the fraternal model of extralocal, nonpartisan associationalism could be adopted as a means of putting electoral pressure on politicians, thus creating a people's lobby, or a new way of mobilizing interests outside the traditional confines of the party system:

> The late nineteenth century . . . saw the multiplication of voluntary associations, many with formal committees dedicated to drafting legislation, lobbying, or cultivating public opinion. These organizations provided arenas in which individuals reconstituted themselves as political actors, learned to articulate demands for specific policies, and then to monitor the responses of elected officials.[17]

Adoption of the already prevalent fraternal model of organization was key to this development, according to Elisabeth Clemens, who portrays the populist uprisings of women, farmers, and workers during the Progressive Era as a primary case in point. By exploiting an "appropriate" organizational form for new, conventionally "inappropriate" purposes, she argues, these groups were able to garner widespread support through the familiar and seemingly innocuous lure of the fraternal lodge while, at the same time, passing relatively unnoticed by their key opponents, party officials and urban elites.[18]

Theda Skocpol is another proponent of the political potential of fraternalism. Focusing on the emergence and growth of "broad-gauged, cross-class" associations, many modeled explicitly after the fraternal lodge system, Skocpol argues that this implicitly apolitical form of social organization actually served many Americans as a vehicle for the communication and articulation of their social and political concerns.[19] Thus, both Skocpol's and Clemens's observations are implicitly motivated by the belief that the origin of grassroots politics in American politics, specifically the potential for a viable, vibrant civil society, were firmly grounded outside of the party system in large, extralocal membership associations founded during the late nineteenth and early twentieth centuries.

Reassessing the Political Development Debate

Alexis de Tocqueville's exemplar of an ideal-typical American political association was a convention of 200 delegates assembled in Philadelphia on October 1, 1831, to express their joint opposition to a tariff bill then under consideration in Washington, D.C. At issue were the competing interests of Northern industrialists (who sought vigorous protectionist legislation) and Southern farmers (who complained that protectionist tariffs made manufactured goods unduly expensive), as well as the latent but hotly debated issue of states' rights. In the final analysis, Tocqueville credits the Philadelphia convention with influencing "the attitude of the malcontents" and preparing them "for the open revolt of 1832 against the commercial laws of the Union," a compromise that only temporarily appeased the Southern secessionists.[20]

I raise this example not for its historical value but because of the light it sheds on several claims made by historical sociologists about the role of associationalism in a later period, the Progressive Era. The simple fact I wish to raise here is that, as in Tocqueville's own discussion of the tariff controversy of the early 1830s, associations representing extrapartisan interests were a natural and frequent entity in American politics before the Progressive Era. More important, Tocqueville's example also illustrates the fact that associationally derived social movements do not have to be large, long-lived, or nationally federated to have a lasting impact on political outcomes.

Nonetheless, whether oriented around class, status, or party, the proliferation of associations in American cities after the Civil War did signify the expansion of the power of special interests in the United States. Capitalizing on the constitutionally derived freedom of association, a freedom duly curtailed in some of the great western European powers, many Americans began realizing, if not cultivating, their segmental interests—as property owners, laborers, religious adherents, ethnics, enthusiasts, do-gooders, and businessmen—through exclusive, voluntary, nonprofit organizations.[21]

Besides providing a locus for communal engagement and fellow feeling, these organizations cultivated the powers that many now associate with the very worst aspects of democracy in America—coercive, fractious enterprises dedicated exclusively to the manipulation of public opinion and political decision making. Not only women, farmers, and workers turned to fraternalism as a way to organize outside the party system; the rich, the powerful, and the well educated all formed clubs of one kind or another with the express aim of influencing political outcomes. Moreover, the rich and powerful often used such organizations to do more than threaten politicians with opposition at the polls; deal making and horse trading were common, though largely undocumented, functions of the early special-interest groups, as they are today.

Fine-tuning the Debate: Four Types of Political Association

We have traveled some distance from the ideal-typical conception of fraternalism discussed in chapters 1–3. The connection between political associations and the fraternal movement comes by way of their common organizational form, not their common aspirations. The political associations discussed in this and the next several chapters encompass a special breed. They constitute a species of American association designed specifically for the pursuit of politics; or in the enlightened words of Max Weber, they are groups that "live in a house of 'power.'"[22] The question that concerns us here is the extent and manner in which politically oriented civic associations influenced the trajectory of American political development.

Four different types of political association deserve mention here, though such an abbreviated list cannot begin to do justice to the many variants and hybrids listed in the city directories of the period. First, *mercantile and commercial organizations* are economically oriented lobby groups such as manufacturers' associations, employers' associations, and mercantile organizations, each of which brings together actors sharing a common market niche for mutually advantageous collusion and cooperation.[23] Such commercial cadres are probably one of the oldest forms of association known to humankind, though their postbellum incarnations are indeed unique in the degree of organizational sophistication they brought to the process. Like the medieval guilds of yore, traders and manufacturers used this form of voluntary organization to represent their collective interests on a wide (and nearly monopolistic) scale. By banding together within and across industries, they could use their collective strength in dealing with clients, employees, and political figureheads alike. As Albert Shaw, eminent political scientist and editor of the widely read *American Review of Reviews*, commented (in 1897), "We are governed in this city today, and governed splendidly, by the New York Chamber of Commerce."[24] Such organizations were an increasingly prominent feature of every American city's political landscape.

During the postbellum era, there arose two interesting variants on this model, each distinguished by the ingenuity with which political maneuvering could be veiled behind the guise of American associationalism. The first, boards of trade, chambers of commerce, industrial exposition associations, and the like, provided a forum for businesspeople in different fields to congregate and mobilize on behalf of their collective interests. To give only one example, the Board of Trade of the City of Newark, founded in 1868, lists its objectives as follows:

> For the promotion of trade, the giving of proper direction and impetus to all commercial movements; the encouragement of intercourse between business men; the improvement of facilities for transportation; the correction of abuses; the diffusion of information concerning the trade, manufactures and other interests of the city of Newark; the co-operation of this with similar societies in other cities, and the promotion and development of the commercial, industrial and other interests of said city.[25]

Though such descriptions make trade organizations out to be apolitical groups working on behalf of the entire population, it should be clear that their primary aim was to see to the interests of prominent manufacturers, brokers, and wholesale traders working in that city. Such interests might well conflict with those of their employees, as well as those involved in other sectors of the city's economy, such as professionals, retailers, and those engaged in the service industries.

Returning once again to the 90-year span of Boston city directories (see appendix for details), we see the number of commercial, mercantile, and trade organizations (excluding those representing laborers and professionals) increasing steadily from 1850 to 1920 and tapering off only slightly over the remaining twenty years (see figure 4.1).

A second, and perhaps more insidious, variety of economic association is the *elite social club*. Such groups are exceedingly difficult to identify in city directories of the period because most elite social clubs did not betray their elitism by name, choosing instead more subtle titles (such as the City, Metropolitan, or Union League Club). I was thus unable to count the number of such organizations in Boston with any accuracy, though I might venture to guess that their number neither increased over time nor was very large to begin with. Nonetheless, according to historian David Hammack, elite social clubs in this period tended to revolve around three interests—those claiming a direct ancestral line to some quasi-mythical, old-city elite; those joined by their wealth and their interest in perpetuating it; and those attached by a common appreciation for the arts and learned pursuits. Although such affiliations did sometimes tend to overlap, members were more likely than not to express their social preferences by joining clubs of one, perhaps two, but rarely all three categories, thus confirming Weber's notion of the social differentiation of status groups within socioeconomic strata.[26]

Once again, European standards set an exceedingly important precedent for the establishment of elite social clubs in American cities. Nearly every feature of America's "top" social clubs was modeled after London's club scene, from membership requirements (women were strictly forbidden, and male guests closely

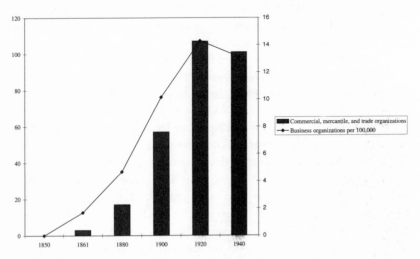

FIGURE 4.1 Commercial, Mercantile, and Trade Organizations in Boston, 1850–1940

monitored) to architecture (McKim and White, foremost architects of America's great nineteenth-century clubhouses, modeled much of their work after the elegant clubs of London's Pall Mall district).[27] On the other hand, American social clubs were less a home away from home than their English forebears and more a place for selective sociability: "There [in England], for the most part, people belong to clubs in order to frequent them, and not by way of reference or passport to high social circles [as in the U.S.]."[28] Like most things in the New World (relative to the Old), American clubs were both easier to join and more instrumental in purpose. Elite club membership was a passport to the highest levels of American society, one that members need feel no embarrassment about using for their own best interests.

Some of these clubs were formed with genuine political purposes in mind. The Union League Clubs which spread across the country during the Civil War were expressly founded to support the Union effort for example, on the other hand, the Union League was not above boosterism, self-promotion, or, influence-peddling.[29] Consider the following apologetic confession in the *Chronicle of the Union League of Philadelphia*:

> Ever since 1875 the Union League had abstained from taking part in the discussion or determination of municipal or State politics or elections.[30] ... The city of Philadelphia was, however, about to pass under the provisions of a new Act of Assembly (the Bullitt Charter), which greatly modified its form of government and the character of the offices to be filled. The mayor of the city was thereafter to be an official of such dignity and power that his qualifications became a matter of vital importance. If nominations had then been made, the Board would simply have urged members to weigh their action carefully, but as no conventions had yet been called it was suggested that a committee of twenty-five members be appointed by the Union League to take public action on the election, selecting a worthy candidate for party support. This resulted in the nomination of Edwin H. Fitler, a member of the Union League, as the Republican candidate and his election as the first mayor of Philadelphia under the Bullitt Charter [1886].[31]

In contrast, a group of prominent New York Democrats established the Manhattan Club in 1865 with the express purpose of countering the political power of the (New York) Union League Club, a known bastion of Republicanism. "None but Democrats" were eligible, and the membership rolls of the Manhattan Club read like an unexpurgated history of Gilded Age excess, numbering among them the leaders of the Tweed ring; various Democratic mayors, governors, and presidents; and a nice handful of robber barons. In his 1873 monograph, *The Clubs of New York*, Francis Gerry Fairfield says the following about the goings-on at the Manhattan Club:

It has been here that most great national questions affecting the Democratic party have been settled; the Manhattan Club being the spider, so to speak, that spins the gossamer webs of policy, and manages the details of campaigns, itself silent within the mahogany doors of its splendid Fifth Avenue den. Here, too, have been incubated the great railroad wars of the last decade. Here Vanderbilt and Drew, both members, have met to play whist, while enacting in Wall Street and the courts the first great railway struggle, and playing the rôles of opposing generals in the great battle of tactics.[32]

Adds Fairfield, "James Fisk, Jr., was not a member, and appears as the only railroad lord who has not made No. 96 a lounging place."[33]

In general, elite club members were among the richest people in the country, and they apparently had few misgivings about collaborating with their comrades in political and economic matters alike. Since the collective wealth and social power of elite club members were simply unmatched elsewhere in society, these clubs proved an important locus for collective mobilization of money and power. The 1894 membership roster of New York's Metropolitan Club includes, for example, "six Harrimans, six Morgans, six Roosevelts, six Cuttings, five Vanderbilts, four Havemeyers, three Duponts, three Auchinclosses, three Frelinghuysens, two Astors and two Rockefellers."[34] Other leading industrialists, such as Charles Schwab, Andrew Carnegie, Henry Clay Frick, and Sir Henry Bessemer, were said to have been frequent guests. Andrew Carnegie's megalithic steel conglomerate, U.S. Steel, is even said to have been "born" in the club library.[35]

The third type of interest group, by far a more legitimate and thus more publicly visible form, was the *professional organization*—medical societies; dental societies; bar associations; teachers' organizations; organizations for civil, mechanical, and electrical engineers; and so on. Professional organizations in Boston grew rapidly in number after 1850, peaking in 1880, dipping, then rising again after 1920 (see figure 4.2). This 1880–1920 dip does seem somewhat surprising, until one considers that both the medical and legal professions were working hard to wrest control over their internal affairs during this period. However, not all nineteenth-century professional organizations were destined to become well-enfranchised national behemoths like the American Bar Association or the American Medical Association. City directories from the late nineteenth century list dozens of professional organizations, representing groups like doctors of homeopathy and eclectic medicine, though the number of such atypical professional organizations did dwindle over time.[36]

Despite such internal disputes, professional groups had a huge stake in local politics, and they were not reluctant to use their sway whenever possible. A good example is the Association of the Bar of the City of New York (ABCNY). Founded in 1870 to represent the interests of a small set of superelite New York lawyers (almost Anglo-Protestant to a man), the ABCNY was active in New York City

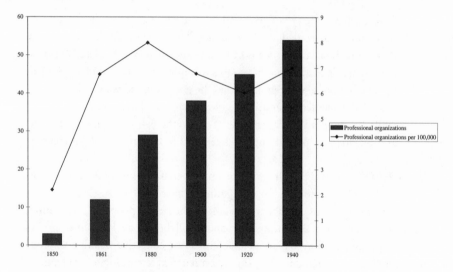

FIGURE 4.2 Professional Organizations in Boston, 1850–1940

politics from the outset, spearheading the Tweed corruption investigation, helping to found various independent councils to investigate city officials, and actively working to gain influential appointments in state and local government
for its members. This was typical of big-city professional organizations. Given
that most locally relevant laws, appropriations, and appointments are made at
the local level under the American system, associations entrenched in local policy
networks can be particularly influential in local affairs.[37]

Neighborhood associations, civic clubs, and citizens' groups represent a fourth
type of political association to emerge during this period (see figure 4.3). This
category of political association is somewhat broad, including a variety of voluntary groups organized around specific political agendas, from prohibition
to tax, tariff, and immigration reform. Such groups sometimes enter politics
through the electoral system, threatening elected officials with retribution if their
interests are ignored. At other times, such groups might resort to other forms of
political maneuvering, cutting deals, trading favors, and generally conspiring in
pursuit of common interests.

The neighborhood association was one form of special-interest group lobbying that became increasingly prevalent in American cities after the Civil War,
when expensive infrastructural improvements and large municipal construction
projects became essential for community growth and prosperity. Because property taxes pay for most municipal improvements and property values fluctuate
with them, local homeowners, merchants, and real estate developers all had a
stake in decisions concerning urban development.[38] Historian Joseph Arnold
notes that in late nineteenth-century Baltimore, "one locality after another sought

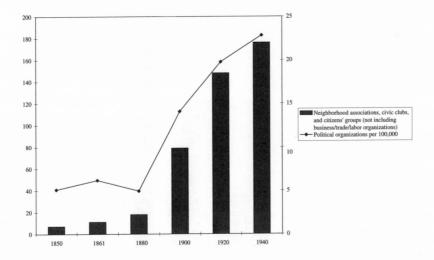

Legend: Neighborhood associations, civic clubs, and citizens' groups (not including business/trade/labor organizations); Political organizations per 100,000

FIGURE 4.3 Neighborhood Associations, Civic Clubs, and Citizens' Groups in Boston, 1850–1940

to organize a nonpartisan neighborhood association of businessmen and property owners. From this organizational effort grew Baltimore's almost century-old tradition of local associationalism—political pressure groups outside the regular party structure."[39] The first neighborhood associations were organized in Baltimore between 1884 and 1886 (the Old Town Merchants and Manufacturers Association and the West Baltimore Improvement Association), and by 1893 there were 21 of them in all, each representing some particular part of the city. Like fraternal lodges, these groups sponsored social events and helped bring community members in contact with one another; but, more important, they represented an early (i.e., preprogressive) form of special interest mobilization outside the confines of the traditional party system.

Rhetoric and Reform in American Associational History

In the abstract, the emergence of political associations in the American polity after the Civil War might seem like something of a good thing (normatively speaking). Veterans mobilized to expand government pension awards for their service in the Civil War (figure 4.4 documents the rise of veterans' groups in Boston, 1850–1940); women organized to fight for maternalist welfare policies and the right to vote (figure 1.6 documents the growth of women's groups in Boston, though it should not be assumed that all or even most of these groups dedicated themselves expressly to the cause of women's rights); and workers, too, founded voluntary organizations to represent their interests in collective bar-

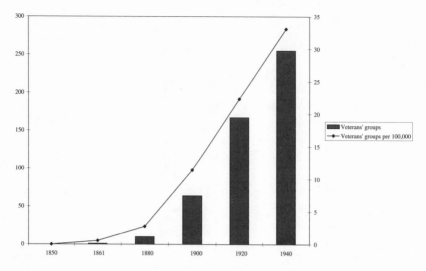

FIGURE 4.4 Veterans Organizations in Boston, 1850–1940

gaining with employers (see figure 4.5). Nonetheless, two important things must be kept in mind in order to weigh the ultimate ramifications of this transformation in American political action.

First, the division of the American polity into ever so many interest-group organizations greatly hindered Americans' ability to unite around what they had in common. Labor, for example, never managed to unify itself as a true political

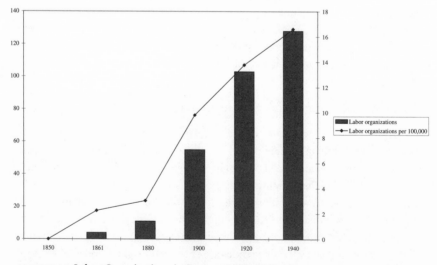

FIGURE 4.5 Labor Organizations in Boston, 1850–1940

coalition by and for workers, relying instead on unions as weak collective-bargaining organizations (see chapter 5). America's ethnic, racial, and religious diversity is often blamed for the failures of its labor unions, but as I show in the next two chapters, the rise of American associationalism actually played a dramatic (and easily overlooked) role in the history of American labor.

Second, it should be mentioned that until the New Deal, American voters were generally reluctant to endorse large-scale, government-run benefit plans, with the exception of an enormous pension scheme for Civil War benefits and short-lived pensions for worthy mothers and their children.[40] Voluntary organizations representing veterans and mothers deserve some of the credit for these legislative successes, but this merely begs the question: Why give benefits to these groups and not others? Why did the rest of the American electorate, namely, the millions of voters who would receive no benefits under either plan, agree to go along with such schemes? The answer lies, I believe, not only in the structure of American government at the time but also in the nature of American social organization, that is, fraternalism.

Fraternal lodges evolved into the primary providers of pension plans for white American males before the early twentieth century (see chapter 2). Millions of dollars were invested in lodge burial and sickness insurance policies, and many fraternities offered health insurance through the lodge system as well. Women, however, were largely excluded from such benefit plans. Thus, social insurance was constructed in the United States as the exclusive privilege of male fraternalists. In the early twentieth century, as the nations of western Europe steadily institutionalized liberal benefit policies for all their citizens, Americans stood by the excesses of fraternal privilege. Working men should buy insurance policies for themselves and their families, they argued; women can rely on their husbands for support, or if that fails, they can appeal to social service agencies for aid. As for those thousands of American men who were either unable to afford or socially ineligible to join fraternities or commercial insurance companies. . . . Well, they would just have to make do.

American labor leaders are often blamed for America's niggardly welfare state. According to many histories of the period, Samuel Gompers and his powerful American Federation of Labor killed national social welfare legislation in the early twentieth century by actively opposing it. This is true to an extent, though the nation's many insurance-providing fraternal orders were equally as vociferous in the fight against expanding benefits for the sick and needy (see chapter 7). The pressing question is not why Gompers opposed national welfare legislation but why such a conservative labor union came to be the primary organization representing the nation's workers in the first place. American workers sometimes experimented with other forms of representation, but they generally failed to hold these organizations together through thick and thin. Part of the problem was the tremendous power factory and railroad owners had to wage war against them (see chapter 6). An even bigger part of the problem was the astronomical number of other fraternal, social, and religious organizations that were competing for their attention (see chapter 5). Thus, associationalism unconsciously rendered obstacles to lasting labor organization at both ends.

Another reason for the difference in American and western European political development was, as Theda Skocpol argues, Americans' fear of big government, more specifically, their distaste for party patronage and the corruption that presumably went with it.[41] Though there is good cause to be skeptical about such antimachine rhetoric, the historical opposition of American voters to the expansion of government services only reinforces the need to appreciate the impact of new elite and commercial interest groups in the postbellum years, for it was exactly such groups that spearheaded the drive in many American cities to disenfranchise ordinary voters.

Arguably, the accusations reformers hurled at the party machines stemmed from their desire to oust party politicians from office, rather than from any genuine interest in reforming politics. The "ward-o-cratic" party system gave special voice to ordinary, working-class voters in the various sections of the city, and under such a system, elites had a tough time getting elected. In response, elites formed reform organizations like New York's Committee of Seventy, a private watch-dog organization put together by leaders of the New York State Chamber of Commerce, Good Government Club, and civil service reforms clubs. One of the committee's primary goals was to lobby for electoral reforms that would limit the power of the parties and their middle- and working-class constituents.[42] There is no more telling example of this type of elite voluntary action than the city manager movement, which swept the country at the beginning of the twentieth century after a terrible storm left the city of Galveston, Texas, in ruins.

Galveston had had its fair share of elite interest groups. The city's Deep Water Committee existed for the sole purpose of lobbying the federal government for subsidies to help improve the city's harbor, a mainstay of the local economy. The Galveston Chamber of Commerce, Citizens' Club, and Good Government Club were all organized around the interests of a select cadre of Galveston elites. And when the hurricane of 1900 left the city with 6,000 dead and $17 million in property damage, they all worked in concert to capitalize on the opportunity to increase their power and influence.

First, members of the Deep Water Committee blamed the existing city government for the wreckage of the hurricane. Then, they began petitioning the Texas State legislature for permission to abolish the popularly elected city council (in which every ward of the city was duly represented by a council member) and replace it with a five-member city commission. Their argument seemed reasonable enough: Representatives of the committee said that they sought simply to reestablish the city's municipal administration on the firm footing of "efficient business practice." On the other hand, they planned to pursue this goal by disenfranchising city voters. Rather than running a citywide election for mayor and city council, the governor would now be empowered to appoint five commissioners to oversee city affairs—a general manager and four commissioners specializing in finance and revenue, police and fire, streets and public property, and waterworks and sewage—a modern-day oligarchy, if you will. Furthermore, the plan granted the commissioners the power to both authorize municipal appropriations and oversee their execution, an invitation for corruption if there ever was one.[43]

Galveston's standing mayor, Walter C. Jones, former chief of police and a favorite of the city's four heavily working-class wards, severely criticized the plan, protesting that it endorsed "government without the consent of the governed."[44] Jones's fears were warranted, but the Deep Water Commission ran a vigorous publicity campaign, using every means at their disposal to convince the city's electorate that the status quo meant disaster, that bankruptcy was staring the city in the face, and that the commission system promised the panacea of sound business methods. And though the system was later modified to popularly elect two of the five commissioners, members of the City Club held those seats for years to come, leading some to call E. R. Cheesborough, director of the City Club, "the boss of Galveston." Writing of the incident to a cousin of his some years later, Cheesborough commented that the statement made him laugh, but "to a certain extent it is true."[45]

As journalist George Kibbe Turner described it in his now-famous October 1906 *McClure's Magazine* article, Galveston's reformist elite had rid the city of vice, crime, and "the ward—*the most vicious political unit in our democratic government.*" Turner concluded (somewhat cynically), "There is in Galveston to-day the most powerful motive in the world for good government—the normal, healthy selfishness of the individual citizen opposed continually to the craft and greed of the exploiters of the community. And it is the new form of administration which made this possible." In Turner's opinion, the Deepwater planners were successful because "they viewed Galveston, not as a city at all, but a great ruined business." Turner went so far as to declare that Galveston was now run by "the proper class of men," predicting that "within two years it is believed that every city of consequence in the State" will have followed suit.[46]

Turner was right. When elites around the country got wind of the successful Galveston coup and muckraking magazines like *McClure's* began running stories on Galveston's battle against the electorate, cities all around Texas began adopting the so-called Galveston plan, as Turner had predicted. Soon, cities outside of Texas even started adopting "reform" plans of their own, such as the Des Moines plan drafted by members of that city's Commercial Club.[47]

For a short time, passion for the Galveston–Des Moines Commission Plan swept the nation. Of 267 cities studied by sociologist David Knoke, 107 adopted some form of the commission plan by 1919, though nearly half of those abandoned it again by 1942.[48] More popular still was the council-manager plan, a related municipal innovation first developed in Staunton, Virginia, in 1908.[49] The council-manager plan combined a popularly elected city council with a professionally trained city manager. It eliminated the old, ward-based system of voting, nonetheless. By 1919, the council-manager plan was incorporated into the National Municipal League's "model city charter," and it gradually emerged as one of the most popular forms of local governance in the United States.[50] Arguably, this streamlined style of municipal governance foreshadowed the broader transformation of American political practice in the later twentieth century, when special-interest lobbies, "policy experts," and single-issue voter blocs would increasingly come to dominate politics at the expense of the ordinary voter.[51]

The origins of this system lie in the period just discussed, when a variety of new interest-group organizations emerged in the midst of the fraternalist fray, many devoted to the pursuit of the segmental self-interest of doctors, lawyers, factory owners, business owners, financiers, and so forth. America's extensive tradition of fraternal organization provided the institutional fodder for these new movements. As exemplified in the case of the city-manager movement, small, exclusive voluntary organizations were created to sell an extrapartisan agenda to the public at large.

In the long run, the emergence of interest-group politics had both positive and negative consequences on American political development. By using organizational innovation to transcend the limits of the normal party system, associations provided new leverage for interest-group organizations in the American political arena. The well-documented successes of temperance reformers, suffragettes, and civil service reformers are important outcomes in this respect. Nonetheless, these same political innovations launched an organizational cascade whereby the extrapartisan efforts of challengers were often matched by their opponents, thus creating a spiraling descent into political gamesmanship, propaganda, and influence peddling. The overall trajectory of the temperance movement provides an excellent illustration in this respect, though similar processes can also be observed in the arenas of labor agitation, institutional reform, and social welfare policy. In each case, one sees a widespread coalition mobilized for social change gradually transformed into a special-interest lobby isolated from its members, not to mention its original mission.[52]

In the next chapter, I examine yet another example of coalition building transformed by organizational pressures, as well as outside competition—the Knights of Labor, one of the most successful and short-lived labor organizations in American history.

THE HIGH COST OF HIGH-EXIT ORGANIZATIONS

The Struggle to Organize American Workers

Labor historians almost unanimously agree that the Knights of Labor, the largest single labor organization in American history, held enormous promise as a means of unifying workers of different ethnic, religious, and racial backgrounds. They see it as a group that had genuine potential to create a viable working-class political coalition capable of forcing labor issues onto the national stage.[1]

Today, the nation's largest labor union, the AFL-CIO (American Federation of Labor and Congress of Industrial Organizations), represents a smaller percentage of American workers than did the Knights of Labor in 1886, when as many as 20 percent of all workers were affiliated with the order.[2] Nonetheless, soon after reaching its height, the Knights' membership began a steady and rapid decline, after which the organization never regained its national prominence or stature. Its collapse, furthermore, had wide-ranging repercussions for American politics, as subsequent workers' organizations took a more conservative tactk toward labor organization:

> Ideologically, the Knights' defeat demoralized those who championed radical reform and classwide organization while empowering those who promoted pragmatic politics and sectional labor unions. Both the demoralized and the empowered drew lessons from the defeat of the order, and these lessons made it much more difficult for radical activists to persuade workers that inclusive unionism was possible or desirable.[3]

Had the Knights of Labor succeeded in organizing (or maintaining organization among) a broad swathe of the American working class, labor unions in America might well have come closer to matching the achievements of their western European counterparts. In fact, argues Kim Voss, the American working class as of the mid-1880s seemed every bit as politically active as their western European rivals.

So why, then, did the Knights collapse, whereas European workers' movements continued to build on existing strengths? Why did American trade unions take such a different course than the labor coalitions of nearly every democratic nation in western Europe?

Current scholarship on the Knights of Labor attributes their calamitous decline to two factors: the persistent tension between skilled craftsmen and unskilled workers[4] and, more decisively, the fierce opposition of employers' associations, which brought various extralegal means of opposition to bear on union activists.[5] Using time-series data on the organizational founding and mortality of Knights' lodges in the state of New Jersey, Kim Voss has examined the salience of both arguments in detail. Her New Jersey data show that it was opposition from employers' associations, not intraclass conflict within the Knights' organization itself, that led to the dissolution of so many Knights' lodges after 1886.[6]

Clearly, there is much truth in Voss's argument. Employers' associations did mount fierce resistance to the labor movement throughout the 1870s, 1880s, and 1890s, breaking numerous strikes and testing the will of striking workers. As I demonstrate in chapter 6, part of the reason for this was actually the nation's long-standing tradition of civilian militias, a legacy that by the 1870s was modified to allow state governments to ban some military organizations (those representing workers, ethnics, and socialists) while encouraging others (those mustered to protect the interests of factory and railroad owners, as well as urban elites).

Beyond the effective opposition hypothesis, most scholarly answers look to the internal characteristics of the Knights' organization to reveal its weaknesses. These include the loose federal structure of the order, variance across local assemblies in structure and form, the divisive issue of whether to admit black workers or not, and the lack of a unifying myth or ideology that would encourage members to persevere in hard times.[7] Although empirically valid and clearly important, these endogenous explanations of the Knights' vulnerability to opposition fail to acknowledge one accompanying feature rarely considered in the literature on American labor history: the exogenous competition to labor from the burgeoning associational sphere, particularly for groups like the Knights, which adopted the fraternal model of organizing at the height of its popularity.

Labor organizations were far from the only groups competing for the loyalty of American workers in the late nineteenth century. Religious societies, fraternal orders, ethnic clubs, and mutual savings societies were all flourishing at the same time. One distinctive feature of the Knights of Labor, as opposed to other labor organizations at the time, was that it self-consciously sought to usurp the functions of these other associations by creating a single, multipurpose fraternity for American workers across the country. This put the Knights in direct competition with the nation's booming fraternal movement, whereas the more successful American Federation of Labor, which survived the 1880s and grew in the decades thereafter, self-consciously avoided such competition by articulating more modest goals and a minimum of rhetoric.

But where the defection argument really proves its worth is in its ability to explain both the success of the AFL and the success of European trade unions and workers' parties in light of the Knights' failure. One major difference between the Knights and its more successful counterparts was that it put itself in direct competition with a thriving form of social affiliation: the fraternal lodge.[8] One chief characteristic of American fraternities was their high defection rates— fraternities were high-exit organizations, thus making them particularly vulnerable to membership defection and decline. The rival AFL self-consciously avoided this liability by representing itself as anything but a fraternal order: It organized workers by occupation and industry, and its sole focus was on earning better wages for members. American workers could thus remain members of the AFL and participate in their local fraternal, religious, and ethnonational organizations at the same time. The overreaching philosophy of the Knights forced members to choose between these competing loyalties.

By this same period, furthermore, European workers had already eschewed the fraternal tradition in favor of trade-based organizations and Christian-worker parties. Though their labor organizations espoused far-reaching goals and ideologies like those of the Knights of Labor, European workers no longer relied on the fraternal form as a model for organization (an overgeneralization, of course, but one generally supported by the literature on political suppression and worker activism in nineteenth-century Europe, as discussed in chapter 1). By the late nineteenth century, European laborers were founding low-exit unions with broad benefits and ambitious political aims. This, coupled with the general absence of competing lodges and associations in the European civic sphere, gave European labor organizations a far better chance of recruiting and retaining members.[9]

But for this defection argument to be truly believable, I must also provide hard evidence to support the notion that defection from the Knights was in fact stimulated by the lure of rival affiliations, as opposed to the brute force of effective opposition (i.e., mercenary armies created by employers' associations). In the following pages, I offer both qualitative and quantitative evidence in support of the argument that defecting Knights flocked to (and founded) dozens of new rival organizations, which better represented their interests by pursuing less ornate and more reasonable goals. In other words, workers eschewed the Knights' one-group/many-functions model and instead joined fraternal lodges for their collegial benefits and trade unions for occupational representation, thus dividing their time between noncompeting groups.

I first outline several key controversies within the Knights that provided a catalyst to defection. These controversies revolved primarily around the existing ethnoreligious differences of worker-members, thus confirming the role of cultural heterogeneity in the trajectory of American labor. But, as I have argued earlier, this is not in itself a satisfactory explanation for the weakness of American labor organizations. Associationalism exacerbated these differences, creating organizational affiliations that then put conflicting demands and constraints on their members. It was these constraints—the American Roman Catholic clergy's demand that Catholics not join the Knights, for example—that made diversity an impediment to the unification of American workers, not their basic diversity as such. Catholic clergy in Europe were not similarly opposed to labor organizations at least partly because European workers were not faced with the same pressure from rival voluntary organizations competing for their time, allegiance, and money. The American clergy saw fraternalism as a threat to American Catholicism, on the other hand, and they responded by creating quasi-fraternal organizations of their own. They also demanded that faithful Catholics break all ties with non-Catholic fraternal orders like the Knights of Labor.

I would not have you believe that Knights left the order simply because quitting was an easy thing to do; nor do I argue that effective opposition from employers was not a powerful impetus for defection. I argue that competitive voluntarism created an atmosphere in which labor activists either had to craft catchall fraternal organizations that could compete with their many rivals at the time or they had to find new, sparsely populated niches where they would face less competition. The Knights chose the former strategy and, after a short boom, quickly faded into obscurity. The AFL, on the other hand, created a new niche in which they could offer laborers something different without pitting themselves against the more popular fraternal orders of the age.

But because I realize that my argument is novel, ambitious, and controversial, I take several additional steps toward making my case. First, I demonstrate, through a brief history of the Knights' ups and downs, how the fraternal character of the organization got it into trouble with its rival, church-based organizations, which in turn forced members (particularly Catholic members) to choose between competing loyalties. (The AFL surely had many Catholic members, but it avoided alienating them by adopting an organizational model inoffensive to church leaders.) Second, I show how the effort to appease Catholic members created further problems for the Knights, as non-Catholic members grew angry at the drive to defraternalize the rites and rituals of the order (i.e., remove the secret oath and generally downplay its fraternal trappings). Third, I show how both constituencies fell into conflict with a third group—members who joined to pursue radical political goals. Thus, one sees in full the internal tensions created by the overreaching goals of the Knights' organization: In trying to be all things to all people, it satisfied none and created the groundwork for a massive defection.

It is an open question to which groups former Knights were most likely to defect (if at all), but in Newark, New Jersey, 60 Knights' lodges folded between

1886 and 1889 and 11 new mutual benefit societies were founded over that same period, as well as 3 new temperance fraternities; 5 new Protestant, nativist fraternities; and 18 new general fraternal orders.[10] This profound growth in Newark's voluntary sector and its temporal correspondence with the collapse of so many Knights' assemblies seems to indicate some significant relationship between the two. If the defection hypothesis is in fact correct, workers would have rejected the generalist aims of the Knights' organization and compartmentalized their various interests in separate associational affiliations, thus differentiating the religious, social, political, and economic elements of their social lives. To test this assumption, I take one last, rather monumental step: Relying on hundreds of pages of city directory listings, I provide a quantitative test of the thesis that cities that were experiencing a drop in Knights' participation experienced a similar and proportional increase in participation in other forms of fraternal and union organizations (as measured by the number of fraternal lodges and non-Knights-affiliated union assemblies in that same city for the following year). I also show that this relationship holds up even when one controls for the potential effect of failed strikes (i.e., effective opposition) on membership defection. Unfortunately, membership data for most Knights' lodges has been lost because of inadequate archiving (i.e., someone's leaky garage), so we must rely on data about the number of lodges listed in annual city directories.[11] The logic of this test will become clear shortly; for now, suffice it to say that I provide several types of empirical evidence that support the notion that defection from the Knights was related to a subsequent increase in related forms of civic participation.

In my own mind, I take this as evidence for the fact that the presence of so-many comparable alternatives provided a stimulus for defection from the Knights. Note, however, that I am not implying a one-to-one correlation between the rise of the golden age of fraternity and the collapse of the Knights of Labor. Clearly, the birth of the fraternal movement preceded the Knights by at least a decade; this is exactly my point, in fact. The Knights of Labor was formed in the prevailing image of the day—the fraternal lodge. Its founders were themselves active participants in other fraternal orders, and their aim in creating the Knights was to found a new fraternity expressly for working men and women. For a time, this strategy worked well; the Knights' early membership drives were helped by the general mania for clubbing. Following a series of internal controversies and external defeats, however, the same recipe that had helped the Knights grow soon led to its demise. Given so many associational alternatives, as well as the ever-present option to form new associations in the face of dissatisfaction, individual Knights began to abandon the order at the first sign of trouble.[12] Thus, the fact that the general growth of associationalism was not confined to the period of the Knights' collapse (roughly 1887–1890) supports, rather than hinders, my argument. The Knights of Labor was a product of its times, and a victim of them as well.

Note, too, that this perspective dovetails nicely with scholarship on the twentieth-century American labor movement, particularly the work of political scientist Ira Katznelson. Katznelson blames the failure of twentieth-century American working-class movements on the "radical separation in people's consciousness, speech, and activity of the politics of work from the politics of community. . . . Most members of the working class thought of themselves as workers at work, but as ethnics (and residents of this or that residential community) at home."[13] Similarly, historian Richard Oestreicher writes that "while there was untapped class sentiment in the electorate, even in explicitly class-oriented campaigns, ethno-cultural factors and organizational resources shaped the potential base of working-class support."[14] Where my work differs from these accounts is in its specific mode of explanation: My account emphasizes the role of associationalism (and its incumbent organizational models) in the fragmentation of the American working class, as opposed to Katznelson's and Oestreicher's focus on electoral outcomes.

In fact, the defection argument goes straight to the heart of current debate about the impact of associationalism on American politics: Ethnocultural historians have gone to great lengths to illustrate the effects of ethnic and religious heterogeneity on American electoral behavior in the late nineteenth century, but they have yet to consider the impact of the myriad civic associations that spawned in their midst.[15] Plainly stated, I argue that the associational tradition in America—lauded by Tocqueville, Schlesinger, Putnam, and Skocpol—had an inhibitory effect on the American labor movement in the late nineteenth century. That is, the profusion of trade unions, religious sodalities, fraternal lodges, benevolent societies, and mutual benefit organizations had the unintended consequence of undermining workers' ability to organize and maintain a vital constituency mobilized for decisive political action. It is through these organizations that American ethnocultural diversity expressed itself, and it is in spite of them that the American labor movement achieved any lasting national profile at all, namely in the guise of the American Federation of Labor.

Indeed, the AFL provides a significant counterexample of successful organization in the face of both competition from rival associations and opposition from employers. Though the AFL took a much more conciliatory attitude toward employers and contract disputes than did the Knights, it was not above organizing strikes and walkouts to pursue specific goals. In this sense, then, it was just as susceptible to effective opposition as was the Knights of Labor. Unlike the Knights, however, the AFL was much more successful in both negotiating with employers and retaining members. Presumably, this success occurred because the AFL organized itself around very different principles than the Knights, prefiguring a new organizational model for American associationalism—the incorporated, focused, unilingual, special-interest group (see chapter 4). In other words, the AFL was designed to pursue very specific ends, as opposed to the

Knights, which espoused any number of goals for labor. Sensing the organizational problems plaguing the Knights—that is, its quasi-fraternal nature and fuzzy agenda—Samuel Gompers, founder of the AFL, described the Knights as a "hodgepodge with no basis for solidarity."[16] Gompers and the AFL staff thus self-consciously rejected the fraternal model on which the Knights was founded.

In his autobiography, *Seventy Years of Life and Labor*, Gompers goes to great lengths to describe the AFL's early struggle to redefine American unionism, particularly in the face of strident opposition from the Knights. Detailing the specific shortcomings of the Knights, Gompers describes it as "an organization with high ideals but purely sentimental and bereft of all practical thought and action." In contrast, Gompers's strategy in founding the AFL was to abandon fraternalism, avoid political posturing, and establish "a business basis for unionism"—low dues and a tightly structured national federation of subservient union locals. Although Gompers's main goal was to promote "the stability of labor organizations," an unintended consequence of this move was to neglect ideologically motivated pursuits, thus minimizing labor's impact on national politics.[17] According to one scholarly account, "Unions affiliated with the AFL in the main chose this [more conciliatory] course of action because their leaders concluded from the experiences of the late nineteenth century that 'pure and simple' craft unionism was the only viable form of working-class organization in the United States as the twentieth century began."[18] Thus, from what was perhaps the nation's most ambitious experiment with labor activism, the Knights of Labor, came a much more modest avatar, one that set the tone of labor politics for decades to come.

One might well consider this to be another downside of competitive voluntarism, that free expression and a welter of affiliations can promote factionalism and dissent, as well as democratization and a more civil society.[19] Given so many types of voluntary association in open competition for members' time and money, many Americans felt that they had to choose between rival allegiances to their religion, their social class, their race, and their ethnic group, among others. In turn, many avoided such conflicts by simply compartmentalizing their various priorities in different (i.e., multiple) associational affiliations.

Qualitative Evidence for the Defection Hypothesis

In his writings on the American labor movement, Friedrich Engels succinctly put his finger on the abiding strengths and weaknesses of the Knights of Labor:

> An immense association spread over an immense extent of the country in innumerable "assemblies," representing all shades of individual and local opinion within the working class; the whole of them sheltered under a platform of corresponding indistinctness and held together much less by their

impracticable constitution than by the instinctive feeling that the very fact of clubbing together for their common cause makes them a very great power in the country.[20]

At its height, in 1886, the Knights had approximately 700,000 members who were affiliated with local assemblies in cities and towns throughout the nation. By July 1887, however, membership had thinned to 510,351, and by the fall of 1888, it was a mere 350,000. As a result, the movement largely disappeared from America's cities, retreating to a still-loyal core of members in the rural, agricultural sectors of the South and Midwest.[21]

At the same time, the American Federation of Labor retained its basic membership and built a solid organizational core for future endeavors. In his presidential address at the St. Louis convention of the AFL in December 1888, Samuel Gompers proudly proclaimed, "In the past year, when the tendency in all other directions of the labour movement to disintegration of membership has been going on and interest in their organisation laxing [*sic*], we may justly pride ourselves when we know that the trade union movement has not only maintained but actually increased its numerical strength."[22] "In contrast to the Knights of Labor," comments labor historian Selig Perlman, "the trade unions [i.e., bread-and-butter unions such as those affiliated with the AFL] met with some success in strikes and lockouts. The great lockout of the building trades in Chicago, May, 1887, although it ended in defeat, nevertheless showed the superiority of the trade union form of organisation."[23] Thus, even in defeat, the various wings of the AFL managed to maintain, if not expand, their membership, which leads to the question of why the Knights' membership was so vulnerable to the opposition of employers' associations.

One of the primary factors in the collapse of the Knights of Labor was its organizational structure, incorporating as it did the aims of both a fraternal lodge and a labor union. Moreover, the Knights adopted the weakest features of both while omitting their strengths. Though organized around fraternal principles of faith and brotherhood, the Knights failed to provide the sickness and burial insurance benefits that most fraternal groups offered. The AFL did not make the same mistake. In the words of Samuel Gompers, "It is noticeable that a great reaction and a steady disintegration is going on in most all organisations of labor which are not formed upon the basis that the experience of past failures teaches, namely, the benevolent as well as the protective features in the unions."[24] Prompted by the Knights' lack of sufficient insurance provisions for members and their families (as well as the order's flagging support for striking locals), a group in Binghamton, New York, actually split from the Knights over this issue and formed its own organization, Excelsior Assembly No. 1, Independent Order of Knights of Labor. A press release issued by the Independent Order declared the following: "The Independent Order of Knights of Labor will help the sick, the orphan and the widow, but will not give one cent to Pennsylvania dema-gogues [i.e., Knights Grand Master Workman Terence Powderly of Scranton, Pa.]. It is intended that it shall be a benefit association."[25] And although this splinter organization was short lived—upon the first death of a member, the group fell into conflict over the $100 benefit promised to the widow—it does attest to the general popularity of fraternal benefit programs at that time, as well as the weakness rendered to the Knights because of its lack thereof.

Similarly, though the Knights aspired to represent the interests of workers of all skills and backgrounds, they wavered in their support for different labor-related political goals, particularly the need for concerted and sometimes mili-tant action in the quest not just for better wages and working conditions but also for better political representation for laborers in the United States. In sum, the organization was neither fish nor fowl—a fraternity without a fraternal benefi-ciary plan and a labor union without tenacity or direction. Thus, when Ameri-can workers faced difficult choices about their representation, many left the Knights, disbanded their local assemblies, and (presumably) joined fraternal beneficiary lodges and trade unions instead.

Exactly these tensions can be seen in several internal controversies that set the Knights against themselves and split the organization into numerous com-peting factions. The first set of issues revolves around the Knights' fraternal ori-entation, specifically, the status of its quasi-Masonic rituals in the face of Catholic opposition. Next, I turn to the Knights' political agenda, or rather its failure to establish one following several hotly contested disputes. Finally, I offer some quantitative evidence in support of the defection hypothesis.

An Organization in Search of Its Mission: Fraternal Brotherhood or Political Activism?

One of the most divisive issues during the Knights' short history was that of the fraternal oath of secrecy, required of all members. Fraternal orders customarily possessed a coterie of handshakes, rituals, and signs that were kept strictly se-cret, and the Knights of Labor was established in this mold. Knights' founder Uriah S. Stephens and the early members of the order were as committed to quasi-Masonic ritualism as they were to bread-and-butter economic issues. In fact, the Knights took to calling their assembly halls the "temple," placed an open Bible on an "altar" at the beginning of each meeting, and referred to their leader as the "Master Workman" and themselves as his assembly of "noble brothers," all terms reminiscent of the Freemasons' own nomenclature. One of the members of the first ritual committee, Robert McCauley, even confessed (later in life) that the ceremony established to initiate new members into the order "was taken verbatim et literatim from that of the Knights of Pythias," another American secret society spun from the Masonic mold.[26]

That confraternity and labor unionism might be combined in a single entity was surely a strong incentive for many joiners. Nonetheless, it also proved to be one of the sources of the Knights' decline. The Catholic clergy had long been suspicious of organizations that required their members to swear an oath of allegiance to any power other than God and the church, and the great rise in fraternal organizations in America after the Civil War was cause for alarm among the episcopate. Thus, from the beginning, the Knights were split between two camps: those loyal to the fraternal origins of the organization as a secret society for workers and those devout Roman Catholics concerned about the spiritual consequences of Freemasonry.[27]

Although the Catholic clergy did not oppose the Knights of Labor as such, they demanded certain alterations in its practices, particularly renunciation of the secret oath. The question of dropping the oath was first mentioned in the Knight's national convention of 1878, though Grand Master Workman Stephens was adamantly opposed to the change. Before his involvement in founding the Knights of Labor, Stephens had been active in the Freemasons, the Odd Fellows, and the Knights of Pythias.[28] Nonetheless, a forceful alliance of Catholic members, upset about the pressure put on them by clergy to change the rites or leave the order, continued to push for changes. In the winter of 1879, Stephens finally resigned from office, citing this controversy as one of his chief reasons for leaving.[29]

The complaints of Catholic members were not unwarranted, given the threats and condemnation coming from the church hierarchy. Catholic missionaries periodically organized "missions" against the Knights, denouncing the order and threatening members with excommunication. In some cities, Catholic Knights were even refused the rite of absolution. In Columbus, Ohio, for example, the bishop of the city began refusing Christian burial for Knights. In Cleveland, Catholic Knights were called off the line in a local parade and denounced from the pulpit. And in every such case, local Knights' lodges experienced subsequent declines in membership.[30] Between 1880 and 1881, the years of the first clerical attacks on the Knights, national membership fell from 28,136 to 19,422, a remarkable 30% decline in a 12-month period.[31] After one such onslaught in his native city, Scranton, Pennsylvania, Stephens's successor, Terence Powderly, complained, "We had a mission here in all the Catholic churches in the city and the *good* Christians are [now] leaving us."[32]

At the national Knights' convention in 1881, Powderly confessed, "Many locals were already working under protest, the alternative of leaving the Order staring them in the face. Night after night have I sat thinking and deliberating this matter over. . . . We *must* admit that we want the men of all religions, and to get them we must make concessions to the church, for its influence is too vast to be idly passed over."[33] A resolution altering the Knights' secret rituals was finally passed at the General Assembly meeting in 1881.[34] But, as Powderly anxiously noted, "You [still] have men in New York who would move heaven and earth to restore the old *Masonic* customs and make the Order again oath bound."[35]

In the meantime, Powderly continued his efforts to appease the Roman Catholic Church by adamantly stumping for a Knights' temperance policy, which angered many members and caused not a few more defections.[36] When one American Catholic clergyman, Cardinal James Gibbons, began defending the Knights, a number of Powderly's enemies, as well as a number of leading Protestant clergymen, launched a counterattack on Powderly for his supposed "popery."[37] Articles in the *Journal of United Labor* and the *Irish World* accused him of packing the executive board of the order with Catholics. In turn, antiprohibitionists, radical socialists, and conservative Protestants began leaving the order in droves. In 1888, Thomas Barry, an influential member of the Knights' Executive Board, even formed his own splinter group, the Brotherhood of United Labor, after he was ousted from the order over the religion question.[38]

The Organization Overreaches: Politics Split the Knights

In its late nineteenth-century incarnation, American socialism was largely associated with (and promulgated by) members of specific immigrant groups, particularly German expatriates. When mixed with the religious controversies already plaguing the labor movement, politics proved fatal for the Knights of Labor.

Disparagingly called atheistic anarchism by opponents, socialism was widely criticized by the American Catholic clergy (among others) throughout the later nineteenth century. Nonetheless, a strong and sometimes strident socialist faction emerged within the Knights in the mid-1880s. Given the ambiguity of the Knights' political agenda, Grand Master Powderly was thus put in the difficult position of having to appease two mutually exclusive constituencies at the same time—devout Catholics and ardent socialists. In granting support for socialist political action, Powderly risked alienating Catholic members, as well as conservative Protestants; on the other hand, in eschewing socialism, he risked losing the support of politicized Germans, among others. Any issue could ignite tension between the rival factions, and Powderly often found himself trying to play both ends against the middle.

Powderly's problems were worsened by the fact that he had so little control over local and district assemblies within the order. Hoping to build as large a labor movement as possible, the Knights admitted workers of any ideological stripe. Membership requirements were gradually watered down, leading some long-time members to complain that new members were being initiated with little or no knowledge of the order or its rituals (there was still a strong and unhappy profraternal faction). And to attract more members, as well as assuage criticism from the Catholic clergy, Powderly continually revised the precepts of the order, shortening rituals, abbreviating oaths, and abolishing secrecy. In turn, internal affairs were increasingly shaken by the presence of Marxists, Lassalleans, anarchists, syndicalists, and single-tax advocates, each of which opposed Powderly for his conservative, antisocialist leanings, as well as his reluctance to advocate militant action of any kind. In his memoir, *Thirty Years of Labor*, Powderly repeatedly expresses his anxiety over the fact that so-called anarchists could easily penetrate the order and wreak havoc from within.[39] Nonetheless, although Powderly himself did not reject socialism outright, he continually tried to play down the socialist presence in the order to appease his Catholic critics and conservative allies.

The year 1886 was a landmark one for labor. Thousands of factories and plants were struck, and workers flocked to the Knights in record numbers. The order was conspicuously unable to manage its own success, however. Earlier that same year, Powderly and his executive committee had hemmed and hawed about supporting a national movement for 8-hour workday legislation. Momentum for the 8-hour day was provided by the rival Federation of Trades (later renamed the American Federation of Labor), but Powderly and his lieutenants could not decide whether to join in or avoid unnecessary confrontation with factory owners. Naturally, lack of consensus among the members only made this decision harder. Eventually, however, events chose for them.

When the Federation of Trades declared May 1st, 1886, as the deadline for their 8-hour pleas, the press falsely credited the Knights with the call for a national strike. Powderly accused anarchist agitators within the Knights of promulgating these rumors, but it was too late. National opinion held the Knights responsible for what would eventually become one of the most violent episodes in all of American labor history—the Haymarket riot of May 4, 1886.[40]

Public outrage over the riot fostered more public animosity toward the Knights. But this was only the beginning in a year fraught with difficulties for Powderly; for that same year he had also to deal with Henry George's mayoral campaign in New York City. George, author of the popular Marxist tract *Progress and Poverty*, was a staunch advocate of a single-tax plan, which, he felt, would redistribute wealth to workers by assessing taxes on the property holdings of the rich. George's 1886 mayoral campaign was watched throughout the nation.[41] Sensing the socialist undertones in George's rhetoric, the Catholic Church condemned his candidacy despite its popular following among Irish Catholic workers and German socialists. Matters only became worse when a Catholic cleric, Dr. Edward McGlynn, defied his superiors and openly backed George's campaign.

Sensing the church's ire at the radical tone of the George platform, Powderly tried to distance himself from the campaign, even though he privately supported it. One of Powderly's aides warned him to guide the Knights away "from any public affiliation with the forces of Henry George lest they agitate the Church."[42] But when rumors got out that he might be opposed to George's candidacy,

Powderly reversed tack and joined the single-tax campaign, going so far as to travel around Manhattan with George and Father McGlynn, stumping for votes.[43]

George eventually lost the mayoral race (though he did out-poll a young Republican candidate, Theodore Roosevelt), but his single-tax campaign continued elsewhere in the nation, uniting workers sympathetic to the idea of a full-time political party expressly dedicated to their interests. Nevertheless, no matter how much Powderly tried to deny it, his affiliation with Henry George cost the Knights many thousands of Catholic members. In the nation's 10 largest cities, for example, membership in Knights' district assemblies fell off by approximately 180,000 members between July 1886 and July 1887. One journal, the *Boston Pilot*, attributed the decline to Powderly's obstinacy on the church question:

> There are tens of thousands of Catholics within the labor camp who have nobly borne their share of the trials and struggles of the past ten years. They have endured the black-list, faced starvation and were always ready to make sacrifices for the common cause. They have proven themselves good and faithful soldiers. Yet today these very men are staggering away from the ranks because of the foul attacks which have been made against their holy religion.[44]

However, although these examples make it clear that members were leaving the Knights because of its factional disputes, I have yet to prove that their departure was followed by reaffiliation in alternate venues. Given that increasing numbers of trade unions and fraternal lodges seem to have coincided with the declining number of Knights' lodges, I have hypothesized that former Knights left the organization to join other lodges and trade unions. More specifically, I argue that the Knights' attempt to meld political representation and social ritual for workers failed and that multiple associational affiliations allowed this same population of American workers more flexibility in decoupling their identities as workers and community members.

Membership in the Knights was declining throughout the country while at the same time new fraternal beneficiary societies, religious groups, trade unions, and ethnic social clubs were forming at an alarming rate. Presumably, members were leaving the order to pursue their objectives elsewhere. Powderly had tried to do too much, appease too many parties, forge too many coalitions, and it was ethnoreligious conflict, bolstered by the lure of alternative affiliations, that ultimately doomed the order.

Quantitative Evidence in Support of the Defection Hypothesis

To test the hypothesis that workers quit the Knights of Labor and joined other types of association, I have compiled annual associational and labor union data from 25 medium-sized American cities (see appendix for details) for the period 1880–1890, the seminal years of the Knights' rise and fall. Associational data were culled from city directories by using a coding scheme designed to enumerate organizational diversity among late nineteenth-century American civic associations.[45] Data on the Knights of Labor itself come from a directory of all local assemblies for the period 1869–1890.[46] In addition, longitudinal data on labor-related strikes were taken from the *Sixteenth Annual Report of the Commissioner of Labor*.[47] All of these sources provide annual longitudinal data on the number of relevant organizations in each of the cities from 1880 to 1890, amounting to some 275 city-years of information.

A simple multivariate time-series regression model was used to test the hypothesis that there was a consistent, significant, and negative relationship between the number of Knights' lodges in each city and the number of other, presumably rival fraternal, labor, and civic associations between the years 1885 and 1890.[48] (Once again, let me remind you that membership data are not available with which to test this hypothesis by tracking individuals.)

Independent variables that represent both the number of rival associations and the number of those same associations in the following year (time $_{t+1}$) are included in the models, examining specific examples of rival associations one at a time (see table 5.1). By substituting different associational variables into the model, we can deduce which types of association appear to have been relevant alternatives for disenchanted Knights. Lagged associational variables are included to account for the hypothesis that defection from a Knights' lodge would precede formation of new alternatives by at least a year. Thus, the same-year association variables serve as baseline controls that account for basic structural differences across and within cities—that is, namely the size of each city and its preexisting associational climate—whereas the lagged association variables provide evidence of probable defections to these groups, if such a process indeed occurred. In addition, a failed-strikes variable is included to account for the effect of demoralization and defeat on the Knights' movement itself. Though the strike data reflect labor activity at the state level only, they nonetheless provide a year-by-year baseline for weighing the notion that effective opposition crushed the Knights' movement in cities across the nation. More specifically, the percentage of strikes in each state that were reported (by the U.S. Commissioner of Labor) as failed strikes is used to test the idea that opposition on the part of employers' associations was significantly related to the dissolution of Knights' lodges in each locale.[49]

The results shown in table 5.1 support the defection hypothesis. That is, the results support the proposition that former Knights may have redirected their associational energies to other types of voluntary organization, net of strike failures.[50]

It is important to note, however, that not all of the hypothesized rival associations appear significantly related to the dissolution of Knights' lodges. The

TABLE 5.1 Coefficients for Weighted Least Squares Regression
on Number of Knights Lodges, U.S. Cities, 1885-1890

	Model 1	Model 2	Model 3	Model 4	Model 5
Constant	15.669*	13.174**	12.310**	13.507**	12.203**
	(2.005)	(2.220)	(1.805)	(1.723)	(2.882)
Failed strikes	.045	4.242*	1.689	.716	2.295
	(1.458)	(1.641)	(1.805)	(1.650)	(1.616)
Trade unions	.118*				
(excluding Knights lodges)	(.056)				
Trade unions—lagged	−.235**				
(excluding Knights lodges)	(.076)				
Fraternal lodges (general)		.111**			
		(.025)			
Fraternal lodges—lagged		−.132**			
		(.028)			
Temperance fraternities			.092		
			(.093)		
Temperance fraternities—			−.003		
lagged			(.099)		
Mutual benefit societies				.059	
				(.096)	
Mutual benefit societies—				−.079	
lagged				(.085)	
All civic associations					.038**
					(.010)
Civic associations—lagged					−.039**
			(.012)		
Number of observations	141	141	141	141	141
Log likelihood	−446.610	−449.002	−452.089	−452.657	−446.998
Wald Chi-square	10.10	24.54	2.04	1.01	13.76
Pr > chi-square	.018	.000	.565	.799	.003

$** = P$ value $< .01$ $* = P$ value $< .05$

All coefficients are unstandardized. Standard errors are reported in parentheses. Lagged variables represent data for x_{t+1}.

data show that the latter were replaced by both general fraternal lodges and trade unions. Though the coefficients for the lagged temperance fraternities and mutual benefit society variables are in the hypothesized (i.e., negative) direction, they are not statistically significant. Thus, we can deduce that former Knights were more likely to join general fraternal lodges and trade unions than temperance fraternities and mutual benefit societies. Though temperance was an issue that sometimes caused dissention within the Knights, the formation of new temperance lodges and mutual benefit societies does not appear to have occurred in direct proportion to the dissolution of Knights' lodges. This does not necessarily mean that former and current Knights were not joining temperance fraternities and mutual benefit societies, but it does indicate that there was not a consistent, direct relationship between the dissolution of Knights' lodges and the formation of new lodges of this type.

It should be added that these findings make logical sense in that the two primary functions of the Knights of Labor—as fraternal lodge and as trade union—were thus divided and reinstated in two separate kinds of organizations, the rise of which appears to have been significantly related to the declining number of Knights' lodges across the sample of 25 medium-sized cities. Nonetheless, these findings also raise an important methodological question: How can we be sure that there was a direct causal link between the declining number of Knights' lodges and the rise of these other types of voluntary organizations? If associations of all types were increasing in number over this period, might not the declining number of Knights' lodges be causally independent of the rising number of alternatives (i.e., a rising tide lifts all boats, except the Knights', which might have dropped for purely endogenous reasons)?

This is certainly a reasonable line of inquiry, but one, unfortunately, that can only be addressed through indirect means. However, by examining slope coefficients for the number of organizations per year, we can see if the rival organizations' yearly rate of growth accelerated in direct proportion to the Knights' decline (1886–1890). I do this through a simple extension of the cross-sectional time-series model above: Using the same sample of cities, I generate generalized least squares coefficients for each time period, regressing $year_{ij}$ on the number of organizations$_{ij}$. The coefficient for the year thus indicates how much the organization in question increased from year to year over the given time span. By comparing the slope coefficients for time-series models of the period just before and just after 1886, we can thus see if the rate of increase of the probable alternatives itself increased over time. In other words, if amid a generally increasing number of associations the rate of growth of the presumed target organizations (general fraternities and trade unions) is greater in $t_{>1885}$ than $t_{<1887}$, we have reason to believe that the decline of the Knights was related to an accelerated rate of increase in the number of target organizations.[51]

The data do, in fact, confirm this hypothesis (see table 5.2a and b). The coefficients for both the fraternal lodges and trade union variables are nearly two-thirds greater for the latter time period than the former. Thus, we can conclude that the growth rate of both types of rival organizations increased significantly in the presence of a declining number of Knights' lodges (i.e., the period beginning 1886).

Though both the quantitative and qualitative results seen here provide only indirect support for the defection hypothesis, it should be noted that direct examination of this process is virtually impossible, given the disappearance of the Knights' membership rolls from this period. What I have tried to demonstrate is that the organizational structure of the Knights' organization might have rendered it unusually susceptible to membership defection. Using cross-sectional time-series data, I have also provided support for the idea that there were clear and consistent negative relationships between the number of Knights' lodges and two types of rival associations over time, thus supplying empirically valid descriptions of both the internal and external causes of membership defection from the Knights. Whether this is a wholly accurate description of the processes underlying the Knights' decline is uncertain, though it would appear to have been at least a contributing factor.

TABLE 5.2A Coefficients for Weighted Least Squares Regression on Number of Fraternal Lodges, U.S. Cities, 1880–1886 and 1886–1890

	Model 1 Fraternal lodges	Model 2 Fraternal lodges
Constant	−11749.64**	−19667.7*
	(4024.688)	(9249.063)
Years (1880–1886)	6.284**	
	(2.137)	
Years (1886–1890)		10.484*
		(9249.063)
Number of observations	175	125
Log likelihood	−954.460	−721.084
Wald chi-square	8.64	4.58
Pr > chi-square	.003	.032

**= P value <. 01 *= P value <. 05

All coefficients are unstandardized. Standard-errors are reported in parentheses.

TABLE 5.2B Coefficients for Weighted Least Squares
Regression on Number of Trade Unions U.S. Cities,
1880–1886 and 1886–1890

	Model 3 Trade Unions	Model 4 Trade Unions
Constant	−3028.923** (734.408)	−4344.264** (1497.364)
Years (1880–1886)	1.614** (.390)	
Years (1886–1890)		2.312** (.793)
Number of observations	175	125
Log likelihood	−656.761	−493.482
Wald chi-Square	17.13	8.50
Pr > chi-square	.000	.003

$** = P$ value $< .01$ $* = P$ value $< .05$
All coefficients are unstandardized. Standard-errors are reported
in parentheses.

Aftermath and Conclusion

In the years after the great upheaval of 1886, the Knights' popularity surged in rural
districts, presumably on the coattails of Henry George's single-tax campaign.
Thirty-seven new district assemblies were formed, mostly in small localities, and
state assemblies were added in Alabama, Florida, Georgia, Indiana, Kansas, Mis-
sissippi, Nebraska, North Carolina, Ohio, West Virginia, and Wisconsin. "After
1887," writes Selig Perlman, "the Knights of Labor lost their hold upon the large
cities with their wage-conscious and largely foreign population, and became an
organisation predominantly of country people, of mechanics, small merchants,
and farmers, an element more or less purely American and decidedly middle-class
in its philosophy."[52] In the years following, Terence Powderly responded in kind
by stumping more actively for Henry George, the Farmers' Alliance, and later the
People's Party, all Populist movements of a decidedly agrarian bent. In essence,
Powderly, always willing to compromise, had found a new constituency less bound
by the issues that had previously plagued his efforts—religion, anarchism, and
ethnic strife. In fact, Powderly eventually broke with the Catholic Church altogether, joined the Freemasons, and accepted a prestigious appointment by President McKinley as commissioner general for immigration.[53]

Unfortunately, American workers were not nearly so fortunate. Labor would never again equal its 1886 peak (at least in terms of membership in a single, unified labor organization), and American workers would miss out on many subsequent opportunities to lobby for serious social reform.

As previously stated, I take the collapse of the Knights to be in some way indicative of the larger shortcomings of the late nineteenth-century fraternal model of associationalism. So grandiose were the Knights' aims, so divided its members, and so diffuse its means that widespread collective action, or even localized coalition building, was virtually impossible. The order was intensely vulnerable to schism and outright defection. And although the number of civic associations increased dramatically during this period, the ability of any single organization to achieve and sustain political goals was mitigated by the countervailing force of opponents, detractors, and rival associations.

In western Europe, by contrast, workers managed to forge more significant political alliances within and among themselves. Owing to centuries of church-state friction and governments' time-tested powers of political suppression, voluntary associations were not nearly so common or so easy to create in Europe as in the United States. Thus, labor unions faced a relatively open niche in which to organize workers, despite concerted opposition. And, in addition, European labor movements also avoided niche problems by either explicitly choosing politics over religion, as they did in France and England, or by explicitly founding unions around religious principles, as they did in Germany.[54]

This points to the need to reassess the trajectory of various national labor movements in light of the presence of competing alternatives for workers' loyalties in each country. Western European labor movements have generally built their successes around the unification of workers within single, unilingual political parties. In the United States, on the other hand, workers seem to have been overwhelmed by the profusion of organizational options open to them. Thus, we see another example of how competitive voluntarism proved a monumental obstacle to the kinds of coalition building necessary for effective political mobilization in the late nineteenth-century United States.

6

COMPETITIVE MILITANCE

Civilian Military Organizations and the Destabilization

of American National Security

It has been customary, since at least the late nineteenth century, to view military power as an extension of the legitimate authority of the state (except, of course, in cases of unsanctioned violence or insurrection).[1] The American experience, however, gives lie to the assumption that there is a clean analytical divide between state and civil society when it comes to military matters. Lacking either a sizable standing army or an effective state militia, nineteenth-century American national defense policy relied on the military preparedness of ordinary citizens in time of need. Until 1903, in fact, when Congress officially reorganized the National Guard, responsibility for defense was loosely divided among federal, state, and independent forces. Among the independents were voluntary militia companies, shooting clubs, and paramilitary organizations, many explicitly organized around ethnoreligious lines. German-American *turner vereine* and *schützenbünde*, the Irish-American Hibernian Guards, and Czech *sokol societies* were all nineteenth-century incarnations of this tradition of ethnic military training and self-protection.[2]

Surprisingly, there is little direct evidence that the proliferation of gun clubs and militias stimulated violence in American cities. The persistent ambiguity of America's nineteenth-century national defense policy and the related decision to promote private gun ownership do seem to be important precursors of late twentieth-century gun culture in the United States, however. In assuming that guns belonged in the hands of the people, and not in those of a professional standing army, America's founding fathers created a tradition of civilian militarism that remains with us to this day.

The division of American national defense forces into myriad independent clubs, guards, and militias further fragmented American national consciousness. Differences of race, ethnicity, religion, and class could easily and legitimately be expressed through the formation of independent military outfits. The founding fathers did not aspire to such a system—they hoped that all able-bodied males could be compelled to serve in local militias organized by the various state governments—but the system gradually evolved into something resembling the organizational hodgepodge of golden age fraternalism. Independent militias proliferated, armed themselves, and marched on the streets of American cities and towns with striking regularity. Eventually, the shortcomings of civilian militance led to the formation of uniformed state police, the expansion of the federal forces and reserves, and the rationalization of the National Guard, but only after lasting legacies of private gun ownership and resistance to government authority were already well entrenched.

Though America's long-standing civilian military tradition predates the associational boom of the late nineteenth century, the two are interrelated in a number of important ways: First, both strands are related in their connection to the ritualistic trappings of late century fraternalism, particularly its members' penchant for fancy dress, elaborate ceremony, and inordinately complex organizational hierarchies. As stated earlier, the fraternal boom was in many ways a product of the Civil War, both in its fixation on the economics of sickness and death and in its fascination with pomp and circumstance. Many orders ran themselves much like military regiments, in fact, and some actually created ancillary groups explicitly devoted to military training and parading. Not surprisingly, then, there was a welter of volunteer militia groups formed in the fraternal mold—private, nonprofit military clubs charged with financing and managing themselves and operating independently of government authority. Moreover, in promoting the creation of rival militias and gun clubs, competitive voluntarism took on a new dimension in cities and towns across the country: Rival groups were now impelled to arm and train themselves in the art of modern warfare, and though few such groups ever succeeded in using these new skills to much effect, the movement to militarize did have a lasting effect on American political culture.

A second connection between fraternalism and civilian militance can be found in the rise of special-interest group politics on the American scene after the Civil War. Nineteenth-century warfare required specialized skills, such as advanced riflery training, that were difficult to acquire under the lax and lazy routine of most militias. Noting how unprepared state militiamen were for service in the Civil War, a group of retired Union army generals founded a voluntary organization devoted to the task of improving the marksmanship of National Guardsmen—the National Rifle Association. The NRA was originally funded with state and federal money, and its aims were limited to improving the preparedness of the nation's state militias (thus leaving the many independent militias out of the picture). Over time, however, the NRA evolved into a full-fledged interest group, claiming to represent the nation's interests vis-à-vis the gun-owning segment of the population. This transformation was typical of many voluntary organizations in the late nineteenth and early twentieth centuries (as described in chapter 4). Once organized to recruit and retain members, collect dues, and hold regular meetings, the progression from service provider to interest protector was a simple if not inevitable affair. And in competing with rival groups for control over decisions of national import, such groups came to hold more and more sway over the nation's political parties. The specific case of the NRA provides a graphic illustration of how competitive voluntarism helped transform the American political system: Issues like national defense, gun control, and law enforcement have become the playground of competing interest-group lobbies, leaving voters little say in the shape of national affairs.

Another, less well-known consequence of competitive militance is the role it played in the emerging struggles between laborers and their employees in the decades after the Civil War. Because the Second Amendment says so little about the types of militia that should and should not be allowable under the Constitution, the courts had great leeway in interpreting and applying the law. In the midst of the violence that ensued between American workers and employers in the closing decades of the nineteenth century, the Second Amendment was frequently interpreted in a manner that allowed government officials to ban militias that were serving the interests of socialists and labor organizers while permitting their use by factory and railway owners. The resulting imbalance of power placed yet another obstacle in the path of American workers, which when coupled with the organizational pressures discussed in the preceding chapter helps explain the relative weakness of working-class consciousness in the United States.

In order to present each of these arguments in some detail, this chapter goes beyond the temporal purview of the book. It begins with the nation's founding and continues in a narrative fashion up through the years preceding World War I. This departure in form and content is justified by the nature of the topic at hand: American military history is not unique to the associational boom of the late nineteenth century, though it is related to it in several important respects. Doing the topic justice thus requires a narrative that weaves the special history of American military institutions together with the aforementioned dynamics of competitive voluntarism. I will make every effort to relate the narrative back to our central concerns wherever possible, though the story of American civilian militias deserves telling in its own right.

A Confederacy of Dunces: 1776–1861

The founding fathers probably worried more about national defense than any other subject. It was a constant topic of debate in the Constitutional Congress, and it helped exacerbate long-standing differences between Federalists and anti-Federalists. In hindsight, the ambiguous wording of the Second Amendment was framed exactly around this debate, that between Federalists eager to see the nation build a strong national military system and Republicans fervent in their belief that state militias manned by citizen-volunteers were essential to the protection of state power.[3] Debate led nowhere, however, and the matter was largely left unsettled until the beginning of the twentieth century, when Congress passed the Dick Act of 1903, which formally organized the National Guard and the federal army as the nation's primary means of defense.[4] Prior to that time, military appropriations were made on a largely ad hoc basis, leaving generals to scramble for men and munitions whenever the need presented itself. Though one president after another observed that the nation's military system was not up to the task, persistent worry over the potential dangers of a standing army forestalled formal action in the name of national defense.[5]

The Revolutionary War itself provided a valuable but largely unheeded lesson in the difficulties of relying on citizen-volunteers in a time of crisis. Volunteers proved worthy in the early battles of the war—at Boston, Fort Ticonderoga, and Quebec City—but their effectiveness dwindled rapidly in the years thereafter. Most volunteers expected to serve for only a few months, and the hardships of weather and war soon took a toll on their enthusiasm for battle. One of General Washington's primary difficulties throughout the war was simply convincing troops to stay the course and remain in situ. Similarly, "Benedict Arnold's assault on Quebec ended ignominiously when more than half his force abruptly departed in December [1775] as their enlistments expired," says historian Jerry Cooper.[6] This would have come as no surprise to experienced veterans like Arnold and Washington; desertion was a common problem in earlier colonial engagements.

In response, the colonial army quickly abandoned hope of mustering a volunteer army and began cultivating professional soldiers among its ranks, enlisting recruits for multiyear commitments and paying them handsomely in return. Comments historian Lawrence Delbert Cress,

> By the summer of 1776 Congress was well on its way toward creating a military establishment that placed a premium on military expertise, avoided the use of militiamen whenever possible, and relied extensively on enlistment bonuses and bounties to fill the ranks of the chronically undermanned American army. Even John Adams [an early advocate of the militia system] was convinced that the states could not "reasonably hope to be a powerful, prosperous, or a free People [without] a permanent Body of Troops."[7]

Given the spotty performance of volunteers in the Revolutionary War, military commanders had justifiably little faith in the citizen-soldier tradition; yet Republicans prevailed after the war in congressional debates on the subject. Drawing on the rich and still memorable history of the English Civil War, American Republican leaders touted radical Whig arguments against the maintenance of standing armies in support of the perennial duty of citizens to serve their republic in time of need.[8] Patrick Henry, harbinger of the Revolution, eloquently professed the dangers of a federal army before the Virginia Ratifying Convention in 1788: "My great objection to this Government is, that it does not leave us the means of defending our rights; or, of waging war against tyrants. . . . Let my beloved Americans guard against that fatal lethargy that has pervaded the universe: Have we the means of resisting disciplined armies, when our only defense, the militia is put into the hands of Congress?"[9]

The persuasiveness of these arguments led to the eventual passage of the famous Second Amendment: "A well regulated Militia, being necessary to the security of a free State, the right of the people to keep and bear Arms, shall not be infringed." There is little if any evidence that this provision was forged to protect individuals' right to bear arms; rather, it appears to have stemmed from a desire to protect states from the tyrannous incursion of national government, as shown above. "Bearing arms was linked to the citizenry's collective responsibility for the republic's defense," comments Cress. "Standard warnings about the threat of standing armies and the need to ensure the subordination of military to civil authority underscored that responsibility."[10]

Surprisingly, few state legislators seemed to fear that their own militia might aspire to tyranny or that such a militia might be turned against the citizenry in governors' hands. Clearly, the debate was focused around states' rights. "Tranferring suspicions directed against the crown during the 1760s and 1770s to the newly formed Continental government, the states remained deeply sensitive to the possibility that the army could become an instrument for the expansion of continental power at the expense of state sovereignty."[11] Although several state conventions, namely, those of Massachusetts, New Hampshire, and Pennsylvania, did briefly consider protecting individuals' right to bear arms, they also acknowledged that there must be reasonable limits to this right (i.e., that it could be revoked in cases in which it presented a danger to society), thus putting the "order and security of society" ahead of the individual's right to bear arms.[12] Given the clarity of hindsight, it was states' rights, and not some ultrapatriotic right to arm individuals, that guided the authors of the Second Amendment.

But statesmen with military experience remained worried about the nation's state of preparedness. In 1790, Secretary of War Henry Knox proposed a new plan that would maintain the militia tradition while placing responsibility for its organization, training, and financing in the hands of the federal government. Even this was too centralized a plan for Congress. "With the failure of the Knox plan," writes Cooper, "the Federalists abandoned efforts to make the militia an effective national institution."[13]

In 1792, Congress finally passed the Militia Act, though the bill did little to change prerevolutionary national defense policy: "The law continued a universal militia obligation for able-bodied men between the ages of eighteen and forty-five. Although it prescribed tactical organization in detail and specifically listed how each militiaman was to equip himself, it provided neither measures for forcing states to comply with the law nor financial support."[14]

In 1803, President Jefferson obtained an amendment requiring state militias to report their enrollments to the War Department, though few adjutants general ever actually complied. In 1808, an annual federal appropriation of $200,000 was passed, to be distributed in arms to the states in proportion to the size of their militia, but money was not enough to overcome their administrative problems. Funds were poorly supervised, inefficiently allocated, and sorely short of the mark in supporting the numerous militias of the states.

In the years preceding the War of 1812, the state militias had numerous opportunities to prove their worth and failed in every respect. Weapons granted to the militias by the federal government were poorly maintained and sometimes sold outright for profit.[15] Few states managed to muster the numbers required of them by Congress and many let requirements for mandatory militia service slide: Recruits were frequently allowed to pay a small fine in return for exemption from military service, for example, hardly the *civitas* Republicans had anticipated. Localism also proved a substantial problem: During both Shay's Rebellion (1786–1787) and the Whiskey Rebellion (1794), state militiamen were reluctant to turn against their brethren in the name of local order. Moreover, civilian militias often spent more time drinking and parading than training for active duty.[16]

With the onset of another round of Anglo-American hostilities, the weaknesses in America's national defense policy became particularly acute. Several states, namely, Massachusetts, Connecticut, and Vermont, ignored a presidential request for assistance, arguing that their respective charters did not require them to serve out of state.[17] On the militarily vulnerable western frontier, furthermore, poor finances and a small population afforded grossly undersized militias. As historian Mark Pitcavage notes, "The weakness of the frontier militias demonstrated during this period the vulnerability of a militia-based defense. If every area had to defend itself, then the system was only as strong as its weakest link. During the period 1801–1812 the system's weakest links happened to be located in some of its most strategically important areas."[18] Indeed, though the militia held firm in the celebrated Battle of New Orleans, state forces fell far short of the mark in many battles of the second Anglo-American war. State militias lost at Detroit and at Queenstown and, after fleeing the battle of Bladensburg, yielded the nation's capital to an outnumbered force of British regulars. Said General William Henry Harrison in 1818, "The late war repeatedly exhibited the melancholy fact, of large corps of militia going to the field of battle without understanding a single elementary principle, and without being able to perform a single evolution."[19]

Thereafter, federal officials largely lost faith in the state militia system, though the federal army did not grow dramatically either, thus leaving the nation's defense in a rather haphazard and vulnerable state:

The national government had done just about all it could do, considering the irrational jealousy involved in the then dominant version of the theory of states' rights. By violations of the spirit of this theory and of the spirit of the Second Amendment and the militia clause, the national government might have saved the militia. Out of respect for the constitutional tradition, however, and out of distaste for the militia itself, the national government left the militia to the states and the states failed in the trust.[20]

Whatever standards prevailed among the state militias before the War of 1812 sadly declined in the years thereafter. Though most states recognized the need to maintain a militia through compulsory service (as outlined in the Militia Act of 1792), resistance ran high, finances ran low, and discipline was virtually nonexistent. Some states relied on fines to enforce mandatory service, but protest and disobedience led many others to replace mandatory service with a small commutation tax for those not wishing to serve.[21] Even in Massachusetts, a state known for its dedicated minuteman tradition, service requirements were gradually lowered and exemptions increased throughout the 1820s and 1830s, which led one contemporary, John Gorham Palfrey, to refer to the Massachusetts milita as "the once efficient and admired, *now apparently expiring* militia system of Massachusetts."[22] In addition, those militias that did actually muster were generally known for their terrible marksmanship, poorly maintained weaponry, and gross inebriation. According to one account, the militiamen of Oxford, Massachusetts, were such poor marksmen that they voted 35 to 5 to end their annual target-shooting exercise for fear of public embarrassment: "Even those with arms lacked experience in their use. Musters were, after all, usually held but once a year; parading, drinking, and partying clearly took priority over target practice; and uniforms evoked far more passion and interest than musket fire."[23]

In lieu of compulsory service, another military tradition took the place of state militias, growing throughout the period after the War of 1812—volunteer, or uniformed militias. As the separate states let their compulsory militias wither in the decades after the War of 1812, volunteer militias began forming in their absence. The volunteer militias were "a form of voluntary association that appealed to young men with an interest in martial arts, a passion for pomp and circumstance, and a desire to socialize with individuals of their own class and ethnicity."[24] In addition, the character of the volunteer militias became increasingly imbued with the populist spirit of the age:

> Before independence [the volunteer militia] was made up largely of a small number of elite companies, whose members were well-to-do Americans from long-established families. "Afterwards many other citizens, some of them working-class German and Irish Americans, organized companies of their own. By the middle of the 19th century, nearly every small town had at least one such company, and some big cities had a dozen or more.[25]

Volunteer militia companies had much in common with the prototypical voluntary associations described by Alexis de Tocqueville in *Democracy in America*. Volunteer militias drafted their own bylaws, elected their own officers, raised their own revenues, and trained and socialized like fraternal brothers. Nonetheless, they also tended to be notoriously unfit for duty, inexcusably selective in their membership parameters, and positively wanton in their search for cold, hard cash:

> It is tempting to make fun of the uniformed [volunteer] militia. Their outlandish uniforms, wholly unfit for field service; their intricate drill tactics, more appropriate to a marching band than a military unit; and their hyperbolic assertions about the fighting prowess of the American citizen soldier—all mocked the serious content of Whig ideology and the realities of 19th-century battlefields.[26]

More significant, however, is the fact that the volunteer militias were almost completely free of government control, private armies free to roam the countryside at will. Because state governments did little to contribute to the support of the voluntary militias, they had little or no control over their actions, training, or deployment.[27] And when deployed, the results were often disastrous, as in the infamous 1844 Philadelphia riots, in which nativist, Irish, and state militias turned against one another in an open street battle.[28] Volunteer militias were also intimately involved in the initial hostilities of the Civil War, seizing federal property in Virginia, South Carolina, Florida, and Texas, as well as initiating the siege of Fort Sumter. Ironically, this same belief in the virtues of voluntary service blocked repeated efforts to bolster the size of the federal army. At the outset of the Civil War, federal forces numbered an abysmal 16,000. The Union army subsequently spent much of the early part of the war scrambling to bolster its forces.[29]

In light of this fact, it is also interesting to note the presence of independent "colored" regiments in Southern cities such as Charleston, South Carolina, after the Civil War (see table 6.1). While it is common knowledge that blacks fought in segregated regiments on both sides of the war, it is surprising to see "colored regiments" listed as independent militia in Southern cities after Reconstruction. I have not myself devoted much time to exploring the frequency with which such groups existed in the postbellum South or their relationship to the state militias, but this is clearly a subject worth serious consideration by historians of the period. In fact, one might question more generally what impact the presence of independent minority group militias had on the politics and psychology of the age. As we see in the next section, ethnic independent militias were sometimes the source of great controversy, particularly when they were allied with labor activism.

TABLE 6.1 Military Groups and Gun Clubs in Four U.S. Cities, 1880

	Independent Militia	Shooting/Gun Clubs	State Militia
Charleston	German Artillery	Butler Guard Rifle Club	State Militia, Fourth Brigade
	Charleston Light Dragons [sic]	Deutsch Schutzen Gesellschaft	*First Regiment—Rifles*
	First Regiment, *Colored*	Charleston Turn Verein	Palmetto Guards
	Infantry Companies A–H		Washington Light Infantry
	Cavalry		Irish Volunteers
	Royal Cavalry		German Fusiliers
			Sumter Guards
			Seventeenth Regiment
			Montgomery Guards
			Charleston Riflemen
			Irish Rifle Club
			Carolina Rifle Battalion
			Company A
			Company B
			First Regiment—Artillery
			Washington Artillery
			LaFayette Battery
			Marion Battery
			Cavalry
			German Hussars
			Sixteenth Regiment Companies A–D

Chicago

Illinois National Guard
First Regiment
    Companies A–K
Second Regiment
    Companies A–G
Sixth Regiment
    Companies A–E
Sixteenth Battalion (*Colored* Infantry)
    Company A
Battery D—First Artillery
First Cavalry
    Companies A–D

Aurora Turn Verein
Bohemian Gymnastic Society
Chicago Scandinavian Turner Society
Chicago Sharpshooters' Mutual Aid Society
Chicago Shooting Club
Chicago Turn Gemeinde
Maksabaw Shooting Club
Northwestern Schuetzen Bund
Tel. Jed. Sokol
Turn Verein Vorwaertz

Alpine Hunters
Clan-Na-Gael Guards
Lackey's Zouaves

("Companies not under State Laws")
Veteran City Guard of Hartford, CT
Hartford Germania Guard Veteran Assn.
First Company Governor's Foot Guard
    Veteran's Corps
Putnam Phalanx
    1st Company
    2nd Company
Cambridge Guards

Hartford

Connecticut National Guard
First Regiment
Governor's Horse Guard
Governor's Foot Guard
Germania Guard
Hillyer Guard
Hartford City Guard
Hartford Light Guard
Hartford Company K
Hartford Company B (*colored*)

Franklin Rifle Club
German Rifle Club of Hartford
Hartforder Turnerbund
Hartford Wesson Rifle Club

(*continued*)

TABLE 6.1 (*continued*)

	Independent Militia	Shooting/Gun Clubs	State Militia
San Francisco	Independent Companies ("Independent of the National Guard of California and not under control of the State military authorities")	California Rifle Assn.	National Guard of California:
		California Wing Shooting Club	First Regiment Infantry:
		Gun Club (pigeon shooting)	City Guard
	Austrian Jaegers	S.F. Long Range Rifle Club	N.G. Company C
	California Jaegers	California Schuetzen Club	Franklin Light Infantry
	French Zouaves	Eureka Turn Verein	Sumner Light Guard
	Garibaldi Guard	Pacific Turn Bezirk	Light Guard
	German Fusileer Guard	S.F. Turn Verein	Company H
	German Dragoons	Swiss Rifle Club	Second Regiment Infantry:
	Juarez Guard		Company B
	Independent McMahon Grenadier Guard		S.F. Fusileers
	Independent Rifles		Germania Rifles
	Italian Sharpshooters		Company F
			Company G
			S.F. Cadets

LaFayette Guard
Sarsfield Guard
Schuetzen Verein
Swiss Sharpshooters
Society of California Volunteers

Third Regiment Infantry:
Montgomery Guard
Shields Guard
Wolfe Tone Guard
Meagher Guard
Emmet Life Guard
McMahon Guard
First Battalion Cavalry:
First Light Dragoons
S.F. Hussars
Jackson Dragoons
Union Guard Gatling Battery
First California Guard Light Battery

Sources: Sholes Directory of the City of Charleston, November 15, 1879 (Charleston, S.C.: Walker, Evans & Cogswell, 1879); *The Lakeside Annual Directory of the City of Chicago, 1880* (Chicago: Chicago Directory Co., 1880); *Geer's Hartford City Directory and Hartford Illustrated; for the Year Commencing July, 1880* (Hartford, Conn.: Elihu Geer, 1880); *Langley's San Francisco Directory for the Year Commencing April, 1880* (San Francisco: Francis, Valentine, & Co., 1880).

Note: Veterans' fraternities like the Grand Army of the Republic are not included here. All spellings of foreign-language words are given as listed in their respective city directories. Also note that these four cities were chosen for their illustrative power and regional diversity and are not intended to represent a generalizable sample of American cities from the period.

Near Anarchy (1865–1903)

Ethnic Militias and Social Order

Along with the voluntarist turn in American military organization came newfound enthusiasm for private military groups made up exclusively of individuals from a specific local ethnic and/or religious community. Not surprisingly, the onset of this trend occurred soon after the great European migration of the 1840s, which brought large numbers of Germans and Irish to America. Given the widespread hostility this immigration evoked from nativist foes, the ethnic militia movement quickly spurred an escalating cycle in the sphere of private military activity reminiscent of that seen in the voluntary sector more generally. "From the mid-1840s on," comments historian Jerry Cooper, "a large number of ethnic companies appeared, most of them German or Irish. Native-born Americans found this development disturbing and organized their own organizations to meet this 'foreign' threat."[30] Note, too, the presence of Austrian, Bohemian and Czech, French, Italian, and Swiss militias in the four city directories summarized in figure 6.1.[31]

One important force behind ethnic militarization was the Turner movement, brought to America by German émigrés in the mid-nineteenth century.[32] The Turners were originally founded by Friedrich Ludwig Jahn, a Prussian patriot prompted to encourage "bodily exercise" and "patriotic ideals" in Prussian youths following the Prussian Army's ignominious defeat at the Battle of Jena in 1806. Though today one is not likely to associate gymnastic exercises with military training, Jahn's motives were clearly militaristic in origin, his primary aim being "to supply his country with a body of young men inspired by patriotism and love of freedom, men who, at the call to arms, would willingly sacrifice their lives to liberate Germany from the tyranny of foreign rule."[33]

Turnvater Jahn's new system was first introduced to America in the 1820s by three of his disciples, one of whom was recruited by medical professors at Harvard College to establish a training program for students there. By the late 1840s, a steady stream of expelled German revolutionaries began arriving in the United States and founding *turnvereine* and *turngemeinde* of their own. The earliest American *turnvereine* were explicitly political in origin, espousing the socialist ideals of 1848, but Turners soon became engaged in other causes as well, actively joining the abolitionist movement and the Republican Party in force.[34]

Turnervereine and their military brethren helped bolster German-American ethnic solidarity in the face of an increasingly hostile nativist movement. They frequently drilled in public, for example, thus evoking a strong mobilized presence in the public sphere.[35] And although I have not been able to verify the frequency with which ethnic and/or nativist militias were involved in episodes of violent conflict, I would venture to guess that the presence of such groups proved a valuable deterrent to, rather than cause of, ethnically motivated violence in American cities of the late nineteenth century. Most volunteer militias of the period were not organized for violence so much as for the public display of their potential for violence. In fact, many more closely resembled social clubs than military organizations: "With self-support the *sine qua non* of unit survival, militiamen naturally devoted themselves to activities that would simultaneously earn money and attract dues-paying members. Some companies fared well in fund-raising and attained stability. Others failed and either collapsed or struggled along ineffectively."[36]

Existing records from postbellum volunteer militias attest to their primary function as social, almost quasi-fraternal organizations where men could gather regularly, dress up in fancy costumes, drink, party, and parade. Stage shows, dances, and plays were regular features of militia activity, and the need to perpetually raise funds for equipment and supplies helped ensure that they would be well done, elaborately staged, and well publicized.[37] Some volunteer companies even hosted circuslike fairs featuring band concerts, beauty pageants, animal shows, chariot races, and drill competitions. One particular specialty of these militia shows were so-called sham battles, staged contests in which militiamen dressed as Indians, Huns, Romans, and so forth. Another common fund-raising strategy of volunteer and state militias alike was to grant honorary memberships to wealthy donors in exchange for exemption from jury duty.[38]

At the same time, German Americans also cultivated a stylized form of gallery shooting called *schuetzen* matches, and so-called *schuetzenvereine* became increasingly common in cities across the nation. Using customized, small-caliber rifles and short-distance shooting ranges, most *schuetzen* matches combined massive Bavarian-style picnics, contest shooting, singing, dancing, and many, many rounds of beer. The North American Schuetzen Bund [*sic*] was, in fact, the oldest shooting organization in America, and "by 1890 *schuetzen* clubs, or *schuetzenbunds* [*sic*], were found in almost every American community where there were more than a few citizens of Teutonic ancestry."[39]

Volunteer Militias and Vigilantism in the Labor Agitation of the Postwar Years

Nineteenth-century volunteer militias were not all revelry and war play, however. Private citizens were generally free to form volunteer militias at will, and private militias could be formed in the service of particular class, as well as ethnonational, interests. Following the Paris Commune of 1871, the panic of 1873, and the railroad strike of 1877, the stakes in American class conflict began to heighten, and elite groups increasingly turned to the citizen-soldier tradition as a way of mobilizing their own counterinsurgency forces (cf. chapter 5 on the power of such opposition in quelling the nascent American labor movement).

In the fall of 1879, New York's Upper East Side basked in the glory of the new Seventh Regiment Armory. Located in a posh new building between East Sixty-sixth and Sixty-seventh Streets, the Armory was home to a regiment of elite young men charged with the protection of one of America's wealthiest neighborhoods.[40] "In the two decades, 1891–1910," writes political scientist William Riker, "New York built armories in forty legislative districts at a cost of nearly twenty million dollars."[41] At the same time, factory and railroad owners in Pennsylvania and Illinois began organizing their own vigilante armies:

> During the 1880s many businessmen and other community leaders formed vigilante groups, generally known as "Law and Order Leagues," to help maintain public order. To counter the armed bands of radicals, some Chicago businessmen set up military outfits for their employees. In one large wholesale house, for example, there was an organization of 150 young men who were armed with Remington rifles and drilled on a regular basis. Even more menacing were the private (or corporate) police forces, the most infamous of which were the Pennsylvania "Railroad Police" and "Coal and Iron Police." Authorized by the state legislature in 1865, these outfits grew rapidly after 1877. Although commissioned by the governor, they were accountable only to the corporations that employed them. Armed with handguns and rifles, these forces patrolled the state much like an occupying army.[42]

Throughout the 1880s and 1890s, both state and voluntary militias would repeatedly serve in police actions designed to break strikes, quell protests, and disband rallies, all with the calculating force of complete legitimacy. Coupled with the fact that state governors could call out the state militia at will, elites now possessed a formidable arsenal in their battle with would-be agitators.[43]

The ironies of this situation are obvious: A tradition of resistance to a standing federal army had given way to something far worse—a tradition of independent armies serving the minority interests of anyone wealthy enough to form one. But the stakes became even higher when, in 1886, the U.S. Supreme Court defended a governor's right to prohibit some militias and permit others. Justice Woods stated in the majority opinion in the landmark case of *Presser v. Illinois* that "the right voluntarily to associate together as a military company or organization or to drill or parade with arms, without, and independent of, an act of Congress or law of the State authorizing the same, is not an attribute of national citizenship."[44]

Given the role of German and Irish activists in the midcentury labor movement, ethnonational militias were often targeted as seditious troublemakers. *Presser* evolved under exactly such circumstances: In 1879, the Illinois State Legislature began debating the merits of a new militia bill designed to bolster the preparedness of local National Guard units. Presumably, this was an indirect response to the labor agitation of 1877, in which the Illinois militia had been hard-pressed to contain strike activity throughout the state. Furthermore, attached to the bill was a controversial statute, which stipulated that all private militias not officially recognized by the governor would be thenceforth prohibited. In other words, the governor would now be entitled to sanction some independent militias, whereas all others not so recognized would be prohibited.

A group of ethnic military organizations in Chicago apparently saw the implications of this proviso, and while the bill awaited final approval in the Illinois State Legislature, a number of them took to the streets in protest. According to the *Chicago Tribune*, members of the *Lehr und Wehr Verein*, the (Irish) Labor Guards, the Bohemian Sharpshooters, the *Jaeger Verein*, numerous nonmilitary labor societies, citizens in express wagons and buggies, and "a loaded beer wagon" took to the streets of Chicago to express their opposition to the pending militia bill.[45] The march proved peaceful despite threats of antilabor violence, though the response of some Chicagoans was less than welcoming. The following day, an article in the *Tribune* glibly commented, "The Bohemians, Poles, and Scandinavians of the Socialist party are demonstrating their 'rights.' They include among these the right to KEEP THE CITY IN A CONSTANT FERMENT; to bear the red flag through its streets; to force the authorities to maintain a regiment under arms, and to retain the police upon duty all day." The unnamed *Tribune* author also accused the marchers of public drunkenness and disturbing the peace:

> The landless and propertyless immigrants of the Lehr und Wehr Verein must be taught here what they apparently failed to learn at home, that law reigns in the United States. Believing that the proper remedy for any evils which may exist in the ballot-box, and that the people of Illinois do not hold with mob-intimidation, the Legislature has under its consideration a bill providing that no body of men, other than those legally authorized, shall drill or parade with arms in any city or town in Illinois without the consent of the Executive. This, of course, means the death of the Lehr und Wehr Verein and all its connections, and it was for the purpose of intimidating the Legislature and preventing them from passing this Militia law that the meeting of yesterday was held.[46]

Nonetheless, despite the protests and parades, the bill quickly passed the legislature with the militia restriction intact.

Several months later the commander of the *Lehr und Wehr Verein*, Herman Presser, was arrested for leading his group on parade through the streets of Chicago in contravention of the new militia restrictions. Presser's actions seemed designed to provoke arrest, and he subsequently took his case all the way to the Supreme Court. *Presser v. Illinois* has since proven to be one of the most controversial Supreme Court decisions in U.S. history, though, as constitutional scholars currently avow, the courts have been fairly consistent in supporting a collectivist reading of the Second Amendment (meaning that they rarely interpret the Second Amendment to support an individual's right to bear arms but see it rather as protection of the state militia system vis-à-vis the federal army).[47] Nonetheless, as the *Socialist* argued in the heady days of 1879, "[The *Lehr und Wehr Verein's*] purpose is not to create riots or *emeutes*, but to protect the workingmen in their Constitutional right to assemble peaceably," a right guaranteed by the First and, arguably, the Second Amendments.[48]

The new militia bill did not stop independent militias from drilling in Illinois or in other states, but the *Presser* decision was indicative of a new trend in the United States whereby the Second Amendment was used against labor insurgents and in support of the state militias meant to control them. Uniformed police forces had been adopted in American cities after the British innovation in the 1850s, and as labor unrest grew in the postbellum years, state militias and new state police forces received newfound support.[49] In addition, the flexibility of antimilitia laws allowed officials to look the other way whenever independent military organizations served their purposes. By this means, private armies of scabs, detectives, and strike-breaking marauders were founded for the express purpose of combating labor.

The National Rifle Association and the State Sponsorship of Militancy

At the same time that the Supreme Court was redefining the scope of the Second Amendment, another innovation in American military policy was just gaining steam, one that would affect the nation to this day—the formation of the National Rifle Association.

The history of the NRA is as complex and poorly understood as any voluntary organization in the United States. It originated as a state-subsidized paramilitary organization founded to support and promote the marksmanship of state and federal troops. Modeled largely after the successful National Rifle Association of Great Britain, the NRA movement in America was spearheaded in 1871 by *New York Sun* publisher William Conant Church, with the backing of New York National Guard Captain George Wood Wingate and New York State Governor John T. Hoffman. Though the ambiguities of American national defense policy had always encouraged a well-armed citizenry, and in fact Union soldiers were allowed to take their rifles home with them after serving in the Civil War, new tactical innovations in military science required marksmanship that most American soldiers were sorely lacking. The surprising 6-week victory of the well-armed, well-trained Prussian armies over the French in 1870 made this only too clear to American generals, as did the generally poor performance of Union army soldiers in the most recent war. The NRA was thus formed expressly for the purpose of improving the marksmanship of America's soldiers and militiamen.[50]

With a $25,000 appropriation from the New York State Legislature and an additional $5,000 each from the cities of New York and Brooklyn, the NRA launched its first project in 1872 by constructing a shooting range at Creedmoor, Long Island. Here, once again, we run headlong into the fuzzy distinction between state and civic organizations in the United States: The NRA was a private, nonprofit concern with clear and self-conscious state backing. Most of its officers were retired military men, and its primary membership for the remainder of the nineteenth century was made up of National Guardsmen. Its aims, furthermore, were explicitly guided by the desire to bolster national security. By 1878, in fact, the NRA's Board of Directors included representatives from all the major national defense institutions, including the commanders of the various army departments, the superintendent of West Point, and the chief of ordinance of the United States.[51]

The NRA had its ups and downs in the final decades of the nineteenth century—in 1880, New York State Governor Alonzo B. Cornell decreed, for example, "There will be no war in my time or in the time of my children. The only need for a National Guard is to show itself in parades and ceremonies. . . . Rifle practice for these men is a waste of money, and I shall not countenance in my presence anything as foolish as a discussion of the rifle shooting at Creedmoor"[52]—but the NRA did succeed in several respects. By sponsoring shooting competitions among the various military regiments of the federal and state armies, American marksmen soon began rivaling, if not besting, their European counterparts.[53]

The 1880s and 1890s also saw a resurgence of nonethnic voluntary militias in certain parts of the country, particularly on the East Coast, where the independent militia tradition began well before the Revolutionary War.[54] Many such groups either resembled fraternal orders or were attached to them directly. So rapid was the proliferation of quasi-fraternal militias that in 1897 journalist W. S. Harwood declared (in the same *North American Review* article that proclaimed the "Golden Age of Fraternity"):

> Perhaps even more significant than the fact that there are so many millions of oath-bound men in the United States is the further fact that auxiliary to and a part of these orders are military branches, having at the present time about two hundred and fifty thousand members in the prime of life, who are trained in military tactics and who know the sword and musket manual as well as does the cleverest "regular," many of them thoroughly informed as to the history, the present needs, and the possibilities of military life."[55]

In Massachusetts, a periodical called *The Volunteer: A Monthly Magazine Devoted to the Interests of the Volunteer Militia of New England* was released in 1889. Its tone is notably defensive in declaring the need to maintain, if not bolster, public support for independent military activity. "Its object," state the editors, "will be not only to defend the militia system as it exists today but to instruct our citizen soldiers in all that pertains to a soldier's duty in order that our militia may be still more worthy of public support than it is at the present time."[56]

The magazine includes how-to sections on military drills, historical sketches of notable companies and commanders, advertisements (primarily from purveyors of "fine" uniforms), and a curious section of self-promoting news excerpts from around the region, including the following announcement for a group called the *East Boston Amazons*:

> The young ladies connected with the East Boston High School organized some six months ago, two companies for the purpose of perfecting themselves in military movements. . . . The first public exhibition was given at East Boston, on Thursday evening, April 25th, in the presence of several thousand interested spectators who liberally applauded the drilling by these young ladies, which was performed in a highly credible manner. . . . A drill by the boys of the school followed at the conclusion of which there was a dress parade and then dancing."[57]

According to the *Volunteer*, paramilitary organizations were common in New England schools at the time.[58] Another *Volunteer* excerpt states, for example, that "there are now over 1200 boys in the Boston School regiment who are regularly drilled, using rifles which are furnished at the expense of the city or state. The regiment will hold their annual parade on the 17th of this month."[59] Nonetheless, success was not always so forthcoming, as in Worcester, where according to another excerpt, "The Wrocester [*sic*] Continentals are in need of recruits, and if some are not immediately obtained it is likely that this organization may disband."[60]

The Rise of the American Gun Culture

Together, the rise of volunteer militias, shooting clubs, and antilabor police tactics provided a climate ripe for America's new gun culture. Historian Michael Bellesiles has provided comprehensive (though controversial) evidence that gun ownership was relatively rare in the United States prior to the Civil War, but this trend was clearly reversed by the end of the century.[61] Since the Ordinance Department was always desperate for reliable, accurate pistols and rifles that could be produced quickly and cheaply in mass quantities, vast improvements were made in the design and manufacture of guns and ammunition. The nation's disorganized array of shooting clubs and independent military organizations also helped create an expansive new market for advanced weaponry. Furthermore, the well-publicized exploits of midcentury explorers, speculators, and Indian fighters contributed mightily to the growing prestige of gun play. As a result, little or no thought was ever given to the issue of gun control; in fact, public policy was explicitly oriented toward promoting gun culture throughout the period before World War I.[62]

Though rifles predominated in most nineteenth-century military and target-shooting circles, pistol design also received its fair share of attention in this period. Given the desire of policemen, naval officers, and ordinary citizens for a weapon that was small but powerful, intense efforts were made by the nation's various gun manufacturers to produce a handgun worthy of the job. The Colt Company, for example, put out an expansive line of Deringers, pocket revolvers, and so-called house pistols in a variety of calibers, barrel lengths, and stock designs.[63]

After the Civil War, a series of international shooting matches endorsed by the NRA became another vehicle for spreading the gospel of American marksmanship, as well as the American-made weapons that made it possible. Press accounts of international shooting matches were florid in their praise for the American team and their guns. "Greek met Greek when the British and American rifle teams struggled for the Centennial trophy throughout the days of the 13th and 14th," declared the *New York Merchants' Journal* (September 22, 1877), "and while, with such shooting as was then exhibited, defeat itself was an honor, the victory which rewarded the magnificent efforts of the Americans was glory indeed." The new and improved Sharps long-range rifle was celebrated as the key to the American victory: "Bruce, the hero of the American team, who, on the last day, made the unheard-of record, 219 out of a possible 225, used this wonderful gun, and, at the conclusion of the match made the emphatic remark that 'SHARPS' Rifle made my record; I only happened to be behind it.'"[64]

Nonetheless, for the time being, the NRA remained committed to training only National Guardsmen, primarily those from the greater New York region.

A New Divide: Centralization of the National Guard and the Proliferation of Civilian Gun Culture

The U.S. military did come closer to a distinct divide between civic and state affairs at the turn of the century, though its reputation was severely tarnished by a prior history of anarchy and decentralization. Throughout the postbellum period, the various state militias had struggled to form themselves into a national body in order to gain greater recognition, funding, and permission to serve alongside the federal army in wartime. The term *National Guard* itself was promoted and diffused across the country by the National Guard Association (NGA), a lobby group founded in the late 1870s by militia officers with two purposes: "to promote military efficiency throughout the active militia of the United States, and to secure united representation before Congress for such legislation as . . . may [be] necessary for this purpose."[65]

Though the NGA had been lobbying for a national militia reform bill for decades, the nation's various militias were still governed (and largely ignored) under the rough parameters of the Militia Act of 1792. However, the Spanish-American War proved to be the turning point in their quest for reorganization:

> The war dispelled the skepticism of those who doubted that the United States would ever fight. It demonstrated the need for a trained reserve by exposing the inadequacies of the militia, who, as volunteers for federal service, reported to their training camps pathetically ill-prepared. It suffused the country with a martial spirit, and it greatly accelerated the development of nationalism, thereby reducing states'-rights opposition to a federal militia act.[66]

In 1903, after years of vigorous lobbying, Senator Charles Dick (former major general of the Ohio National Guard), finally saw the enactment of federal legislation to reform the National Guard—the Dick Act of 1903 (H.R. 11654). In a speech noteworthy for both its self-promotion and self-deprecation, Senator Dick proclaimed:

> The present law governing the militia has been on the statute books for one hundred and ten years and has long since been inoperative and obsolete. . . . For over one hundred years Congress has made no adequate provision for organizing, arming, and disciplining the militia, and the matter has been left entirely in the hands of the States and Territories. . . . And while the troops are generally known and described as the National Guard, they are in no proper sense a national guard, but are strictly State militia, and are not subject to supervision and control by the War Department. It was believed that these State troops would be promptly available for national defense in case of an emergency. The experience of the country during the war with Spain showed that these expectations were not fully realized.[67]

The Dick Act served the interests of the National Guard Association in several ways: First, it dramatically increased federal appropriations to state militias, enabling them not only to buy new weapons and supplies but also to expand training for recruits; second, the National Guard had chafed for some time under its primary role as domestic riot police, and the Dick Act created a formal place for the National Guard in the nation's armed forces, thus enabling its officers to train with their federal counterparts and serve alongside them in time of war. (This last complaint stemmed from the fact that domestic riot duty was not only violent and dangerous but also often inimical to the interests of recruits, many of whom were laborers themselves.[68])

A third function of the Dick Act proved more controversial, however, and this once again highlights the dangers of America's ambiguous military policy: Whereas the Dick Act aimed to reintegrate independent and state militias under the single aegis of the National Guard, provisions for doing so were notoriously unclear. Standards were proposed to establish eligibility requirements for militias that were seeking formal recognition (and thus subsidization) under the bill, but repeated plans to implement such standards were opposed by the militias themselves, who resented "efforts to centralize control over them because they justifiably believed their organizations were more the products of their own time, energy, and money."[69] Furthermore, the Dick Act failed to make clear how the volunteer militia's private arms and armories would be subsumed under the new system. Colonel Thomas F. Edmands of Boston's First Corps of Cadets, for example, adamantly demanded (in a letter to Congress) a guarantee that the corps' private property would not be stripped from them under the new act.[70]

Furthermore, despite the reorganization of the National Guard, thereby precluding the need for volunteer militias, the federally funded race to arm the nation continued apace. Sensing that its mission to encourage better marksmanship in the military was complete, the NRA now turned its sights on bigger game: the general public.[71]

The NRA's campaign began with the passage of a 1903 bill creating the National Board for the Promotion of Rifle Practice, about which Secretary of War Elihu Root said, "The board therefore respectfully recommends the encouragement by the War Department of the organization of rifle clubs composed of those who would be eligible for service in time of war, but without special obligation for war service on account of such membership."[72] In 1905, Public Law 149 bolstered the campaign by authorizing the sale (at cost) of surplus military weapons to rifle clubs that met the specifications of the new national board.[73] Why the NRA and the federal government felt it so necessary to encourage civilian riflery when the military had taken such pains to improve its own training facilities remains an open question.

In 1903, the NRA also adopted a resolution stating that "the National Rifle Association of America deems it expedient to take immediate steps to secure the affiliation with it of colleges, universities and other educational institutions of the United States for the purpose of stimulating and encouraging rifle practice among the American youth."[74] In 1905, former NRA president General George W. Wingate started a competitive rifle-shooting program in the New York City public schools, with the additional sponsorship of the Grand Army of the Republic. In the years following, the NRA became increasingly involved in the organization and sponsorship of interscholastic and intercollegiate shooting matches.[75]

The year 1910 was yet another landmark for American gun culture: "Throughout 1910 the NRA concentrated on organizing schoolboy clubs through the United States," write historians Trefethen and Serven. "It mailed circulars to the principals and superintendents of high schools in every state and frequently followed them with personal visits."[76] Furthermore, that same year saw the passage of a bill sponsored by Iowa Congressman John Albert Tiffin Hull authorizing the War Department to issue free rifles and ammunition to any and all rifle clubs affiliated with the NRA:

> It was the first time that individual members at large of the NRA were given access to government equipment. Earlier distribution had been only to af- filiated military clubs, and ownership of the weapons was retained by the War Department. These rifles, however, were sold outright to individual [NRA] members who could "sporterize" them for hunting, "accurize" them for target work, or scrub off the cosmoline and use them as they were. The only restriction was that they not be acquired for the purpose of resale.[77]

One only wonders how many guns were put into distribution around the na- tion through this federal subsidy program.

Conclusion

By the onset of World War I, the organization of the American military had undergone a number of major transformations: Republican aspirations for a civic army of part-time citizen-soldiers were quelled; private military organizations were fostered, though those favoring the interests of enfranchised elites gained a decided advantage over time; and through the concerted efforts of state and civic leaders alike, a national gun culture was cultivated in high schools, shooting clubs, and volunteer militias throughout the nation.

Though far from a complete history of militia policy, this brief tour supports three simple claims about the relationship between American associationalism and national security:

1. Concerns about state and federal integration in the early years of the Republic created an institutional vacuum later occupied by populist and elite militias alike, both of which have received scant (but noteworthy) attention in the annals of American social and political history.
2. The proliferation of ethnic- and labor-based militias led to counter- legislation aimed at suppressing some civilian militias while encourag- ing others, a trend that contributed greatly to the political weakness of American labor in the late nineteenth century.
3. The ambiguities of American military policy both reflected and fostered a tradition of latent hostility to the federal government, as seen in the vagar- ies of civilian and professional military training before World War I.

Fleshing out this argument will require the concerted effort of military histo- rians and scholars of American political development. A number of questions remain unanswered: How did the centralization of federal forces and the cre- ation of federal intelligence agencies in the early twentieth century relate to the rise of right-wing militias and organized crime thereafter? What were the long-

and short-term effects of weapons-training programs in American schools? Were American cities more or less prone to outbreaks of ethnic violence in the presence of ethnic civilian militias? And what role did the public gun distribution programs sponsored by the NRA and the federal government play in the proliferation of privately owned weapons and the rise of organized opposition to gun control?

In addition to derailing American national security for over 100 years and creating artificial obstacles to the pursuit of labor-related political goals, one major ramification of the American legacy of civilian military organization is a nation in which gun ownership is an important and well-protected right. Given the ambiguities of the Constitution and the history of government support for private gun ownership, contemporary gun lobby advocates can indiscriminately draw on an invented tradition of Americans and their guns—one that will likely linger for many years to come.

WHITHER COMPREHENSIVE SOCIAL INSURANCE
IN THE UNITED STATES?

Antistatism and Associationalism before the New Deal

Thus far, I have endeavored to convince you that the rise of the fraternal model of social organization had several adverse effects on American political development: It fostered division of the polity into numerous groups that represented narrowly defined special interests, it helped fracture the nascent labor movement along sectarian lines, and it helped nurture a nation afraid of itself and enamoured with guns. This chapter aims to outline yet another underappreciated consequence of the golden age: the defeat of a national campaign to enact compulsory health insurance during the 1910s. More specifically, it touches once again on two prominent themes of this volume:

1. the manner in which competitive voluntarism in general and the rise of fraternalism in particular encouraged the formation and articulation of special interests in American political culture
2. the relationship between the rising popularity of sectarian fraternal benefit plans and subsequent resistance to government plans that would collectivize risk and redistribute income across sectarian lines.

Competitive voluntarism entailed more than just competition among rival fraternal orders, religious sodalities, and ethnonational clubs; it also involved competition between voluntary groups and those other organizations that sought to usurp their function, that is, government and for-profit insurance agencies. In the long run, nonprofit insurance providers won the battle against government insurance while losing the war to the commercial insurers. But whereas commercial insurance has improved on many of the shortcomings of the fraternal insurance system, namely, the management of investors' premiums, it shares with the fraternal system a penchant for eligibility restrictions and limited coverage—yet another unintended legacy of the golden age.

Why Don't More Americans Have Health Insurance Today?

The years just before and after World War I were an auspicious time for social welfare legislation in America. Over the preceding several decades, a new generation of Americans dedicated to social welfare reform had founded think tanks, reform organizations, and social welfare agencies in cities and towns across the nation. The reformers were unusually well-educated men and women committed not only to providing better social services to needy Americans but also to researching the causes and consequences of various policy options in depth. Western Europe was obviously a role model in this respect. American public policy reformers spent vast amounts of time traveling to and from Europe to study the latest innovations in labor relations, public health, affordable housing, old-age pensions, poor relief, and something they called *sickness* insurance— which we now, perhaps overoptimistically, refer to as *health* insurance.[1]

European approaches to these problems obviously varied enormously, which only provided additional directions for American reformers. By 1911, Great Britain, American reformers' strongest role model, had enacted compulsory national policies that granted workers' compensation and unemployment insurance for all laborers, old-age insurance for the indigent elderly, and sickness insurance for all residents of the Commonwealth. Germany enacted similar policies, with the exception of unemployment insurance, and most other western European nation-states, as well as Canada, Australia, and New Zealand were busy following suit.[2] Citing these as precedents, American reformers and social activists lobbied vigorously for comparable social welfare legislation in the United States in the first two decades of the twentieth century.

One of the most politically important social welfare campaigns on this side of the Atlantic revolved around the prospects for a state-run health insurance system:

> Between 1915 and 1920 compulsory health insurance was one of the most controversial, widely debated social issues in the United States. Identified primarily with the American Association for Labor Legislation, and its Committee on Social Insurance, it reached an advanced legislative stage in New York and California. The AALL published tentative standards for health insurance in the summer of 1914, followed in November 1915 by the first draft of a bill. Versions were introduced into the New York, Massachusetts, and New Jersey legislatures in 1916, and into those of fifteen other states in 1917.[3]

The failure of the health insurance campaigns of 1915–1920 bolstered the power of the medical industry to set its own standards and fees and encouraged the creation of commercial health insurance funds for those who could afford to buy them: "Of the immense variety of political coalitions ruling state governments," writes medical sociologist Terry Boychuk, "not one of them devised a legislative program for universalizing hospital insurance."[4] Understanding why the quest for universal health insurance failed in the United States is a question of great import for policy historians and policymakers alike, though most have yet to consider one key piece of the puzzle: the concerted opposition of the nation's many fraternal orders and lodge brothers.

Existing Explanations of the Failed Social Insurance Campaign of 1915–1920

Theda Skocpol's brilliant history of American social welfare legislation, *Protecting Soldiers and Mothers: The Political Origins of Social Policy in the United States*, highlights two crucial points about the nature of early twentieth-century Americans' approach to social insurance: First, she dispels the myth that Americans have always been opposed to social welfare legislation—the enormous pensions granted to Union army veterans of the Civil War were part of one of the largest social welfare programs on either side of the Atlantic before 1900.[5] Second, Skocpol shows how successive attempts to build on this legacy were defeated in all but one domain—benefits for indigent mothers and their children. American industrial leaders also later capitulated on the issue of workers' compensation, having been driven to it by fear of class-action suits and/or government regulation; but except for workers' compensation and aid to indigent mothers, campaigns for new social welfare programs were soundly defeated in state legislatures across the country before the New Deal. Even minimum wage laws and regulations on the maximum length of the industrial workday only came piecemeal.

Considering its almost exclusive focus on the welfare of women with children, Skocpol aptly characterizes American welfare policy as "maternalist" in focus, and she offers a compelling explanation for this unusual outcome: On the one hand, she argues, Americans' experience with veterans' pensions, and their fear of government corruption in general, lent an atmosphere of fear and suspicion to any and all proposals for new government programs. Decades of party patronage and graft had purportedly soured Americans on the idea of state-run anything: "Their [reformists'] broadsides against democratic patronage parties and the 'horrors' of social spending for the masses helped to ensure that Civil War benefits would become an obstacle rather than an entering wedge for more general old-age pensions and workingmen's insurance in the United States."[6]

On the other hand, the strength of this particular explanation of failed welfare reform is weakened by two facts relevant to the period in question: First, it overlooks the fact that at this time, in the early decades of the twentieth century, American voters were busily endorsing vast increases in municipal public health and infrastructure, as well as national defense spending, all three of which had equal potential for political misappropriation.[7] Moreover, shortly afterward, Americans *did* endorse state pensions for indigent mothers, no less an invitation to graft and scandal than pensions for workingmen or the elderly (see table 7.1).

Though Progressive Era reformers often spoke of the need to eliminate graft and corruption from the nation's governmental institutions, one needs to exercise some caution in interpreting their complaints. Opposition to party patronage came largely from a group of educated elites resentful of the loyalty urban voters displayed toward their ward officials and party representatives. And despite the prevalence of antipatronage sentiment among elite reformers of the Progressive Era, the so-called party machines continued to flourish throughout the 1910s and 1920s and beyond.[8] In other words, the language of party patronage might well be seen as a political canard used to fool voters into temporarily ousting working-class politicians and replacing them with self-righteous (and largely unsuccessful) business reformers.

In addition, whereas opponents of compulsory health insurance labeled it many things, from a threat to workers' manliness to an invitation to state socialism, I have found only passing references to the issue of party graft and/or corruption in published speeches, essays, and articles on this topic.[9] Rhetoric about policy legacies can indeed play a powerful role in political debate, as it sometimes did during the Progressive Era, but one should never mistake rhetoric for the underlying reasons that bring it to the lips of advocates. If reformists

TABLE 7.1 Relationship Between Occupational and Fraternal Organizations and Social Welfare Policy Outcomes, Circa. 1890–1930

Strength by type of organization	United States	United Kingdom	France	Germany
Labor unions	Weak	Strong	Strong	Strong
Fraternals	Strong	Weak	Weak	Weak
Timing of social policy outcomes				
Old-age pensions	none	1908–1925	1910–1930	1889
Sickness insurance	none	1911	1930	1883
Unemployment insurance	none	1911–1920	1914	1927
Mothers' pensions	1911–1920	none	none	none

Sources: Peter Flora and Arnold J. Heidenheimer, eds. *The Development of Welfare States in Europe and America* (New Brunswick, NJ: Transaction Books, 1981); Susan Pedersen, *Family, Dependence, and The Origins of the Welfare State: Britain and France, 1914–1945* (Cambridge: Cambridge University Press, 1993); Theda Skocpol, *Protecting Soldiers and Mothers: The Political Origins of Social Policy in the United States* (Cambridge: Belknap, 1992).

used the patronage label to smear proposals for some social insurance schemes and not others, we need to explore the logic of action across different policy domains. More important, such discrepancies beg the question of why voters would have bought into such rhetoric in the first place: Millions of American families benefited from Civil War pensions, however profligate they may have been. Why didn't they lobby harder for similar benefits for all Americans?

In *Protecting Soldiers and Mothers*, Skocpol argues, more convincingly, that a second factor behind the defeat of social welfare legislation in the 1910s was the fervent opposition of several major American business constituencies. The commercial insurance lobby is one obvious villain here (assuming that you, like me, agree that some kind of guaranteed health insurance for all Americans would have been a desirable policy outcome).[10] Doctors, represented by the mighty American Medical Association (AMA), were another enemy of social insurance. The AMA fought long and hard to protect the lucrative professional autonomy that doctors had worked so hard to achieve in the late nineteenth century.[11] Manufacturers and business owners also came out in force against the idea of compulsory insurance, and they did so through their increasingly powerful mercantile and commercial lobbying groups.[12] Of course, not all employers fought compulsory social welfare programs simply because of their cost. Many larger firms created private pension and benefit programs for their own employees. Such efforts only stimulated their opposition to state-mandated reforms, however. Employers were extremely reluctant to cede a bargaining tool as valuable as employee benefits to state agencies. In the words of historian Andrea Tone, "although businessmen may have been divided in their support of acts establishing the Federal Trade Commission, the Federal Reserve System, and more comprehensive meat inspection, they stood united, almost without exception, in their animosity toward social welfare and labor legislation."[13]

By far the most damning and best documented opponent of state-run health insurance was the American Federation of Labor, the very union that had risen from the ashes of the fallen Knights of Labor (see chapter 5). Samuel Gompers, long-time head of the AFL, was one of the nation's most vocal opponents of compulsory health insurance, and he brought the loyalty of his many followers to bear on the insurance debate as it played out in New York, California, and elsewhere in the 1910s. Publicly, Gompers denounced compulsory insurance as a threat to the autonomy of trade unions, but privately he was a lifelong Freemason and a personal advocate of private insurance. According to historian David Beito, Gompers professed to a 1918 convention of the National Casualty and Surety Agents, "I wish that there would be more of that insurance of a fraternal and mutual character."[14] At the Social Insurance Session of the National Civic Federation's annual meeting in April 1920, Gompers clarified his stance on social insurance beyond a shadow of a doubt: "It has come to me that recently some person has declared that Gompers has been won over to compulsory health insurance. I have already made my answer, which is that I am unalterably opposed to it."[15]

Gompers had built his career on the principle that unions should stick to the business of contract negotiations and stay out of politics (see chapter 5). His public declarations on the health insurance issue were touted by opponents of health insurance reform as the final word on the issue: If the leader of the nation's largest labor union was against it, how could anyone stand for it? Arguably, Gompers was backed into taking such an ardent stand by circumstance, as well as conviction. Anticommunist rhetoric was at a fever pitch following the Bolshevik Revolution in Russia and the onset of war with Germany. Any sign of support for compulsory insurance on Gompers's part might well have been labeled subversive by enemies of labor, thus leaving the AFL open to outright persecution. In fact, the very same issue of the *National Civic Federation Review* that printed Gompers's "unalterable" opposition to compulsory health insurance also featured a story entitled "Revolutionary Forces in Our Midst: Peace with Bolshevist Regime Would Aid Efforts Toward World Revolution—Red Propaganda Active in America—Bolshevism and Socialism Identical."[16] At the same time, Gompers also faced a potential revolt within the AFL's ranks over the health insurance issue. At least 15 state branches of the AFL came out in support of health legislation, and the extent to which Gompers went out of his way to publicize his opposition to it may indicate a more subtle attempt to combat insurgency within the AFL.[17] Either way, the strength of the labor opposition argument is mitigated by the presence of internal divisions over this issue within the labor movement as a whole.

One can salvage from all this at least one strong, empirically verifiable explanation of the failure of the health insurance campaigns of 1915–1920: Whereas a powerful constituency of reform-minded lobbyists and academics supported the notion of state-run health insurance, an equally if not more powerful constituency of doctors, employers, insurance underwriters, and labor leaders came out against it.

In retrospect, one might have expected such mighty adversaries to come to a draw on the issue, prompting successful compromise in those states where universal insurance advocates had a slight edge. But history tells a different story: Health insurance legislation failed in every state where it was proposed. Why, then, were its adversaries so successful in blocking universal health insurance (as well as old-age pensions and unemployment insurance)?

An obscure article buried in the *New York Times* of March 20, 1919, provides one tentative answer: "UNITE IN ATTACK ON HEALTH INSURANCE" affirms the headline, and the first paragraph reads, "Compulsory health insurance as proposed in the Davenport-Donohue bill was attacked as un-American, unsound, and unconstitutional by its opponents at a hearing before the [New York] Senate Judiciary Committee this afternoon. Manufacturers, merchants, physicians, and

representatives of fraternal organizations appeared in opposition, while representatives of labor argued for it."[18] Thus we find an often overlooked clue, that fraternal organizations joined the fray in the battle against state-sponsored health
insurance: Special-interest groups representing doctors, manufacturers, commercial insurers, and laborers are often cited as the chief opponents of social insurance, but one should keep in mind that by 1919, at the height of the insurance
debate, the fraternal movement comprised millions of members, organized in
every state of the union. Fraternal opposition to health insurance may thus be
the missing link in the search for a viable explanation of the failure of health
insurance campaigns in states across the nation.

Fraternal Opposition to Health Insurance Legislation

Historical accounts of the health insurance question have generally failed to
explain why the mainstream American voter was so swayed by the opposition,
lobby pressure notwithstanding. The 1910s saw increasing public momentum
in support of some reorganization of the public welfare system. Presumably, state-
sponsored health insurance should have been appealing to a majority of Americans at that time. Many states even considered instituting voluntary programs,
which would have afforded residents a choice among competing health insurance options. But, for some reason, all such bills were defeated. In addition to
the corporate interests involved, we must look for some larger reason why so
many Americans failed to respond to the lure of universal health coverage.

One account, the *History and Operation of Fraternal Insurance,* provides some
clues: Though its author, Walter Basye, admits that "organized fraternalism takes
little interest in legislation" beyond that "directed mainly to obtaining exemptions from taxation and for maintaining the second-class mailing privileges for
the official society journals," he proudly recalls that "recently [c. 1919] the societies have waged a strong fight against social and government insurance. . . .
Several million [fraternal] members are convinced that socialistic and paternal-
istic legislation is a menace to them and their children, and their opposition is
expressed through the societies."[19]

Basye's account was clearly drafted to weigh in on the health insurance debate then raging around the country. Acknowledging the tendency to overlook
fraternities' political potential in light of the interest-group titans involved, he
states that "the fraternal system possesses a powerful influence of its own":

> This is based on the fact that practically all of the members of such societ-
> ies are voters, and *when they vote together their influence at the polls is tre-*
> *mendous.* Another factor of the influence exerted by the societies is in the
> fact that fraternalists are often very active in politics. Some of the societies
> claim as members United States senators, governors, congressmen and State

legislators. The author has in mind the legislature of one State in which all the members of both Senate and House were members of one or more of the established fraternal benefit societies.[20]

It is somewhat puzzling that fraternal opposition to compulsory health insurance has received so little attention from historians of the period.[21] Fraternal spokespeople were active in debates on the issue: A. C. McLean, president of the National Fraternal Congress of America sat on the 11-person Social Insurance Committee convened by the National Civic Federation, for example.[22] Nor did fraternalists fail to make their voices heard in state legislatures. When Alice B. Locke testified before the Labor and Industries Committee of the New York Senate on behalf of the Woman's Benefit Association of the Maccabees (a women's fraternity with 30,000 members in New York State), for example, she made her point loud and clear:

> Since when do three-quarters of a million citizens of the State of New York, who are insured in the fraternal benefit societies, have to accept for their "superior" intelligence, any kind of "raw" legislation that paid uplifters and Socialists may see fit to hand out to us? Since when must the members of the State Grange, the Federation of Women's Clubs, and the hundreds of thousands of other loyal 100 per cent Americans cower under the lash of the men and women who are seeking to push through our legislature this bill, which is obnoxious to millions of patriotic, self-respecting independent citizens?[23]

Recall, too, that the fraternal system had been growing in membership and geographical scope since the early 1870s. Historians make the conservative estimate that one in three adult males belonged to at least one fraternal lodge as of 1920 and that members carried a total of about $9 billion in fraternal life insurance at that time.[24] Over the years, fraternalism had also gained the respect and deference of American politicians. In March 1915, when a bill was proposed in New York City to revoke the property tax exemption granted to all churches and voluntary associations, for example, fraternal associations were explicitly omitted from any such tax increases, an "oversight" that prompted at least one angry letter to the editors of the New York Times: "Upon what principle are 'fraternal associations' to be continued in exemption from taxes, when churches, synagogues, monasteries, convents, schools, colleges, asylums, homes, hospitals, cemeteries, and libraries are to be taxed, according to the so-called 'Sullivan bill' in the legislature?"[25] The Sullivan bill was never made law, but the special dispensation granted to the city's fraternal associations reflects a deep respect for their presence in the politics of the day.

Similar respect is evident in an address by Texas Senator Morris Sheppard at a ceremony for the Woodmen of the World in Durham, North Carolina, June

1916: "The fraternal spirit will ultimately solve all economic problems and defend the country against monarchies and destruction," he said, adding that "the fraternal orders of America [represent] a power greater than the strength of all armaments and naval powers of the Earth."[26] Under ordinary circumstances, one might simply overlook such an obvious effort at flattery. The details of Sheppard's speech deserve a bit more consideration, however, for Sheppard was the very same senator later responsible for passage of the Sheppard-Towner Infancy and Maternity Protection Act of 1921, a child welfare scheme often cited by historians as the cornerstone of America's maternalist approach to social welfare.[27]

The connection is obscure but vitally important in understanding the politics behind fraternal opposition to compulsory insurance: Most fraternal orders in America excluded women from membership: the Woodmen of the World, for example, the very group Sheppard was so busy flattering, did not admit women as members until 1928.[28] This meant that sickness and burial insurance were difficult services for most women to acquire. At the same time, compulsory insurance programs such as those being proposed in the 1910s threatened to usurp one of the primary benefits of fraternal membership—cheap sickness and/or burial insurance for men. (Representatives of those organizations that did provide women with such benefits, such as the Women's Benefit Association of the Maccabees, were also opposed to compulsory health insurance.) Thus, one sees the makings of an obvious tradeoff in the works: Under Sheppard's maternalist welfare scheme, fraternalists would preserve the right to provide insurance to their members in return for two things: (1) a strong presence in the battle against compulsory state insurance and (2) tacit approval of subsequent measures aimed at giving needy women and their children some insurance benefits through state-run, tax-funded social service programs. Indigent women needed help, in other words, whereas gainfully employed men should be expected to rely on the "manly" virtues of fraternalism to provide for themselves and their families.

Fraternal opponents of compulsory insurance leaned heavily on this gendered notion of citizenship. In a 1918 address before the National Fraternal Congress of America in Philadelphia, John Sullivan, a member of the Modern Woodmen of America, repeatedly spoke of the threat social insurance presented to American manhood:

> Such assumption of power by Government, un-mans the citizen, in that undertaking to dictate and manage his personal affairs, on theory it can do so better than he himself, taking from him the responsibility, and man-building element of human nature, of thinking for himself, acting for himself, carried to the full conclusion of the idea involved, of government assuming lines of individual prerogative, decadence in the individual obtains and a species of soul-abhorring serfdom in citizenship results. Such

idea of Government applied to American institutions would take the red out of the Stars and Stripes.[29]

Given the force and rhetoric of this speech, I do not think Sullivan was merely using "man" as a diminutive for "human." In making the connection between manhood and self-insurance, Sullivan implied that American fraternalism was part of the divine order as God intended it:

> *True manhood obtains through contest.* God placed *man* upon earth endowed with brain and brawn giving him nature's wealth in the rough upon which to use his talents and efforts for his sustenance. . . . The recognized necessity and prudence of so doing so [*sic*] to save, accumulate and guard against the pit falls of life, keeping in view the demands and uncertainties of old age which leads men to utilize all talents and spurs him on to effort, wrestling with, struggling with, and enduring whatever hardships may materialize which makes health minded men, high minded men, and such composing its citizenship is the bulwark of the Republic.[30]

By threatening the principal basis of fraternalism, state-run benefit programs threatened to emasculate American men, or so it was argued.

I am not an intellectual historian, nor am I an expert on the history of American social policy, but this does appear to me to be a clear harbinger of contemporary American antistatism today. Fraternal critics of compulsory insurance accused the government of wanting to make everyone a "ward of the state." Compulsory insurance was likened to state socialism, and state socialism was equated with immorality and femininity. And beneath the rhetoric, it is clear that there were indeed a number of important interests at stake: State-run sickness and old-age insurance threatened the very cornerstone of American fraternalism. It would devalue the insurance policies of millions of American fraternalists, if not render them totally worthless.

To bolster their case, fraternal spokesmen like John Sullivan looked to the legacy of social insurance provision in Germany for examples of the evils of state welfare programs:

> Social insurance propaganda is of European origin. . . . The great purpose of the Imperial Government was to disarm the Socialists and to work out a plan which would make the masses of German people, under allurement of financial help from the State, subservient to the government. . . . There is no more potent and copper-riveted tyrannical power devisable over a dejected and helpless spirit than that obtaining in the hands controlling the treasury box. There is no condition which will more un-man the man, devitalize him, destroy his spirit equal to that of being dependent and subservient to somebody else, be such government or individual.[31]

Similarly, a 1919 editorial in a national fraternal periodical, *Fraternal Monitor*, described how "wily Bismarck took the situation in hand and, while appeasing the socialists, foisted upon the people . . . a system that made them mentally, morally and industrially subservient to the Junkers."[32] Such anti-German rhetoric was part of the emerging anti-immigrant sentiment at the time, as well as a newfound fear of Bolshevism in Russia. Using just such rhetoric, elites, professionals, employers, and fraternalists allied against both the specter of state-run social insurance and the continued permissiveness of U.S. immigration policy.

How Did Fraternalists Defeat Compulsory Health Insurance?

Though American fraternalism had never before faced a threat of this magnitude, the leaders of the fraternal movement clearly saw the specter of government intervention. They were ready and waiting with a vast organization of politically-minded leaders and advocates when agitation for compulsory insurance began to hit its stride in the mid-1910s.

Despite decades of argument and schism, the nation's fraternal organizers had worked hard to build a solid federation of associated fraternal groups, the National Fraternal Congress of America (NFCA). Though the NFCA aimed to address a wide array of issues relevant to the fraternal enterprise, the specter of government oversight was clearly a strong incentive for creating a national lobby, representing fraternities near and far. The NFCA, founded in 1913, was actually the avatar of the earlier National Fraternal Congress (NFC), founded in 1886 "to oppose legislation which was inimical to [fraternal] societies."[33] State governments had long since tried to place some constraints on the business practices of fraternal organizations, particularly given the frequency with which charlatans had taken to walking away with ordinary people's savings. Nonetheless, the NFC's Committee on Legislation recommended in 1890 that "no legislation subjecting the fraternal orders to State control in any way should be permitted to be enacted," and the fight to block further efforts at government regulation proved a constant source of momentum for fraternal lobby organizers.[34]

Later, when the struggle over state welfare provisions grew hotter, fraternal groups were ready to leap into action, effectively mobilizing their members—plus an arsenal of national periodicals, spokespersons, parades, and conventions—in the fight against state involvement in social insurance for all but destitute women and children. "The leading fraternal publications, such as the *Fraternal Monitor* and the *Western Review*, provide ample evidence of a continuing aversion to intrusive bureaucracy and paternalism," comments historian David Beito. "This hostility greatly intensified when the NFCA and other fraternal organizations launched a vigorous and ultimately successful campaign against proposals for compulsory health insurance."[35]

Figure 7.1 details the official resolutions adopted by the National Fraternal Congress of America on the very same day as Sullivan's address on social insurance. The resolutions clearly state the NFCA's united opposition to any legislation that would adopt state-run social insurance, voluntary or involuntary. (Both would provide unwanted competition for fraternal benefit plans.) The NFCA resolution also draws on anti-German sentiment ("State social insurance is paternal, socialistic and distinctly pro-German in character") and targets debate among British reformers over the success of their own recently erected sickness insurance plan ("Its burden and coming failure are easily seen in its complete lack of success in preventing poverty and distress among the people of the British Empire"). The NFCA resolutions end, "Resolved: That the constituent societies of the Congress and various officers and committees of the Congress use all honorable means to prevent the enactment into law in any form of a plan for social insurance through State or National control."[36]

Resolutions adopted by National Fraternal Congress of America at Philadelphia, Pa., August 28, 1918, opposing Social Insurance:

Resolved: That the National Fraternal Congress is unalterably opposed to the propaganda for State or National, voluntary or involuntary, social insurance, now being considered by the United States Congress, and which at this time is before the people of California, in the form of a constitutional amendment.

State social insurance is paternal, socialistic and distinctly pro-German in character. Its workings are well illustrated by the thorough and complete enslavement of the German people through State insurance.

Its burden and coming failure are easily seen in its complete lack of success in preventing poverty and distress among the people of the British Empire.

The platform of American Labor demands fair wages and living conditions that the laborer may in his own way care for himself and his family, and the experience of fraternal and beneficial orders demonstrates that all the needs of the individuals can be better met through private co-operation or cooperative means than through any species of State or National compulsion.

Resolved: That the constituent societies of the Congress and various officers and committees of the Congress use all honorable means to prevent the enactment into law in any form of a plan for social insurance through State or National control.

FIGURE 7.1 Resolutions Adopted by the National Fraternal Congress of America at Philadelphia, August 28, 1918, Opposing Social Insurance

Ultimately, the NFCA, together with professional lobbies that represented American doctors, insurance brokers, manufacturers, and business owners, defeated health insurance legislation wherever it was proposed:

> By the end of 1917 fraternal opposition to compulsory insurance had come into its own. The societies had joined forces with their old enemies, the commercial insurers, to form umbrella organizations. Despite past differences the coalition was a natural one. Both fraternal and commercial insurers had long stressed the dangers of excessive governmental paternalism and the virtues of self-reliance.[37]

The Insurance Federation of America (IFA) was one such umbrella organization that actively opposed state insurance in any form. The better-funded, more moderate Insurance Economics Society of America (IESA) focused more explicitly on the health insurance issue, bringing its considerable resources to bear. The IESA provided seed money to lobby organizations like the New York League for Americanism and the California Research Society of Social Economics, for example, prominent advocacy organizations in key states where health insurance legislation was on the agenda. Recognizing that fraternalists were an enormous constituency that could easily be mobilized in opposition to health insurance legislation, these umbrella organizations "took special pains to stress the dangers of compulsory insurance to fraternal orders. The bulletins received wide circulation in the fraternal world."[38] Indeed, in California, one of the states where health insurance legislation was deemed most likely to pass, insurance opponents even ran full-page ads in newspapers, such as the *San Francisco Chronicle*, that were directed explicitly at fraternal voters. Printed under the headline "Social Insurance Monopoly Is Opposed," the text reads, "Strong opposition to the adoption in California of the Leipzig, or German, plan of compulsory, monopolistic social insurance. . . . is voiced by thousands who oppose the scheme because, among other reasons, they say, it would destroy the usefulness of the many splendid fraternal benefit societies, some of which have been operating in the State for over fifty years." Sounding as if it were an actual news story, as opposed to a paid advertisement, the column continues, "If compelled to carry State 'social' insurance, many of these members declare they will reluctantly be obliged to terminate their membership in the fraternal societies. Thus cold-blooded compulsion, it is pointed out, will take the place of brotherly love."[39] These campaigns were obviously intended to ensure that every person holding a fraternal benefit policy in America knew that state-mandated health insurance was something they should oppose.

The obvious irony here is that the very same federated fraternal networks that women, farmers, and workers were using to organize pressure for progressive state legislation had here allowed a very different set of political actors to veto similarly progressive legislation, legislation that would have provided millions of Americans with much-needed health benefits and created a platform for future improvements in state social provisions.

The Making and Meaning of Fraternal Opposition to Social Insurance

The American social insurance and health care market had been growing for nearly 50 years by the time the progressives proposed its reformation. Like the contemporary health care debates of today, everyone knew that something had to be changed, but no one was quite sure how best to do it.

After decades of relying on private, sectarian organizations for social services, most Americans had little desire to see social services collectivized as new government programs, particularly those who had already paid into fraternal, work-based, and/or commercial insurance plans. Though many interests were involved in the struggle over early twentieth-century social insurance, the existing popularity of fraternal insurance plans, coupled with the rising popularity of commercial insurance, created a platform for concerted opposition to a new set of government initiatives that would use taxpayers' money to create new competition in the insurance market. Ultimately, commercial underwriters won the bulk of the insurance market—coupled with modest state and federal income assistance and benefits programs for the poor and indigent—but in the meantime, they successfully goaded fraternalists into cooperating in the struggle against state-run insurance for all Americans. One disappointed supporter of social insurance observed in 1917 that "in California, the insurance companies apparently have been egging on the fraternals to urge that under health insurance there should be free competition between all classes of carriers. And the fraternals fell for it!"[40]

This interest-based argument works equally well in explaining the passage of mothers' pensions and workers' compensation programs during the same period. Since there was little money to be made by supporting widows and private charitable organizations were generally too weak to stave off adverse welfare legislation at the time, mothers' pensions were allocated to the states. Similarly, businesses yielded to the states on workers' compensation because without it, they were exceedingly vulnerable to liability suits from injured employees. In neither case did doctors, fraternal orders, or commercial insurers have all that much to lose. Not so for national health insurance: Here, there were simply too many viable, ongoing concerns to turn the till over to the government.

This approach may explain why leaders of the fraternal and commercial insurance industries were willing to see mothers' pensions pass and not sickness insurance, but it still does not explain why the average American voter would have consented to this logic. Given the vagaries of life in a time when old age was rare, work was dangerous, and politics could be violent, the average American (male) worker had just two priorities vis-à-vis social policy: burial insurance, since death was always just around the corner; and disability insurance, since on-the-job injuries were commonplace.[41] Their first concern, burial insurance, was already widely available through fraternal lodges, unions, employers, and increasingly commercial agencies. All offered cheap burial insurance for white working men. Disability insurance, on the other hand, was actually an amalgam of two kinds of benefits: Ordinary sickness insurance was often supplied by local fraternal, mutual benefit, or trade organizations; but injuries on the job were also common, and liability for so-called industrial accidents became the duty of the state through workmen's compensation. Here, American voters had every interest in supporting state aid for disabled workers since those injuries might wind up being their own. For all other illnesses and disabilities, however, Americans stood behind the voluntary system of private insurance.

However, in addition to this simple economistic rationale, there was a much deeper issue underlying fraternal opposition to social insurance: sectarianism, or self-segregation.

Private, fraternal insurance had been the norm in America until the turn of the (last) century. This meant that the majority of Americans' insurance savings were tied up in sectarian social organizations based on relatively exclusive grouping of co-ethnics, co-religionists, and so forth. Seen from this perspective, social welfare programs like compulsory health insurance would not only have undermined the mission of fraternal organizations but also would have collectivized everyone's social insurance dollars under one umbrella organization, the U.S. government.

Government itself was not the problem, though it received much of the blame. The problem was that government sponsorship of social service programs would implicitly transform the "social" from something based on sectarian affiliation to one based merely on income. Collectivization would transcend the lines fraternalists had worked so hard to draw over the preceding decades. In the words of historian Lizabeth Cohen, who has extensively studied immigrant community organizations in early twentieth-century Chicago, "Because mutual assistance had long provided an institutional base for ethnicity, threats to its survival endangered the viability of ethnic communities."[42] Nonethnic (i.e., mainstream white) fraternalists presumably felt the same way: "Each man for his Brother first, and Heaven, then, for each."[43]

State-run social insurance constituted one such threat to sectarianism, though by the 1930s, amid the financial difficulties of the Great Depression and the waning significance of American ethnicity, voters consented to several major social insurance initiatives. In the meantime, however, state-run insurance was portrayed as a threat to the sectarian comforts of fraternal self-insurance, even for those Americans who were not members of specific ethnic or religious communities. In other words, compulsory health insurance not only threatened the material interests of the fraternal organizations themselves but also threatened to supercede some of the divisions in American society rent by ethnoreligious competition, racism, sexism, and nativism, all of which were bolstered by the prevalence of fraternal organizations.

Of course, not all fraternalists were unanimous in this position, nor were they all opposed to national health insurance. (It would be an incredibly difficult but worthwhile endeavor to explore the extent to which specific fraternal orders, lodges, and participants supported or opposed compulsory insurance; at least one national order, the Fraternal Order of Eagles, did campaign for old-age and mothers' pensions, for example.[44]) However, the general lay of the land seems clear: (1) Collectivization scared both 'ethnics' and WASPS because of the social and fiscal mingling it would entail, and (2) government itself was increasingly associated with the ethnic menace of Germans, Russians, and Jews, the main proponents of socialism at home and troubling adversaries abroad.

In the meantime, the extent and quality of care provided by existing fraternal organizations and ethnoreligious nonprofit agencies was substandard at best. First, membership in one or more fraternal orders and/or mutual benefit societies was an obvious prerequisite for benefits, and as previously mentioned, membership was not always easy to obtain. Women generally had a harder time than men in procuring fraternal benefits, for example, and until 1917 fraternal groups rarely if ever offered policies for the children of members.[45] Furthermore, even those white men fortunate enough to be eligible for inclusion generally needed to be between 16 and 60 years of age and in good physical condition to qualify. As one account of the Ancient Order of United Workmen's health policy proudly proclaims:

> Fraternal benefit societies have made good use of the medical examination, and the result has been the acquiring of a splendid class of risks. . . . Had no restrictions been placed upon the admission of new members, physically impaired persons would have rushed to join and a speedy end to fraternal protection would have followed. . . . In this respect it has been well that the charitable zeal of some of the early members [of the AOUW] was tempered by the good sense of the leaders.[46]

The slack caused by the fraternal groups' foreshortened charitable zeal must have presented real problems for those unable to join, and recognizing this need, municipalities made what provisions they could for the poor through public clinics and subsidies to private charitable organizations.[47] Needless to say, many such clinics were as interested in saving souls as in saving lives. The tiny Chinese Hospital of Brooklyn is one such example, a five-bed hospital established by a missionary group, the King's Daughters of China, "Christian people engaged in the work of evangelizing" immigrant Chinese. Historian David Rosner writes that, "medicine and morality were so closely tied together in this institution that two sets of statistics were kept: One reported on the number of patients successfully treated by what was called 'Western Science,' and another gave the number of patients who were converted or who 'heard the Gospel' for the first time."[48]

Nonetheless, even those lucky enough to belong to a fraternal lodge or mutual aid organization that provided health benefits could not always count on the best of care. Rather than paying a doctor for each and every visit to a member, some lodges contracted with doctors for full coverage on a capitation basis. However, only the neediest (i.e., least skilled) doctors would accept such lodge practices, as they were a perpetual source of derision within the medical community.[49] Naturally, as any contemporary reader might imagine, the "lodge doctor" had every incentive to cut corners and avoid extraneous visits, since he or she would collect the same fee regardless. At the same time, social and technological changes in the medical industry caused the price of adequate care to skyrocket.[50] Thus, while the health care business was being undermined by competition and the social function of the hospital transformed by new technology, fraternals themselves were faced with spiraling costs and diminishing demand. As we see in the next chapter, on the decline of fraternal insurance in America, there was little these groups could do by way of salvage; most simply got out of the insurance business and devoted themselves exclusively to charity and brotherhood.

Conclusion

Until the New Deal brought widespread shifts in the American polity and inaugurated a new era of government-sponsored social services, the only successful campaigns for compulsory social services were those for workers' compensation, veterans' pensions, and limited relief for mothers in poverty. The fraternals held their ground over government intervention, but they were soon to face an even greater challenge on another front—private, commercial insurance. While the fraternal groups were involved in organizing themselves to oppose national health insurance, their competitors were threatening them in the market for private burial, sickness, and life insurance policies. By this time, the fraternals had so steeped themselves in the rhetoric of free, open-market competition that there was little they could do to oppose their new rivals. Thus, long before the Great Depression lowered the curtain on the fraternal industry, commercial firms had begun to undermine them, the subject to which I turn next.

Part Three

SOCIAL CHANGE, SOCIAL CAPITAL,

AND THE FUTURE OF DEMOCRACY IN AMERICA

Thus far, I have tried to frame the golden age in a revisionist light. More specifically, I have focused on changes in the market for burial and sickness after the Civil War, as well as the influx of new immigrants (and freed slaves and free-thinking women) in explaining the rising popularity of fraternalism in late nineteenth-century America. The presence of a readily available, easily replicable fraternal organizational form, coupled with a newfound demand for mutual aid and self-segregation, fueled a competitive boom in America's voluntary sector that lasted through the first decades of the twentieth century.

But forming an adequate explanation of the rise of competitive voluntarism requires an adequate and symmetrical explanation of its decline, as I have been at some pains to assert. Here lies the strength of the aforementioned approach, for the same factors that fueled the rise of fraternalism can easily be related to its ensuing decline: When commercial insurers entered the market for low-cost sickness and life insurance, fraternal groups lost much of their appeal for would-be members; and when immigration to this country came to a halt in the years after World War I, assimilation began breaking down some of the barriers that fraternal self-segregation had helped to erect.

My goal in the next few chapters is to convince you that my explanation of the rise of American associationalism is equally relevant in explaining its fall—as I show in chapter 8. But in chapter 9 and the conclusion, I am forced to confront far more ambiguous material, such as the desirability and functionality of associationalism as a means of collective organization. There are obviously no easy or clear-cut answers to these questions, though I try to support my own opinions with empirical observations whenever possible. Needless to say, I am crossing into dangerous territory here, ground that some social scientists might rather I left untouched. However,

I would feel remiss in arguing so fervently for a specific interpretation of the golden age without saying what relevance it has for my understanding of contemporary affairs. My answers may do no more than raise new questions; but if all I achieve here is to raise questions about the purported effects of competitive voluntarism, I will have accomplished something quite worthwhile indeed.

COMPETITIVE CONSUMERISM

Commercial Insurance, Ethnic Assimilation,

and the Decline of American Fraternalism

Late twentieth-century American associationalism is only a ghost of its former self. Americans are still among the most religious people in the developed world, but the size and scope of American voluntarism has changed enormously over the past 100 years.[1] Union participation in the United States is abysmally low, for example; and except for religious affiliations, Canadians, Norwegians, Swedes, and Dutch all report participation rates in voluntary organizations as high or higher than those of Americans.[2] Those that do participate are increasingly satisfied with "checkbook voluntarism," or the vicarious pursuit of social endeavor through third-party advocacy organizations furthermore.[3] According to political scientist Robert Putnam, America's declining rates of voluntary participation may actually be linked to a host of social ills, from voter apathy to crime, unhappiness, and poor health.[4]

There may be many reasons for Americans' declining interest in voluntarism, but at least two common explanations are not generally supported by the facts: American fraternalism, once the core of voluntarism in the United States, did not disappear because Americans lost interest in their communities, nor did the growth of government social welfare programs push them out, as conservatives would have us believe. Fraternalism declined because Americans found better alternatives, or so I argue here. On the one hand, commercial banks and insurance companies began offering working families sound, stable asset management services in the early decades of the twentieth century, something that had never been a strong point of fraternal benefit plans. On the other hand, the declining salience of ethnicity, religion, and gender among white Americans after World War I meant that the segregated confines of the lodge hall began to lose some of their allure. Nonetheless, although Americans increasingly saw less and less reason to segregate themselves along fraternal lines, the associational boom would have a lasting effect on U.S. political development— in the maternalist focus of its welfare state, the divisiveness of its labor movement, and the latent hostility of its citizens toward gun control and the redistribution of income.

Associationalism in Search of Itself, 1900–1929

The transformation of American fraternalism began as early as the 1890s, when lobby organizations like the National Fraternal Congress began working to rationalize what had previously been a disorganized mass of independent organizations. The coming struggles over government regulation and universal health insurance lent an air of sobriety and mission to the fraternal enterprise as well. Over time, many orders sought to distance themselves from their bacchanalian reputations of yore. The Benevolent and Protective Order of Elks eschewed its drinking-club origins and turned toward the serious business of civic action, for example. "The apron went in 1895," said one Elks historian. "The 'secret password' expired in 1899. The badge and grip died natural deaths in 1902 and 1904 respectively. The test oath and a few other extraneous things disappeared and the Elk began to be themselves and look less like a cross between the Masons and a college fraternity."[5] In fact, the internal transformation of the Elks predates a new kind of quasi-fraternal organization on the American scene—the service or luncheon club.

Unlike fraternal orders, service clubs met for lunch instead of dinner. They met in public restaurants rather than elaborate lodge halls. And, most important, service clubs cultivated a clientele of businessmen and community leaders, not workingmen and their drinking companions. Three of the nation's most prominent service clubs were formed in the early decades of the twentieth century: Rotary International in 1905, Lions International in 1917, and Kiwanis International in 1915.[6] By 1929, sociologists Robert and Helen Lynd would observe that the more prosperous inhabitants of "Middletown" (actually Muncie, Indiana) still belonged to fraternal lodges, but "the man who goes weekly to Rotary will confess he gets around to the Masons 'only two or three times a year.'"[7]

The chatty, collegial atmosphere of the service club was meant to cater to established career men like George F. Babbitt, the cold-blooded real estate agent portrayed in Sinclair Lewis's comic novel, *Babbitt*. Lewis's protagonist is a member of both the local Elks and Booster clubs, both of which he uses to parlay illegal real estate deals. "The International Organization of Boosters' Clubs has become a world-force for optimism, manly pleasantry, and good business," writes Lewis, tongue firmly in cheek. "Chapters are to be found now in thirty countries. Nine hundred and twenty of the thousand chapters, however, are in the United States."[8] Lewis goes to great pains to satirize the comings and goings of an average Booster Club luncheon:

The second March lunch of the Zenith Boosters' Club was the most important of the year, as it was to be followed by the annual election of officers. . . . As each of the four hundred Boosters entered he took from a wallboard a huge celluloid button announcing his name, his nickname, and his business. There was a fine of ten cents for calling a Fellow Booster by anything but his nickname at a lunch, and as Babbitt jovially checked his hat the air was radiant with shouts of "Hello, Chet!" and "How're you, Shorty!" and "Top o' the mornin', Mac!"[9]

Lewis is obviously exaggerating for comedic effect, though there is surely a hint of truth: Service clubs assumed a membership that no longer needed help in buying insurance, a membership, furthermore, that no longer needed a special private place for late-night drinking and revelry. (Babbitt does plenty of that on his own.) Service clubs assumed a membership, in other words, that was decidedly middle class and determined to stay that way.

Documenting the Decline in Fraternal Organizational Density

Organizational density is a weak indicator of membership density—it reflects only the rise and fall in the number of lodges per capita, not the changing number of members who are participating in each one—but in the absence of widespread membership data, it is the best indicator we have of changing trends in American fraternal activity. As discussed in chapter 2, the density of fraternal organizations varied across the four cities I examined (see figures 2.1–2.4). In Boston and San Francisco, for example, the number of fraternal lodges per capita peaked in 1900, dropping in the 40 years thereafter. New Orleans experienced a huge growth in its fraternal sector between 1900 and 1920, only to drop back again by 1930. Milwaukee, on the other hand, began experiencing a secular decline in organizational density as early as 1880, though the raw number of lodges in that city continued increasing through 1940. It is hard to draw any definite conclusions from these data, but it is clear that the declining presence of fraternal lodges began well before 1965—or before the New Deal, for that matter.

From this information on organizational density, there are several conclusions from which to choose:

1. Fraternal membership continued to increase, despite a decreasing number of lodges.
2. Membership began to decrease at a rate equal to the declining number of lodges.
3. Membership was actually decreasing faster than the total number of lodges, given the likelihood that individual lodges would fight to stay open even in the face of declining membership.

Membership data from one large North American fraternal organization, the International Order of Odd Fellows, provide additional clues, though these data continue only through 1930 and conflate information from the United States and Canada. Nonetheless, economic historians George and J. C. Emery have compiled these data in such a way as to at least allow us to examine the changing number of IOOF lodges, members, and (estimated) members per lodge over time.[10] The results are shown in figure 8.1.

Surprisingly, the membership of the IOOF continued to increase through 1920 and then began to decline,[11] although the number of IOOF lodges began to fall one decade earlier, in 1910. A rough estimate of the number of members per lodge (calculated by dividing total membership by the total number of lodges) reveals an interesting trend: Whereas (average) lodge size had been growing steadily since at least 1870, it, too, begins to drop off after 1920. Thus, there is reason to believe that increasing lodge size helped to compensate for the decrease in the number of lodges for a short period of time (1910–1920). In other words, the total membership of the IOOF continued to grow during this interval despite a decrease in the aggregate number of lodges. Thereafter, however, IOOF membership itself began to decline. In real terms, IOOF lodge membership fell 23.5% between 1920 to 1930, declining from 1,863,000 to 1,425,000 members. Moreover, the IOOF's 1930 membership was 6.4% lower than its 1910 level, evidence of an incipient decline in participation.

One major problem with these data is that they combine U.S. and Canadian figures, thus conflating a number of causal factors that might help ex-

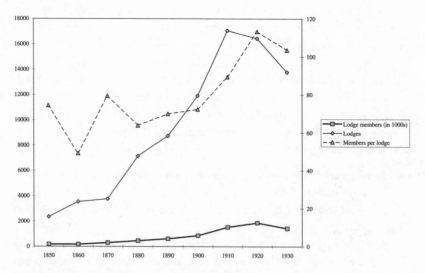

FIGURE 8.1 International Order of Odd Fellows' Lodge Membership in the United States and Canada, 1850–1930

plain the decline. Nonetheless, we can consider at least one important causal factor endogenous to the IOOF's organization itself (and therefore equally applicable to the American and Canadian cases): its decision to make sickness insurance an optional feature of lodge practice in the mid-1920s. According to Emery and Emery, "In 1863 the SGL [Supreme Grand Lodge] had described the sick benefit as 'a distinguishing characteristic of the Order and one of its fundamental principles.' In 1925, in contrast, its assembled grand representatives held 'the general opinion . . . that the stipulated sick benefit system [had] outlived its usefulness.'"[12]

Though Emery and Emery go on to profess ambivalence about the root cause of the IOOF's transnational decline, their description of the order's changing attitude toward the provision of fraternal benefits confirms two themes of this book: First, it seems clear that the desire to purchase inexpensive burial and/or sickness insurance was a major, if not the major, motivating force behind the huge growth of fraternalism in the late nineteenth century. From this, a second observation logically follows: A profound change in the markets for sickness and burial insurance might have had a devastating effect on the future of fraternalism. It is exceedingly hard to estimate changes in consumer demand for different forms of insurance, but there is clear evidence that there were important changes in the commercial insurance industry that go a long way toward explaining why fraternalism lost its luster for so many Americans (and possibly Canadians) in the decades before World War II.

The Transformation of American Social Insurance

Given that the financial backbone of most fraternal orders was their commitment to providing affordable burial, and in some cases sickness and unemployment, insurance, fraternal benevolence might well have survived the ravishes of the Great Depression had it not been for the rising competition of commercial insurers. However, the real onset of commercial competition in the underwriting business coincides almost exactly with the nascent decline of fraternalism in the United States—1900 to 1910. Presumably, the two are causally, as well as temporally, connected. In 1870, for example, commercial firms held 99.85% of the nation's life insurance monies, just over $2 billion (see figures 8.2 and 8.3 for graphical illustration). By 1900, that percentage had dropped to 54.7%, largely because of competition from fraternal lodges (42.4%) and mutual aid societies (2.7%), though the total life insurance market had grown to a whopping $14 billion (a 694% increase over 30 years). By 1917, however, commercial insurers had regained their advantage over fraternal groups: 72.7%, or $25.7 billion, of the nation's life insurance was now held by commercial firms, as opposed to 25.8%, or $9.1 billion, in fraternal life insurance. The advent of government insurance during World War I temporally altered the market for both sectors,

CHART IV

LIFE INSURANCE IN FORCE IN THE UNITED STATES, 1814–1937

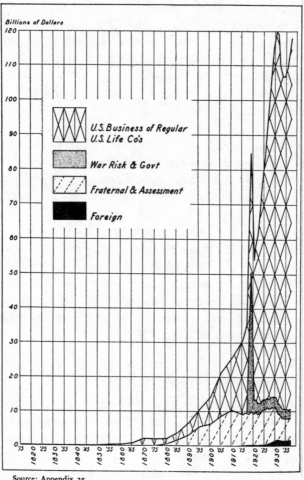

Source: Appendix 25.

FIGURE 8.2 Life Insurance in Force in the United States, 1814–1937
Source: J. Owen Stalson, *Marketing Life Insurance: Its History in America* (Cambridge: Harvard University Press, 1942).

though from 1920 on the percentage of American life insurance held in commercial policies continued to grow, whereas the percentage held in fraternal and mutual assessment policies dropped precipitously. In 1928, at the peak of economic expansion, Americans held $93.3 billion of commercial life insurance, whereas the fraternal insurance market had barely grown at all, reaching a total of just $9.3 billion, or 8.68% of the market for that year.[13]

Several innovations in the life insurance industry fostered this transformation: In the years after the Civil War, Americans came to find social insurance

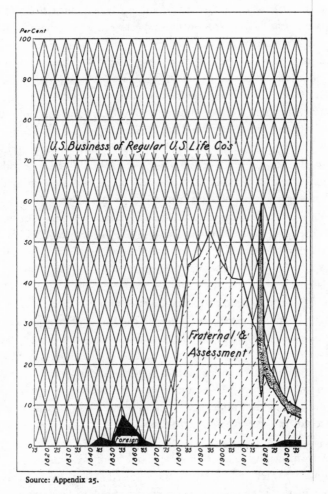

CHART V

LIFE INSURANCE IN FORCE IN THE UNITED STATES, 1814-1937,
ON PERCENTAGE BASIS

Source: Appendix 25.

FIGURE 8.3 Life Insurance in Force in the United States, 1814–1937, on Percentage Basis
Source: J. Owen Stalson, *Marketing Life Insurance: Its History in America* (Cambridge: Harvard University Press, 1942).

indispensable for those who could afford it. Vast sums went into life insurance, but sickness and disability insurance were also finding new proponents, especially by the early twentieth century. In his 1942 overview of the life insurance enterprise, business historian J. Owen Stalson notes (with no small hint of pride), "On the credit side we must acknowledge that the [fraternal assessment] system did take the life insurance idea to millions of Americans; it continued the education of the public to the needs of life insurance."[14] Although Stalson surely overestimates the natural superiority of commercial as opposed to fraternal life insurance, he was correct in pointing out the changing dynamics of the life insurance industry. Fraternalism had emerged in the American context as a response to the pressures of postbellum urbanization and industrialization, thrived for a time, and was then usurped by more specialized entities, namely, commercial life and health insurance collectives.

There were obvious fiscal benefits to commercial insurance, professional management and government regulation being two of them. Arguably, however, it was not the economic benefits alone that encouraged Americans' conversion from fraternal to commercial insurance; as with all consumer phenomena of the twentieth century, one cannot overlook the impact of mass marketing.

Before 1905, American life insurance had catered primarily to wealthy, elite customers.[15] Late nineteenth-century commercial life insurers were also fond of speculating with policyholders' money. So-called tontine plans split policyholders' money into two pools, one devoted to purchasing insurance on the life of the policyholder, the other devoted to the investment whims of the insurance company itself. The expectation was that the policyholder would receive a handsome return on his or her investment after a predetermined span of time had elapsed, but there were, as always, no guarantees. ("You Don't Have to Die To Win," claimed one 1884 ad for a tontine investment plan offered by the New York Life company, evidence that gambling was also part of the lure for tontine investors.[16]) Despite its popularity, however, tontine insurance became the subject of a 1905 investigation in the New York State Legislature led by State Senator William W. Armstrong and counsel Charles Evans Hughes (who defeated William Randolph Hearst in the race for governor the following year). According to economic historians Roger Ransom and Richard Sutch, companies offering tontine policies came under investigation because they were using investors' capital "to enhance the social status, political influence, and personal wealth of industry leaders."[17]

The Armstrong investigation eliminated one lucrative sector of the commercial insurance market, and industry leaders started looking for new ways to expand their market share. Given the enormous popularity of fraternal sickness and burial insurance, one obvious possibility was the millions of workingmen currently buying insurance from fraternal lodges and mutual benefit societies. And, not wanting to wait for the laws of the marketplace to convince consumers that commercial policies were more fiscally sound than fraternal policies, industry leaders quickly unleashed an army of salesmen on the American public, trained to sell low-cost life insurance door to door.

The door-to-door approach not only allowed salesmen the chance to make the most of face-to-face contact but also provided a convenient means for collecting money from existing policyholders. Salesmen received incentives for cultivating new customers and collecting their payments, thus allowing the insurance agencies themselves to focus on the business of investing. It was this new army of door-to-door salesmen that allowed commercial insurers to penetrate working- and middle-class communities far and wide. Though many individuals seem to have held on to their fraternal benefit plans out of loyalty, little new money was invested in such policies after 1910 (see figure 8.2). The commercial underwriters essentially beat the fraternals at their own game—building a wide network of modest but loyal customers through face-to-face contact:

> The trend toward informed selling and sales management has probably been the most significant development in the total life insurance operation since 1906. . . . At the heart of the whole movement are two concepts from which many others flow: (1) life insurance is a vital and unique opportunity for every person who has financial plans, and (2) selling life insurance is an art which can be taught.[18]

The first organized classes for beginning salesmen were started by the Equitable Life Assurance Society of the United States in 1902. Students who showed promise were then offered jobs in the firm. Several competitors, facing the same problem of cultivating qualified salesmen from within their ranks, began imitating the Equitable system. Soon, agency training grew into its own little industry, including formal courses of instruction at Harvard and Yale and the inauguration of the eponymous Cerf School of Salesmanship at the Mutual Benefit of New Jersey's New York office, famous for its essay-writing contests on "The Advantages of Life Insurance as a Profession."[19]

Although it may seem surprising that the life insurance industry took so long to realize the potential of mass marketing, remember that marketing itself was a relatively new science at the turn of the century, as was the idea that ordinary working families could be a worthwhile venture for commercial underwriters.[20] In addition, according to Stalson,

> The unfavorable publicity which accompanied the legislative hearings in New York and elsewhere from 1905 through 1907 prompted life men to think of offsetting action. The National Association of Life Underwriters, for instance, became energetic advocates of the idea of life insurance selling as a profession. The life agent was called a missionary; his many opportunities for career satisfactions were frequently discussed. The position of the solicitor was to be elevated.[21]

By 1916, the study of "scientific" salesmanship was a full-blown industry, culminating in the foundation of the national Association of Life Agency Officers and the corporate-sponsored Bureau of Salesmanship Research at the Carnegie Institute of Technology.[22]

From this standpoint, one can only wonder how fraternal groups survived such concerted competition, for their members were exactly the type of people that the new "life men" were trying so hard to sell to, but survive they did. As seen in figure 8.4, which relies on data from Richard De Raismes Kip's *Fraternal Life Insurance in America*, the total number of fraternal life insurance policies held in the United States stayed about the same from 1904 through 1940, increasing slightly in the 1910s and 1920s and then falling during the Great Depression. At the same time, however, the number of industrial, group, and ordinary commercial policies skyrocketed. The most likely explanation seems to be that whereas many lodge members maintained long-standing fraternal policies out of allegiance and "brotherhood," they also began investing the bulk of their insurance dollars in commercial policies.[23]

Figures 8.5 and 8.6 bear this out: Though industrial life policies were by far the largest in terms of sheer numbers throughout the period, their average policy size was actually quite small (in fact, industrial insurance was commonly referred to as penny insurance). Commercial and group policies were rather large, on the other hand, and both continued to increase in size relative to fraternal policies. In fact, the average size of fraternal policies declined consistently throughout this period (see figure 8.5). Furthermore, when these same data are viewed in terms of total life insurance in force (see figure 8.6), the gradual ascendancy of ordinary commercial insurance is quite evident: Beginning around 1910, the commercial insurance industry grew exponentially, followed by a short decline around 1930 and then by continued resurgence.

Whereas working-class Americans seemed increasingly aware of the need for insurance of some sort, the heightened competition of commercial sales was clearly changing their behavior. One history of fraternal insurance notes (rather forlornly):

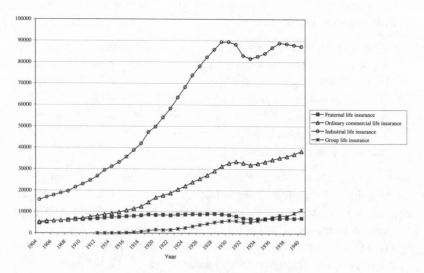

FIGURE 8.4 Number of Policies in Force by Type of Insurance, 1904–1940

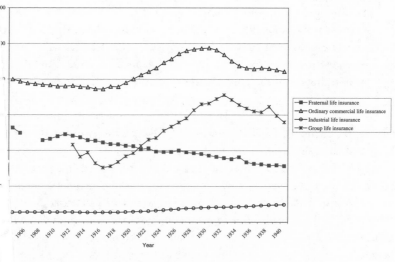

RE 8.5 Average Size Policy by Type, 1904–1940

There is a big difference between the methods of [fraternal] deputies in the early years and the field work of to-day [1919]. A. R. Talbot, Head Consul of the Modern Woodmen of America, has remarked that in the old days a deputy could enter a town, employ the brass band to parade up the main street following a banner announcing that a lodge would be established in the evening and the result would be the organization of a good-sized lodge. Prospective members would appear at the meeting of their own volition.

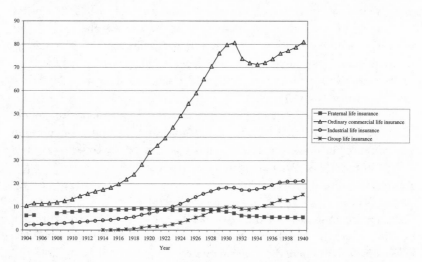

FIGURE 8.6 Life Insurance in Force (in Billions of Dollars) by Type, 1904–1940

> To-day every member must be obtained by solicitation. This makes a deputy's work more difficult and more important. The prospect of to-day wants to know all about insurance plans and other features. He may have his choice of a number of societies and he wants the one which offers most. And in these days the public rarely subscribes to any enterprise without being solicited.[24]

Clearly, the economic basis of fraternalism had been undermined, though the lodge system itself muddled on.

As described in the previous chapter, many fraternities fought hard to maintain their place in American life. Improved facilities for members, including special hospitals, sanitoria, and orphanages, were constructed at great cost, though few realized their full potential because of problems of geography and management. The Security Benefit Association raised money from members to build a fraternal hospital that would be free to all members "as long as they kept up their life insurance payments," for example, but the location of the hospital, in Topeka, Kansas, made it expensive and difficult to reach for members outside the region. At the same time, an aging membership base put new strains on the fiscal stability of the lodges, forcing many to adopt age-graded assessments and/or increased premiums for all.[25]

Broader changes in the American economy also took their toll on the fraternals: Affluent suburbanites tended to look down on the rough-and-tumble climate of the lodge hall; employers increasingly provided the benefits sought by working families; and, of course, the new pleasures of mass media provided alternate venues for leisure-time activity (though I doubt that the effect of new media was as drastic as many believe).[26] Although the radio and the movie house may have siphoned some potential members from the associational pool, one should remember that in the era of their incipient decline—the 1910s, 1920s, and 1930s—most movie houses offered only one feature a week, and radio itself was a new and still relatively underexploited medium.[27] One might even hypothesize that the social capital theorists have it backward: Perhaps television and radio evolved to fill the gaps in American social life increasingly vacated by fraternalism.

By far a better candidate on the leisure side of the equation is Prohibition. Although the Eighteenth Amendment is not something generally considered in academic accounts of American associationalism, its relevance seems justified in light of the role drinking played in many fraternal lodges. According to one pamphlet published by the International Reform Federation (in 1927), for example, "The Loyal Order of Moose generally derided 'dry' laws. Last July 21, Federal prohibition agents raided 18 of their lodges in the vicinity of Pittsburgh and the stewards of 17 of these lodges plead [sic] 'guilty' and paid fines of $1,000 each, while nearly 100 of their officials plead [sic] 'guilty' and were paroled for two years by the U.S. court."[28] The Fraternal Order of Eagles was another major

American fraternal organization charged with violating the Eighteenth Amendment: "During one month prior to January 16, 1927, prohibition agents in one state raided 32 aeries of the Fraternal Order of Eagles and made liquor seizures in 32 aeries. Brewing and distilling were found in half a dozen of these clubhouses."[29] Prohibition surely dealt a major blow to wet fraternities as illegal lodge bars were busted up by federal marshals; it also relieved many so-called temperance fraternities and total abstinence societies of their primary reason for being.

Still more significant, however, was the effect of ethnic assimilation on the children of immigrant parents, children who increasingly looked past the neighborhood and the clan for social attachments. In some cases, particularly those of oppressed minorities (e.g., Irish, Italians, Jews, and Chinese), ethnicity maintained its salience as a source of social life and identification, but by the end of World War II, even these bastions of ethnic fraternization began a long, slow decline.[30]

During the golden age, fraternal orders and mutual benefit societies representing every ethnonational and ethnoreligious identity imaginable popped up in America. Competitive voluntarism accentuated those features of social identity that were mutable, and thus worth competing over. Following World War I and its subsequent spate of nativism, anti-Semitism, and red-baiting, many white ethnics actively strove to shed the trappings of their immigrant roots. More recently, there have been various ethnic revivals of sorts, particularly on college campuses and among certain lower middle-class urban communities, but in the prescient words of sociologist Orlando Patterson, "Modern American ethnicity is *revivalist* . . . in the importance it attaches to the value of being different; in the mythology that real differences exist; in the support of these claims by an affirmation of the virtues of segregated living; by the exaggeration and celebration of the social correlates of the urban ghetto; and by the reinvestment of archaic symbols with ideological potency."[31] Modern-day ethnicity has more salience as a political weapon and rhetorical tool than it does as a meaningful basis for social exchange and identity formation.

Religion, on the other hand, has waxed and waned in its sociological significance. Seen as the basis of personal identity and social affiliation, religion is more mutable than ethnicity; thus it became a central, if not *the* central, piece of identity politics underlying the perceived need to create voluntary organizations that would help retain and/or recruit members in the late nineteenth century. Interdenominational competition still persists today, but its dynamics have changed noticeably. Mainline Protestants no longer proselytize as they once did, for example, and the social trappings of religious recruitment have largely turned from building clubs and fraternities to offering self-help groups, youth programs, and informal social gatherings. Judaism, too, has changed its character as a basis for American social identity, though not in the same way as Christianity. What was once a byword for racial and ethnic differentiation is now resolutely presented as a matter of religion and nationhood. Modern-day Jews differentiate themselves not by place of origin but by degree of orthodoxy and support for the Jewish state. Similarly, most contemporary Jewish-American associations revolve around political concerns, Jewish fraternalism and self-help having fallen by the wayside.

In the nineteenth-century context, race and gender were only vestigial features of fraternal segregation—blacks and women were generally shunted to the side, self-consciously ignored by the fraternal majority—and ethnicity and religion were the primary characteristics around which fraternalists affiliated. But as the social salience of ethnicity and religion have faded (at least as primary means of social differentiation), race and gender have come to the fore. Even among new immigrants, who once again began flocking to the United States after the gates were reopened in 1965, race would appear to be a defining parameter: white immigrants, especially those from western Europe, face far fewer obstacles to acceptance and assimilation than do black, Hispanic, and Asian immigrants from around the globe. Gender, too, has been on the ascendance as an important and hotly disputed component of identity politics. American feminists first began to gain ground in organizing themselves and creating a self-conscious political identity for women in the midst of the golden age. For a time, American women fought gender segregation by founding clubs and orders for themselves. Today, however, their struggles are being waged in courts, board rooms, churches, and living rooms all across America.[32]

Conclusion

The return of many veterans from World War II gave new life to the fraternal movement, though it was a noticeably different kind of organization than it had been in its golden age. Some orders managed to maintain or even revive their role as exclusive members-only clubhouses, but just as many, perhaps more, had already folded or, in some cases, converted themselves into for-profit organizations. When the once mighty Security Benefit Association (SBA) found itself under investigation by the Nebraska Insurance Commission, for example, "The board of directors concluded that the fraternal method of operation was not viable and started conversion to a mutual company." Reorganized as the Security Benefit Life Company, the group was soon forced to sell its old lodge hospital, though the company itself still exists today, since reorganized as the Security Benefit Group of Companies.[33] In fact, many contemporary savings banks, insurance, and mortgage companies are actually avatars of the golden age.[34]

Amid the dramatic changes in the American insurance industry, furthermore, the conditions for ethnic and racial integration were changing dramatically in the post–World War II period. In 1965, federal immigration quotas were finally loosened for the first time since the 1920s. The end of such draconian restrictions has had two significant ramifications: First, the intervening period of low immigration accelerated the assimilation of white ethnics into the American mainstream. Without the reinforcement of new arrivals, bringing with them the need for foreign-language social and occupational outlets, white ethnics lost touch with Old World traditions and became increasingly assimilated into the American mainstream. The succeeding generations, those who came of age in the 1950s and 1960s, largely eschewed their parents' clubs and organizations in lieu of work, family, and the pursuit of higher education for themselves and their children. Baby-boomers and their children appear to have little time and even less inclination for the club life of yore.[35]

Second, this new, post-1965 influx of immigrants has significantly watered down the pool of would-be associationalists. Many remaining fraternal and/or civic organizations were by this period resolutely "American" in outlook; some, like the Veterans of Foreign Wars (VFW), were open only to those who had served in the American armed forces, and others clung perilously to legal statutes that entitled them to self-segregation. Without the impetus to form or join their own ethnic fraternities, the offerings at hand must have appeared unattractive or merely unattainable to many new immigrants, particularly because so few of them were of European descent. Furthermore, many new immigrants now seem more reluctant than their forebears to lean on the comforts of voluntary organization in their quest for success. Whereas advocacy organizations for many minority communities have flourished, there has been a general decline in service-providing organizations that serve those same communities. Some new immigrant groups, most notably Korean Americans, have turned to rotating-credit organizations to help pool capital and thus nurture their ethnic economy, but new immigrants generally rely on services provided by the government and/or their employers, rather than forming voluntary organizations by and for themselves.[36]

Thus one sees the overlap and interplay between public and private, for-profit and nonprofit in the American social landscape. Over time, the American social insurance market changed from one grounded in sectarian mutualism to one grounded in nonsectarian professionalism and a guaranteed (though niggardly) social safety net. These transformations occurred because of changing wants; changing needs; and, most important, changing demographic and market pressures. But the legacy of competitive voluntarism is with us still. It shapes the way Americans think about the nation, its government, and their relationship to it. And, more important, it played a huge and often overlooked role in shaping the way in which American insurance markets evolved in the pivotal years of the early twentieth century.

In the next chapter I look more carefully at the variable role voluntary organizations have played and might continue to play in various minority communities in the United States. This should help give you a fuller appreciation of the ways in which competitive voluntarism can help and hinder those communities looking to use mutualism as a source of socioeconomic and political empowerment. Only then will our journey through the golden age be truly complete.

ETHNOGENESIS

Social Capital, Racial Protectionism, and

Sectarian Social Organization

Thus far, I have argued that competitive voluntarism contributed to sectarianism and self-segregation in the United States by providing organizational boundaries dedicated to the perpetuation thereof. Admittedly, however, American associationalism may not have flourished without the impetus of racial hatred, religious disrespect, gender segregation, and ethnic suspicion fueling it from below. In the face of such outward hostility and discrimination, many identity groups turned inward, relying on fraternal organizations and mutual aid societies for help and support in an otherwise hostile world. As one history of the Knights of Columbus organization declares, "Fraternalism was the chosen medium for fashioning a unique expression of Catholic Americanness.... The ceremonials of the Order instructed the initiates in these lessons and satisfied their need for forging strong fraternal ties in an otherwise antagonistic social and cultural climate."[1]

Seen in this light, sectarianism might have been far more efficacious than I have portrayed it. That is, self-segregation was a somewhat logical response to closed doors, unwelcoming faces, and "——— need not apply" signs. Surely, there is dignity in distinction, and self-segregation need not be portrayed as an absolute evil, all things considered:

> Traditionally, the [Knights of Columbus] Order reflected the social mentality associated with what was called "*ghetto Catholicism*." However, its fraternal sense of Catholic peoplehood was not expressed in diffident tones of defensiveness but in tones of confidence in the essential legitimacy of American Catholicism, symbolized by Columbus's act of consecrating the New World. The Knights did not view the "ghetto" as a refuge from the mainstream of American life, but rather as a healthy preserve of Catholic culture.[2]

But if self-segregation was, for some groups at some times, a self-conscious choice made by minority communities, what can we learn from my account of the unintended consequences of American associationalism? Of what utility is a term like *competitive voluntarism* in explaining a process forged by choice? "Ethnicity is a communalistic form of social affiliation, depending, first, upon an assumption of a special bond among people of like origins, and, second, upon the obverse, a disdain for people of dissimilar origins," write sociologists Edna Bonacich and John Modell. "Ethnicity is, above all, a form of commitment," says Orlando Patterson; "it is an ideology, or more properly, a faith."[3] If most forms of social identity revolve around similar choices, why quibble about a people's chosen way of life, let alone put it under the sociological microscope?

The first reason lies in the fact that identity is more than a simple choice or product of parentage. Identity results from a combination of endogenous and exogenous factors, ranging from choice and parentage to residential and occupational segregation. Some forms of identity are more mutable than others, and the presence or absence of entry and exit options further complicates this process.[4] Voluntary organizations contribute to this mix by providing incentives to attract and retain members, as well as creating restrictions that differentiate those eligible and ineligible for membership.

The contrasting experiences of African Americans, Japanese Americans, and Chinese Americans with organization building before World War II provide a useful trichotomy of different organizational responses to hostility and discrimination. Japanese Americans commanded a fairly rigid discipline of community members through vertically integrated economic organizations, namely, agricultural and retail business collectives. Culturally, the Japanese-American community promoted assimilation and accommodation, however, and the economic bonds of community market building did not extend far into other sectors of immigrant life.[5]

Chinese Americans, in contrast, erected a more all-encompassing social system for members of their community; in fact, they used economic and social organizations to enforce cooperation and participation in community-sanctioned activities. Sociologist Stanford Lyman refers to this Chinese-American organization-building strategy as "communalism," and he describes it as "community-wide domination of the people in question by a group of institutional elites" who pursue policies "directed toward maintaining the *separateness* of the community and their own authority over the 'subjects.' Both of these conditions existed in Chinatown," he adds, "neither in 'Little Tokyo.'"[6] Thus, whereas both systems provided valuable incentives to help maintain the loyalty of Japanese and Chinese immigrants to their ethnoracial communities, the Chinese generally asked more of their members and also made it much more difficult for existing members to depart at will.

In contrast, African Americans did not generally have great success in forming organizations capable of widespread economic cooperation, nor did they manage to effect much community-wide social integration. In African-American communities, voluntary organizations proliferated in great numbers, though none held sway over a significant percentage of the black population. Operating in the predominant fraternal mode of the day, most were high-exit organizations and faced hefty competition from rival groups, meaning that they could not be overly demanding of their existing members.

These observations are not intended as judgments of the various communities in question, but they do highlight the role voluntary organizations can play in community building and social cohesion. Although not without costs of their own, the low-exit models of the Japanese- and Chinese-American prewar communities would appear to demonstrate viable alternatives to the competitive voluntary system of black and white ethnic communities. African Americans faced challenges not experienced by Asian immigrants—there were far more blacks in the United States at the time, for one thing, and blacks also faced broader, better entrenched discrimination than did Asians—but the comparisons offered here are not intended to lay blame or pass judgment on one or the other community, only to draw lessons from lived experience in the hope of adding to our larger understanding of human agency and social process. In this chapter, I provide more detailed descriptions of these three modes of organization building with the aim of elucidating their differences. Thereafter, I turn more specifically to the issue of social capital and the prospects for new immigrant communities.

Lessons from the Experience of American Minorities

Just to be clear, let me restate the preceding argument before delving into the details. The process we are trying to understand or explain is the relative strength of community identity, that is, the likelihood that those eligible for membership will actively choose to take up such identities and participate in related community functions and organizations. Alternatively, members may choose other identity-group affiliations or pursue no such affiliations at all. In some cases, as in those of race or class, eligible individuals will have more difficulty in escaping their ascribed identity than they might like. My concern, however, is with the way in which various forms of voluntary organizations might influence the actions of large numbers of eligible individuals; in other words, I try to assess the prospects for various forms of community building by extrapolating from the potential response of ideal-typical individuals to the presumed costs and benefits of each alternative.

As described in chapter 4, my primary concern has been with three organizational facets of the identity-formation process:

1. The degree to which there is active competition for individual affiliation

2. The degree to which those eligible for membership encounter negative stereotypes and adverse action based on that eligibility (e.g., racism, sexism, anti-Semitism, and nativism
3. The degree to which quitting a given organization or exiting a given community is hampered by the threat of negative sanctions and/or the loss of positive rewards

I might further divide organizational competition into several related factors:

4. The ease with which eligible members can join existing organizations
5. The number of comparable organizations competing for the same pool of members at the same time
6. The ease with which eligible members can form altogether new organizations in lieu of joining existing ones
7. The attractiveness of the incentives being offered by such organizations

Let it be assumed, furthermore, that organizations that offer obvious benefits to members will generally fare better than those that do not offer such benefits, and that such benefits will not only attract new members but help retain existing members as well. The threat of negative sanction, on the other hand, will not only not help recruit new members (except in extreme cases) but will also hamper efforts to retain existing members in the event that comparable options are open to them.[7] (Why stay and accept punishment when there are equally attractive alternatives elsewhere?) The ecological perspective helps elucidate such dynamics in light of competition between rival organizations for limited resources, opportunities, and members.

Japanese Americans capitalized on the social stigma they experienced in the United States before World War II in several most ingenious (and associationalist) ways. Instead of allowing white farmers to run herd on them, Japanese immigrants organized themselves into *kenjinkai* labor gangs, or work teams organized among descendants of the same Japanese prefecture (*ken*). Each gang was organized by a gang boss who negotiated contracts with would-be employers. "Rancher and farm laborer confronted one another only through the mediation of the boss," writes sociologist Ivan H. Light. This system not only helped mute ethnic conflict but also served Japanese workers well, for "[Japanese] agricultural bosses were outspokenly mercenary on behalf of their crews. They negotiated with the [white] employers concerning the wage rate and unhesitatingly allocated their crew to whichever rancher offered the men the best terms."[8]

Independent (i.e., non-*kenjinkai*) Japanese farmers also formed collective organizations to represent their interests in the California agricultural community:

Almost every Japanese farmer belonged to some Japanese agricultural organization. These associations were organized along the familiar lines of

the trade guild, taking as their purpose the marketing of members' produce, control of prices and wages, regulation of labor disputes and of internal competition, protection of farmers' interest, and guardianship of the
social welfare of members' families.

A conglomeration of these groups united in 1929 as the Japanese Cooperative
Farm Industry (JCFI) of Southern California. Together, Japanese agricultural
laborers took control of produce distribution at the California Flower Market
and the City Market of Los Angeles.[9]

Nonetheless, the Japanese-American internal economy also had some drawbacks. The collected members of an agricultural association were entitled to
oversee and even intervene in the management of any single Japanese-owned
farm, for example, and the truly wayward could be banished from the local farm
economy on the basis of a group decision. Japanese often exploited Japanese
under this system, particularly in cities where the Japanese-American economy
operated largely like a *kenjinkai* cartel. "To receive a job . . . was to become
the recipient of a benevolence bestowned upon one by virtue of social connections," writes Light. In turn, workers had few civil rights, even within their
own community. "Complaining, striking, and quitting—the defense of the Western worker against exploitation—were denied to the Japanese employee of a
Japanese-owned firm."[10] Thus, the loyalty and obedience of Japanese-American
workers to the Japanese-American community was reinforced by the absence of
options (save repatriation, an issue to which I return shortly).

On the other hand, Japanese-American mutualism before the war generally
limited itself to economic matters and thus held limited sway over community
members. *Tanomoshi-ko*, or rotating-credit societies, circulated capital among
members, but once each contributor had received his alloted portion, the organization was dissolved. As members of the Japanese-American community in
Los Angeles got on better financial footing, the *ko* willingly gave way to more
commercial institutions, which could better supply the needs of the rapidly growing economy.[11] "Mutual aid societies among Japanese in America have been
limited in purpose and short-lived," comments sociologist Stanford Lyman.
"Kenjinkai limited their activity to providing mutual aid and death benefits and
did not exercise executive, legislative, or judicial power over the Japanese."[12]

Although both Japanese- and African-American communities relied on voluntary associations to pool and redistribute capital, differences in their social
structure and the structure of their associational ventures brought about very
different results, each with incumbent strengths and weaknesses. Despite the
racist belief that freed slaves and their descendents lack the initiative or knowhow
to foster self-help and mutual aid in their urban communities, African Americans actually have a long though checkered history of voluntary organization.
Between 1884 and 1935, for example, at least 134 banking institutions were es-

tablished by and for blacks, primarily in the Deep South. Many had fraternal origins: Black fraternities such as the Knights of Honor and the True Reformers both established banks of their own. Nonetheless, despite the ardent hopes of turn-of-the-century black leaders, by 1929 only 21 black-owned banks still survived.[13]

Recruiting well-trained black administrators was one problem, as was a general lack of liquid capital in communities already saddled with poverty and debt. Another issue facing black-owned banks and savings societies was what to do with their credit in order to keep it circulating, and thus growing, within their respective communities. Real estate investment in poor urban real estate was one venture in which black-owned banks lost lots of money, as were community development plans organized around the central vehicle of the fraternal order. Arguably, all of these problems might have been rectified by a *kenjinkai*-style attachment among black entrepreneurs, black workers, and black bankers. Japanese mutual savings organizations not only offered attractive incentives for participation but also discouraged defection through a system of community-wide organizations. In contrast, black-owned banks exerted little control over their capital, and black consumers showed little loyalty to black-owned businesses. In a sense, the structure of their community organizations left too many options for those interested in working, spending, or banking outside the community.

Commentators on the fate of African Americans in the United States clearly recognized these shortcomings in the black community before World War II. Business historian Abram Harris coined the term *racial protectionism* in his book, *The Negro as Capitalist*, to describe the need for low-exit organizations in the face of isolation and discrimination.[14] Harris's study of the black banking industry in the Deep South carefully documents its persistent failures. Harris found, for example, that most of the money invested in black-owned banks did not remain with them for long and that "the white bank is the final resting place of the funds lent by the Negro bank." One might argue that black-owned banks had limited investment options outside of their own community because of widespread discrimination, although, as Harris points out,

> there is no obstacle in the way of the Negro bank's investing some of its idle cash in government bonds and other securities that can be easily liquidated in emergencies. In fact, wise banking practice shows that idle cash invested in this way helps to maintain liquidity. We found, however, that only a few Negro banks made any considerable investments of this nature, and it is likely that the banks in the far South were not exceptional in this respect.[15]

To make matters worse, black banks took little interest in directing their capital toward intensive community development. Harris states that "although ostensibly sponsored as the means of self-help or racial coöperation, as it was sometimes called, through which the masses were to be economically emancipated, Negro business enterprise was motivated primarily by the desire for private profit and looked toward the establishment of a Negro capitalist employer class."[16] These centrifugal aspirations siphoned precious labor, capital, and knowhow from a community not otherwise welcome in America at large. W. E. B. Du Bois arrived at similar conclusions: "The Negroes are unused to co-operation with their own people and the process of learning it is long and tedious. Hitherto, their economic activities have been directed almost entirely to the satisfaction of wants of the upper classes of white people, and, too, of personal and house-hold wants."[17]

This is not to say that racial protectionism is altogether desirable from a nor-mative standpoint. In fact, I have argued, perhaps too subtly thus far, that such intensive forms of social organization tend to have large negative repercussions, or externalities, on their members, as well as on society as a whole. A third case from the same period, that of Chinese-American immigrants in the early twen-tieth century, helps draw out the most salient characteristics of intensive social organizations, as well as their costs and benefits, for those minority groups that employ them.

Before World War II, virtually all Chinese immigrants to the United States came from one of seven districts in the South China province of Guangdong. Every American city with a reasonable Chinese population was subsequently divided among immigrants from these districts, each of which formed a district association represented at a citywide Chinese-American board of governance. (In San Francisco, for example, this group was commonly referred to as the Six Companies and officially called the Chinese Consolidated Benevolent Associa-tion.) Once here, Chinese immigrants maintained strict, nearly exclusive ties to their district associations. Members paid dues and fealty in exchange for which they could count on a steady supply of employment. Individuals could then form rotating-credit associations with fellow district members to secure safe, low-interest loans for carefully regulated purposes. Unlike black-owned fraternal insti-tutions or Japanese-American business collectives and rotating-credit associations, however, "The Chinese Six Companies and constituent district associations were *not* voluntary organizations. The officials of these institutions claimed that every Chinese in the United States was 'automatically' a member of the Six Companies through his 'automatic' membership in the district association representing him."[18]

Within each district association, members were divided into "surname asso-ciations," or *tsu*, each of which claimed the loyalty of all those with the same last name. In San Franciso's Chinatown, for example, members of the Chan, Lee, and Wong *tsu* generally dominated. These clans became the basis of specific communities, founding businesses, credit associations, relief organizations, and community leadership by and for their kin. Individual Chinese immigrants were thus forced to rely on clan and kin representatives as intermediaries when dealing with whites.[19]

The costs and benefits of such a rigid, clan-oriented system are clear: Through the Six Companies and their various village and surnamed-based affiliates, Chinese immigrants overcame many of the obstacles of American racism. They founded viable working communities and occupational niches. More important, the strict boundaries of internal segregation provided specific boundaries within which to conduct business: Competition was strictly regulated, credit was carefully distributed, apprentices and trainees were easily secured, and everyone benefited from a firm commitment to the internal economy.[20] But this system had obvious negative aspects, too: Faced with such strong internal barriers to action, compliance with community norms was very strictly enforced; all personal and financial exchanges were closely regulated; and operating a business outside the established guilds or violating community standards could be cause for punishment or, in extreme cases, community-sanctioned homicide. Such rigid barriers to entry and exit even gave rise to a de facto minority within the Chinese community—those unattached to any of the clans. Chinese immigrants from towns outside of those represented in the clan system were thus excluded from full participation in the Chinese community. In turn, some alienated Chinese formed illicit gangs, or *tongs*—supracommunal clan organizations that came to dominate the underworld of most major Chinatown districts at the time.[21]

One can argue that the clan system ultimately hampered Chinese and Japanese business expansion:

> So long as they were locked into exclusive village, territorial, and family groupings, Chinese and Japanese workers were unable to shift their membership support to any leadership that pleased them. Hence, the rank and file could not readily control unresponsive territorial elites by playing them off against one another. Moreover, so long as the Old World loyalties remained lively, mutual distrust tended to prevent disgruntled people of different immigrant backgrounds from making common cause against conservative elites.[22]

In addition, such intensive clan systems tended to keep Japanese Americans and Chinese Americans strictly isolated from mainstream society. Lacking a stronger presence in white communities, both groups encountered heightened hostility and discrimination during World War II, whereas blacks actually made significant strides toward political recognition during that same period.

Once again, contrast the nature of Chinese community organizations with those of African Americans: Though clearly as experienced with racial exclusion as their Chinese and Japanese counterparts (if not much more so), African Americans lacked the close ties of clan division characteristic of Asian-American immigrant groups before World War II. This stems partly from the distinctive

patterns of black migration from the Old South. Though large numbers of Southern blacks found themselves living side by side in cities of the industrial Northeast, Midwest, and Pacific Coast, they generally failed to form anything like a
clan system for themselves and newcomers. Presumably, one's state of origin
might have lent itself as one basis for intrasocial solidarity, much as village of
origin served Chinese immigrants from Guangdong province. For whatever reason (and I am definitely not qualified to offer one), no such networks developed
among black migrants once they settled outside of the South, at least no such
networks that would provide obvious, a priori means of compelling strangers to
welcome one another on the basis of common ancestry. Though there are clearly
many reasons for the apparent differences in the experiences of blacks and Japanese and Chinese immigrants in the United States before World War II, the
absence of binding, intracommunal social ties among migrant black workers does
seem to have contributed to their lack of intensive social organization, and thus
the failure of racial protectionism. Because black mutual aid and fraternal
organizations always needed to remain popular with members, they had difficulty in making the unpopular sorts of demands necessary to the fiscal uplift
of an oppressed community. In contrast, Japanese- and especially Chinese-
American communities enforced fiscal discipline on their members by con-
trolling the flow of jobs, credit, and capital.

Social Capital or Social Control?

This invariably brings us to the issue of social capital, or the "features of social
organization, such as trust, norms, and networks, that can improve the efficiency
of society by facilitating coordinated actions."[23] Social capital theory has become
something of an academic cottage industry of late, though there is as yet little
consensus among social scientists about what exactly this term means, let alone
how one might detect its presence in a community, country, or organization.[24]
Nonetheless, the issue is an important one, and it bears directly on the fore-
going discussion of intensive social forms and the organizational characteristics
that tend to encourage and discourage them.

Put aside the issue of recruitment for a moment, as well as the involuntary
basis for membership in organizations that revolve around ascribed identities
such as race, gender, and place of birth, and consider only the effect voluntarism
has on existing organizations and their members: Because members always have
three options—exit, voice, and loyalty—organizations must either meet their
needs or risk defection. This limits the internal norms the association is able to
command of its members:

> The first and most serious limitation of voluntary association . . . is its ca-
> pacity to enroll only those who voluntarily join. . . . Scurrying for ever

broader support, the organizational elite is in no position to impose strin-
gent life style rules on their transient and calculating members. On the
contrary, they must work persistently to reduce the ratio of organizational
demands to benefits in order to maintain fickle loyalties of persons already
supporting them and to court the favor of those supporting some rival
organization. [In other words] *rationalized membership competition erodes
internal solidarity.*[25]

As you may recall (from chapter 5), this was one of the things that distinguished a successful labor union like the American Federation of Labor from its
unsuccessful rival, the Knights of Labor. The AFL asked less of members and
seriously attended to the "what's-in-it-for-me" problem. The Knights demanded
total loyalty from members but offered little in return. As a result, the AFL survived and grew, whereas the Knights withered and collapsed. In the long run,
however, material incentives like those offered by the AFL lose some of their allure
particularly when members are continually faced with organizational alternatives.
The AFL eventually found itself struggling to compete with the recruitment efforts of an equally incentivized rival, the Congress of Industrial Organizations
(CIO), and in lieu of continued competition for the allegiance of American
workers, the two organizations eventually devised a noncompetition agreement
in the form of a flexible merger, the AFL-CIO.[26]

Nonetheless, incentives for recruitment and retention can sometimes provide the glue necessary to hold an organization together. This works particularly well when threats and sanctions might simply push members into the arms
of less punitive rivals.[27] In other cases, however, particularly those in which
would-be participants have precious few alternatives, negative sanctions can
be used to good effect. Whereas members with choices will probably defect in
the face of sanctions, the threat of punishment can serve to convince members without such options that the costs of defection would be higher than those
of loyalty.[28]

This latter scenario describes the situation of racially ascribed American minority groups fairly well. The chief characteristic separating the successful experience of Japanese- and Chinese-American associations from the unsuccessful
experience of African Americans was not the presence of investment capital or
selective incentives but the ability to place enforceable constraints on the behavior
of individual members. Japanese-American associations tended to limit themselves to control over the economic activities of members, in contrast to the all-
encompassing Chinese-American system, but the price of defection from either
community was the same: alienation from the one group in society that would
knowingly welcome them. African-American organizations did not extract nearly
so much discipline, fiscal or otherwise, from community members. The result
was both more freedom and a less vibrant internal economy. African Americans

have made great strides in political organization over the past five decades, though their efforts have succeeded best when they upped the stakes of affiliation by offering tangible benefits for loyalty such as a social and political voice (i.e., representation through active and widely recognized political organizations) and creating tangible disincentives for exit such as social stigma and alienation from the black community itself.[29]

Note, however, how different this perspective is from the sentimental conception of social capital one finds in the writings of many contemporary theorists, who equate knowing a person, or participating in a club together, with being able to count on him or her in time of need. Seen in the light of American ethnic history, social capital is actually something born out of competition and discipline, not acquaintance.[30] In fact, participation in high-exit associations might have been seen as a obstacle to social capital formation, rather than an aid thereto. Fraternalism, for the most part, fared poorly as a vehicle for social capital formation. In the face of perpetual competition, most fraternal orders were unable to demand much of their members, and thus, one might presume, most members were unable to demand much of one another in turn. At the same time, fraternalism did contribute mightily to the stratification of the American populace by race, ethnicity, gender, and religion. Therefore, it seems foolhardy to believe that fraternalism might be a quick fix for contemporary American anomie, though many would have us believe otherwise.

Future Prospects for New Immigrant Communities in the United States

As applied to the contemporary American scene, the legacy of the golden age offers several tentative lessons about the future prospects of new immigrant groups here and elsewhere. The organizational structure of a community can have important consequences for its social and economic status vis-à-vis the mainstream. Blacks, Japanese Americans, and Chinese Americans all faced enormous barriers to entry in the American economy before World War II, for example, but discrimination alone was not enough to create internal cohesion in each community. Internal barriers to exit, coupled with rigid norms of intracommunal social ascription and behavior, created strong, cohesive communities among Japanese and Chinese immigrants. Without the privilege of voice within their respective communities, however, each remained vulnerable to defection once the barriers to assimilation diminished. Given the choice among exit, voice, or loyalty, many if not most Chinese and Japanese immigrants chose exit, or assimilation, once such opportunities became widely available.

In the abstract, one can imagine at least three factors relevant to new immigrants' choices concerning their identity affiliations here in the United States: First and most prominent is the option of *separatism*, or self-segregation. Under conditions of systematic exclusion and discrimination, internal discipline can be a vital asset for communities looking to circle their wagons and develop endogenously. It creates strong incentives for joiners and tall barriers for would-be quitters, thus guaranteeing the loyalty and obedience of all. But, as sociologist Orlando Patterson argues, the notion that ethnic separatism is the best, or even a viable, path to equality "is a dangerous myth. The comparative sociology of ethnic relations strongly suggests that separate always means unequal for the mass of minority group members." Furthermore, "The only members of minority groups to benefit from such a system are leaders who enjoy the collective spoils permitted by the dominant group as a payoff for keeping the groups separate."[31] Separatism is an organizationally intensive affair, in other words, competitive voluntarism notwithstanding. It makes work for organizers but does not necessarily benefit their brethren.

A second path, *assimilation*, generally entails spatial and cultural immersion in the mainstream. The goal, if it can be said to have a goal, would be the virtual elimination of difference. Total assimilation has been a viable strategy for some white immigrants from European communities. Intermarriage among members of white ethnic groups mixed their norms and networks to such an extent that questions of ethnic identity were largely reduced to matters of preference rather than ascription.[32] On the other hand, it is acknowledged that assimilation is not always or even generally an option for many new immigrants, particularly those who bear the social stigma of racialized identities. For them and for others that so choose, there is a third option: *symbolic ethnicity*. Under this rubric, members of ethnic groups strike a compromise between their desire to maintain some sense of their heritage and the need to gain full access to the mainstream society. Holidays and religious practices are adapted and maintained, for example, but occupational and residential segregation are generally avoided. Those ethnic or ritualistic practices that might be offensive or just particularly visible to the mainstream are also eschewed or adapted in order to ease passage in and out of the mainstream.[33] For the descendants of the late nineteenth- and early twentieth-century immigration waves to America, this last option generally seems to have been the most prevalent (as described in chapter 8).

New immigrants to America will face similar choices in the future, though they do have one additional exit option not yet discussed: Recent immigrants can, under circumstances to be outlined shortly, choose to exit their American communities and simply return home, or *repatriate*. Repatriation probably has cross-cutting effects on the solidarity of immigrant communities. On the one hand, the viability of this exit option means that manpower and resources will perpetually flow out of immigrant communities here in the United States. Thus, a strong exit option such as repatriation puts pressure on community organizers to provide and maintain conditions of relative satisfaction to would-be returnees. On the other hand, and perhaps more important, repatriation and serial migration maintain active ties to the homeland, thus helping to preserve the traditions, rituals, and commitments of the immigrant community itself. To the extent that exit options such as repatriation and serial migration vary across immigrant groups, one might thus hypothesize that those new immigrant groups farthest from their homeland and/or least able to return will be most likely to assimilate into mainstream American patterns of life. Lacking active ties to their homeland, as well as a steady stream of migrants traveling back and forth, community loyalty seems likely to dissipate with the second and third generations, if not before. Russian, Vietnamese, and Chinese immigrants might thus be seen as less likely to maintain sectarian social organizations than their Mexican, Caribbean, and Latin American counterparts, who can, and often do, repatriate with great frequency.

It has been my presumption throughout this text that social affiliation, or identity formation, is related to the number of identity options available to would-be members, as well as the positive and negative incentives related to each option. Being born black, Jewish, or Italian is no guarantee that one will actively choose to participate in any of these communities as an adult. The number of choices, or options, open to an individual, as well as their costs and benefits, will help shape the future of these communities in addition to the individual's own life course and worldview. Though new immigrants do not face anything like the pressure for religious conversion or ethnic loyalty that immigrants at the end of the nineteenth century did, it is still fair to say that several ethnic options are open to them here in the United States.[34] In the case of, say, Vietnamese Americans, immigrants essentially have three such options: (1) They can remain in the United States but cling to the comforts of ethnic solidarity, thus forging what one might call a Vietnamese-American identity; (2) they can pull up stakes and try to return to their country of origin (despite obstacles like distance and expense), thus re-creating their original Vietnamese identity; or (3) they can choose to remain here but forge ahead in the quest for assimilation into mainstream American society. (Clearly, there is a huge middle ground between the first and third options, but the contrast is worth considering in light of the preceding discussion of intensive social forms.)

Given these three options and the relative difficulty of option 2 (repatriation), one might thus suppose that leaders in the Vietnamese-American community will have a fair chance of maintaining a cohesive ethnic community in their midst, particularly as long as members of their community face linguistic obstacles to further interaction with English speakers. Moreover, if new immigrants continue to arrive from Vietnam, the salience of their ethnic distinctiveness will continually be replenished and reinforced.[35]

When contrasted with the ethnic options of, say, Russian Americans, the ramifications of ethnic options become clearer still: A large number of Russian immigrants, Russian Jews specifically, come to the United States because of religious oppression in their homeland. As American settlers, Russian Jews have not three but five ethnic options: They can join the larger Russian community here in the United States, thus becoming Russian Americans; they can form a separate ethnoreligious enclave of Russian-American Jews; they can try to assimilate into the mainstream religious enclave of American Jews; they can attempt to repatriate to Russia, thus becoming simply Russian-Russian Jews again; or they can relinquish all such options and simply try to assimilate as unhyphenated Americans. Furthermore, non-Jewish Russian immigrants lack three of these five options but make up for it with three of their own (becoming Russian Orthodox Americans here, returning home as Orthodox Russians, or returning home as nonreligiously defined Russians). The difficulty of creating and maintaining distinctive ethnic communities in the face of so many identity options seems to be considerable, particularly if immigration from Russia begins to decline in coming years.

A more extreme example can be found in the case of so-called Hispanics, or Spanish-speaking Americans. Though there are political movements afoot to unify Spanish speakers as a single political bloc in the United States, the potential for such a community to survive setbacks, defeats, or internal disagreements is severely weakened by the range of ethnonational identity options that are available. When difficulties arise, as they often do in the world of community organizations, there will be significant temptations for Guatemalans, Nicaraguans, Cubans, Mexicans, Columbians, Peruvians, and so on to express their dissatisfaction by retreating to their own ethnonational enclaves. My own sense is that the contemporary movement for Hispanic political organization is implicitly intended to represent Mexican Americans first and foremost, with the expectation that other communities of Spanish speakers will join the cause out of linguistic solidarity. The lessons of exit, voice, and loyalty would seem to predict, on the other hand, that such a panlinguistic movement is likely to fail in the face of defection and that an explicit focus on the concerns of Mexican Americans would pay better returns for Mexican Americans and have beneficial effects that would spill over to the wider Spanish-speaking community.

Of course, local voluntary associations can play a big role in tipping the scales of identity in one way or another, as this text has been at great pains to illustrate. In Boston, for example, advocacy and service organizations for Portuguese speakers seem to reinforce the loyalty of local Brazilians to their ethnonational community. Haitians seem similarly unified around community organizations specific to themselves. Language barriers alone do not explain such loyalty, furthermore, for within the local Portuguese-speaking community, Brazilians and native Portuguese tend to go their separate ways, each gravitating toward their local cultural and religious organizations.[36] Regardless, it is indeed true that community organizations with high exit barriers and strong incentives for loyalty tend to fare best in securing the identification and participation of would-be members.

Returning to the issue of American political history, one sees how both endogenous and exogenous factors helped create incentives and disincentives for community loyalty in the face of marginalization from the mainstream. Although the United States is currently experiencing an immigration wave comparable in size and scope to that of the late nineteenth and early twentieth centuries, the obstacles to successful integration are somewhat different. A significant number of the earlier generation of immigrants, for example, came from English-speaking countries, namely England and Ireland. Furthermore, the majority of new immigrants were regarded as more or less "white," which facilitated their eventual acceptance into the American mainstream. With the passing of generations, many of the barriers to entry that fostered white-ethnic associationalism were torn down by legislation, by intermarriage, and by assimilation. As sociologist Mary Waters has shown, intermarriage among European Americans has traditionally afforded to many contemporary whites a variety of ethnic identities from which to choose (i.e., it is not uncommon for white Americans to have mixed European parentage). Faced with so many options, the descendants of European immigrants tend to take up those ethnic identities that bear the highest social status, as opposed to those that make up the largest portion of their genealogy.[37]

Whether new immigrants from Africa, Asia, and South America will achieve similar options is largely a question of time. Racial differences may prove to be an obstacle to assimilation, though rising rates of interracial marriages (particularly between Asians and whites) seem to indicate that this is not so high a barrier as it might seem. On the other hand, intensive ethnonational organizations may slow this process by encouraging new immigrants to remain loyal to their communities at the expense of successful assimilation. In all likelihood, however, new immigrants will forge loose ethnic options much like white immigrants of the earlier period.

In sum, contemporary calls for reinvigorating American civil society through community organization building ignore the variegated experiences of hyphenated Americans and mistake cause for effect: The basis of social cohesion, or social capital, lies in the organizational capacity to enforce community-minded thinking, or at least obedience to communal dictate. Amicability has little if any part in such a process, though it may well be a result thereof. Loyalty, reciprocity, but also fear and constraint foster social capital among individuals; mere association is not enough.

CONCLUSION

I've a good mind to join a club . . .

and beat you over the head with it.

—GROUCHO MARX, *Duck Soup*

"There is a state of mind," writes William James, "known to religious men, but to no others, in which the will to assert ourselves and hold our own has been displaced by a willingness to close our mouths and be as nothing in the floods and waterspouts of God."[1] Such exalted states reflect an individually embodied reification of the social, according to James, the negation of self in lieu of the collectivity.

One might argue that many social phenomena can be explained in this manner, particularly those involving intensive social organizations. Historian William McNeill has devoted an entire monograph to the world history of such phenomena, and employing his own Jamesian lense, he has singled out "muscular bonding" as a unique and historically transverse form. McNeill's idea is simply that regimented physical activity in close coordination with others instills a certain esprit de corps in individuals. (Of his own experience in the U.S. army, McNeill writes, "Words are inadequate to describe the emotion aroused by the prolonged movement in unison that drilling involved. A sense of pervasive well-being is what I recall; more specifically, a strange sense of personal enlargement; a sort of swelling out, becoming bigger than life, thanks to participation in collective ritual."[2]) Thus, as with James's religious aspirants, muscular bonding stems from the suppression of individual freedom in the service of organizationally derived goals.

Though only one example of many possible forms of social discipline, the point of McNeill's example is exceedingly relevant to the issue at hand—the performance of different types of organizations in the facilitation of coopera-tion among otherwise independent individuals. Both James and McNeill were struck by the myriad ways in which collective action could be helped or hindered by the presence of unique social organizations. Surprisingly, however, social capital theory tends to pay less attention to the effects of different forms of so-cial organization than to the need for more of them.

What remains distinct about associationalism in late nineteenth-century America is the way in which organizations competed for members, not their numbers alone. In a few well-known cases, large organizations, encompassing members from across the country, achieved great and meaningful change: women's successful lobby for the right to vote, for example, and African Ameri-cans' 100-year struggle for civil rights. But in the bigger picture, the political gains of specific associational lobbies were far outweighed by the negative (and largely unintended) consequences competitive voluntarism had on the American so-cial landscape. Individual group differences were accentuated by self-segrega-tion. Millions of poor and needy people were cruelly harassed by high-minded "moral reformers." Benefit groups held social insurance legislation hostage to their special interests. And an entire nation temporarily lost the right to drink. (I am not being facetious here. Prohibition was one of the worst legislative deci-sions ever made in American history. It stifled freedom, promoted racketeering, and forever changed one of the great social service agencies of the nineteenth century—the saloon, which once proudly served the masses as restroom, soup kitchen, and employment agency all in one.[3]) More important and more to the point, the rise of fraternal participation in American cities and towns was di-rectly linked to the rise of a fragmented political system based around special interests rather than common interests. This period in American history was unique not because Americans suddenly turned to one another for faith and succor but because faith and succor were suddenly turned into matters of orga-nizational self-segregation.

Fortunately, the decline of American associationalism can be at least partly explained by the fact that contemporary Americans are increasingly more com-fortable in associating with those of different ethnic, racial, and religious backgrounds than they once were. Americans did not stop caring about their com-munities when they stopped clubbing together; clubbing has simply lost much of its appeal, both socially and financially. One might go so far as to say that the more we become a nation of equals, the less we need be a nation of joiners.

In lieu of fraternalism, Americans have increasingly turned to associational networks built on common interests rather than common heritage. Accord-ing to sociologist Robert Wuthnow, for example, 4 out of every 10 Americans belong to a small group of one kind or another, from self-help groups to sports and hobby clubs, book groups and Bible study meetings, youth and singles groups, and so on. More important, small groups have become so popular

because they cater to the diverse interests, needs, and lifestyles of the public. . . . In short, the variety of small groups, coupled with the ease of moving into and out of them, enhances their appeal. We are, after all, a mobile
society, not only in the ways we move ourselves around, but also in the ways
in which our interests and orientations adapt to new situations. Small
groups allow us to find something suitable to our tastes at a given moment
and then to move on when our interests change.[4]

The proliferation of such groups is not without its own costs—Wuthnow notes
among them a competitive dynamic all their own, one in which organization
building has once again become a goal in and of itself[5]—but the stakes appear
far less grave. Competitive voluntarism is less a matter of survival, bigotry, and
self-segregation today than it is one of comfort, leisure, and philosophical inquiry.

Although some are bothered by the fact that contemporary Americans increasingly identify themselves by what they buy, watch, and consume, our
nineteenth-century predecessors did not have the luxury to choose their friends
and enemies, let alone their favorite TV shows. In their world, exclusive social
organizations fueled mutual distrust, if not outright hostility. In ours, identity
has largely become an indulgence, something we cling to when it serves our purposes (as opposed to something that clings to us because we serve its purposes).
The speed with which most upwardly mobile, hyphenated Americans have re-
linquished the trappings of exclusion is a testament to the social friction caused
by associational self-segregation. Given the choice, most contemporary Americans prefer to embrace composite identities made up of bits and pieces of various preferences and affiliations. And given the choice, most would rather not
affiliate with the organizational avatar of American self-segregation—the fraternal lodge.

The Impact of Associationalism on American Political Development

The etymology of a word often has deep-seated relevance for understanding its
meaning in contemporary parlance. Consider the etymology of *lodge*, the base
unit of most fraternal organizations. The medieval Latin root, *lobia*, denotes a
"covered walk or cloister." In modern language, this most closely translates into
the words *loge* or *lobby*, that is, a covered space in which individuals can seek
refuge or protection.[6] This sense of the word does indeed reflect what I take to
be the true origins of the associational tradition in the late nineteenth-century
United States. Fraternal lodges were a form of self-protection for many Americans at the time—a refuge from poverty, an escape from interaction with those
of different roots and preferences, and a simple guarantee that one would not
end up in potter's field. Following the carnage of the Civil War, the rapid expansion of America's economic and industrial base, and the massive influx of

immigrants and freed slaves, there arose a growing perception that certain such protections were necessary, if not merely desirable. As some individuals began banding together for such purposes, a dormant Masonic movement was resurrected in the form of full-blown fraternalism.

The fraternal movement grew in the 1870s and 1880s as the perceived need for lodge protection diffused and expanded. Simple, easily replicable organizational models made emulation simple and easy, which lent the movement more momentum still. Though originally founded by white Protestant men for white Protestant men, new immigrants drew on their own indigenous burial society traditions and transformed them into fraternalistic, ethnoreligious lodges. Soon, there were Catholic lodges for Catholics, French lodges for Frenchmen, colored lodges for African Americans, womens' lodges for women, Jewish lodges for Jews, Alsatian lodges for Alsatians, ancestral lodges for "ancestors of the Pilgrims," and on and on: The American social landscape literally filled with sectarian organizations designed for self-protection, self-segregation, and self-aggrandizement.

There were exceptions, of course—nonsectarian lodges that welcomed members of all stripes and backgrounds. Most fraternal lodges were never truly open to any and all, however. Membership had to be granted by current members, and dues had to be paid promptly and regularly. Exclusion, rather than inclusion, was the norm of the day. Sectarian social organization, as rooted in the fraternal system, ensured that the ties of race and birth origin would not only be perpetuated but also have means of transmission across generations and over vast expanses of territory.

At the same time, the American economy was undergoing a vast and meaningful transformation of its own. Railroads and telegraphy had laid out the spinal cord of intranational communications and transportation before the Civil War, and afterward the manufacturing, commercial, and professional sectors literally exploded with new technological and organizational innovations. It is interesting, however, that whereas the American economy quickly caught up to its western European rivals in terms of output and scale, it sorely lagged behind in the cultivation of its service sector. Unlike European cities, which had age-old service economies and in some cases were literally governed by the denizens of occupational guilds, the antebellum American economy had been built largely around overseas trade and agricultural production, and its cities were still relatively backward in cultural, professional, and social options.[7] This, in fact, goes a long way toward explaining the unique proliferation of fraternal lodges and political associations in the United States after the Civil War: Whereas European tradesmen and professionals could rely on ancient territorial and occupational organizations to protect and serve their interests, Americans had no such traditions. Seeing all the good that guilds, lodges, and friendly societies provided for English workingmen, Americans began building voluntary organizations of their own, assisted, to be sure, by British immigrants themselves.

Americans created their associational movement in the British image, though with one major difference: Whereas in Europe the organizational diffraction of the economy was a natural and indigenous part of its social fabric, the U.S. service sector coevolved with the mass migration of new settlers to its cities and towns. Members of different ethnonational and ethnoreligious groups gravitated toward particular industries, industries in which they could rely on in-group solidarity to give themselves protection and security. In many cases, blacks and foreigners were tacitly barred from participation in coveted sectors of the economy, thus relegating them to occupations like the laundry trade, the restaurant business, and other less-than-glamorous backwaters of the service and manufacturing sectors.[8] Whereas European workers could rely on their already extensive traditions of occupational organization in facing the new threat of wage labor, Americans had no such organizational framework with which to build a diverse, broad-based organizational coalition for artisans and laborers. Instead, American workers divided themselves along ethnic, racial, and religious lines. In turn, American labor organizations like the American Federation of Labor focused exclusively on such bread-and-butter issues as wage hikes and hiring practices to avoid the larger differences that divided members in their nonworking lives.

Fraternities helped reinforce these extraoccupational barriers to communication and consensus. Social issues such as temperance, school reform, poor relief, and compulsory national health insurance played into fraternally based hostility and further divided the polity along ethnoreligious rather than socioeconomic lines. As a consequence, American workers were never truly able to mobilize behind worker-friendly politics in this period. Thus, although the United States was every bit as ripe for widespread social welfare legislation as its European counterparts in the 1870s and 1880s, by the turn of the century, when the idea of government-sponsored social welfare legislation really took hold in the Western world, populist legislation was stymied in the United States as Europeans began half a century of sustained policy innovation.[9]

The truly interesting question is whether the early twentieth-century American political landscape would have looked the same without the initial input of whites, blacks, and foreigners divvying up the polity into so many associational baskets. On the one hand, Europe had a strong tradition of mutual aid and burial societies of its own, though in most European countries the practice of associationalism had already been weakened by decades of adverse legislation by the end of the nineteenth century. In France and Germany, for example, close surveillance of independent associations had long since driven fraternities and mutual benefit societies underground, or at least rendered them subservient to the dictates of an authoritarian (and highly suspicious) state.[10] Though England abandoned such restrictions in the 1830s and never practiced the same kind of antiassociationalism characteristic of France and Germany, even the British "friendly society" tradition had largely withered by the dawn of the twentieth century.[11] In all three cases, associational remnants of the medieval guild system were in decline long before the turn of the century, having been replaced by workplace organizations oriented toward state-sponsored social welfare legislation.

In the United States, on the other hand, fraternities were just coming into their own when the window of national social welfare legislation opened. The American labor movement was still struggling to find its place within this system, and the absence of antiquarian trade guilds, commercial cadres, and professional organizations only accelerated the pace of associational development, thus facilitating the growth of special-interest groups in American politics. Though such divisions would have been likely in any country as heterogeneous as the United States, the associational movement of the postbellum era accentuated the lines that divide and hardened Americans' resistance to collectivization of risks and resources. As a result, America missed its primary opportunity to join western Europe in the adoption of people-friendly social policies.[12]

Many modern-day civic associations undoubtedly do Americans (and the rest of the world) a lot of good. They cultivate social ties and civic commitment that might otherwise lie dormant. They operate summer camps and swimming pools and after-school programs. And they do provide much-needed social services for a significant minority who might not find them elsewhere. But, of course, that is exactly the problem. America's nineteenth-century experience with voluntarism is responsible in part for the very insufficiencies contemporary neo-Tocquevillians seek to address with voluntarism—poor schools, insufficient health care and social services, and a general lack of interest in the commonweal.

APPENDIX

U.S. City Directories Consulted

This appendix documents all of the city directories consulted in the course of research on this project. Most were acquired from the United States City Directories Microfilm Collection produced by Research Publications, Inc. The remaining directories were acquired from the collections of the New York, Boston Public, and Widener Libraries. Most city directories are made up primarily of alphabetical listings of all the inhabitants of that city, though most also contain fairly comprehensive listings of government agencies, public services, civic associations, clubs, and societies, as well as a directory of businesses resident in that city. For my purposes, I scanned each directory for all listings pertaining to voluntary organizations and/or local militia. Generally, these listings were grouped together in one obvious place in the directory, thus making it relatively certain that I did not miss any pertinent listings. To be sure, however, I also searched the business and government sections of each directory for separate listings that might have been omitted elsewhere (such as voluntary organizations that listed themselves as incorporated mutual benefit or savings and loan societies).

Data collection was done in three waves, as described in the introduction. Though my coding scheme was modified somewhat over time, my aim was generally to count all the voluntary organizations listed in each city directory, as well as to code them according to a typology that differentiated them by purpose or function. The data thus allow one to view the prevalence of arts and cultural organizations independently from those organizations dedicated to fraternal benevolence, military training, business cooperation, and so on. With the exception of the Boston data, in which the name of every organization was recorded individually, my data do not make it possible to track the trajectory of specific organizations (i.e., most of the entries do not include the name of specific organizations, only the number counted within each category). Nonetheless, they do provide a rough picture of the organizational density in these many cities over time.

A copy of the basic coding scheme follows a bibliographic listing of all the city directories consulted for this project. In a few select cases, specific bibliographic data were lost or unavailable and are noted as such.

Cross-sectional Study of Cities, 1880 and 1890

(Includes all cities with an 1890 population greater than 50,000, listed by 1890 population size.)

New York
> *Trow's New York City Directory for the Year Ending May 1, 1880* (New York: Trow City Directory Company, 1880).
> *The New York City Register* (New York: Trow City Directory Company, 1890).

Chicago
> *The Lakeside Annual Directory of the City of Chicago, 1880* (Chicago: Chicago Directory Company, 1880).
> *The Lakeside Annual Directory of the City of Chicago, 1890* (Chicago: Chicago Directory Company, 1890).

Philadelphia
> *Gopsill's Philadelphia City Directory for 1880* (Philadelphia: James Gopsill, 1880).
> *Gopsill's Philadelphia City Directory for 1890* (Philadelphia: James Gopsill's Sons, 1890).

Brooklyn, N.Y.
> *The Brooklyn Directory for the Year Ending May 1st, 1880* (Brooklyn: Lain, 1880).
> *Lain's Brooklyn Directory for the Year Ending May 1st, 1890* (Brooklyn: Lain, 1890).

St. Louis, Mo.
> *Gould's St. Louis Directory for 1880* (St. Louis: David B. Gould, 1880).
> *Gould's St. Louis Directory for 1890* (St. Louis: Gould Directory Co., 1890).

Boston
> *The Boston Directory . . . for the Year Commencing July 1, 1880* (Boston: Sampson, Davenport, 1880).
> *The Boston Directory . . . for the Year Commencing July 1, 1890* (Boston: Sampson, Davenport, 1890).

Baltimore
> *Wood's Baltimore City Directory* [for 1880] (Baltimore: John W. Woods, 1880).
> *R. L. Polk & Co's Baltimore City Directory for 1890* (Baltimore: Nichols, Killam & Maffitt, 1890).

San Francisco
> *Langley's San Francisco Directory for the Year Commencing April, 1880* (San Francisco: Francis, Valentine, 1880).
> *Langley's San Francisco Directory for the Year Commencing April, 1890* (San Francisco: Francis, Valentine, 1890).

Cincinnati
> *Williams' Cincinnati Directory* (Cincinnati: Williams, 1880).
> *Williams' Cincinnati Directory* (Cincinnati: Williams, 1890).

Cleveland
> *The Cleveland City Directory for the Year Ending June, 1881* (Cleveland: Cleveland Directory Co., 1880).
>
> *The Cleveland City Directory for the Year Ending July, 1891* (Cleveland: Cleveland Directory Co., 1890).

Buffalo, N.Y.
> *Buffalo City Directory for the Year 1880* (Buffalo: Courier Co., 1880).
>
> *Buffalo City Directory for the Year 1890* (Buffalo: Courier Co., 1890).

New Orleans
> *Soards' New Orleans City Directory for 1880* (New Orleans: L. Soards, 1880).
>
> *Soards' New Orleans City Directory for 1890* (New Orleans: L. Soards, 1890).

Pittsburgh
> *Directory of Pittsburgh and Allegheny Cities, 1880–1881* (Pittsburgh: J. F. Diffenbacher, 1880).
>
> *J. F. Diffenbacher's Directory of Pittsburgh and Allegheny Cities for 1890* (Pittsburgh: J. F. Diffenbacher, 1890).

Washington, D.C.
> *Boyd's Directory of the District of Columbia . . . 1880* (Washington, D.C.: Wm. H. Boyd, 1880).
>
> *Boyd's Directory of the District of Columbia . . . 1890* (Washington, D.C.: William H. Boyd, 1890).

Detroit
> *Detroit City Directory for 1880* (Detroit: J. W. Weeks, 1880).
>
> *Detroit City Directory for 1890* (Detroit: R. L. Polk, 1890).

Milwaukee
> *The Milwaukee Directory for 1880* (Milwaukee: William Hogg, 1880).
>
> *Wright's Directory for Milwaukee for 1890* (Milwaukee: Alfred G. Wright, 1890).

Newark, N.J.
> *Holbrook's Newark City Directory for the Year Ending April 1, 1881* (Newark: A. Holbrook, 1880).
>
> *Holbrook's Newark City and Business Directory, Official for the Year Ending May 1, 1891* (Newark: A. M. Holbrook, 1890).

Minneapolis
> *Minneapolis City Directory for 1880–1881* (Minneapolis: Johnson, Smith & Harrison, 1880).
>
> *Minneapolis City Directory for 1890–'91* (Minneapolis: Harrison & Smith, 1890).

Jersey City, N.J.
> No title page (Jersey City: William H. Boyd, 1880).
>
> *Gopsill's Jersey City . . . Directory, 1890–91* (Washington, D.C.: W. Andrew Boyd, 1890).

Louisville, Ken.
> *Caron's Directory for the City of Louisville for 1880* (Louisville: C. K. Caron, 1880).
>
> *Caron's Directory for the City of Louisville for 1890* (Louisville: C. K. Caron, 1890).

Omaha, Neb.
> *Wolfe's Omaha City Directory, 1880–81* (Omaha: J. M. Wolfe, 1880).
>
> *Omaha and South Omaha City Directory for 1890* (Omaha: J. M. Wolfe, 1890).

Rochester, N.Y.

The Rochester Directory . . . for the Year Beginning July 1, 1880 (Rochester: Drew, Allis, 1880).

The Rochester Directory . . . for the Year Beginning July 1, 1890 (Rochester: Drew, Allis, 1890).

St. Paul, Minn.

St. Paul City Directory, 1880–81 (St. Paul: R. L. Polk and J. D. Leonard, 1880).

R. L. Polk & Co's St. Paul City Directory, 1890–91 (St. Paul: R. L. Polk, 1890).

Kansas City, Mo.

Ballenger & Hoye's Tenth Annual City Directory . . . City of Kansas, Mo., 1880 (Kansas City: Ramsey, Millett & Hudson, 1880).

Hoye's City Directory of Kansas City, Mo., 1890–1891 (Kansas City: Hoye Directory Co., 1890).

Providence, R.I.

The Providence Directory . . . for the Year Commencing July 1, 1880 (Providence: Sampson, Davenport, 1880).

The Providence Directory . . . for the Year Commencing July 1, 1890 (Providence: Sampson, Murdock, 1890).

Denver, Col.

No directories consulted.

Indianapolis, Ind.

R. L. Polk & Co's Indianapolis Directory for 1880 (Indianapolis: R. L. Polk, 1880).

R. L. Polk & Co's Indianapolis Directory for 1890 (Indianapolis: R. L. Polk, 1890).

Allegheny, Pa.

Directory of Pittsburgh and Allegheny Cities, 1880–1881 (Pittsburgh: J. F. Diffenbacher, 1880).

J. F. Diffenbacher's Directory of Pittsburgh and Allegheny Cities for 1890 (Pittsburgh: J. F. Diffenbacher, 1890).

Albany, N.Y.

The Albany Directory for the Year 1880 (Albany: Sampson, Davenport, 1880).

The Albany Directory for the Year 1890 (Albany: Sampson, Murdock, 1890).

Columbus, Ohio

Columbus City Directory for 1880 (Columbus: G. J. Brand, 1880).

R. L. Polk & Co's Columbus City Directory, 1890–91 (Columbus: R. L. Polk, 1890).

Syracuse, N.Y.

Boyd's Syracuse City Directory, 1880–1881 (Syracuse: Boyd's Directory Corp., 1880).

Boyd's Syracuse City Directory, 1890–1891 (Syracuse: Boyd's Directory Corp., 1890).

New Haven, Conn.

Benham's New Haven City Directory, 1880 (New Haven: Price, Lee, 1880).

Benham's New Haven City Directory, 1890 (New Haven: Price, Lee, 1890).

Worcester, Mass.

The Worcester Directory . . . for the Year Beginning January 15, 1880 (Worcester: Drew, Allis, 1880).

The Worcester Directory . . . for the Year Beginning January 15, 1890 (Worcester: Drew, Allis, 1890).

Toledo, Ohio

R. L. Polk & Co's Toledo City Directory for 1879–80 (Toledo: R. L. Polk, 1879).

R. L. Polk & Co's Toledo City Directory for 1890–91 (Toledo: R. L. Polk, 1890).

Richmond, Va.
> *Chataigne's Richmond City Directory for the Years 1879–'80* (Richmond: J. H. Chataigne, 1879).
> No 1890 directory located.

Paterson, N.J.
> *Boyd's Patterson Directory . . . 1880–81* (Washington, D.C.: Wm. H. Boyd, 1880).
> *Boyd's Patterson Directory . . . 1890–91* (Paterson: George S. Boudinot, 1890).

Lowell, Mass.
> *The Lowell Directory, 1880* (Boston: Sampson, Davenport, 1879).
> *The Lowell Directory, 1890* (Boston: Sampson, Murdock, 1890).

Nashville, Tenn.
> *Nashville Directory . . . 1880* (Nashville: Marshall & Bruce, 1880).
> *Nashville Directory . . . 1890* (Nashville: Marshall & Bruce, 1890).

Scranton, Pa.
> *Lant Brothers' Scranton City Directory, 1880* (Scranton: M. W. Lant, 1880).
> *Williams' Scranton Directory for the Year 1890* (Scranton: J. E. Williams, 1890).

Fall River, Mass.
> *The Fall River Directory, 1880* (Boston: Sampson, Davenport, 1880).
> *The Fall River Directory, 1890* (Boston: Sampson, Davenport, 1890).

Cambridge, Mass.
> *Greenough's Cambridge Directory for 1880* (Boston: Greenough, 1880).
> *The Cambridge Directory, 1890* (Boston: W. A. Greenough, 1890).

Atlanta, Ga.
> *Sholes' Directory of the City of Atlanta for 1880* (Atlanta: A. E. Sholes, n.d.).
> *Atlanta City Directory for 1890* (Atlanta: R. L. Polk, 1890).

Memphis, Tenn.
> *Sholes' Memphis Directory for 1880* (Memphis: S. C. Toof, 1880).
> *Dow's City Directory of Memphis, for 1890* (Memphis: Harlow Dow, n.d.).

Wilmington, Del.
> *The Wilmington City Directory for 1880–81* (Wilmington: Ferris Bros., 1880).
> *The Wilmington City Directory for 1890* (Wilmington: W. Costa, 1890).

Dayton, Ohio
> *Proudfoot & Urquhart's Directory of Dayton . . . for 1880–81* (Dayton: Proudfoot & Urquhart, 1880).
> *Williams' Dayton City and Montgomery County Directory for 1890–91* (n.p.: Williams, 1890).

Troy, N.Y.
> *The Troy Directory, for the Year 1880* (Troy : Sampson, Davenport, 1880).
> *The Directory of Troy . . . for the Year Commencing June 15, 1890* (Troy: Sampson, Murdock, 1890).

Grand Rapids, Mich.
> *Grand Rapids City Directory, 1880–81* (Grand Rapids: R. L. Polk, 1880).
> *R. L. Polk & Co's Grand Rapids Directory, 1890* (Grand Rapids: R. L. Polk, 1890).

Reading, Pa.
> *Boyd's Reading City Directory . . . 1880–1881* (Reading: W. Harry Boyd, 1880).
> *Reading City Directory . . . 1890–1891* (Reading: W. H. Boyd, 1890).

Camden, N.J.
No directories consulted.

Trenton, N.J.
Fitzgerald's Trenton and Mercer County Directory, 1880 (Trenton: Thomas F. Fitzgerald, 1880).
Fitzgerald's Trenton and Mercer County Directory, 1889 (Trenton: Thomas F. Fitzgerald, 1889).

Lynn, Mass.
No title page (Boston: Sampson, Davenport, 1880).
The Lynn Directory, 1890 (Boston: Sampson, Murdock, 1890).

Lincoln, Neb.
No directories consulted.

Charleston, S.C.
Sholes' Diretory of the City of Charleston, November 15, 1879 (Charleston: A. E. Sholes, 1879).
The Charleston City Directory, 1890 (Charleston: Walker, Evans & Cogswell, 1890).

Hartford, Conn.
Geer's Hartford City Directory . . . July, 1880 (Hartford: Elihu Geer, 1880).
Geer's Hartford City Directory . . . July, 1890 (Hartford: Hartford Printing Co., 1890).

St. Joseph, Mo.
No directories consulted.

Evansville, Ind.
Williams' Evansville City Directory for 1880 (Evansville: Williams, 1880).
Bennett & Co's Evansville City Directory for 1890 (Evansville: Courier Co., 1890).

Los Angeles
Los Angeles City Directory for 1879–80 (Los Angeles: Morris & Wright, 1879).
Los Angeles City Directory, 1890 (Los Angeles: W. H. L. Corran, 1890).

Des Moines, Iowa
Bushnell's Des Moines Residence and Business City Directory, 1881–1882 (Des Moines: J. P. Bushnell, 1881).
Bushnell's Des Moines City Directory, 1890 (Des Moines: Bushnell, 1890).

Time-Series Study of Medium-Sized Cities, 1880 through 1890

(Includes all cities with an 1880 population between 45,000 and 250,000, listed by 1880 population size.)

San Francisco
Langley's San Francisco Directory . . . (San Francisco: Francis, Valentine, 1880–1890).

New Orleans
Soards' New Orleans City Directory (New Orleans: L. Soards, 1880–1890).

Cleveland, Ohio
The Cleveland City Directory (Cleveland: Cleveland Directory Co., 1880–1890).

Pittsburgh
Directory of Pittsburgh and Allegheny Cities, 1880–1881 (Pittsburgh: J. F. Diffenbacher, 1880).

J. F. Diffenbacher's Directory of Pittsburgh and Allegheny Cities (Pittsburgh: J. F. Diffenbacher, 1882–1890).

Buffalo, N.Y.
Buffalo City Directory (Buffalo: Courier Co., 1880–1890).

Washington, D.C.
Boyd's Directory of the District of Columbia (Washington, D.C.: Wm. H. Boyd, 1880–1890).

Newark, N.J.
Holbrook's Newark City Directory (Newark: A. M. Holbrook, 1880–1890).

Louisville, Ken.
Caron's Directory for the City of Louisville (Louisville: C. K. Caron, 1880–1890).

Jersey City, N.J.
No title page (Jersey City: William H. Boyd, 1880).
Gopsill's Jersey City . . . Directory (Washington, D.C.: W. Andrew Boyd, 1881–1890).

Detroit
Detroit City Directory (Detroit: J. W. Weeks, 1880–1885).
Detroit City Directory (Detroit: R. L. Polk, 1886–1890).

Milwaukee, Wisc.
The Milwaukee Directory for 1880 (Milwaukee: William Hogg, 1880).
The Milwaukee Directory for 1881 (Milwaukee: Hogg, Wright, 1881).
Wright's Directory for Milwaukee (Milwaukee: Alfred G. Wright, 1882–1890).

Providence, R.I.
The Providence Directory . . . (Providence: Sampson, Davenport, 1880–1884).
The Providence Directory . . . (Providence: Sampson, Murdock, 1885–1890).

Albany, N.Y.
The Albany Directory (Albany: Sampson, Davenport, 1880–1885).
The Albany Directory (Albany: Sampson, Murdock, 1886–1890).

Rochester, N.Y.
The Rochester Directory . . . (Rochester: Drew, Allis, 1880–1890).

Allegheny, Pa.
Directory of Pittsburgh and Allegheny Cities, 1880–1881 (Pittsburgh: J. F. Diffenbacher, 1880).
J. F. Diffenbacher's Directory of Pittsburgh and Allegheny Cities (Pittsburgh: J. F. Diffenbacher, 1882–1890).

Indianapolis, Ind.
R. L. Polk & Co's Indianapolis Directory (Indianapolis: R. L. Polk, 1880–1890).

Richmond, Va.
Complete series unavailable.

New Haven, Conn.
Benham's New Haven City Directory (New Haven: Price, Lee, 1880–1890).

Lowell, Mass.
The Lowell Directory (Boston: Sampson, Davenport, 1879–1881, 1883–1885).
No 1882–1883 directory published.
The Lowell Directory (Boston: Sampson, Murdock, 1886–1890).

Worcester, Mass.
The Worcester Directory . . . (Worcester: Drew, Allis, 1880–1890).

Troy, N.Y.
> *The Troy Directory* (Troy: Sampson, Davenport, 1880–1885).
> *The Directory of Troy* . . . (Troy: Sampson, Murdock, 1886–1890).

Kansas City, Mo.
> *Ballenger & Hoye's Tenth Annual City Directory* . . . *City of Kansas, Mo., 1880* (Kansas City: Ramsey, Millett & Hudson, 1880).
> *Hoye's Kansas City Directory for the Year 1881* (Kansas City: Ramsey, Millett & Hudson, 1881).
> *Hoye's City Directory of Kansas City, Mo.* (Kansas City: Hoye Directory Co., 1882–1890).

Cambridge, Mass.
> *Greenough's Cambridge Directory* (Boston: Greenough, 1880–1883).
> *The Cambridge Directory* (Boston: W. A. Greenough, 1884–1890).

Syracuse, N.Y.
> *Boyd's Syracuse City Directory* (Syracuse: Boyd's Directory Corp., 1880–1890).

Columbus, Ohio
> *Columbus City Directory* (Columbus: G. J. Brand, 1880–1882).
> *Williams' Columbus City Directory* (Columbus: Williams, 1883–1886).
> *Wiggins' Columbus City Directory* (Columbus: J. Wiggins, 1887–1888).
> *R. L. Polk & Co's Columbus City Directory* (Columbus: R. L. Polk, 1889–1890).

Paterson, N.J.
> *Boyd's Patterson Directory* . . . (Washington, D.C.: Wm. H. Boyd, 1880–1888).
> *Boyd's Patterson Directory* . . . (Paterson: George S. Boudinot, 1889–1890).

Toledo, Ohio
> *R. L. Polk & Co's Toledo City Directory* (Toledo: R. L. Polk, 1879–1890).

Charleston, S.C.
> Complete series unavailable.

Fall River, Mass.
> Complete series unavailable.

Minneapolis, Minn.
> *Minneapolis City Directory* (Minneapolis: Johnson, Smith & Harrison, 1880–1886).
> *Minneapolis City Directory* (Minneapolis: Harrison & Smith, 1887–1890).

Longitudinal Study of Four Major Cities, 1850–1940

Boston
> *The Directory of the City of Boston* . . . *from July 1850, to July 1851* (Boston: George Adams, 1850).
> Boston directory for 1861 (no bibliographic data).
> *The Boston Directory* . . . *for the Year Commencing July 1, 1880* (Boston: Sampson, Davenport, 1880).
> *The Boston Directory* . . . *for the Year Commencing July 1, 1900* (Boston: Sampson, Murdock, 1900).
> *The Boston Directory* . . . *for the Year Commencing July 1, 1920* (Boston: Sampson, Murdock, 1920).
> *The Boston Directory* . . . *for the Year Commencing August 1, 1930* (Boston: Sampson, Murdock, 1930).
> *The Boston Directory* . . . *for the Year Commencing July 1, 1940* (Boston: R. L. Polk, 1940).

Milwaukee, Wisc.

The Milwaukee City Directory for 1851–2 (Milwaukee: Parsons & Van Slyck, 1851).

1860–61 Directory of the City of Milwaukee (Milwaukee: Starr & Son, 1860).

The Milwaukee Directory for 1880 (Milwaukee: William Hogg, 1880).

Wright's Directory of Milwaukee for 1900 (Milwaukee: Alfred G. Wright, 1900).

Wright's Milwaukee City Directory . . . 1920 (Milwaukee: Wright Directory Co., 1920).

Milwaukee Directory for 1930 (no bibliographic data).

Wright's Milwaukee City Directory, 1940 (Milwaukee: Wright Directory Co., 1940).

New Orleans

Cohen's New Orleans and Lafayette Directory . . . 1850 (New Orleans: n.p., 1849).

Gardner's New Orleans Directory for 1861 (New Orleans: Charles Gardner, 1861).

Soards' New Orleans City Directory for 1880 (New Orleans: L. Soards, 1880).

Soards' New Orleans City Directory for 1900 (New Orleans: Soards Directory Co., 1900).

Soards' New Orleans City Directory for 1920 (New Orleans: Soards Directory Co., 1920).

Soards' New Orleans City Directory for 1930 (New Orleans: Soards Directory Co., 1930).

Polk's New Orleans City Directory for 1940 (New Orleans: R. L. Polk, 1940).

San Francisco, CA

The San Francisco City Directory . . . September 1, 1850 (San Francisco: Charles P. Kimball, 1850).

The San Francisco Directory for the Year Commencing September, 1861 (San Francisco: Valentine, 1861).

Langley's San Francisco Directory for the Year Commencing April, 1880 (San Francisco: Francis, Valentine, 1880).

Crocker-Langley San Francisco Directory for the Year Commencing May, 1900 (San Francisco: H. S. Crocker Co., 1900).

San Francisco Directory for 1920 (no bibliographic data).

San Francisco Directory for 1930 (no bibliographic data).

San Francisco Directory for 1940 (no bibliographic data).

Sample Coding-Scheme

City Name:

Directory Date of Publication:

Comments:

Benefit Clubs: _____(total)

_____F1   Masonic

_____F2   Veterans

_____F3   Non-Masonic

_____B6   Pay-in insurance (nonfraternal)

_____F8   Temperance fraternity

_____F4   patriotic/nativist fraternity (e.g., American Protestant Association)

Charitable Organizations: _____ (total)

_____B1   Charitable-general

_____B2   Charitable-religious

_____B3   Charitable-veterans

_____B4   Charitable-occupational

_____B5   Charitable-ethnic/national

Commercial Organizations: _____ (total)

_____C2   Commercial group (white collar)

_____C4   Professional organization

Labor/Farm Organizations: _____ (total)

_____C1   Unions/trade organization (blue collar)

_____F9   Labor fraternity

_____C6   Agricultural

Cultural Clubs: _____ (total)

_____M1   Arts/music/literary club

_____M2   Sporting club (nonmilitary)

_____M3   Scientific/learned society

_____M4   National, ethnic, or racial (nonbenefit)

_____M5   Local social club

_____M6   Militias/military training group

_____M7   Horticultural

_____M8   Political/reform

Religious Groups: _____ (total)

_____R1   Catholic Church

_____R2   Protestant Church

_____R2a   Colored (Protestant) Church

_____R3   Non-Christian Congregation

_____R5   Temperance/reform (nonfraternal)

_____R6   Proselytizing organization

_____R7   Church-related social group

Unknown (unidentifiable): _____ (total)

_____U1   Unknown:

Total: _____

Groups of Note:

NOTES

Introduction

1. Arthur M. Schlesinger, "Biography of a Nation of Joiners," *American Historical Review*, vol. 50, no. 1 (October 1944): 1–25. In all honesty, the noun *associationalism* may be a word of my own construction, borrowed from casual references elsewhere in the literature to the thing that people do when they are in the habit of forming associations. The *Oxford English Dictionary*, 2nd ed. (online) does contain a reference to this word but refers to it as a variant of the philosophical term *associationism*, or "the doctrine that mental and moral phenomena may be accounted for by association of ideas."

2. W. S. Harwood, "Secret Societies in America," *North American Review*, vol. 164, no. 486 (May 1897): 622–623, emphases added.

3. David T. Beito, *From Mutual Aid to the Welfare State: Fraternal Societies and Social Services, 1890–1967* (Chapel Hill: University of North Carolina Press, 2000); Robert D. Putnam, *Bowling Alone: The Collapse and Revival of American Community* (New York: Simon & Schuster, 2000); Theda Skocpol, "The Tocqueville Problem: Civic Engagement in American Democracy," *Social Science History*, vol. 21, no. 4 (Winter 1997): 455–479.

4. Putnam, *Bowling Alone*, pp. 383–384 and all of chap. 23, "Lessons of History: The Gilded Age and the Progressive Era." Also Gerald Gamm and Robert D. Putnam, "The Growth of Voluntary Associations in America, 1840–1940," *Journal of Interdisciplinary History*, vol. 29, no. 3 (1999): 511–557.

5. Schlesinger, "Biography of a Nation of Joiners," p. 1; emphasis added.

6. Alexis de Tocqueville, *Democracy in America*, George Lawrence, trans. (New York: Harper & Row, [1966] 1988), p. 515.

7. See, for example, Benjamin R. Barber, "An American Civic Forum: Civil Society Between Market Individuals and the Political Community," *Social Philosophy and Policy*, vol. 13, no. 1 (1996): 269–283; Beito, *From Mutual Aid to the Welfare State*; Jean L. Cohen and Andrew Arato, *Civil Society and Political Theory* (Cambridge, Mass.: MIT Press, 1994); Amitai, Etzioni, ed., *Rights and the Common Good: The Communitarian Perspective* (New York: St. Martin, 1995); Marvin Olasky, *The Tragedy of American Compassion* (Wheaton, Ill.: Crossway Books, 1992); James Q. Wilson, "The Rise of the Bureaucratic State," *Public Interest*, vol. 41 (Fall 1975): 88–89.

8. Tocqueville, *Democracy in America*, p. 515.

9. Robert D. Putnam, with Robert Leonardi and Raffaella Y. Nanetti, *Making Democracy Work: Civic Traditions of Modern Italy* (Princeton, N.J.: Princeton University Press, 1993), p. 167. Another classic text in this tradition is Edward C. Banfield, *The Moral Basis of a Backward Society* (Glencoe, Ill.: Free Press, 1958). Banfield frequently contrasts the vibrant associational life of Americans to the "amoral familism" of Southern Italy—"the inability of the villagers to act together for their common good or, indeed, for any end transcending the immediate, material interest of the nuclear family" (p. 10).

10. Tocqueville, *Democracy in America*, p. 517.

11. For a general overview of these competing depictions of American associationalism, see Jason Kaufman, "Three Views of Associationalism in 19th Century America: An Empirical Examination," *American Journal of Sociology*, vol. 104, no. 5 (March 1999): 34–83. Also see Bob Edwards, Michael W. Foley, and Mario Diani, eds., *Beyond Tocqueville: Civil Society and Social Capital in Comparative Perspective* (Hanover, N.H.: University Press of New England, 2001); and Amy Gutmann, ed., *Freedom of Association* (Princeton, N.J.: Princeton University Press, 1998). For a view that attempts to brace both conceptions of associations in action, see Jane J. Mansbridge, *Beyond Adversary Democracy* (Chicago: University of Chicago Press, 1980).

12. James Madison, "Federalist Paper No. 10," *The Federalist Papers*, Clinton Rossiter, ed. (New York: Mentor, [1788] 1961), p. 79; emphasis added.

13. George Miller Calhoun, *Athenian Clubs in Politics and Litigation* (Austin: University of Texas, 1913), p. 2. Also Josiah Ober, *Mass and Elite in Democratic Athens: Rhetoric, Ideology, and the Power of the People* (Princeton, N.J.: Princeton University Press, 1989); I. F. Stone, *The Trial of Socrates* (Boston: Little, Brown, 1988), p. 142.

14. For example, Benjamin R. Barber, *A Place for Us: How to Make Society Civil and Democracy Strong* (New York: Hill & Wang, 1998); Amitai Etzioni, ed., *The Essential Communitarian Reader* (Lanham, Md.: Rowman & Littlefied, 1998); Olasky, *Tragedy of American Compassion*; Robert D. Putnam, "Bowling Alone: America's Declining Social Capital," *Journal of Democracy*, vol. 6 (1995): 65–78; Putnam, *Bowling Alone*. For survey research on American civic participation, see Gabriel A. Almond and Sidney Verba, *The Civic Culture: Political Attitudes and Democracy in Five Nations* (Princeton, N. J.: Princeton University Press, 1963); Seymour Martin Lipset, *Continental Divide: The Values and Institutions of the United States and Canada* (New York: Routledge, 1990); Sidney Verba, Kay Lehman Schlozman, and Henry E. Brady, *Voice and Equality: Civic Voluntarism in American Politics* (Cambridge, Mass.: Harvard University Press, 1995); Robert Wuthnow, *Sharing the Journey: Support Groups and America's New Quest for Community* (New York: Free Press, 1994).

15. Skocpol, "Tocqueville Problem." Also John P Heinz, Edward O. Laumann, Robert L. Nelson, and Robert H. Salisbury, *The Hollow Core: Private Interests in National Policy Making* (Cambridge, Mass.: Harvard University Press, 1993); Darrell M. West and Burdett A. Loomis, *The Sound of Money: How Political Interests Get What They Want* (New York: Norton, 1999). Cf. Michael Schudson, *The Good Citizen: A History of American Civic Life* (New York: Free Press, 1998).

16. Glenn R. Carroll, "Organizational Ecology," *Annual Review of Sociology*, vol. 10 (1984): 71–93; Michael T. Hannan and John Freeman, *Organizational Ecology* (Cambridge, Mass.: Harvard University Press, 1989); Debra C. Minkoff, *Organizing for Equality: The Evolution of Women's and Racial-Ethnic Organizations in America, 1955–1985* (New Brunswick, N.J.: Rutgers University Press, 1995); Jitendra V. Singh and Charles Lumsden, "Theory and Research in Organizational Ecology," *Annual Review of Sociology*, vol. 16 (1990): 161–195.

17. Paul J. DiMaggio and Walter W. Powell, "The Iron Cage Revisited: Institutional Isomorphism and Collective Rationality in Organizational Fields," *American Sociological Review*, vol. 48 (1983): 147–160; John Meyer and Bryan Rowan, "Institutionalized Organizations: Formal Structure as Myth and Ceremony," *American Journal of Sociology*, vol. 83 (1977): 340–363; Arthur L. Stinchcombe, "Social Structure and Organizations," in James March, ed., *Handbook of Organizations* (New York: Rand McNally, 1965).

18. John Freeman and Michael T. Hannan, "Growth and Decline Processes in Organizations," *American Sociological Review*, vol. 40 (1975): 215–228; John Freeman and Michael T. Hannan, "Niche Width and the Dynamics of Organizational Populations," *American*

Journal of Sociology, vol. 88 (1983): 1116–1145; Hannan and Freeman, *Organizational Ecology*; Michael T. Hannan and John Freeman, "The Population Ecology of Organizations," *American Journal of Sociology*, vol. 82 (1977): 929–964.

19. By 1915, the order reportedly had 128,000 members. Alvin J. Schmidt, *Fraternal Organizations* (Westport, Conn.: Greenwood, 1980), p. 181.

20. Roger Finke and Rodney Stark, *The Churching of America: Winners and Losers in our Religious Economy* (New Brunswick, N.J.: Rutgers University Press, 1992); Peter Dobkin Hall, "A Historical Overview of the Private Nonprofit Sector," in Walter W. Powell, ed., *The Nonprofit Sector: A Research Handbook* (New Haven, Conn.: Yale University Press, 1987); Jason Kaufman, "The Political Economy of Inter-Denominational Competition in Late 19th Century American Cities," *Journal of Urban History* (forthcoming); R. Laurence Moore, *Selling God: American Religion in the Marketplace of Culture* (New York: Oxford University Press, 1994); Michael P. Young, "Confessional Protest: The Evangelical Origins of Social Movements in the United States, 1800–1840," PhD. dissertation, Department of Sociology, New York University, New York, 2000.

21. See Peter M. Blau, *Inequality and Heterogeneity: A Primitive Theory of Social Structure* (New York: Free Press, 1977); Claude S. Fischer, "The Subcultural Theory of Urbanism: A Twentieth-Year Assessment," *American Journal of Sociology*, vol. 101, no. 3 (1995): 543–577; Janet Tai Landa, *Trust, Ethnicity, and Identity: Beyond the New Institutional Economics of Ethnic Trading Networks, Contract Law, and Gift-Exchange* (Ann Arbor: University of Michigan Press, 1994); Noah Mark, "Beyond Individual Differences: Social Differentiation from First Principles," *American Sociological Review*, vol. 63 (1998): 309–330; J. Miller McPherson and James R. Ranger-Moore, "Evolution on a Dancing Landscape: Organizations and Networks in Dynamic Blau Space," *Social Forces*, vol. 70, no. 1 (1991): 19–42; Mancur Olson, *The Logic of Collective Action* (Cambridge, Mass.: Harvard University Press, 1965); Susan Olzak, *The Dynamics of Ethnic Competition and Conflict* (Stanford, Cal.: Stanford University Press, 1992); Pamela A. Popielarz and J. Miller McPherson, "On the Edge or in Between: Niche Position, Niche Overlap, and the Duration of Voluntary Association Memberships," *American Journal of Sociology*, vol. 101, no. 3 (1995): 698–720; Robert H. Salisbury, "An Exchange Theory of Interest Groups," *Midwest Journal of Political Science*, vol. 13, no. 1 (1969): 1–32; Charles Tilly, *Durable Inequality* (Berkeley: University of California Press, 1998).

22. This is a central assertion of Robert Putnam's best-selling *Bowling Alone*.

23. Louis Hartz, *The Liberal Tradition in America: An Interpretation of American Political Thought Since the Revolution* (New York: Harcourt, Brace & World, 1955); Samuel P. Huntington, *Political Order in Changing Societies* (New Haven, Conn.: Yale University Press, 1968).

24. Richard Franklin Bensel, *Sectionalism and American Political Development, 1880–1980* (Madison: University of Wisconsin Press, 1984); Elizabeth Sanders, *Roots of Reform: Farmers, Workers, and the American State, 1877–1917* (Chicago: University of Chicago Press, 1999).

25. Richard Franklin Bensel, *Yankee Leviathan: The Origins of Central State Authority in America, 1859–1877* (Cambridge: Cambridge University Press, 1990); Theda Skocpol, *Protecting Soldiers and Mothers: The Political Origins of Social Policy in the United States* (Cambridge: Belknap, 1992); Stephen Skowronek, *Building a New American State: The Expansion of National Administrative Capacities, 1877–1920* (Cambridge: Cambridge University Press, 1982).

26. Elisabeth S. Clemens, *The People's Lobby: Organizational Innovation and the Rise of Interest Group Politics in the United States, 1890–1925* (Chicago: University of Chicago Press, 1997); J. P. Nettl, "The State as a Conceptual Variable," *World Politics*, 1967–1968, 559–592;

Martin Shefter, "Party and Patronage," *Politics and Society*, vol. 7(1977): 404–451; Skocpol, *Protecting Soldiers and Mothers*.

27. Frederick Jackson Turner, *The Frontier in American History* (New York: H. Holt, 1920). Also Richard Hofstadter and Seymour Martin Lipset, eds., *Turner and the Sociology of the Frontier* (New York: Basic Books, 1968).

28. Daniel Bell, *The End of Ideology: On The Exhaustion of Political Ideas in the Fifties* (Glencoe, Ill.: Free Press, 1960); Lipset, *Continental Divide*.

29. Robert R. Alford, "Class Voting in the Anglo-American Political Systems," in Seymour Martin Lipset and Stein Rokkan, eds., *Party Systems and Voter Alignments: Cross-National Perspectives* (New York: Free Press, 1967); Nathan Glazer and Daniel P. Moynihan, *Beyond the Melting Pot*, 2nd ed. (Cambridge, Mass.: MIT Press, 1963); Ira Katznelson and Aristide R. Zolberg, eds., *Working-Class Formation: Nineteenth-Century Patterns in Western Europe and the United States* (Princeton, N.J.: Princeton University Press, 1986); Jeff Manza and Clem Brooks, *Social Cleavages and Political Change: Voter Alignments and U.S. Party Coalitions* (New York: Oxford University Press, 1999); Seymour Martin Lipset and Gary Marks, *It Didn't Happen Here: Why Socialism Failed in the United States* (New York: Norton, 2000). Naturally, it is a vast overstatement to say that American society lacked, or lacks, vivid class distinctions. As historian Sven Beckert has shown, American merchants and manufacturers frequented many elite social clubs toward the end of the nineteenth century. Nonetheless, those eligible for membership in such organizations represent a tiny fraction of the total American population at the time. See Sven Beckert, *The Monied Metropolis: New York City and the Consolidation of the American Bourgeoisie, 1850–1896* (New York: Cambridge University Press, 2001); and Stuart M. Blumin, *The Emergence of the Middle Class: Social Experience in the American City, 1760–1900* (Cambridge: Cambridge University Press, 1989).

30. John Bodnar, *The Transplanted: A History of Immigrants in Urban America* (Bloomington: University of Indiana Press, 1985); Will Herberg, *Protestant—Catholic—Jew: An Essay in American Religious Sociology* (Garden City, N.Y.: Doubleday, 1955); John Higham, *Strangers in the Land: Patterns of American Nativism, 1860–1925* (New Brunswick, N.J.: Rutgers University Press, 1955). For more theoretically informed accounts of how this process might work, see Michael Hechter, "Group Formation and the Cultural Division of Labor," *American Journal of Sociology*, vol. 84, no. 2 (September 1978): 293–318; Mark, "Beyond Individual Differences"; McPherson and Ranger-Moore, "Evolution on a Dancing Landscape"; Popielarz and McPherson, "On the Edge or in Between." For an exceedingly intelligent defense of associational exclusivity, see Nancy L. Rosenblum, *Membership and Morals: The Personal Uses of Pluralism in America* (Princeton, N.J.: Princeton University Press, 1998), in which she says, "Loathsome groups can be lifelines" (p. 22). Exclusive groups nurture pluralism, she argues, because they help contain diverse points of view, even those we would rather do without. For an equally nuanced rebuttal, see Michael Walzer, "On Involuntary Association," in Amy Gutmann, ed., *Freedom of Association* (Princeton, N.J.: Princeton University Press, 1998). An article by Rosenblum follows Walzer's, restating her position on this matter.

31. Schlesinger, "Biography of a Nation of Joiners," p. 23.

32. *Boston Directory . . . for the Year Commencing July 1, 1900* (Boston: Sampson, Murdock, 1900), pp. 2104–2114. Information on the membership requirements of these lodges was then derived from Schmidt, *Fraternal Organizations*.

33. Albert O. Hirschman, *Exit, Voice, and Loyalty : Responses to Decline in Firms, Organizations, and States* (Cambridge, Mass.: Harvard University Press, 1970); Mark E. Warren, *Democracy and Association* (Princeton, N.J.: Princeton University Press, 2001).

34. For an excellent comparative history of identity construction in two very different democratic societies, I recommend Donald L. Horowitz and Gérard Noirel, *Immigrants in Two Democracies: French and American Experience* (New York: New York University Press, 1992). For a comparable account of contemporary differences in identity construction among French and American men, see Michele Lamont, *Money, Morals, and Manners: The Culture of the French and American Upper-Middle Class* (Chicago: University of Chicago Press, 1992); and Michele Lamont, *The Dignity of Working Men: Morality and the Boundaries of Race, Class, and Immigration* (Cambridge, Mass.: Harvard University Press, 2000).

35. Indeed, although the Progressive Era reforms are one viable product of the associational boom, they are notable for their regulatory, rather than redistributive, approaches to government action.

36. For a sampling of recent scholarly work that views American political development from a comparative-historical perspective, see Francis G. Castles, ed., *The Comparative History of Public Policy* (Cambridge: Polity Press, 1989); Gary Marks, *Unions in Politics: Britain, Germany, and the United States in the Nineteenth and Early Twentieth Centuries* (Princeton, N.J.: Princeton University Press); Ann Shola Orloff, *The Politics of Pensions: A Comparative Analysis of Britain, Canada, and the United States, 1880–1940* (Madison: University of Wisconsin Press, 1993); Daniel T. Rodgers, *Atlantic Crossings: Social Politics in a Progressive Age* (Cambridge: Belknap, 1998); Skocpol, *Protecting Soldiers and Mothers*; Margaret Weir, Ann Shola Orloff, and Theda Skocpol, eds., *The Politics of Social Policy in the United States* (Princeton, N.J.: Princeton University Press, 1988).

37. The analysis described here is outlined in my 1999 article, "Three Views of Associationalism," pp. 1296–1345.

38. The initial results of these two studies are detailed in my 1999 article with Steven J. Tepper, "Groups or Gatherings? Sources of Political Engagement in 19th Century American Cities," *Voluntas: The International Journal of Voluntary and Nonprofit Organizations*, vol. 10, no. 4 (December): 299–322; and in my own "Rise and Fall of a Nation of Joiners: The Knights of Labor Revisited," *Journal of Interdisciplinary History*, vol. 31, no. 4 (Spring 2001): 553–579. Students in my spring 2000 junior tutorial in the Sociology Department at Harvard College on civil society and participatory democracy provided invaluable assistance in collecting and coding much of these data, as did Gian Pangaro, Evelina Fedorenko, and David Weintraub, all of whom worked as research assistants on this project.

39. Though some may question my choice of Boston as a test case, given its twentieth-century tradition of racial intolerance and segregation, it presented itself as a good opportunity for an in-depth analysis for several reasons: (1) The population of Boston was fairly stable over this period (relative to other American cities); (2) it was fairly diverse, both ethnically and religiously, and its tradition of sectarian conflict seemed to offer a good opportunity to ponder the contribution of Boston's many civic associations to its political landscape; (3) it is reputed to have had a long tradition of civic and political activism; (4) the city itself has a well-documented social and political history; and (5) Boston exists in living color just outside my office window, temptation enough for any curious historian. Nonetheless, disparities surely exist between Boston and other cities.

40. *Langley's San Francisco Directory for the Year Commencing April, 1880* (San Francisco: Francis, Valentine, 1880), p. 1117; emphasis added. See chapter 2 for a full explication of the data I used to confirm this assertion.

41. I relied primarily on Schmidt, *Fraternal Organizations*; and Albert C. Stevens, *The Cyclopedia of Fraternities* (New York: E. B. Treat, 1907), though other such references abound.

Chapter 1

1. H. Morton Bodfish, ed., *History of Building and Loan in the United States* (Chicago: United States Building and Loan League, 1931), pp. 33–34. Also Frank P. Bennett, Jr., *The Story of Mutual Savings Banks* (Boston: Frank P. Bennett, 1924); Heather A. Haveman and Hayagreeva Rao, "Structuring a Theory of Moral Sentiments: Institutional and Organizational Coevolution in the Early Thrift Industry," *American Journal of Sociology*, vol. 102 (1997): 1606–1651; John Lintner, *Mutual Savings Banks in the Savings and Mortgage Markets* (Boston: Andover Press, 1948).

2. Bodfish, *History of Building and Loan*, p. 34.

3. Text reprinted ibid., p. 36.

4. Alexis de Tocqueville, *Democracy in America*, George Lawrence, trans. (New York: Harper & Row, [1966] 1988), p. 514.

5. Ibid., p. 189.

6. Quoted in Bodfish, *History of Building and Loan*, p. 49.

7. Most of the members of the Oxford Provident were employees of Frankford's textile mills. Many subsequent building and loan societies were founded around ethnic, ethnonational, and ethnoreligious lines, such as the Amerikanischer Darlehen and Bau Verein [*sic*], founded in 1846 by and for Philadelphia's burgeoning German population. It was not until 1848 that any building and loan in America (Philadelphia's Abolition Association) even considered accepting African Americans as members, though it is not known whether any black members were actually ever admitted. See ibid., pp. 78–79.

8. See, for example, *Moose Lodge No. 107 v. Irvis*, 407 U.S. 163 (1972); *Cornelius v. Benevolent Protective Order of the Elks*, 382 F. Supp. 1182 (1974); *Roberts v. Jaycees*, 468 U.S. 609 (1984); *Rotary International v. Rotary Club of Duarte*, 481 U.S. 537 (1987); *New York State Club Assn. v. City of New York*, 487 U.S. 1 (1988). Two recent scholarly articles that describe and defend the fraternal right of exclusion are Douglas O. Linder, "Comment: Freedom of Association After *Roberts v. United States Jaycees*," *Michigan Law Review*, vol. 82 (1984): 1878–1903; Nancy L. Rosenblum, "Compelled Association: Public Standing, Self-Respect, and the Dynamic of Exclusion," in Amy Gutmann, ed., *Freedom of Association* (Princeton, N.J.: Princeton University Press, 1998).

9. *Moose Lodge v. Irvis*; the opinion cited was written by Justice Rehnquist. The statute from the Constitution and General Laws of the Loyal Order of the Moose is excerpted from the published court opinions in the case of *Cornelius v. Elks*. Note, however, that the Moose made some effort to revise their membership requirements in 1973, opening the lodge to all males over 25 years of age, following the proceedings in *Moose Lodge v. Irvis*.

10. My source for this quote is Alvin J. Schmidt, *Fraternal Organizations* (Westport, Conn.: Greenwood, 1980), p. 103. Schmidt mentions reading the *Proceedings* of the Elk's annual grand lodge sessions but does not offer an exact citation for this quote. Nonetheless, the blackball is a quintessential element of fraternal practice. Whether or not every Elks' lodge in the country might blackball nonwhite candidates, the potential for such practices surely exists.

11. For contrasting views on the presence of class solidarity in American voluntary organizations, see E. Digby Baltzell, *The Protestant Establishment: Aristocracy and Caste in America* (New York: Random House, 1964); Sven Beckert, *The Monied Metropolis: New York City and the Consolidation of the American Bourgeoisie, 1850–1896* (New York: Cambridge University Press, 2001); Stuart M. Blumin, *The Emergence of the Middle Class: Social Experience in the American City, 1760–1900* (Cambridge: Cambridge University Press, 1989); Mary Ann Clawson, *Constructing Brotherhood: Class, Gender, and Fraternalism* (Princeton, N.J.: Princeton University Press, 1989); Peter Dobkin Hall, *The Organization of American Cul-*

ture, 1700–1900: Private Institutions, Elites, and the Origins of American Nationality (New York: New York University Press, 1982); David C. Hammack, *Power and Society: Greater New York at the Turn of the Century* (New York: Russell Sage Foundation, 1982); Ira Katznelson, *City Trenches: Urban Politics and the Patterning of Class in the United States* (Chicago: University of Chicago Press, 1982); Ira Katznelson and Aristide R. Zolberg, eds., *Working-Class Formation: Nineteenth-Century Patterns in Western Europe and the United States* (Princeton, N.J.: Princeton University Press, 1986).

12. Lodge information for 1900 comes from *The Boston Directory . . . for the Year Commencing July 1, 1900* (Boston: Sampson, Murdock, 1900). Information on the membership requirements of these lodges was derived from Schmidt, *Fraternal Organizations*. Lodges that could not be found in Schmidt (or elsewhere) are listed here as "no data" unless there was good reason to believe that they would have had race-, religion-, or gender-specific preferences (e.g., a group by and for Irishmen would be presumed to be for men only and for Christians only, though this could not be confirmed with secondary source material). Such groups were listed as having de facto exclusionary policies since specific restrictions were not described in their membership requirements. De facto barriers to entry may have been intentional, as in the case of nativist orders, or unintentional, as in the case of orders created for explicit ethnic and religious groups (such as the Scottish Order of Clans or the Sons of Hermann). A good number of the "no data" groups probably had similar de facto policies, though the figures offered here err on the safe side by making no assumptions about groups with unlisted membership policies.

13. There were 56 orders in Boston in 1900, with a total of 854 separate lodges.

14. The French Archives Nationales are filled with nineteenth-century police surveillance records that reported on the activities of local associations. Precise information about the size and scope of French associational activity is amazingly difficult to come by, however. I consulted a copy of the April 10th, 1834, decree on the loi sur les Associations in the Bibliothèque Nationale. For more general information on the history of French associationalism, I have relied on the "Association" entry in the *Pierre Larousse Grand Dictionaire Universel du XIX⁹ Siecle, Vol. I, deuxieme partie* (Geneve: Slatkine, [1866–1879] 1982), p. 798.

15. Robert J. Goldstein, *Political Repression in 19th Century Europe* (Totowa, N.J.: Barnes & Noble, 1983), pp. 47–48; Gérald Noirel, "Difficulties in French Historical Research on Immigration," in Donald L. Horowitz and Gérard Noirel, eds., *Immigrants in Two Democracies: French and American Experience* (New York: New York University Press, 1992).

16. P. H. J. H. Gosden, *The Friendly Societies in England, 1815–1875* (Manchester: Manchester University Press, 1961); Roy Lubove, *The Struggle for Social Security, 1900–1935* (Pittsburgh: University of Pittsburgh Press, 1986); Ann Shola Orloff, *The Politics of Pensions: A Comparative Analysis of Britain, Canada, and the United States, 1880–1940* (Madison: University of Wisconsin Press, 1993); Theda Skocpol, *Protecting Soldiers and Mothers: The Political Origins of Social Policy in the United States* (Cambridge, Mass.: Harvard University Press, 1992); Neil J. Smelser, *Social Change in the Industrial Revolution: An Application of Theory to the British Cotton Industry* (Chicago: University of Chicago Press, 1959); George Steinmetz, *Regulating the Social: The Welfare State and Local Politics in Imperial Germany* (Princeton, N.J.: Princeton University Press, 1993).

17. Clawson, *Constructing Brotherhood*; Louis Galambos, "The Emerging Organizational Synthesis in American History," *Business History Review*, vol. 44 (1970): 279–290; Charles Perrow, "A Society of Organizations," *Theory and Society*, vol. 20 (1991): 725–762; William G. Roy, *Socializing Capital: The Rise of the Large Industrial Corporation in America* (Princeton, N.J.: Princeton University Press, 1997); Arthur M. Schlesinger, "Biography of a Nation of

Joiners," *American Historical Review*, vol. 50, no. 1 (October 1944): 1–25; Ronald E. Seavoy, *The Origins of the American Business Corporation, 1784–1855: Broadening the Concept of Public Service During Industrialization* (Westport, Conn.: Greenwood, 1982); Sidney Tarrow, "'The Very Excess of Democracy': State Building and Contentious Politics in America," in Anne N. Costain and Andrew S. McFarland, eds., *Social Movements and American Political Institutions* (Lanham, Md.: Rowman & Littlefield, 1998).

18. *Boyd's Directory of the District of Columbia* (Washington, D.C.: William H. Boyd, 1890), p. 965; *Boyd's Paterson Directory, 1890–1891* (n.p.: George S. Boudinot, 1890), p. 620; *The Albany Directory for the Year 1880* (Albany, N.Y.: Sampson, Davenport, 1880), p. 365.

19. I explain the nature of these different types of organization in detail in the chapters to follow, as well as provide estimations of the number of associations per capita in Boston and three other cities over time.

20. David T. Beito, *From Mutual Aid to the Welfare State: Fraternal Societies and Social Services, 1890–1967* (Chapel Hill: University of North Carolina Press, 2000); Mark C. Carnes, *Secret Ritual and Manhood in Victorian America* (New Haven, Conn.: Yale University Press, 1989); Clawson, *Constructing Brotherhood*; Lynn Dumenil, *Freemasonry and American Culture, 1880–1939* (Princeton, N.J.: Princeton University Press, 1984); Clifford Putney, "Service Over Secrecy: How Lodge-Style Fraternalism Yielded Popularity to Men's Service Clubs," *Journal of Popular Culture*, vol. 27, no. 1 (Summer 1993): 179–190; Schlesinger, "Biography of a Nation of Joiners".

21. W. S. Harwood, "Secret Societies in America," *North American Review*, vol. 164, no. 486 (May 1897): 622.

22. Charles Edward Ellis, *An Authentic History of the Benevolent and Protective Order of Elks* (Chicago: Self-published, 1910), pp. 29–30; emphasis in original.

23. W. J. Rorabaugh, *The Alcoholic Republic: An American Tradition* (New York: Oxford University Press, 1979), p. 207; also Andrew Barr, *Drink: A Social History of America* (Carroll & Graf, 1999); Mark Edward Lender and James Kirby Martin, *Drinking in America: A History* (New York: Free Press, 1982).

24. This quote is attributed to "a German minister" as recorded by Royal L. Melendy, "The Saloon in Chicago, Part II," *American Journal of Sociology*, vol. 6, issue 4 (January 1901): 436. Unfortunately, Melendy's account of drinking in the turn of the century in Chicago sends mixed messages about the role of alcohol in lodge life. Though he refers to the fact that many lodge meetings were held in brewer-subsidized halls located above saloons, he also observes in other neighborhoods that "in many localities where lodges are very abundant the saloons are correspondingly scarce" (p. 435). It would appear that Melendy's opinion is that lodges might provide a viable, "dry" alternative to saloons, though he attests to the prevalence of many "wet" fraternities as well. On the social activities of turn-of-the-century lodges and saloons, see Carnes, *Secret Ritual and Manhood*; Clawson, *Constructing Brotherhood*; Perry Duis, *The Saloon: Public Drinking in Chicago and Boston, 1880–1920* (Urbana: University of Illinois Press, 1983); Putney, "Service Over Secrecy"; Roy Rosenzweig, *Eight Hours for What We Will: Workers and Leisure in an Industrial City, 1870–1920* (Cambridge: Cambridge University Press, 1983); Luc Sante, *Low Life: Lures and Snares of Old New York* (New York: Vintage, 1991).

25. Nicola Beisel, "Class, Culture, and Campaigns Against Vice in Three American Cities, 1872–1892," *American Sociological Review*, vol. 55 (February 1990): 44–62; Jed Dannenbaum, *Drink and Disorder: Temperance Reform in Cincinnati from the Washingtonian Revival to the WCTU* (Urbana: University of Illinois Press, 1984); Joseph R. Gusfield, *Symbolic Crusade: Status Politics and the American Temperance Movement* (Urbana: University of Illinois Press, 1963); K. Austin Kerr, *Organized for Prohibition: A New History of the Anti-Saloon League* (New Haven, Conn.: Yale University Press, 1985).

26. "Liquor Dealers Ruled Out," *Buffalo Evening News*, September 1, 1894; Melendy, "Saloon in Chicago," p. 435; "Pythians Opposed to Liquor Dealers," *New York Times*, September 6, 1894.

27. The "secret society" moniker is a constant source of confusion in talking about the golden age. Fraternal orders were anything but secretive about their existence; the secret was what exactly went on inside the lodge hall.

28. Harwood, "Secret Societies in America," p. 622.

29. Tocqueville, *Democracy in America*, vol. 2, pt. 2, chaps. 8 and 9.

30. Andrew Abbott, *The System of Professions: An Essay on the Division of Expert Labor* (Chicago: University of Chicago Press, 1988); Magali Sarfatti Larson, *The Rise of Professionalism* (Berkeley: University of California Press, 1977); Roy Lubove, *The Professional Altruist: The Emergence of Social Work as a Career, 1880–1930* (Cambridge, Mass.: Harvard University Press, 1965); Paul Starr, *The Social Transformation of American Medicine* (New York: Basic Books, 1982).

31. Clarence E. Bonnett, *Employers' Associations in the United States: A Study of Typical Associations* (New York: Macmillan, 1922); Oscar Handlin and Mary F. Handlin, "The Origins of the American Business Corporation," *Journal of Economic History*, vol. 5 (1945): 1–23; Kim Voss, *The Making of American Exceptionalism: The Knights of Labor and Class Formation in the Nineteenth Century* (Ithaca, N.Y.: Cornell University Press, 1994).

32. Beckert, *Monied Metropolis*; Chi-nien Chung, "Networks and Governance in Trade Associations: AEIC and NELA in the Development of the American Electricity Industry, 1885–1910," *International Journal of Sociology and Social Policy*, vol. 17 (1997): 57–110; Jessica I. Elfenbein, *Civics, Commerce, and Community: The History of the Greater Washington Board of Trade, 1889–1989* (Dubuque, Iowa: Kendall/Hunt, 1989); Louis Galambos, *Competition & Cooperation: The Emergence of a National Trade Association* (Baltimore: Johns Hopkins University Press, 1966); Mark Granovetter and Patrick McGuire, "The Making of an Industry: Electricity in the United States," in Michel Callon, ed., *The Law of Markets* (Oxford: Blackwell, 1998); David Hammack, *Power and Society: Greater New York at the Turn of the Century* (New York: Russell Sage Foundation, 1982); Samuel P. Hays, "The Changing Political Structure of the City in Industrial America," *Journal of Urban History*, vol. 1, no. 1 (November 1974): 6–38; Roy, *Socializing Capital*.

33. The National Funeral Directors' Association was founded in 1882, following several decades of exponential growth in the cost of a "proper" burial. See James J. Farrell, *Inventing the American Way of Death, 1830–1920* (Philadelphia: Temple University Press, 1980), 146–183.

34. Morton Keller, *The Life Insurance Enterprise, 1885–1910: A Study in the Limits of Corporate Power* (Cambridge: Belknap, 1963); Francis De Raismes Kip, *Fraternal Life Insurance in America* (Philadelphia: College Offset Press, 1953); Charles Kelley Knight, "The History of Life Insurance in the United States to 1870," University of Pennsylvania, Philadelphia, PhD. dissertation, 1920; J. Owen Stalson, *Marketing Life Insurance: Its History in America* (Cambridge, Mass.: Harvard University Press, 1942); Viviana A. Rotman Zelizer, *Morals and Markets: The Development of Life Insurance in the United States* (New York: Columbia University Press, 1979). David Beito's *From Mutual Aid to Welfare State* focuses specifically on the health and death benefits provided by fraternal orders to their members.

35. The chief texts in this vein are Thomas McKeown, *The Role of Medicine: Dream, Mirage, or Nemesis?* (Princeton, N.J.: Princeton University Press, 1979); and Charles E. Rosenberg, *The Cholera Years: The United States in 1832, 1849, and 1866* (Chicago: University of Chicago Press, 1962), though the topic itself has served as the basis for a cottage in-

dustry of sorts among medical historians. On the rising cost of health care in the late nineteenth century, see Charles E. Rosenberg, *The Care of Strangers: The Rise of America's Hospital System* (New York: Basic Books, 1987); David Rosner, *A Once Charitable Enterprise: Hospitals and Health Care in Brooklyn and New York, 1885–1915* (Princeton, N.J.: Princeton University Press, 1982); Morris Vogel, *The Invention of the Modern Hospital: Boston, 1870–1930* (Chicago: University of Chicago Press, 1980).

36. Beito, *From Mutual Aid to the Welfare State*), chap. 6, "The Lodge Practice Evil Reconsidered"; Terry Boychuk, *The Making and Meaning of Hospital Policy in the United States and Canada* (Ann Arbor: University of Michigan Press, 1999); Starr, *Social Transformation of American Medicine*, pp. 206–209. It is interesting that the American Medical Association was opposed to "lodge practices," objecting, according to Starr (p. 208), to doctors who provided "unlimited service for limited pay and the 'ruinous competition' it 'invariably' introduced." He adds, "Many county medical societies refused membership to any doctor who contracted with a lodge."

37. Beito, *From Mutual Aid to the Welfare State*; George Emery and J. C. Herbert Emery, *A Young Man's Benefit: The Independent Order of Odd Fellows and Sickness Insurance in the United States and Canada, 1860–1929* (Montreal: McGill-Queen's University Press, 1999); Francis B. Forbes, "Notes on the Fraternal Beneficiary Corporations Doing Business in Massachusetts," *Publications of the American Statistical Association*, vol. 8, no. 57 (1902): 1–29.

38. Katznelson and Zolberg, *Working-Class Formation*; Seymour Martin Lipset, *Political Man: The Social Bases of Politics* (New York: Anchor Books, 1963); Seymour Martin Lipset and Stein Rokkan, eds., *Party Systems and Voter Alignments: Cross-National Perspectives* (New York: Free Press, 1967); Jeff Manza and Clem Brooks, *Social Cleavages and Political Change: Voter Alignments and U.S. Party Coalitions* (New York: Oxford University Press, 1999); Skocpol, *Protecting Soldiers and Mothers*.

39. Timothy L. Smith, "Religion and Ethnicity in America," *American Historical Review*, vol. 83, no. 5 (1978): 1155–1185, especially 1170–1171. The Catholic clergy actually worked long and hard to bring the nation's many ethnonational Catholic churches together under the control of their local dioceses, though they were never wholly successful in doing so.

40. Yaakov Ariel, *Evangelizing the Chosen People: Missions to the Jews in America, 1880–2000* (Chapel Hill: University of North Carolina Press, 2000); Dorothy M. Brown and Elizabeth McKeown, *The Poor Belong to Us: Catholic Charities and American Welfare* (Cambridge, Mass.: Harvard University Press, 1997); Hasia R. Diner, *A Time for Gathering: The Second Migration, 1820–1880* (Baltimore: Johns Hopkins University Press, 1992); Roger Finke and Rodney Stark, *The Churching of America: Winners and Losers in our Religious Economy* (New Brunswick, N.J.: Rutgers University Press, 1992); John Higham, *Strangers in the Land: Patterns of American Nativism, 1860–1925* (New Brunswick, N.J.: Rutgers University Press, 1955); Jason Kaufman, "The Political Economy of Inter-Denominational Competition in Late 19th Century American Cities," *Journal of Urban History* (forthcoming); John W. Mohr, "Soldiers, Mothers, Tramps and Others: Discourse Roles in the 1907 New York City Charity Directory," *Poetics*, vol. 22 (1994): 327–357; R. Laurence Moore, *Religious Outsiders and the Making of Americans* (New York: Oxford University Press, 1986); Stephen J. Shaw, *The Catholic Parish as a Way-Station of Ethnicity and Americanization: Chicago's Germans and Italians, 1903–1939* (New York: Carlson, 1991).

41. Henry Coyle, Theodore Mayhew, and Frank S. Hickey, eds., *Our Church, Her Children and Institutions*, vol. 3 (Boston: Angel Guardian Press, 1908); Christopher J. Kauffman, *Faith and Fraternalism: The History of the Knights of Columbus*, rev. ed. (New York: Simon & Schuster, 1992); Kaufman, "Political Economy of Inter-Denominational Competition";

Deborah Dash Moore, *B'nai B'rith and the Challenge of Ethnic Leadership* (Albany: SUNY Press, 1981); Michael R. Weisser, *A Brotherhood of Memory: Jewish Landsmanshaftn in the New World* (New York: Basic Books, 1985).

42. Roger Waldinger, *Still the Promised City? African-Americans and New Immigrants in Postindustrial New York* (Cambridge, Mass.: Harvard University Press, 1996), p. 25. Conversely, assimilation into the mainstream is fostered by the entrance of immigrants and their children into personal relationships with members of their host society; see Raymond Breton, "Institutional Completeness of Ethnic Communities and the Personal Relations of Immigrants," *American Journal of Sociology*, vol. 70, no. 2 (September 1964): 193–205; Michael Hechter, "Group Formation and the Cultural Division of Labor," *American Journal of Sociology*, vol. 84, no. 2 (September 1978): 293–318.

43. Josef J. Barton, *Peasants and Strangers: Italians, Rumanians, and Slovaks in an American City, 1890–1950* (Cambridge, Mass.: Harvard University Press, 1975); John Bodnar, *The Transplanted: A History of Immigrants in Urban America* (Bloomington: University of Indiana Press, 1985); Dino Cinel, *From Italy to San Francisco: The Immigrant Experience* (Stanford, Cal.: Stanford University Press, 1982); Lizabeth Cohen, *Making a New Deal: Industrial Workers in Chicago, 1919–1939* (Cambridge: Cambridge University Press, 1990); Kathleen Neils Conzen, *Immigrant Milwaukee, 1836–1860: Accomodation and Community in a Frontier City* (Cambridge, Mass.: Harvard University Press, 1976); Guido Andre Dobbert, *The Disintegration of an Immigrant Community: The Cincinnati Germans, 1870–1920* (New York: Arno, [1965] 1980); Virginia Yans-McLaughlin, ed., *Immigration Reconsidered: History, Sociology, and Politics* (New York: Oxford University Press, 1990). As many as one-half of all immigrants actually returned to their country of origin, and many more surely planned to return at some point. (Italian immigrants were among the most likely to attempt a return; Jews were among the most likely to stay in the United States.) Thus many ethnonational fraternal and relief organizations served more as way stations for transatlantic migrant workers than stable bases of American identity formation.

44. Edna Bonacich and John Modell, *The Economic Basis of Ethnic Solidarity: Small Business in the Japanese American Community* (Berkeley: University of California Press, 1980); Ivan H. Light, *Ethnic Enterprise in America: Business and Welfare Among Chinese, Japanese, and Blacks* (Berkeley: University of California Press, 1972); Ivan H. Light and Edna Bonacich, *Immigrant Entrepreneurs: Koreans in Los Angeles, 1965–1982* (Berkeley: University of California Press, 1988); Min Zhou, *Chinatown: The Socioeconomic Potential of an Urban Enclave* (Philadelphia: Temple University Press, 1992).

45. Jose Amaro Hernandez, *Mutual Aid for Survival: The Case of the Mexican American* (Malabar, Fla.: Krieger, 1983), p. 83.

46. William A. Muraskin, *Middle-Class Blacks in a White Society: Prince Hall Freemasonry in America* (Berkeley: University of California Press, 1975); Edward Nelson Palmer, "Negro Secret Societies," *Social Forces*, vol. 23, no. 2 (1944): 207–214.

47. John Silbey Butler, *Entrepreneurship and Self-Help Among Black Americans: A Reconsideration of Race and Economics* (Albany: SUNY Press, 1991); Abram L. Harris, *The Negro as Capitalist: A Study of Banking and Business Among American Negroes* (College Park, Md.: McGrath, [1936] 1968); Booker T. Washington, *The Negro in Business* (Chicago: Afro-Am Press, [1907] 1969).

48. R. L. Moore, *Religious Outsiders and the Making of Americans*, pp. 185–186.

49. Clawson, *Constructing Brotherhood*, p. 200.

50. See, for example, Elisabeth S. Clemens, *The People's Lobby: Organizational Innovation and the Rise of Interest Group Politics in the United States, 1890–1925* (Chicago: University of Chicago Press, 1997); Kenneth D. Rose, *American Women and the Repeal of Prohibition*

(New York: New York University Press, 1996); Theda Skocpol, "The Tocqueville Problem: Civic Engagement in American Democracy," *Social Science History*, vol. 21, no. 4 (1997): 455–479.

51. Ellen M. Henrotin, "The Attitude of Women's Clubs and Associations Toward Social Economics," *Bulletin of the Department of Labor*, no. 23 (July 1899): 502–503. For further debate on the impact of women's organizations in American public policy, see Theda Skocpol, Christopher Howard, Susan Goodrich Lehmann, and Marjorie Abend-Wein, "Women's Associations and the Enactment of Mothers' Pensions in the United States," *American Political Science Review*, vol. 87 (1993): 686–699; and Cheryl Logan Sparks and Peter R. Walniuk, "The Enactment of Mothers' Pensions: Civic Mobilization and Agenda Setting or Benefits of the Ballot?" *American Political Science Review*, vol. 89 (1995): 710–720, on the potential impact of women's associations in the struggle for mother's pensions.

52. Skocpol, "Tocqueville Problem."

53. Higham, *Strangers in the Land*; Eugene Zieber, ed., *Ancestry: The Objects of the Hereditary Societies and the Military and Naval Orders of the United States* (Philadephia: Bailey, Banks & Biddle, 1895).

54. For an extremely lucid explication of the polity centered, see Skocpol's *Protecting Soldiers and Mothers*, pp. 41–62.

55. Beito, *From Mutual Aid to Welfare State*; L. Cohen, *Making a New Deal*, pp. 53–97; Robert Cunningham III and Robert M. Cunningham, Jr., *The Blues: A History of the Blue Cross and Blue Shield System* (Dekalb: Northern Illinois University Press, 1997); Haveman and Rao, "Structuring a Theory of Moral Sentiments"; Keller, *Life Insurance Enterprise*; Rosenberg, *Care of Strangers*; Stalson, *Marketing Life Insurance*; Starr, *Social Transformation of American Medicine*; Zelizer, *Morals and Markets*.

56. John Freeman and Michael T. Hannan, "Growth and Decline Processes in Organizations," *American Sociological Review*, vol. 40 (1975): 215–228; John Freeman and Michael T. Hannan, "Niche Width and the Dynamics of Organizational Populations," *American Journal of Sociology*, vol. 88 (1983): 1116–1145; Michael T. Hannan and John Freeman, *Organizational Ecology* (Cambridge, Mass.: Harvard University Press, 1989).

57. Richard D. Alba, *Italian Americans: Into the Twilight of Ethnicity* (Upper Saddle River, N.J.: Prentice Hall, 1985); Dobbert, *Disintegration of an Immigrant Community*; Joshua A. Fishman, *Language Loyalty in the United States* (New York: Arno, 1978); Nathan Glazer and Daniel P. Moynihan, *Beyond the Melting Pot*, 2nd ed. (Cambridge, Mass.: MIT Press, 1963); Noel Ignatiev, *How the Irish Became White* (New York: Routledge, 1995); Matthew Frye Jacobson, *Whiteness of a Different Color: European Immigration and the Alchemy of Race* (Cambridge, Mass.: Harvard University Press, 1998); Stanley Lieberson, *A Piece of the Pie: Blacks and White Immigrants Since 1880* (Berkeley: University of California Press, 1980); Eva Morawska, *Insecure Prosperity: Small-Town Jews in Industrial America, 1890–1940* (Princeton, N.J.: Princeton University Press, 1996).

58. Lisa Suhay, "Moose and Elk: Endangered Species?" *New York Times*, N.J. ed. August 29, 1999, sec. 14.

59. Richard Abanes, *American Militias* (Downers Grove, Ill.: InterVarsity Press, 1996); Michael A. Bellesiles, *Arming America: The Origins of a National Gun Culture* (New York: Knopf, 2000); Jerry Cooper, *The Rise of the National Guard: The Evolution of the American Militia, 1865–1920* (Lincoln: University of Nebraska Press, 1997); Lawrence Delbert Cress, "An Armed Community: The Origins and Meaning of the Right to Bear Arms," *Journal of American History*, vol. 71, issue 1 (June 1984): 22–42; Jason Kaufman, "'Americans and Their Guns': Civilian Military Organizations and the Destabilization of American National Security," *Studies in American Political Development*, vol. 15 (Spring 2001): 88–102; Kenneth S.

Stern, *A Force Upon the Plain: The American Militia Movement and the Politics of Hate* (New York: Simon & Schuster, 1996); James B. Trefethen and James E. Serven, *Americans and Their Guns: The National Rifle Association Story Through Nearly a Century of Service to the Nation* (Harrisburg, Pa.: Stackpole, 1967).

60. William James, *The Varieties of Religious Experience*, Martin E. Marty, ed. (New York: Penguin, [1902] 1982), p. 22.

Chapter 2

1. Robert H. Wiebe, *The Search for Order, 1877–1920* (New York: Hill & Wang, 1967); see also Stuart M. Blumin, *The Emergence of the Middle Class: Social Experience in the American City, 1760–1900* (Cambridge: Cambridge University Press, 1989); Paul Boyer, *Urban Masses and Moral Order in America, 1820–1920* (Cambridge, Mass.: Harvard University Press, 1978); Mark C. Carnes, *Secret Ritual and Manhood in Victorian America* (New Haven, Conn.: Yale University Press, 1989); Mary Ann Clawson, *Constructing Brotherhood: Class, Gender, and Fraternalism* (Princeton, N.J.: Princeton University Press, 1989); Don H. Doyle, "The Social Function of Voluntary Associations in a Nineteenth-Century American Town," *Social Science History*, vol. 1, no. 3 (Spring 1977): 333–355; Lynn Dumenil, *Freemasonry and American Culture, 1880–1939* (Princeton, N.J.: Princeton University Press, 1984); Clifford Putney, "Service Over Secrecy: How Lodge-Style Fraternalism Yielded Popularity to Men's Service Clubs," *Journal of Popular Culture*, vol. 27 (Summer 1993): 179–190; Arthur M. Schlesinger, *The Rise of the City, 1878–1898* (New York: Macmillan, 1933).

2. Arthur L. Stinchcombe, "The Conditions of Fruitfulness of Theorizing About Mechanisms in Social Science," *Philosophy of the Social Sciences*, vol. 21, no. 3 (September 1991): 385–386. For a similar, sociologically based argument, see Charles Tilly, *Big Structures, Large Processes, Huge Comparisons* (New York: Russell Sage Foundation, 1984).

3. Elisabeth S. Clemens, *The People's Lobby: Organizational Innovation and the Rise of Interest Group Politics in the United States, 1890–1925* (Chicago: University of Chicago Press, 1997); Elisabeth S. Clemens, "Organizational Repertoires and Institutional Change: Women's Groups and the Transformation of U.S. Politics, 1890–1920," *American Journal of Sociology*, vol. 98, no. 4 (January 1993): 755–798; Theda Skocpol, *Protecting Soldiers and Mothers: The Political Origins of Social Policy in the United States* (Cambridge: Belknap, 1992); Theda Skocpol, "The Tocqueville Problem: Civic Engagement in American Democracy," *Social Science History*, vol. 21, no. 4 (Winter 1997): 455–479; Theda Skocpol, Marshall Ganz, and Ziad Munson, "A Nation of Organizers: The Institutional Origins of Civic Voluntarism in the United States," *American Political Science Review*, vol. 94, no. 3 (September 2000): 527–546.

4. Clemens, *People's Lobby*; Samuel P. Hays, *The Response to Industrialism, 1885–1914* (Chicago: University of Chicago Press, 1957); Richard Hofstadter, *The Age of Reform: From Bryan to F.D.R.* (New York: Knopf, 1955).

5. Leon Fink, *Workingmen's Democracy: The Knights of Labor and American Politics* (Urbana: University of Illinois Press, 1983); Richard Schneirov, *Labor and Urban Politics: Class Conflict and the Origins of Modern Liberalism in Chicago, 1864–1897* (Urbana: University of Illinois Press, 1998); Kim Voss, *The Making of American Exceptionalism: The Knights of Labor and Class Formation in the Nineteenth Century* (Ithaca, N.Y.: Cornell University Press, 1993); Norman J. Ware, *The Labor Movement in the United States, 1860–1895: A Study in Democracy* (New York: D. Appleton, 1929); Robert E. Weir, *Beyond Labor's Veil: The Culture of the Knights of Labor* (University Park: Pennsylvania State University Press, 1988).

6. Nicola Beisel, "Class, Culture, and Campaigns Against Vice in Three American Cities, 1872–1892," *American Sociological Review*, vol. 55 (February 1990): 44–62; Jed Dannenbaum, *Drink and Disorder: Temperance Reform in Cincinnati from the Washingtonian Revival to the WCTU* (Urbana: University of Illinois Press, 1984); Joseph R. Gusfield, *Symbolic Crusade: Status Politics and the American Temperance Movement* (Urbana: University of Illinois Press, 1963); K. Austin Kerr, *Organized for Prohibition: A New History of the Anti-Saloon League* (New Haven, Conn.: Yale University Press, 1985).

7. See, for example, Amy Gutmann and Dennis Thompson, *Democracy and Disagreement* (Cambridge: Belknap, 1996); Jane J. Mansbridge, *Beyond Adversary Democracy* (Chicago: University of Chicago Press, 1980); Nancy L. Rosenblum, *Membership and Morals: The Personal Uses of Pluralism in America* (Princeton, N.J.: Princeton University Press, 1998); Carmen Sirianni and Lewis Friedland, *Civic Innovation in America: Community Empowerment, Public Policy, and the Movement for Civic Renewal* (Berkeley: University of California Press, 2001); David B. Truman, *The Governmental Process: Political Interests and Public Opinion* (New York: Knopf, 1951).

8. Alexis de Tocqueville, *Democracy in America*, George Lawrence, trans. (New York: Harper & Row, [1966] 1988), p. 515. David T. Beito, *From Mutual Aid to the Welfare State: Fraternal Societies and Social Services, 1890–1967* (Chapel Hill: University of North Carolina Press, 2000); Marvin Olasky, *The Tragedy of American Compassion* (Wheaton, Ill.: Crossway Books). See also Benjamin R. Barber, "An American Civic Forum: Civil Society Between Market Individuals and the Political Community," *Social Philosophy and Policy*, vol. 13, no. 1 (1996): 269–283; Amitai Etzioni, ed., *Rights and the Common Good: The Communitarian Perspective* (New York: St. Martin, 1995); Michael S. Joyce and William A. Schambra, "A New Civic Life," in Michael Novak, ed., *To Empower People: From State to Civil Society*, 2nd ed. (Washington, D.C.: AEI Press, 1996); James Q. Wilson, "The Rise of the Bureaucratic State," *Public Interest*, vol. 41 (Fall 1975), 88–89.

9. Max Weber, *Economy and Society*, vol. 1, Guenther Roth and Claus Wittich, eds. (Berkeley: University of California Press, 1978), pp. 19–20.

10. Max Weber, "The Protestant Sects and the Spirit of Capitalism," in H. H. Gerth and C. Wright Mills, eds., *From Max Weber: Essays in Sociology* (New York: Oxford University Press, 1946). Weber finished work on his landmark study, *The Protestant Ethic and the Spirit of Capitalism* (first published as a two-part article in the *Archiv für Sozialwissenschaft und Sozialpolitik*), at about the same time he visited the United States (1904–1905), and though it would be unjustified to say that this trip helped formulate his ideas on the origins of capitalism, it would certainly be plausible to argue that the topic was much on his mind during his American travels.

11. Max Weber, "A Biographical View," in H. H. Gerth and C. Wrigt Mills, eds., *From Max Weber: Essays in Sociology* (New York: Oxford University Press, 1946), p. 15. Weber was also kind enough to note the contrast between those "towering bulks of capitalism" and "the tiny homes of American college professors."

12. M. Weber, "Protestant Sects and Spirit of Capitalism," pp. 307–308.

13. Political scientists Gerald Gamm and Robert Putnam agree with Weber's conclusions about the "small town" basis of lodge-based fraternity; see "The Growth of Voluntary Associations in America, 1840–1940," *Journal of Interdisciplinary History*, vol. 29, no. 3 (Winter 1999): 511–557. For different perspectives on the geographical origins of lodge-based fraternalism, see Skocpol, Ganz, and Munson, "Nation of Organizers"; Jason Kaufman and David Weintraub, "The Spatial Distribution of Sectarian Civic Associations: New Evidence on the Geographical Loci of Civic Associational Activity," *Mobilization* (forthcoming).

14. For example, Clawson, *Constructing Brotherhood*; Viviana A. Rotman Zelizer, *Morals and Markets: The Development of Life Insurance in the United States* (New York: Columbia University Press, 1979).

15. James J. Farrell, *Inventing the American Way of Death, 1830-1920* (Philadelphia: Temple University Press, 1980), pp. 148, 181; David Charles Sloane, *The Last Great Necessity: Cemeteries in American History* (Baltimore: Johns Hopkins University Press, 1991).

16. Farrell, *Inventing the American Way of Death*, p. 151.

17. Ibid., p. 174.

18. Josef Maria Baernreither, *English Associations of Working Men*, English ed. (London: S. Sonnenschein, 1889); P. H. J. H. Gosden, *The Friendly Societies in England, 1815-1875* (Manchester: Manchester University Press, 1961); Eric J. Hobsbawm, *Primitive Rebels: Studies in Archaic Forms of Social Movement in the 19th and 20th Centuries* (New York: Norton, 1959), pp. 153-162; T. S. Newman, *The Story of Friendly Societies and Social Security: Past, Present, Future* (London: Hearts of Oak Benefit Society, 1945); E. P. Thompson, *The Making of the English Working Class* (London: Victor Gollancz, 1963), pp. 418-429.

19. Gosden, *Friendly Societies in England*, p. 2, writes, "The increased rate of industrial development in the second half of the eighteenth century and the needs of the growing number of industrial workers [in Britain] account for this [much more] rapid rate of growth."

20. Ibid., pp. 211-220.

21. Clawson, *Constructing Brotherhood*; Dumenil, *Freemasonry and American Culture*.

22. Albert C. Stevens, *The Cyclopedia of Fraternities* (New York: E. B. Treat, 1907), p. xxii. At least one historian of American associationalism, Walter Basye, openly denies the relevance of British precedent in Americans' decision to adopt fraternalism, though this may only be the result of early twentieth-century ethnocentrism, as Basye's account was published in 1919, just after the conclusion of the World War I. In addition, Basye's history of American fraternalism was clearly coined in light of the rising movement for universal health insurance and thus tries to differentiate American fraternalism from the socialistic systems of Germany and Britain. See Walter Basye, *History and Operation of Fraternal Insurance* (Rochester, N.Y.: Fraternal Monitor, 1919).

23. Morton Keller, *The Life Insurance Enterprise, 1885-1910: A Study in the Limits of Corporate Power* (Cambridge: Belknap, 1963), p. 9. See also Francis De Raismes Kip, *Fraternal Life Insurance in America* (Philadelphia: College Offset Press, 1953); Robert Whaples and David Buffum, "Fraternalism, Paternalism, the Family, and the Market: Insurance a Century Ago," *Social Science History*, vol. 15, no. 1 (Spring 1991): 97-122; Zelizer, *Morals and Markets*. Further evidence of the American obsession with death-related benefits is provided by Skocpol's masterful *Protecting Soldiers and Mothers*.

24. Clawson, *Constructing Brotherhood*, pp. 222-223.

25. Lawrence M. Friedman, *A History of American Law*, 2nd ed. (New York: Simon & Schuster, 1985), pp. 301-302.

26. W. S. Harwood, "Secret Societies in America," *North American Review*, vol. 164, no. 486 (May 1897): 617.

27. *Langley's San Francisco Directory for the Year Commencing May, 1890* (San Francisco: Francis, Valentine, 1890). Cross-sectional membership data on the actual size of individual fraternal lodges are exceedingly hard to come by, given that most city directories of the period do not offer this information.

28. The mean size of all 48 lodges was 297.

29. Data on the total membership of the International Order of Odd Fellows (IOOF) in the United States and Canada give an average lodge size of 70 members for 1890, a number comparable to my estimate of 73. The data are found in George Emery and J. C. Herbert

Emery, *A Young Man's Benefit: The Independent Order of Odd Fellows and Sickness Insurance in the United States and Canada, 1860–1929* (Montreal: McGill-Queen's University Press, 1999). See my figure 8.1 for a detailed analysis of IOOF membership figures, 1850–1930.

30. All census figures reported here are from Robert P. Porter, *Compendium of the 11th Census: 1890* (Washington, D.C.: Government Printing Office, 1892).

31. If, on the other hand, I use the larger estimate of 297 members per lodge (the mean of those actually giving a tally of their membership rolls in *Langley's Directory*), I get an estimated 164,310 participants, or 55% of the population of San Francisco.

32. See, for example, Doyle, "Social Function of Voluntary Associations," pp. 333–355; Emery and Emery, *Young Man's Benefit.*

33. On the other hand, if I include the entire population of San Francisco in the denominator and assume an average of two policies per policyholder, only about 11% of the population participated in such plans, or [(67990/2)/298,997 = .1137].

34. Emery and Emery, *Young Man's Benefit*, p. 44; Gamm and Putnam, "Growth of Voluntary Associations." I return to this topic in chapter 3.

35. Gamm and Putnam, "Growth of Voluntary Associations," p. 524.

36. Note that the time periods along the *x* axis are not perfectly symmetrical. Though my original research plan was to examine city directory listings at 20-year intervals, I decided to add a 1930 wave of data in order to examine the potential impact of the Great Depression and New Deal on the decline of fraternalism.

37. Beito, *From Mutual Aid to the Welfare State*; Clawson, *Constructing Brotherhood*; Gamm and Putnam, "Growth of Voluntary Associations." Both Lizabeth Cohen, *Making A New Deal: Industrial Workers in Chicago, 1919–1939* (Cambridge: Cambridge University Press, 1990), and Mark Carnes, *Secret Ritual and Manhood*, argue that, in Carnes's words (p. 151), "The institutional foundations of the fraternal movement collapsed during the depression of the 1930s," though my data do not show nearly so dramatic a decline and in fact date the beginning of the end several decades earlier.

38. One fine account of mid-nineteenth-century fraternal unrest is Mary P. Ryan, *Civic Wars: Democracy and Public Life in the American City During the Nineteenth Century* (Berkeley: University of California Press, 1997). Nonetheless, Ryan is rather enamored with the cantankerous spirit of the age, choosing to see the numerous examples of violence, protest, and general unrest as signs of collective effervescence rather than incipient disorder.

39. Georg Simmel, "The Secret Society," *The Sociology of Georg Simmel*, Kurt H. Wolff, trans. (New York: Free Press, 1950), p. 345; emphases in original.

40. Ibid., p. 359.

41. Roger L. Ransom and Richard Sutch, "Tontine Insurance and the Armstrong Investigation: A Case of Stifled Innovation, 1868–1905," *Journal of Economic History*, vol. 47, no. 2 (June 1987): 379–390.

42. An excellent review of the age question as it relates to fraternal insurance is Emery and Emery, *Young Man's Benefit.*

43. For example, Francis B. Forbes, "Notes on the Fraternal Beneficiary Corporations Doing Business in Massachusetts," *Publications of the American Statistical Association*, vol. 8, issue 57 (March 1902): 1–29; Frederick L. Hoffman, "Fifty Years of American Life Insurance Progress," *Publications of the American Statistical Association*, vol. 12, issue 95 (September 1911): 667–712; Charles A. Jenney, *Report on Insurance Business in the United States at the Eleventh Census: 1890, Part II. Life Insurance* (Washington, D.C.: U.S. Government Printing Office, 1895); B. H. Meyer, "Fraternal Beneficiary Societies in the United States," *American Journal of Sociology*, vol. 6, no. 5 (March 1901): 646–661.

44. Alvin J. Schmidt, *Fraternal Organizations* (Westport, Conn.: Greenwood, 1980), p. 10.

45. *Fraternal Monitor,* November 1, 1919, pp. 21–23.

46. Judge John C. Karel, "New Blood for a Fraternal Society," *Fraternal Monitor,* November 1, 1919, p. 22.

47. Clawson, *Constructing Brotherhood,* pp. 216–217.

48. Emery and Emery, *Young Man's Benefit.*

49. F. H. Hankins, "Fraternal Orders," *Encyclopedia of the Social Sciences,* vol. 6 (New York: Macmillan, 1935), pp. 424–425.

50. F. L. Hoffman, "Fifty Years of American Life Insurance Progress," p. 675. In exploring the age distribution of joiners and quitters among the Odd Fellows' insured population, Emery and Emery (*Young Man's Benefit*) find that contrary to popular belief (or at least contemporary standards), fraternal life insurance policies were most appealing to poor young men just starting their careers, as opposed to older men whose families could rely on their accumulated savings, commercial insurance, and grown children for secondary income.

51. Henry Coyle, Theodore Mayhew, and Frank S. Hickey, eds., *Our Church, Her Children and Institutions,* vol. 3 (Boston: Angel Guardian Press, 1908), p. 32, "The Ladies' Catholic Benevolent Association." Note that this was not the first fraternal organization incorporated for women in America but the first reputed to have been incorporated for the purpose of providing women with the kinds of insurance benefits routinely offered by male fraternal organizations. I have not been able to confirm Coyle, Mayhew, and Hickey's claim that the Ladies' Catholic Benevolent Association was in fact the first such mutual benefit organization for women in the United States, though a cursory glance at the city directories of the period would seem to confirm this assertion, or at least the fact that this was a new phenomenon as of the early 1890s.

52. Ibid., p. 92.

53. Elisabeth S. Clemens, "Organizational Repertoires and Institutional Change: Women's Groups and the Transformation of U.S. Politics, 1890–1920," *American Journal of Sociology,* vol. 98, no. 4 (January 1993): 755–798; Rosemary Crompton, ed., *Restructuring Gender Relations and Employment: The Decline of the Male Breadwinner* (Oxford: Oxford University Press, 1999); Linda Gordon, "Social Insurance and Public Assistance: The Influence of Gender in Welfare Thought in the United States, 1890–1935," *American Historical Review,* vol. 97, no. 1 (1992): 19–54; Linda K. Kerber, *No Constitutional Right to Be Ladies: Women and the Obligations of Citizenship* (New York: Hill & Wang, 1998); Julia S. O'Connor, Ann Shola Orloff, and Sheila Shaver, eds., *States, Markets, Families: Gender, Liberalism, and Social Policy in Australia, Canada, Great Britain, and the United States* (New York: Cambridge University Press, 1999); Skocpol, *Protecting Soldiers and Mothers.*

54. Emery and Emery, *Young Man's Benefit,* p. 12.

55. The mean expense ratio for all the organizations studied was about 8%. Forbes, "Notes on the Fraternal Beneficiary Corporations," pp. 22–29.

56. Ibid., p. 2.

57. Coyle, Mayhew, and Hickey, *eds., Our Church,* pp. 2–4, "The Knights of Columbus: One of the Grandest Fraternal Organizations Ever Instituted."

58. Ibid., p. 13, "Catholic Order of Foresters."

59. Harwood, "Secret Societies in America," p. 622. See also Clawson, *Constructing Brotherhood,* pp. 213–214.

60. Beisel, "Class, Culture, and Campaigns Against Vice"; Dannenbaum, *Drink and Disorder,* Gusfield, *Symbolic Crusade;* Kerr, *Organized for Prohibition;* Royal L. Melendy, "The Saloon in Chicago, Part II," *American Journal of Sociology,* vol. 6, no. 4 (1901): 433–464.

61. William H. McNeill, *Keeping Together in Time: Dance and Drill in Human History* (Cambridge, Mass.: Harvard University Press, 1995).

62. William H. Sewell, Jr., *Work and Revolution in France: The Language of Labor from the Old Regime to 1848* (Cambridge: Cambridge University Press, 1980), pp. 203–205. For slightly contrasting positions, see Lynn Hunt and George Sheridan, "Corporatism, Association, and the Language of Labor in France, 1750–1850," *Journal of Modern History*, vol. 58, no. 4 (December 1986): 813–844; Isser Woloch, *The New Regime: Transformations of the French Civic Order, 1789–1820s* (New York: Norton, 1994), pp. 289–293. See also Ronald Aminzade, *Class, Politics, and Early Industrial Capitalism: A Study of Mid-Nineteenth Century Toulouse, France* (Albany: SUNY Press, 1981); Roger V. Gould, *Insurgent identities: Class, Community, and Protest in Paris from 1848 to the Commune* (Chicago: University of Chicago Press, 1995); Michael P. Hanagan, *Nascent Proletarians: Class Formation in Post-Revolutionary France* (New York: Oxford University Press, 1989); Cynthia Maria Truant, *The Rites of Labor: Brothers of Compagnonnage in Old and New Regime France* (Ithaca, N.Y.: Cornell University Press, 1994); Judith Eisenberg Vichniac, *The Management of Labor: The British and French Iron and Steel industries, 1860–1918* (Greenwich, Conn.: JAI Press, 1990).

63. Naturally, there were exceptions to worker-oriented associations in France, though strict government surveillance of religious and/or "subversive" groups did keep their scope noticeably narrower than those in America.

64. Robert J. Goldstein, *Political Repression in 19th Century Europe* (Totowa, N.J.: Barnes & Noble, 1983).

65. Peter Flora and Arnold J. Heidenheimer, eds., *The Development of Welfare States in Europe and America* (New Brunswick, N.J.: Transaction Books, 1981); Ira Katznelson and Aristide R. Zolberg, eds., *Working-Class Formation: Nineteenth-Century Patterns in Western Europe and the United States* (Princeton, N.J.: Princeton University Press, 1986); Gary Marks, *Unions in Politics: Britain, Germany, and the United States in the Nineteenth and Early Twentieth Centuries* (Princeton, N.J.: Princeton University Press, 1989); Bruce Western, *Between Class and Market: Postwar Unionization in the Capitalist Democracies* (Princeton, N.J.: Princeton University Press, 1997).

66. George Steinmetz, *Regulating the Social: The Welfare State and Local Politics in Imperial Germany* (Princeton, N.J.: Princeton University Press, 1993), p. 125.

67. Neil J. Smelser, *Social Change in the Industrial Revolution: An Application of Theory to the British Cotton Industry* (Chicago: University of Chicago Press, 1959).

68. Gosden, *Friendly Societies in England*, p. 215.

69. Smelser, *Social Change in the Industrial Revolution*, p. 370.

70. Max Weber, "Class, Status, and Party," in H. H. Gerth and C. Wright Mills, eds., *From Max Weber: Essays in Sociology* (New York: Oxford University Press, 1946), p. 194.

Chapter 3

1. *Oxford English Dictionary*, 3rd ed. (online), entry: "community."

2. William Caxton, *The Game of Chesse* (1474), p. 91; cited in the *Oxford English Dictionary*, 2nd ed. (online), entry: "commonty."

3. Prominent examples of recent communitarian thought include Benjamin R. Barber, *A Place for Us: How to Make Society Civil and Democracy Strong* (New York: Hill & Wang, 1998); David T. Beito, *From Mutual Aid to the Welfare State: Fraternal Societies and Social Services, 1890–1967* (Chapel Hill: University of North Carolina Press, 2000); Peter L. Berger and Richard John Neuhaus, *To Empower People: From State to Civil Society*, 20th anniversary ed., Michael Novak, ed. (Washington, D.C.: AEI Press, [1977] 1996); Amitai Etzioni,

ed., *Rights and the Common Good: The Communitarian Perspective* (New York: St. Martin, 1995); Michael S. Joyce and William A. Schambra, "A New Civic Life," in Michael Novak, ed., *To Empower People: From State to Civil Society*, 2nd ed. (Washington, D.C.: AEI Press, 1996); Marvin Olasky, *The Tragedy of American Compassion* (Wheaton, Ill: Crossway Books).

4. Josef J. Barton, *Peasants and Strangers: Italians, Rumanians, and Slovaks in an American City, 1890–1950* (Cambridge, Mass.: Harvard University Press, 1975); Dino Cinel, *From Italy to San Francisco: The Immigrant Experience* (Stanford, Cal.: Stanford University Press, 1982); Guido Andre Dobbert, *The Disintegration of an Immigrant Community: The Cincinnati Germans, 1870–1920* (New York: Arno, 1980); Victor Greene, *For God and Country: The Rise of Polish and Lithuanian Ethnic Consciousness in America, 1860–1910* (Madison: State Historical Society of Wisconsin, 1975); Ivan H. Light, *Ethnic Enterprise in America: Business and Welfare Among Chinese, Japanese, and Blacks* (Berkeley: University of California Press, 1972); La Vern J. Rippley, *The German-Americans* (Boston: Twayne Publishers, 1976).

5. Richard D. Alba, *Ethnic Identity: The Transformation of White America* (New Haven, Conn.: Yale University Press, 1990); Richard M. Bernard, *The Melting Pot and the Altar: Marital Assimilation in Early Twentieth-Century Wisconsin* (Minneapolis: University of Minnesota Press, 1980); Walter Licht, *Getting Work: Philadelphia, 1840–1950* (Cambridge, Mass.: Harvard University Press, 1992); Stanley Lieberson, *A Piece of the Pie: Blacks and White Immigrants Since 1880* (Berkeley: University of California Press, 1980); Stephan Thernstrom, *The Other Bostonians: Poverty and Progress in the American Metropolis, 1880–1970* (Cambridge, Mass.: Harvard University Press, 1973); Roger Waldinger, *Still the Promised City? African-Americans and New Immigrants in Postindustrial New York* (Cambridge, Mass.: Harvard University Press, 1996); Mary C. Waters, *Ethnic Options: Choosing Identities in America* (Berkeley: University of California Press, 1990); Olivier Zunz, *The Changing Face of Inequality: Urbanization, Industrial Development, and Immigrants in Detroit, 1880–1920* (Chicago: University of Chicago Press, 1982).

6. Dorothy M. Brown and Elizabeth McKeown, *The Poor Belong to Us: Catholic Charities and American Welfare* (Cambridge, Mass.: Harvard University Press, 1997); Will Herberg, *Protestant—Catholic—Jew: An Essay in American Religious Sociology* (Garden City, N.Y.: Doubleday, 1955); John Higham, *Strangers in the Land: Patterns of American Nativism, 1860–1925* (New Brunswick, N.J.: Rutgers University Press, 1955); R. Laurence Moore, *Religious Outsiders and the Making of Americans* (New York: Oxford University Press, 1986); Stephen J. Shaw, *The Catholic Parish as a Way-Station of Ethnicity and Americanization: Chicago's Germans and Italians, 1903–1939* (New York: Carlson, 1991).

7. Sociologists Roger Finke and Rodney Stark have been the most vocal supporters of an emerging paradigm in the sociology of religion that emphasizes the role of competition between denominations during this period of American history; see *The Churching of America: Winners and Losers in our Religious Economy* (New Brunswick, N.J.: Rutgers University Press, 1992); also R. Stephen Warner, "Work in Progress Toward a New Paradigm for the Sociological Study of Religion in the United States," *American Journal of Sociology*, vol. 98, issue 5 (March 1993): 1044–1093. Relying heavily on the imagery of neoclassical economics, Finke and Stark describe American religious history as a form of social market for members. Nonetheless, whereas Finke and Stark have set forth a compelling model, it relies primarily on a psychosocial mode of explanation, which requires us to believe that "when successful sects are transformed into churches, that is, *when their tension with the surrounding culture is greatly reduced*, they soon cease to grow and eventually begin to decline" (p. 148; emphasis added). Implicit here is an argument about the spiritual needs that drive churchgoers to join a sect or church: Churches that actively attempt to address the commonplace, material needs of their constituents are doomed to extinction, or at least to a mass

228 NOTES TO PAGES 57–59

outflow of members. Although I agree wholeheartedly with the emphasis Finke and Stark place on the role of interdenominational competition in American religious history, the analysis offered here differs from theirs in stressing the material, as opposed to the ideological, bases of religious competition. For more details, see my article "The Political Economy of Inter-Denominational Competition in Late 19th Century American Cities," *Journal of Urban History* (forthcoming).

8. Hasia R. Diner, *A Time for Gathering: The Second Migration, 1820–1880* (Baltimore: Johns Hopkins University Press, 1992), p. 109; John O'Dea, *History of the Ancient Order of Hibernians and Ladies' Auxiliary* (Notre Dame, Ind.: University of Notre Dame Press, 1995); Rippley, *German-Americans*; Daniel Soyer, *Jewish Immigrant Associations and American Identity in New York, 1880–1939* (Cambridge, Mass.: Harvard University Press, 1997); Michael R. Weisser, *A Brotherhood of Memory: Jewish Landsmanshaftn in the New World* (New York: Basic Books, 1985).

9. Higham, *Strangers in the Land*. This last category of patriotic-nativist fraternal groups is not to be confused with hereditary societies such as the Sons and Daughters of the American Revolution, which did not generally offer financial benefits. See Eugene Zieber, ed., *Ancestry: The Objects of the Hereditary Societies and Military and Naval Orders of the United States* (Philadelphia: Bailey, Banks & Biddle, 1895).

10. Nicola Beisel, "Class, Culture, and Campaigns Against Vice in Three American Cities, 1872–1892," *American Sociological Review*, vol. 55 (February 1990): 44–62; Jed Dannenbaum, *Drink and Disorder: Temperance Reform in Cincinnati from the Washingtonian Revival to the WCTU* (Urbana: University of Illinois Press, 1984); Joseph R. Gusfield, *Symbolic Crusade: Status Politics and the American Temperance Movement* (Urbana: University of Illinois Press, 1963); K. Austin Kerr, *Organized for Prohibition: A New History of the Anti-Saloon League* (New Haven, Conn.: Yale University Press, 1985).

11. An additional incentive for many religiously grounded fraternal organizations was the preexisting moral stigma of life insurance, considered by many American religious leaders to be an alternate form of gambling. Fraternal organizations thus offered a morally acceptable means of attaining life insurance for many in this position. See Christopher J. Kauffman, *Faith and Fraternalism: The History of the Knights of Columbus*, rev. ed. (New York: Simon & Schuster, 1992); Viviana A. Rotman Zelizer, *Morals and Markets: The Development of Life Insurance in the United States* (New York: Columbia University Press, 1979).

12. Ira Katznelson, *City Trenches: Urban Politics and the Patterning of Class in the United States* (Chicago: 1982); Jeff Manza and Clem Brooks, *Social Cleavages and Political Change: Voter Alignments and U.S. Party Coalitions* (New York: Oxford University Press, 1999).

13. All of the above examples are taken from the 1880 and 1900 Boston city directories (see appendix). Two books devoted specifically to the evangelization question are Brown and McKeown, *The Poor Belong to Us*, and Yaakov Ariel, *Evangelizing the Chosen People: Missions to the Jews in America, 1880–2000* (Chapel Hill: University of North Carolina Press, 2000).

14. Given both exogenous and endogenous pressures to maintain group boundaries, these communities might be said to display both closure and appropriable social organization, two traits featured by sociologist James S. Coleman in the formation and maintenance of social capital. See Coleman's "Social Capital in the Creation of Human Capital," *American Journal of Sociology*, vol. 94 (1988): S95–S120; see also Raymond Breton, "Institutional Completeness of Ethnic Communities and the Personal Relations of Immigrants," *American Journal of Sociology*, vol. 70, no. 2 (September 1964): 193–205; Michael Hechter, "Group Formation and the Cultural Division of Labor," *American Journal of Sociology*, vol. 84, no. 2 (September 1978): 293–318; Alejandro Portes and Patricia Landolt, "The Downside of So-

cial Capital," *American Prospect*, vol. 26 (May–June 1996): 18–21; Charles Tilly, *Durable Inequality* (Berkeley: University of California Press, 1998).

15. John Bodnar, *The Transplanted: A History of Immigrants in Urban America* (Bloomington: Indiana University Press, 1985), p. 125.

16. Ibid., pp. 53–54.

17. Ibid., p. 128.

18. Ibid., p. 140.

19. Barton, *Peasants and Strangers*, pp. 70–71.

20. Kathleen Neils Conzen, *Immigrant Milwaukee, 1836–1860: Accommodation and Community in a Frontier City* (Cambridge, Mass.: Harvard University Press), pp. 154–155; also Bodnar, *Transplanted*, pp. 124–125.

21. Greene, *For God and Country*, p. 3.

22. Ibid., pp. 11–12; also Barton, *Peasants and Strangers*; Cinel, *From Italy to San Francisco*; Conzen, *Immigrant Milwaukee*; Shaw, *Catholic Parish as a Way-Station*.

23. See, for example, Dobbert, *Disintegration of Immigrant Community*; Finke and Stark, *Churching of America*; Herberg, *Protestant—Catholic—Jew*.

24. Bodnar, *Transplanted*, pp. 125–126.

25. Kathleen Neils Conzen, "Germans," in Stephan Thernstrom, ed., *Harvard Encyclopedia of American Ethnic Groups* (Cambridge: Belknap, 1980), p. 416; Diner, *Time for Gathering*, p. 87.

26. Deborah Dash Moore, *B'Nai B'rith and the Challenge of Ethnic Leadership* (Albany: SUNY Press, 1981), pp. 12, 54; see also Diner, *Time for Gathering*; Soyer, *Jewish Immigrant Associations*.

27. *Hebrew-American*, vol. 1, no. 1 (March 16, 1894): 1.

28. Ibid.

29. Ibid. All of the above headlines are taken from this issue.

30. "American Hebrew vs. Hebrew American," *Hebrew American*, March 30, 1894.

31. Bodnar, *Transplanted*, pp. 138–139.

32. Ibid., p. 130.

33. Gerald Gamm, *Urban Exodus: Why The Jews Left Boston and the Catholics Stayed* (Cambridge, Mass.: Harvard University Press, 1999).

34. An obvious exception overlooked by Gamm's thesis is the fact that Orthodox Jews must live within walking distance of their temple in order to attend Shabbat services, but this is only a minor point and does not refute his general argument.

35. Gamm, *Urban Exodus*, p. 21; see also Portes and Landolt, "Downside of Social Capital."

36. Albert O. Hirschman, *Exit, Voice, and Loyalty : Responses to Decline in Firms, Organizations, and States* (Cambridge, Mass.: Harvard University Press, 1970); Mancur Olson, *The Logic of Collective Action* (Cambridge, Mass.: Harvard University Press, 1965); Sidney Verba, Kay Lehman Schlozman, and Henry E. Brady, *Voice and Equality: Civic Voluntarism in American Politics* (Cambridge, Mass.: Harvard University Press, 1995); Mark E. Warren, *Democracy and Association* (Princeton, N.J.: Princeton University Press, 2001).

37. The originator of WASP is commonly believed to be E. Digby Baltzell, *The Protestant Establishment: Aristocracy and Caste in America* (New York: Random House, 1964), though the *OED* lists Erdman B. Palmore as the very first person to use the term in writing, in "Ethnophaulisms and Ethnocentrism," *American Journal of Sociology*, vol. 67, no. 4. (January 1962): 442–445.

38. Leonard Dinnerstein and David M. Reiners, *Ethnic Americans: A History of Immigration and Assimilation* (New York: Harper & Row, 1982).

39. Waters, *Ethnic Options*, p. 18.

40. Elisabeth S. Clemens, "Organizational Repertoires and Institutional Change: Women's Groups and the Transformation of U.S. Politics, 1890–1920," *American Journal of Sociology*, vol. 98, no. 4 (January 1993): 755–798; Michael B. Katz, *In the Shadow of the Poorhouse: A Social History of Welfare in America* (New York: Basic Books, 1986); Kenneth D. Rose, *American Women and the Repeal of Prohibition* (New York: New York University Press, 1996); Theda Skocpol, *Protecting Soldiers and Mothers: The Political Origins of Social Policy in the United States* (Cambridge: Belknap, 1992); Diane Winston, *Red-Hot and Righteous: The Urban Religion of the Salvation Army* (Cambridge, Mass.: Harvard University Press, 1999).

41. I consider Judaism to be a quasi-racial category, however, because the formal precepts of the Jewish religion designate membership as a question of lineage (by most definitions, one is a Jew if one's mother is a Jew). Though self-imposed through tradition and consensus, the criterion for membership in the Jewish community thus appears strangely similar to the "one-drop" rules created to differentiate blacks and whites in the early days of the slave trade. Judaism is a community of blood more than a community of faith. I take this to be a central distinction between race-based and ethnoreligiously based communities.

42. For a more complete statement on this topic see Kaufman, "Political Economy of Inter-Denominational Competition," and Finke and Stark, *Churching of America*.

43. Ariel, *Evangelizing the Chosen People*, p. 3.

44. George Emery and and J. C. Herbert Emery. *A Young Man's Benefit: The Independent Order of Odd Fellows and Sickness Insurance in the United States and Canada, 1860–1929* (Montreal: McGill-Queen's University Press, 1999), pp. 44–46.

45. I am eternally grateful to sociologist Mary Ann Clawson for so graciously showing copies of this Pythian directory to me. She uncovered it several years ago while researching her own book on the subject, *Constructing Brotherhood: Class, Gender, and Fraternalism* (Princeton, N.J.: Princeton University Press, 1989).

46. Sociologist Stanley Lieberson offers a method for doing this in *A Matter of Taste: How Names, Fashions, and Culture Change* (New Haven, Conn.: Yale University Press, 2000). The obvious complications in determining the ethnoreligious diversity of such lodges are (a) finding reliable means of identifying the racial and/or ethnoreligious background of club members and (b) proving that the homogeneity of membership was the result of systematic exclusion.

47. "Pythian Supreme Lodge," *Buffalo Evening News*, September 5, 1894.

48. "Encampment of Pythians," *New York Times*, August 28, 1894.

49. "Baltimore German Pythians in Revolt," *New York Times*, December 26, 1894.

50. Gerald Gamm and Robert D. Putnam, "The Growth of Voluntary Associations in America, 1840–1940," *Journal of Interdisciplinary History*, vol. 29, no. 3 (Winter 1999): 538. See also Emery and Emery, *Young Man's Benefit*, especially pp. 44–45. My own data confirm the observation that there is a negative relationship between city size and lodge density, though this relationship is not terribly robust.

51. This last figure represents only those clubs organized outside the fraternal realm—that is, nonfraternal clubs and societies that bear some explicit reference to an ethnic group of some kind in their titles. Fraternal groups were not counted in this way because, as just illustrated, it is often hard to know with any certainty whether a specific order or lodge is organized around ethnic lines.

52. When one controls for the percentage of whites in each city's population, there is a statistically significant negative correlation (−.443) between the percentage of foreign-born and the number of nativist fraternities per capita ($p = .001$).

53. Emery and Emery, *Young Man's Benefit*, p. 44.

54. Lewis Atherton, *Mainstreet on the Middle Border* (Bloomington: Indiana University Press, 1954), pp. 290–291.

55. Louis Dwight Harvell Weld, "Social and Economic Survey of a Community in the Red River Valley." University of Minnesota, Current Problems No. 4 (January 1915): 74–75; quoted ibid., p. 292.

56. The most precise study of late nineteenth-century lodge affiliation to date is that of Emery and Emery, *Young Man's Benefit.*

57. Elisabeth S. Clemens, *The People's Lobby: Organizational Innovation and the Rise of Interest Group Politics in the United States, 1890–1925* (Chicago: University of Chicago Press, 1997); Putnam, *Bowling Alone: The Collapse and Revival of American Community* (New York: Simon & Schuster, 2000); Theda Skocpol, "The Tocqueville Problem: Civic Engagement in American Democracy," Social Science History, vol. 21, no. 4 (Winter 1997): 455–479. For a fine example of a debate over the specific impact of women's associations on the emergence of state pensions for mothers, see Cheryl Logan Sparks and Peter R. Walniuk, "The Enactment of Mothers' Pensions: Civic Mobilization and Agenda Setting or Benefits of the Ballot?" *American Political Science Review*, vol. 89 (1995): 710–720; and Theda Skocpol, Christopher Howard, Susan Goodrich Lehmann, and Marjorie Abend-Wein, "Women's Associations and the Enactment of Mothers' Pensions in the United States," *American Political Science Review*, vol. 87 (1993): 686–699.

58. Edward Nelson Palmer, "Negro Secret Societies," *Social Forces*, vol. 23, no. 2 (December 1944): 211–212.

59. William A. Muraskin, *Middle-Class Blacks in a White Society: Prince Hall Freemasonry in America* (Berkeley: University of California Press, 1075), p. 41; emphasis added.

60. Dorothee Schneider, *Trade Unions and Community: The German Working Class in New York City, 1870–1900* (Urbana: University of Illinois Press, 1994), p. 29.

61. See, for example, Alba, *Ethnic Identity*; Bernard, *Melting Pot and Altar*; Licht, *Getting Work*; Lieberson, *Piece of the Pie*; Thernstrom, *Other Bostonians*; Waldinger, *Still the Promised City?*; Waters, *Ethnic Options*; Zunz, *Changing Face of Inequality.*

62. Erik Kirschbaum, *The Eradication of German Culture in the United States: 1917–1918* (Stuttgart: Verlag Hans-Dieter Heinz, 1986).

63. Roosevelt, quoted in Rippley, *German-Americans*, p. 191; see also pp. 180–195; and H. C. Peterson and Gilbert C. Fite, *Opponents of War, 1917–1918* (Madison: University of Wisconsin Press, 1957).

64. Heinz Kloss, "German-American Language Maintenance Efforts," in Joshua A. Fishman, ed., *Language Loyalty in the United States* (New York: Arno, [1966] 1978), pp. 248–249.

65. Rippley, *German-Americans*, p. 180.

66. Alba, *Ethnic Identity*; Bernard, *Melting Pot and Altar*; Licht, *Getting Work*; Lieberson, *Piece of the Pie*; Thernstrom, *Other Bostonians*; Zunz, *Changing Face of Inequality.*

67. Barton, *Peasants and Strangers*, p. 87.

Part II

1. See, for example, Geoffrey Hawthorn, *Plausible Worlds: Possibility and Understanding in History and the Social Sciences* (Cambridge: Cambridge University Press, 1991).

Chapter 4

1. Alfred D. Chandler, Jr., *Strategy and Structure: Chapters in the History of the Industrial Enterprise* (Cambridge, Mass.: MIT Press, 1962); Morton J. Horowitz, *The Transformation of American Law, 1870–1960: The Crisis of Legal Orthodoxy* (New York: Oxford

University Press, 1992); Charles Perrow, "A Society of Organizations," *Theory and Society*, vol. 20 (1991): 725–762; William G. Roy, *Socializing Capital: The Rise of the Large Industrial Corporation in America* (Princeton, N.J.: Princeton University Press, 1997).

2. Edward W. Bemis, ed., *Municipal Monopolies, A Collection of Papers by American Economists and Specialists* (New York: Crowell, 1899); Hendrik Hartog, *Public Property and Private Power: The Corporation of the City of New York in American Law, 1730–1870* (Ithaca, N.Y.: Cornell University Press, [1983] 1989); Louis Hartz, *Economic Policy and Democratic Thought: Pennsylvania, 1776–1860* (Cambridge, Mass.: Harvard University Press, 1948); Seymour Mandelbaum, *Boss Tweed's New York* (New York: Wiley, 1965); Eugene P. Moehring, *Public Works and the Patterns of Urban Real Estate Growth in Manhattan, 1835–1894* (New York: Arno, 1981); Eric H. Monkkonen, *The Local State: Public Money and American Cities* (Stanford, Cal.: Stanford University Press, 1995).

3. Michael McGerr, *The Decline of Popular Politics: The American North, 1865–1928* (New York: Oxford University Press, 1986); Michael Schudson, *The Good Citizen: A History of American Civic Life* (New York: Free Press, 1998).

4. Terry Nichols Clark and Lorna Crowley Ferguson, *City Money: Political Processes, Fiscal Strain, and Retrenchment* (New York: Columbia University Press, 1983); Philip J. Ethington, *The Public City: The Political Construction of Urban Life in San Francisco, 1850–1900* (Cambridge: Cambridge University Press, 1994); David C. Hammack, *Power and Society: Greater New York at the Turn of the Century* (New York: Russell Sage Foundation, 1982); Samuel P. Hays, "The Changing Political Structure of the City in Industrial America," *Journal of Urban History*, vol. 1, no. 1 (1974): 6–38; Mandelbaum, *Boss Tweed's New York*; Moehring, *Public Works*; Monkkonen, *Local State*; Margaret Susan Thompson, "Corruption—or Confusion? Lobbying and Congressional Government in the Early Gilded Age," *Congress and the Presidency*, vol. 10, no. 2 (Autumn 1983): 169–193.

5. On the changing corporate structure of voluntary, nonprofit organizations, see Peter Dobkin Hall, "A Historical Overview of the Private Nonprofit Sector," in Walter W. Powell, ed., *The Nonprofit Sector: A Research Handbook* (New Haven, Conn.: Yale University Press, 1987), pp. 3–26.

6. In results not presented here, I have established through multivariate regression a statistically significant relationship between the growth in the number of professional, mercantile, and civic associations in a cross section of American cities and the growth in related areas of municipal finance across a 53-case sample of medium- to large-sized cities between 1880 and 1890. See Jason Kaufman, "Economic Associations and Interest-Group Formation in American Political Development, 1865–1900," unpublished paper, Department of Sociology, Harvard University, Cambridge, Mass., Spring 2001.

7. Arthur Cecil Bining and Thomas C. Cochran, *The Rise of American Economic Life*, 4th ed. (New York: Scribner, 1964).

8. Elisabeth S. Clemens, *The People's Lobby: Organizational Innovation and the Rise of Interest Group Politics in the United States, 1890–1925* (Chicago: University of Chicago Press, 1997).

9. James Madison, "Federalist Paper No. 10," *The Federalist Papers*, Clinton Rossiter, ed. (New York: Mentor, [1788] 1961); cf. Clemens, *People's Lobby*; Theda Skocpol, Marshall Ganz, and Ziad Munson, "A Nation of Organizers: The Institutional Origins of Civic Voluntarism in the United States," *American Political Science Review*, vol. 94, no. 3 (September 2000): 527–546; Theda Skocpol, "The Tocqueville Problem: Civic Engagement in American Democracy," *Social Science History*, vol. 21, no. 4 (Winter 1997): 455–479.

10. Alexis de Tocqueville, *Democracy in America*, George Lawrence, trans. (New York: Harper & Row, 1988 [1966]), p. 190.

11. Ibid.

12. Ibid.

13. Ibid., p. 515.

14. For example, Edwin Amenta, Bruce G. Carruthers, and Yvonne Zylan, "A Hero for the Aged? The Townsend Movement, the Political Mediation Model, and U.S. Old-Age Policy, 1934–1950," *American Journal of Sociology*, vol. 98, no. 2 (September 1992): 308–339; Clemens, *People's Lobby*; Elisabeth S. Clemens, "Organizational Repertoires and Institutional Change: Women's Groups and the Transformation of U.S. Politics, 1890–1920," *American Journal of Sociology*, vol. 98, no. 4 (January 1993): 755–798; Theda Skocpol, *Protecting Soldiers and Mothers: The Political Origins of Social Policy in the United States* (Cambridge: Belknap, 1992); Skocpol, "Tocqueville Problem"; Theda Skocpol, Christopher Howard, Susan Goodrich Lehmann, and Marjorie Abend-Wein, "Women's Associations and the Enactment of Mothers' Pensions in the United States," *American Political Science Review*, vol. 87 (1993): 686–699; Skocpol, Ganz, and Munson, "Nation of Organizers."

15. James Bryce, *The American Commonwealth* (London: Macmillan, 1888); Martin Shefter, "Party and Patronage," *Politics and Society*, vol. 7 (1977): 404–451.

16. Mark C. Carnes, *Secret Ritual and Manhood in Victorian America* (New Haven, Conn.: Yale University Press, 1989); Mary Ann Clawson, *Constructing Brotherhood: Class, Gender, and Fraternalism* (Princeton, N.J.: Princeton University Press, 1989); Lynn Dumenil, *Freemasonry and American Culture, 1880–1939* (Princeton, N.J.: Princeton University Press, 1984); Arthur M. Schlesinger, "Biography of a Nation of Joiners," *American Historical Review*, vol. 50, no. 1 (October 1944): 1–25.

17. Clemens, *People's Lobby*, pp. 2–3.

18. Ibid., pp. 41–64; also Clemens, "Organizational Repertoires and Institutional Change."

19. Skocpol, "Tocqueville Problem"; Skocpol, Ganz, and Munson, "Nation of Organizers."

20. Tocqueville, *Democracy in America*, p. 193.

21. I say "exclusive" because membership was a carefully guarded privilege (to different degrees, naturally); "voluntary" because no man or woman could be coerced into participation in these groups by any power under law; "nonprofit" because the organizations themselves were not oriented around capital accumulation, though their members often were (indeed, this was often the very motivation for joining); and "organizations" because these groups were by and large governed by systematic rules and regulations that set forth institutional goals, capabilities, and limitations.

22. Max Weber, "Class, Status, and Party," in H. H. Gerth and C. Wright Mills, eds., *From Max Weber: Essays in Sociology* (New York: Oxford University Press, 1946), p. 194.

23. Chi-nien Chung and Mark Granovetter, "Trade Associations as an Organizational Form: NELA and the Development of the Early American Electricity Industry," paper presented at the 1999 Annual Meeting of the American Sociological Association, Chicago, August 6–10, 1999; Chi-nien Chung, "Networks and Governance in Trade Associations: AEIC and NELA in the Development of the American Electricity Industry, 1885–1910," *International Journal of Sociology and Social Policy*, vol. 17 (1997): 57–110; Jessica I. Elfenbein, *Civics, Commerce, and Community: The History of the Greater Washington Board of Trade, 1889–1989* (Dubuque, Iowa: Kendall/Hunt, 1989); Hays, "Changing Political Structure of the City."

24. Letter, Albert Shaw to William Howe Tolman, March 12, 1897, Shaw Papers, New York Public Library, quoted in Hammack, *Power and Society*, p. 13.

25. *Holbrook's Newark City and Business Directory for the Year Ending April 1, 1883*, vol. 48 (Newark, N.J.: Holbrooks' Steam Press, 1882), p. 1011.

26. David Hammack has rendered the study of social class in late nineteenth-century American cities a great service with his careful study of membership in New York's elite social clubs between 1892 and 1896 (*Power and Society*, pp. 72–77); Weber, "Class, Status, and Party," p. 189; emphasis added. For an alternative account that emphasizes the consolidation of interests among the elite of New York City rather than their segmentation, see Sven Beckert, *The Monied Metropolis: New York City and the Consolidation of the American Bourgeoisie, 1850–1896* (New York: Cambridge University Press, 2001).

27. Paul Porzelt, *The Metropolitan Club of New York* (New York: Rizzoli, 1982), pp. 2–6. Porzelt adds that the Union Club of New York, "the Mother of Clubs," was formed in 1836 after a group of wealthy New Yorkers traveled abroad together and "had become acquainted with the social clubs of the West End of London." Apparently, one of the founders, diarist and mayor of New York Philip Hone, wrote at the time, "If this club can be gotten up like the English clubs it may succeed; little short of that will meet the views of the members."

28. Francis Gerry Fairfield, *The Clubs of New York* (New York: Arno, [1873] 1975), p. 15.

29. In addition to stoking up public support for the war effort, the Union League of Philadelphia sponsored and recruited several so-called Union League regiments by offering enlistees cash bounties. Following the creation of the Massachusetts' Fifty-fourth Colored Troops, they also sponsored a "colored" Philadelphia regiment. See *Chronicle of the Union League of Philadelphia, 1862–1902* (Philadelphia: Wm. F. Fell, 1902), pp. 83–101; also see Beckert, *Monied Metropolis*.

30. In 1875, the members of the Union League had taken a public stand against those they considered to be "undesirable candidates" in the Republican Party and to express their dismay at the Democrats' first majority in the commonwealth's House of Representatives for 16 years. Nonetheless, this effort at intraparty reform failed, and the Union League was aggressively attacked for its presumptuousness by local newspapers and the city's Republican Party bosses. This defeat, coupled with declining membership and the financial hardships of the mid-1870s, seems to have elicited the political withdrawal referred to in the above passage. See *Chronicle of the Union League*, pp. 197–199.

31. Ibid., p. 227. A similar profile is offered of the Union League Club of New York in Harold F. Gosnell, *Boss Platt and His New York Machine* (Chicago: University of Chicago Press, 1924), pp. 127–128.

32. Fairfield, *Clubs of New York*, p. 143.

33. Ibid.

34. Porzelt, *Metropolitan Club*, p. 105.

35. Ibid., p. 107.

36. Andrew Abbott, *The System of Professions: An Essay on the Division of Expert Labor* (Chicago: University of Chicago Press, 1988); Magali Sarfatti Larson, *The Rise of Professionalism* (Berkeley: University of California Press, 1977); Paul Starr, *The Social Transformation of American Medicine* (New York: Basic Books, 1982).

37. Michael Powell, From *Patrician to Professional Elite: The Transformation of the New York City Bar Association* (New York: Russell Sage Foundation, 1988).

38. See, for example, Hammack, *Power and Society*, and Moehring, *Public Works*.

39. Joseph L. Arnold, "The Neighborhood and City Hall: The Origin of Neighborhood Associations in Baltimore, 1880–1911," *Journal of Urban History*, vol. 6, no. 1 (November 1979): 11.

40. Skocpol, *Protecting Soldiers and Mothers*; Ann Shola Orloff, *The Politics of Pensions:*

A Comparative Analysis of Britain, Canada, and the United States, 1880–1940 (Madison: University of Wisconsin Press, 1993).

41. Skocpol, *Protecting Soldiers and Mothers*; also Shefter, "Party and Patronage"; Martin Shefter, "Party, Bureaucracy and Political Change in the United States," in Louis Maisel and Joseph Cooper, eds., *Political Parties: Development and Decay* (Beverly Hills, Cal.: Sage, 1978).

42. Hammack, *Power and Society*, pp. 148–151.

43. William Bennett Munro, *The Government of American Cities* (New York: Macmillan, 1916), pp. 22, 294–299; also Amy Bridges, *Morning Glories: Municipal Reform in the Southwest* (Princeton, N.J.: Princeton University Press, 1997), pp. 57–58; Ernest S. Griffith, *A History of American City Government: The Progressive Years and Their Aftermath, 1900–1920* (New York: Praeger, 1974), pp. 56–58; Bradley Robert Rice, *Progressive Cities: The Commission Government Movement in America, 1901–1920* (Austin: University of Texas Press, 1977), pp. 3–18.

44. Jones's quotation is from Galveston, *Record of Proceedings*, February 4, 1901, cited in Rice, *Progressive Cities*, p. 13.

45. E. R. Cheesborough to Clara Holmes, May 30, 1910, and an unidentified clipping circa 1908 enclosed with letter; John Cheesborough Papers, cited in Rice, *Progressive Cities*, pp. 16, 130; also pp. 5, 10–12, 14–15.

46. George Kibbe Turner, "Galveston: A Business Corporation," *McClure's Magazine*, vol. 27, no. 6 (October 1906), pp. 610, 619, 612, 620, 610; emphasis added.

47. Griffith, *History of American City Government*, p. 56; Munro, *Government of American Cities*, pp. 22, 304–319; G. K. Turner, "Galveston: A Business Corporation," p. 612; James Weinstein, "Organized Business and the City Commission and Manager Movements," *Journal of Southern History*, vol. 28 (February–November 1962): 169–170. For examples of muckraking pieces in support of the city-manager plan, see C. Arthur Williams, "Governing Cities by Commission," *World To-Day*, vol. 11 (September 1906): 945; "Galveston's Government," *Tradesman*, June 15, 1906, p. 50; both cited in Rice, *Progressive Cities*, p. 17.

48. David Knoke, "The Spread of Municipal Reform: Temporal, Spatial, and Social Dynamics," *American Journal of Sociology*, vol. 87, no. 6 (1982): 1325. Knoke notes that, of those cities abandoning the commission plan, twice as many switched to the newer council-manager plan (a further refinement on the centralization of authority theme, begun in Staunton, Va., in 1908) as returned to the mayor-council plan.

49. There is some cause for confusion over this last set of developments: Staunton passed the nation's first city-manager plan, but it did not incorporate the idea of a related commission elected at large, as adopted from the earlier Galveston-Des Moines plan.

50. Knoke, "Spread of Municipal Reform," p. 1315; Rice, *Progressive Cities*, pp. 101–103.

51. Kenneth Finegold, *Experts and Politicians: Reform Challenges to Machine Politics in New York, Cleveland, and Chicago* (Princeton, N.J.: Princeton University Press, 1995); Hays, "Changing Political Structure of the City"; Robert L. Lineberry and Edmund P. Fowler, "Reformism and Public Policies in American Cities," *American Political Science Review*, vol. 61, no. 3 (September 1967): 701–716; Lowi, *At the Pleasure of the Mayor: Patronage and Power in New York City, 1898–1958* (London: Free Press, Collier-Macmillan, 1964).

52. Skocpol, "Tocqueville Problem."

Chapter 5

An earlier draft of this chapter was published as "Rise and Fall of a Nation of Joiners: The Knights of Labor Revisited." *Journal of Interdisciplinary History*, vol. 31, no. 4 (Spring 2001): 553–579.

1. Leon Fink, *Workingmen's Democracy: The Knights of Labor and American Politics* (Ur-

bana: University of Illinois Press, 1983); Philip S. Foner, *History of the Labor Movement in the United States*, vol. 2 (New York: International Publishers, 1947); Victoria C. Hattam, *Labor Visions and State Power: The Origins of Business Unionism in the United States* (Princeton, N.J.: Princeton University Press, 1993); J. Rogers Hollingsworth, "The United States," in Raymond Grew, ed., *Crises of Political Development in Europe and the United States* (Princeton, N.J.: Princeton University Press, 1978); John M. Laslett and Seymour Martin Lipset, eds., *Failure of a Dream: Essays in the History of American Socialism* (Garden City, N.Y.: Anchor Press, 1974); Richard Oestreicher, "Urban Working-Class Political Behavior and Theories of American Electoral Politics, 1870–1940," *Journal of American History*, vol. 74 (1988): 1257–1286; Michael Shalev and Walter Korpi, "Working Class Mobilization and American Exceptionalism," *Economic and Industrial Democracy*, vol. 1 (1980): 31–61; Werner Sombart, *Why Is There No Socialism in the United States?* (White Plains, N.Y.: M. E. Sharpe, 1976); Kim Voss, *The Making of American Exceptionalism: The Knights of Labor and Class Formation in the Nineteenth Century* (Ithaca, N.Y.: Cornell University Press, 1993); Robert E. Weir, *Beyond Labor's Veil: The Culture of the Knights of Labor* (University Park: Pennsylvania State University Press, 1996).

2. Weir, *Beyond Labor's Veil*, p. 16, n. 32.

3. Voss, *Making of American Exceptionalism*, p. 241.

4. Foner, *History of the Labor Movement*; Gerald N. Grob, *Workers and Utopia: A Study of Ideological Conflict in the American Labor Movement, 1865–1900* (Chicago: Quadrangle Books, 1969); Victoria Hattam, "Economic Visions and Political Strategies: American Labor and the State, 1865–1896," *Studies in American Political Development*, vol. 4 (1990): 82–129; Selig Perlman, "Upheaval and Reorganization (Since 1876)," in John R. Commons, ed., *History of Labour in the United States*, vol. 2 (New York: Macmillan, 1926); Lloyd Ulman, *The Rise of the National Trade Union* (Cambridge, Mass.: Harvard University Press, 1955).

5. Voss, *Making of American Exceptionalism*; Weir, *Beyond Labor's Veil*.

6. Voss, *Making of American Exceptionalism*.

7. Joseph H. Gerteis, "Class and the Color Line: The Sources and Limits of Interracial Class Coalition, 1880–1896," Ph.D. dissertation, Department of Sociology, University of North Carolina, Chapel Hill, 2000; Gwendolyn Mink, *Old Labor and New Immigrants in American Political Development: Union, Party, and State, 1875–1920* (Ithaca, N.Y.: Cornell University Press, 1986); Kim Voss, "The Collapse of a Social Movement: The Interplay of Mobilizing Structures, Framing, and Political Opportunities in the Knights of Labor," in Doug McAdam, John D. McCarthy, and Mayer N. Zald, eds., *Comparative Perspectives on Social Movements: Political Opportunities, Mobilizing Structures and Cultural Framings* (New York: Cambridge University Press, 1996), pp. 227–258; Kim Voss, "Labor Organization and Class Alliance: Industries, Communities, and the Knights of Labor," *Theory & Society, 1988*, vol. 17, no. 3 (May 1988): 329–364; Weir, *Behind Labor's Veil*.

8. Other labor organizations founded on this fraternal model include the Knights of St. Crispin, the Supreme Mechanical Order of the Sun, the Brotherhood of the Footboard, and the Sons of Vulcan. Martin Shefter notes that "the fraternalism that characterized such organizations was quite similar to the spirit of mutual assistance among brother workers that labor unions drew upon and sought to strengthen among their members," in "Trade Unions and Political Machines: The Organization and Disorganization of the American Working Class in the Late Nineteenth Century," in Ira Katznelson and Aristide R. Zolberg, eds., *Working-Class Formation: Nineteenth-Century Patterns in Western Europe and the United States* (Princeton, N.J.: Princeton University Press, 1986), pp. 221–222.

9. Katznelson and Zolberg, *Working-Class Formation*; Michael P. Hanagan, *Nascent Proletarians: Class Formation in Post-Revolutionary France* (New York: Oxford University

Press, 1989); Gary Marks, *Unions in Politics: Britain, Germany, and the United States in the Nineteenth and Early Twentieth Centuries* (Princeton, N.J.: Princeton University Press, 1989); George Steinmetz, *Regulating the Social: The Welfare State and Local Politics in Imperial Germany* (Princeton, N.J.: Princeton University Press, 1993); Bruce Western, *Between Class and Market: Postwar Unionization in the Capitalist Democracies* (Princeton, N.J.: Princeton University Press, 1997).

10. Jonathan Garlock, *Guide to the Local Assemblies of the Knights of Labor* (Westport, Conn.: Greenwood, 1982); *Holbrook's Newark City and Business Directory for the Year Ending April 1, 1883*, vol. 48 (Newark, N.J.: Holbrooks' Steam Press, 1886–1889).

11. I owe Joe Gerteis great thanks for this invaluable though rather dispiriting piece of information.

12. Arthur M. Schlesinger, "Biography of a Nation of Joiners," *American Historical Review*, vol. 50, no. 1 (October 1944): 23.

13. Ira Katznelson, *City Trenches: Urban Politics and the Patterning of Class in the United States* (Chicago: University of Chicago Press, 1982), p. 18.

14. Oestreicher, "Urban Working-Class Political Behavior," p. 1281.

15. For examples of ethnocultural, historical accounts of American labor politics see Lee Benson, "Group Cohesion and Social and Ideological Conflict," *American Behavioral Scientist*, vol. 16 (1973): 741–767; Paul Kleppner, "From Ethnoreligious Conflict to 'Social Harmony': Coalitional and Party Transformations in the 1890s," in Seymour Martin Lipset, ed., *Emerging Coalitions in American Politics* (San Francisco: Institute for Contemporary Studies, 1978); Paul Kleppner, ed., *The Evolution of American Electoral Systems* (Westport, Conn.: Greenwood, 1981); Samuel T. McSeveney, *The Politics of Depression: Political Behavior in the Northeast, 1893–1896* (New York: Oxford University Press, 1972); Mink, *Old Labor and New Immigrants*; Oestreicher, "Urban Working-Class Political Behavior." Critiques of the ethnocultural perspective on American political history include Allan J. Lichtman, "Political Realignment and 'Ethnocultural' Voting in Late Nineteenth Century America," *Journal of Social History*, vol. 16 (1983): 55–83; Richard L. McCormick, "Ethno-Cultural Interpretations of Nineteenth Century American Voting Behavior," *Political Science Quarterly*, vol. 89 (1974): 351–377; James E. Wright, "The Ethnocultural Model of Voting: A Behavioral and Historial Critique," *American Behavioral Scientist*, vol. 16 (1973): 653–674.

16. Samuel Gompers, *Seventy Years of Life and Labor: An Autobiography of Samuel Gompers*, Nick Salvatore, ed. (Ithaca, N.Y.: ILR Press, [1925] 1984), p. 76.

17. Ibid., pp. 284–285.

18. Shefter, "Trade Unions and Political Machines," p. 259.

19. See also Jason Kaufman, "Three Views of Associationalism in 19th Century America," *American Journal of Sociology*, vol. 104 (1999), 1296–1345; Jason Kaufman, "The Political Economy of Inter-Denominational Competition in Late 19th Century American Cities," *Journal of Urban History* (2002).

20. Quoted in Kenneth Lapides, ed., *Marx and Engels on the Trade Unions* (New York: Praeger, 1987), pp. 141–142.

21. Henry J. Browne, *The Catholic Church and the Knights of Labor* (Washington, D.C.: Catholic University of America Press, 1949), p. 288; Perlman, "Upheaval and Reorganization," p. 482.

22. Perlman, "Upheaval and Reorganization," 473. It should also be noted that Gompers was himself a former member of the Knights, having joined in 1873 while working as a shoemaker in New York City. Despite his many subsequent feuds with Knights' leader Terence Powderly, Gompers proudly boasted that he had never nor would ever reveal the secrets of the order (Gompers, *Seventy Years of Life and Labor*, p. 27). For a general history of the AFL,

see Lewis L. Lorwin, *The American Federation of Labor: History, Policies, Prospects* (Washington, D.C.: Brookings Institution, 1933).

23. Perlman, "Upheaval and Reorganization," p. 423.

24. American Federation of Labor, *Proceedings, 1887* (Bloomington, Ind.: AFL, 1887), p. 11; quoted in Perlman, "Upheaval and Reorganization," p. 413. See also Frank Dobbin, "The Origins of Private Social Insurance: Public Policy and Fringe Benefits in America, 1920–1950," *American Journal of Sociology* vol. 97, no. 2 (1992): 1416–1450.

25. November 26, 1883; reproduced in Terence V. Powderly, *Thirty Years of Labor* (New York: A. M. Kelley [1890] 1967), p. 295.

26. Weir, *Beyond Labor's Veil*, p. 27; Browne, *Catholic Church and Knights of Labor*, pp. 35–36.

27. Browne, *Catholic Church and Knights of Labor*, pp. 21, 45; Charles W. Ferguson, *Fifty Million Brothers: A Panorama of American Lodges and Clubs* (New York: Farrar & Rinehart, 1937), pp. 296–301. Note, however, that Catholics also had their share of fraternal organizations, church groups, and mutual benefit associations.

28. The other founders of the order had similar fraternal backgrounds (Weir, *Beyond Labor's Veil*, p. 22): Cofounders Robert Keen and Robert Macauley belonged to the Grand Army of the Republic and the Knights of Pythias, respectively. Charles Lichtman, who served as Grand-General Secretary from 1878 to 1881 and from 1886 to 1887 was a members of the Pythians, the Masons, the Odd Fellows, the Improved Order of Red Men, the Royal Arcanum, and the Order of the Golden Cross. Terence Powderly himself was a member in the Workingmen's Benevolent Association, the Ancient Order of Hibernians, and the Irish Land League.

29. Albert C. Stevens, *The Cyclopedia of Fraternities* (New York: E. B. Treat, 1907), p. 392.

30. Browne, *Catholic Church and Knights of Labor*, pp. 82–83.

31. Perlman, "Upheaval and Reorganization," pp. 343–344.

32. Browne, *Catholic Church and Knights of Labor*, p. 59.

33. Ibid., p. 62.

34. Foner (*History of the Labor Movement*, p. 90) comments that "the members of the Knights of Labor and the American working class as a whole paid a costly price for the decision from Rome in the form of a reactionary drive by the leadership of the order against militant trade unionism and those who espoused this policy."

35. Browne, *Catholic Church and Knights of Labor*, p. 91, author's emphasis.

36. Opponents of Powderly's stance on the temperance question included several assemblies of brewery employers and excluded liquor dealers and the large numbers of German members hostile to the idea of prohibition of any kind (Powderly, *Thirty Years of Labor*, pp. 313, 319).

37. Browne, *Catholic Church and Knights of Labor*, pp. 252, 302–304; Weir, *Beyond Labor's Veil*, pp. 95–96.

38. Perlman, "Upheaval and Reorganization," p. 299.

39. See Powderly, *Thirty Years of Labor*.

40. Henry David, *The History of the Haymarket Affair: A Study in the American Socio-Revolutionary and Labor Movements* (New York: Farrar & Rinehart, 1936).

41. For more on the Henry George-Abram Hewitt campaign of 1886, see Louis F. Post and Fred C. Leubuscher, *Henry George's 1886 Campaign: An Account of the George-Hewitt Campaign in the New York Municipal Election of 1886* (Westport, Conn.: Greenwood, [1887] 1961); and David C. Hammack, *Power and Society: Greater New York at the Turn of the Century* (New York: Russell Sage Foundation, 1982), pp. 112–117, 174–176.

42. Browne, *Catholic Church and Knights of Labor*, p. 292.

43. Post and Leubuscher, *Henry George's 1886 Campaign*, pp. 118–119.

44. *Boston Pilot,* July 16, 1887; quoted in Browne, *Catholic Church and Knights of Labor,* p. 288.

45. For more information, see Kaufman, "Three Views of Associationalism"; Jason Kaufman and Steven J. Tepper, "Groups or Gatherings? Sources of Political Engagement in 19th Century American Cities," *Voluntas: The International Journal of Voluntary and Nonprofit Organizations,* vol. 10, no. 4 (1999): 299–322.

46. Garlock, *Guide to Local Assemblies.*

47. Commissioner of Labor, *Sixteenth Annual Report of the Commissioner of Labor: Strikes and Lockouts* (Washington, D.C.: Government Printing Office 1901).

48. The time span 1885–1890 was chosen because it reflects the period between the Knights' peak membership and the end of the lodge-level data presented by Garlock in *Guide to Local Assemblies.* Nonetheless, similar analyses were run with both earlier and later start dates and provided comparable results. Because of the likelihood of serial correlation within cities over time and across cities for each year, a generalized least squares algorithm was constructed, allowing for a unique correlation parameter for each city (as opposed to applying the same correlation parameter across all cities). In addition, it was assumed that standard errors were heteroskedastic across cities (but not correlated across them). These adjustments were made to account for the unique combination of cross-sectional and longitudinal parameters in the data.

49. Note that this method of weighing effective opposition varies somewhat from Voss's approach. Because her primary aim was to reexamine traditional arguments about intraclass conflict leading to the Knights' demise, Voss accumulated an impressive array of longitudinal information about Knights' lodges in New Jersey. The variable on which her own effective opposition argument rests records only whether there was an employers' association in the locale in question (*Making of American Exceptionalism,* p. 191). To provide a better test of this hypothesis, one would need to compare strikes in which employers fought Knights, as opposed to other trade unions, and examine their subsequent impact on membership in both. Though I was unable to collect either type of data for my sample of 25 major cities, I use the percentage of strikes initiated that were subsequently declared failures to test Voss's idea that failed strikes demoralized the Knights and subsequently led to the dissolution of many local assemblies.

50. As is evident from the results reported in figure 5.1, the coefficient for the failed strikes variable was only significant in one of the four models examined here. Thus, it may be that effective opposition was relevant only under certain conditions or that the lone significant coefficient reflects some underlying noise in the model.

51. The year 1886 was included in both regressions because of its role as a pivotal year in the rise and fall of the Knights' organization. Otherwise put, 1886 was part and parcel of both the rise and fall in the total number of Knights' assemblies in cities across the country.

52. Perlman, "Upheaval and Reorganization," pp. 422–423.

53. Browne, *Catholic Church and Knights of Labor,* pp. 354–355.

54. R. E. M. Irving, *The Christian Democratic Parties of Western Europe* (London: Allen & Unwin, 1979); Katznelson and Zolberg, *Working-Class Formation*; Marks, *Unions in Politics*; Joya Misra and Alexander Hicks, "Catholicism and Unionization in Affluent Postwar Democracies: Catholicism, Culture, Party, and Unionization," *American Sociological Review,* vol. 59 (1994): 304–326; Western, *Between Class and Market.*

Chapter 6

An earlier draft of this chapter was published in *Studies in American Political Development,* vol. 15 (Spring 2001): 88–102. I owe special thanks to Katsch Belash for help with

German-language materials related to this project. All spellings of foreign words are given as in their original context.

1. Theda Skocpol, *States and Social Revolutions* (Cambridge: Cambridge University Press, 1979); Charles Tilly, "War Making and State Making as Organized Crime," in Peter B. Evans, Dietrich Rueschemeyer, and Theda Skocpol, eds., *Bringing the State Back In* (Cambridge: Cambridge University Press, 1985); Max Weber, "The Types of Legitimate Domination," in Guenther Roth and Claus Wittich, eds., *Economy and Society* (Berkeley: University of California Press, 1978).

2. William H. McNeill, *Keeping Together in Time: Dance and Drill in Human History* (Cambridge, Mass.: Harvard University Press, 1995), p. 140; Henry Metzner, *A Brief History of the American Turnerbund*, Theodore Stempfel, Jr., trans. (Pittsburgh: National Executive Committee of the American Turnerbund, 1924); James B. Trefethen and James E. Serven, *Americans and Their Guns: The National Rifle Association Story Through Nearly a Century of Service to the Nation* (Harrisburg, Pa.: Stackpole, 1967), p. 111.

3. Lawrence Delbert Cress, *Citizens in Arms: The Army and the Militia in American Society to the War of 1812* (Chapel Hill: University of North Carolina Press, 1982); Mark Pitcavage. "Ropes of Sand: Territorial Militias, 1801–1812," *Journal of the Early Republic*, vol. 13 (Winter 1993): 481–500.

4. Prior to the Dick Act, military matters were left to the states and often went unfulfilled, given a persistent lack of enthusiasm, manpower, and money. With the exception of Massachusetts and Connecticut, most states rarely met the standards expected of them by Congress. This is ironic, however, because their many representatives in the early congresses had lobbied vigorously to protect their right to muster and maintain state militias of their own, as opposed to a national militia system run by the federal government.

5. Jerry Cooper, *The Rise of the National Guard: The Evolution of the American Militia, 1865–1920* (Lincoln: University of Nebraska Press, 1997); Cress, *Citizens in Arms.*

6. Cooper, *Rise of the National Guard*, pp. 4–6.

7. Cress, *Citizens in Arms*, p. 58—from John Adams to Henry Knox, August 25, 1776.

8. Lawrence Delbert Cress, "An Armed Community: The Origins and Meaning of the Right to Bear Arms," *The Journal of American History*, vol. 71, issue 1 (June 1984): 22–42; Cress, *Citizens in Arms*; Pitcavage, "Ropes of Sand."

9. Ralph Ketcham, ed., *The Anti-Federalist Papers and the Constitutional Convention Debates* (New York: Penguin, 1986), Patrick Henry, "5 June 1788," p. 202.

10. Cress, "Armed Community," p. 34.

11. Cress, *Citizens in Arms*, p. 63.

12. Cress, "Armed Community," p. 34.

13. Cooper, *Rise of the National Guard*, p. 9.

14. Ibid.

15. As late as 1839, Secretary of War Joel R. Poinsett would complain that a "majority of [the militia] are armed with walking canes, fowling pieces, or unserviceable muskets"; quoted in Michael A. Bellesiles, "The Origins of American Gun Culture in the United States, 1760–1865," *The Journal of American History*, vol. 83, no. 2 (September 1996): 435. See also Michael A. Bellesiles, *Arming America: The Origins of a National Gun Culture* (New York: Knopf, 2000).

16. William H. Riker, *Soldiers of the States: The Role of the National Guard in American Democracy* (Washington, D.C.: Public Affairs Press, 1957), pp. 28–29; Pitcavage, "Ropes of Sand," pp. 496–497; Bellesiles, "Origins of American Gun Culture," pp. 431–435.

17. Riker, *Soldiers of the States*, p. 37; Alexis de Tocqueville, *Democracy in America*, George Lawrence, trans. (New York: Harper & Row, [1966] 1988), p. 169.

18. Pitcavage, "Ropes of Sand," pp. 493–494, 500.

19. II *American State Papers: Military Affairs*, pp. 663–664, quoted in Riker, *Soldiers of the States*, p. 37.

20. Riker, *Soldiers of the States*, pp. 39–40.

21. Lena London, "The Militia Fine, 1830–1860," *Military Affairs*, vol. 15 (Fall 1951): 133–144; Cooper, *Rise of The National Guard*, pp. 13–14.

22. John Gorham Palfrey, "A Plea for the Militia System in a Discourse Delivered Before the Ancient and Honorable Artillery Company, on its CXCVIIth anniversary, June 1, 1835" (Boston: Dutton & Wentworth, 1835), p. 5–7; emphasis added.

23. Bellesiles, "Origins of American Gun Culture," pp. 435, 434–438.

24. Robert M. Fogelson, *America's Armories: Architecture, Society, and Public Order* (Cambridge, Mass.: Harvard University Press, 1989), pp. 4–5.

25. Ibid., p. 5.

26. Cooper, *Rise of the National Guard*, p. 16.

27. Ibid., p. 17.

28. Michael Feldberg, *The Philadelphia Riots of 1844: A Study of Ethnic Conflict* (Westport, Conn.: Greenwood, 1975).

29. Fogelson, *America's Armories*, p. 4.

30. Cooper, *Rise of the National Guard*, pp. 15–16.

31. It should be noted that the four cities represented in this table might overrepresent the actual prevalence of civilian militia organizations at the time. Unfortunately, my interest in such organizations was piqued only after much of the data collection had already been completed. Militia groups are usually recorded in a separate section of city directories than fraternal, civic, and benevolent organizations, and thus through my own oversight, I failed to copy militia records for the majority of cities in this study. The cities of Hartford, Charleston, Chicago, and San Francisco are highlighted here, in figure 6.1, both because I did happen to have copied the militia sections of their respective city directories and because they appeared to present an interesting array of such organizations. However, these results should in no way be seen as representative of militia activity across the country.

32. Note that the verb *turnen* (to perform gymnastic exercises) is not originally of German origin but was adopted as such by Jahn, who is credited with coining the term.

33. Henry Metzner, *A Brief History of the American Turnerbund*, Theodore Stempfel, Jr., trans. (Pittsburgh: National Executive Committee of the American Turnerbund, 1924), p. 40.

34. Robert Knight Barney, "Knights of Cause and Exercise: German Forty-eighters and Turnvereine in the United States During the Antebellum Period," *Canadian Journal of the History of Sport*, vol. 2 (1982): 62–79; Albert Bernhardt Faust, *The German Element in the United States*, vol. 2 (New York: Steuben Society of America, 1927), pp. 387–390; Horst Ueberhorst, "Die Nordamericanischen Turner und Ihr Jahnbild," *Stadion*, vol. 4, no. 1 (1978): 358–364; McNeill, *Keeping Together in Time*, pp. 137–139. Some Turners in the Deep South, however, did side with and fight for the Confederate cause during the war. I owe great thanks to Katsch Belash and Felix Elwert for serving as able translators of and commentators on the German texts in question.

35. Robert Knight Barney, "German-American Turnvereins and Socio-Politico-Economic Realities in the Antebellum and Civil War Upper and Lower South," *Stadion*, vol. 10 (1984): 135–181; Annette R. Hofmann, "The Turners' Loyality for their New Home Country: Their Engagement in the American Civil War," *International Journal of the History of Sport*, vol. 12, no. 3 (December 1995): 153–168.

36. Cooper, *Rise of the National Guard*, p. 17.

37. The collection at the Houghton Library of Harvard University includes, for example, programs from an 1891 New York National Guard performance of Shakespeare's *As You*

Like It, an 1874 minstrel show put on by a local encampment of the New York Grand Army of the Republic, two 1877 comedies performed by the Boston Navy Yard Dramatic Club, and an 1874 play by the Boston Light Infantry.

38. Cooper, *Rise of the National Guard*, pp. 79–80; Fogelson, *America's Armories*, p. 6.

39. Trefethen and Serven, *Americans and Their Guns*, pp. 111–112. See, for example, Madison Schützenverein, *Constitution, Neben-Gesetz und Regeln des Madison Schuetzenvereins* (Madison: Wisconsin Staats-Zeitung, 1895).

40. Fogelson, *America's Armories*, p. 17; Sven Beckert, *The Monied Metropolis: New York City and the Consolidation of the American Bourgeoisie, 1850–1896* (New York: Cambridge University Press, 2001).

41. Riker, *Soldiers of the States*, p. 60. Though the concept of armories as warehouses, fortresses, and training grounds for militias was certainly nothing new at the time, most civilian military groups had previously relied on small rented quarters for such purposes. Before the late 1870s, "only Brooklyn [of the nation's big cities] came close to providing adequate quarters for the volunteer militia." New York's Tweed ring was infamous for its practice of obtaining unoccupied buildings and then renting them at exorbitant rates to state- and city-funded militia groups. Even Boston's prestigious First Corps of Cadets had had to make do in the MIT gymnasium. Writes Riker, "What rivers and harbors were to Congress— that is, a device to distribute pork barrel to the district of every Congressman—armories became to many state legislatures. Whenever they could, National Guard officials of course took full advantage of the pork barrel."

42. Fogelson, *America's Armories*, p. 28.

43. Ibid., p. 1–2, 28; also Clarence Bonnett, *Employers' Associations in the United States* (New York: Vantage, 1956); Kim Voss, *The Making of American Exceptionalism: The Knights of Labor and Class Formation in the Nineteenth Century* (Ithaca, N.Y.: Cornell University Press, 1993).

44. 116 U.S. 2552 (1886).

45. "A Menace," *Chicago Tribune*, April 21, 1879.

46. Ibid.

47. Steven H. Gunn, "Second Amendment Symposium: A Lawyer's Guide to the Second Amendment," *Brigham Young University Law Review*, vol. 35 (1998): 34–46; Thomas Halpern and Brian Levin, *The Limits of Dissent: The Constitutional Status of Armed Civilian Militias* (Amherst, Mass.: Aletheia Press, 1996).

48. "Military Despotism," *Socialist*, March 1, 1879.

49. Eric H. Monkkonen, *Police in Urban America, 1860–1920* (Cambridge: Cambridge University Press, 1981).

50. Bellesiles, "Origins of American Gun Culture," pp. 452–453; also Trefethen and Serven, *Americans and Their Guns*.

51. Trefethen and Serven, *Americans and Their Guns*, pp. 36–41.

52. Ibid., p. 88.

53. Ibid., pp. 67–78.

54. Independent Company of Cadets, *Roll of the Independent Company of Cadets—1814* (Boston: n.p., 1814); Massachusetts Militia, First Division, Independent Company of Cadets, *The Constitution of the Independent Company of Cadets, Attached to the First Division, Mass. Volunteer Militia* (Boston: Franklin Printing House, 1857); Massachusetts, 1st Corps of Cadets, *The One Hundred and Fiftieth Anniversary of the Foundation of the First Corps Cadets, Massachusetts Volunteer Militia, October 19, 1891* (Boston: N. Sawyer, 1892); Joseph Antenucci, Christopher Hugh Ripman, and Kurt Zumwalt, *Armory, First Corps of Cadets, 1887–1973, at the Corner of Arlington Street and Columbus Avenue, Boston, Massachusetts*

(Boston: Veteran Association of the First Corps of Cadets, 1973). Many of the extant papers of the First Corps of Cadets are currently housed in the Special Collections Division, Mugar Library, Boston University (which houses all of the collections of the former Military Historical Society of Massachusetts).

55. W. S. Harwood, "Secret Societies in America," *North American Review*, vol. 164, no. 486 (May 1897): 617.

56. *Volunteer*, vol. 1, no. 2 (May 1889); this was the only edition of the *Volunteer* available in the holdings of the former Military Historical Society of Massachusetts, and I have not been able to ascertain how long it remained in publication.

57. Ibid., pp. 75–77.

58. Whether such clubs commonly existed for women, as did the East Boston Amazons, is a question that clearly deserves more detailed historical investigation.

59. *Volunteer*, vol. 1, no. 2 (May 1889): 77.

60. Ibid., p. 78. Another excerpt reads, "Chelsea is the only city in Massachusetts which fails to provide her local militia with a rifle range, while the armory which is provided for Co. H, 1st regiment, would be an utter disgrace to any country village" (p. 78).

61. Bellesiles, "Origins of American Gun Culture," pp. 425–455; Bellesiles, *Arming America*, chap. 9.

62. Bellesiles, "Origins of American Gun Culture," pp. 447–452; Philip B. Sharpe, *The Rifle in America* (New York: William Morrow, 1938), pp. 175, 187.

63. Charles T. Haven and Frank A. Belden, *A History of the Colt Revolver and Other Arms Made by Colt's Patent Fire Arms Manufacturing Company from 1836 to 1940* (New York: William Morrow, 1940).

64. Quoted in Sharpe, *Rifle in America*, p. 197; see also Trefethen and Serven, *Americans and Their Guns*, pp. 67–78.

65. Martha Derthick, *The National Guard in Politics* (Cambridge, Mass.: Harvard University Press, 1965), p. 20.

66. Ibid., p. 22; see also Cooper, *Rise of The National Guard*, pp. 87–127; Riker, *Soldiers of the States*, pp. 60–66; Stephen Skowronek, *Building a New American State: The Expansion of National Administrative Capacities, 1877–1920* (Cambridge: Cambridge University Press, 1982), pp. 85–120;

67. *Congressional Record*, June 30, 1902, quoted in Col. Thomas F. Edmands, "Memorial or Protest to Congress by First Corps Cadets, on the Effect of the Bill Known as 'H.R. 11654, 57th Congress, 1st Session'" (Set A315, Boston University Mugar Library, Department of Special Collections), p. 8453.

68. Cooper, *Rise of the National Guard*, pp. 108–112; Derthick, *National Guard in Politics*, pp. 24–29; Riker, *Soldiers of the States*, pp. 60–63.

69. Cooper, *Rise of the National Guard*, p. 83; see also Skowronek, *Building a New American State*, p. 94.

70. Edmands, "Memorial or Protest to Congress." The Supreme Court's 1886 *Presser v. Illinois* decision affirmed a state's right to require express approval of all military groups organized there, but such groups could continue to muster as long as they did not provoke state action against them. City directories of the 1910s and 1920s confirm the fact that some still existed, though there are notably fewer listed than before the turn of the century.

71. Trefethen and Serven, *Americans and Their Guns*, p. 132.

72. Ibid., p. 128.

73. Ibid., pp. 128–130.

74. Ibid., p. 134.

75. Ibid.

244 NOTES TO PAGES 141–147

76. Ibid., p. 158.

77. Ibid., p. 162.

Chapter 7

1. Dietrich Rueschemeyer and Theda Skocpol, eds., *States, Social Knowledge, and the Origins of Modern Social Policies* (Princeton, N.J.: Princeton University Press, 1996); Daniel T. Rodgers, *Atlantic Crossings: Social Politics in a Progressive Age* (Cambridge: Belknap, 1998).

2. Francis G. Castles, ed., *The Comparative History of Public Policy* (Cambridge: Polity Press, 1989); Peter Flora, and Arnold J. Heidenheimer, eds., *The Development of Welfare States in Europe and America* (New Brunswick, N.J.: Transaction Books, 1981); Roy Lubove, *The Struggle for Social Security, 1900–1935* (Pittsburgh: University of Pittsburgh Press, 1986); Ann Shola Orloff, *The Politics of Pensions: A Comparative Analysis of Britain, Canada, and the United States, 1880–1940* (Madison: University of Wisconsin Press, 1993); Theda Skocpol, *Protecting Soldiers and Mothers: The Political Origins of Social Policy in the United States* (Cambridge: Belknap, 1992). There is, in fact, an enormous literature on this issue, though I will spare you the details except when absolutely necessary. Rodgers and Skocpol represent two of the latest and best contributions to this area of comparative history.

3. Lubove, *Struggle for Social Security*, p. 67; also I. M. Rubinow, "20,000 Miles Over the Land: A Survey of the Spreading Health Insurance Movement," *Survey*, vol. 37 (March 3, 1917): 631–635.

4. Terry Boychuk, *The Making and Meaning of Hospital Policy in the United States and Canada* (Ann Arbor: University of Michigan Press, 1999), p. 159.

5. Skocpol, *Protecting Soldiers and Mothers*, chap. 2, "Public Aid for the Worthy Many: The Expansion of Benefits for Veterans of the Civil War."

6. Ibid., p. 532.

7. On turn of the century opinions toward state-run enterprises in public health and urban infrastructural development, see Edward W. Bemis, ed., *Municipal Monopolies: A Collection of Papers by American Economists and Specialists* (New York: Crowell, 1899); Rodgers, *Atlantic Crossings*, chaps. 3–5.

8. On the persistence of of so-called party machines throughout the period in question, see M. Craig Brown and Charles N. Halaby, "Machine Politics in America, 1870–1945," *Journal of Interdisciplinary History*, vol. 17, no. 3 (Winter 1987): 587–612; see also M. Craig Brown and Charles N. Halaby, "Bosses, Reform, and the Socioeconomic Bases of Urban Expenditure, 1890–1940," in Terrence J. McDonald and Sally K. Ward, eds., *The Politics of Urban Fiscal Policy* (Beverly Hills, Cal.: Sage, 1984); and Rebecca Menes, "Public Goods and Private Favors: Patronage Politics in American Cities During the Progressive Era, 1900–1920," Ph.D. dissertation, Harvard University, Cambridge, Mass., 1996.

9. Most of Skocpol's (*Protecting Soldiers and Mothers*) examples of this kind of rhetoric come from debate on the issue of old-age pensions. David Beito offers one example of such rhetoric concerning health insurance, an article in the *Fraternal Monitor* that lambasts Tammany Hall support for compulsory health insurance because it would "provide over fifty thousand jobs to the faithful." Note, however, that this specific commentary is equally as dismissive of social workers and policy analysts who supported such legislation: "So long as the scheme was supported only by impractical reformers and the various kinds of social workers supported by the Russell Sage Foundation the menace was afar off. Everybody realized that professional social workers must make a noise in order to earn their salaries, and this resulted in a disposition among legislators to allow them to rant." See "Menace of So-

cial Insurance," *Fraternal Monitor*, vol. 30 (November 1, 1919), p. 5; quoted in David T. Beito, *From Mutual Aid to Welfare State: Fraternal Societies and Social Services, 1890–1967* (Chapel Hill: University of North Carolina Press, 2000), p. 150. Beito also cites a similar comment by Mary MacEachern Baird in the *Ladies Review*, vol. 25 (March 1919), n.p. Overall, however, arguments of this sort do not feature prominently in the literature on the issue, at least not in those that I have reviewed.

10. Frederick L. Hoffman, who appeared earlier (in chapter 2) as an ardent critic of fraternal insurance, gave speeches all across the country in the 1910s, denouncing compulsory health insurance as socialism, despotism, and worse. At the time, Hoffman was vice president and statistician for the Prudential Insurance Company of America. It is also worth noting Hoffman's opinions on the race question, as they relate to the exclusionary nature of self-insurance in the United States at the time:

> When the ever increasing white population has reached a stage where new conquests are necessary, it will not hesitate to make war upon those races who prove themselves useless factors in the progress of mankind. A race may be interesting, gentle and hospitable; but if it is not a useful race in the common acceptation of that term, it is only a question of time when a downward course must take place. . . . All the facts prove that a low standard of sexual morality is the main and underlying cause of the low and anti-social condition of the [black] race at the present time. All the facts prove that education, philanthropy and religion have failed to develop a higher appreciation of the stern and uncompromising virtues of the Aryan race. . . . In the meantime, however, the presence of the colored population is a serious hindrance to the economic progress of the white race.

Race Traits and Tendencies of the American Negro (New York: Publications of the American Economic Association, 1896), pp. 329–330.

11. Paul Starr, *The Social Transformation of American Medicine* (New York: Basic Books, 1982), pp. 198–235; Ronald L. Numbers, *Almost Persuaded: American Physicians and Compulsory Health Insurance, 1912–1920* (Baltimore: Johns Hopkins University Press, 1978).

12. On May 26, 1919, a committee was formed by the Social Insurance Department of the National Civic Federation to discuss alternatives to the proposed health bill before the New York State legislature. One of the 11 committee members was Mark A. Daly, general secretary of the Associated Manufacturers and Merchants of New York; another was M. W. Alexander, managing directory of the National Industrial Conference Board; and the chair of the committee was Dr. Alvah H. Doty, medical director for the Western Union Telegraph Company. The committee's report is reprinted in "If Not Compulsory Insurance—What?" *National Civic Federation Review*, vol. 14, no. 15 (June 5, 1919).

13. Andrea Tone, *The Business of Benevolence: Industrial Paternalism in Progressive America* (Ithaca, N.Y.: Cornell University Press, 1997), p. 8; also Beatrix Hoffman, *The Wages of Sickness: The Politics of Health Insurance in Progressive America* (Chapel Hill: University of North Carolina Press, 2001); Steven A. Sass, *The Promise of Private Pensions* (Cambridge, Mass.: Harvard University Press, 1997).

14. "Casualty and Surety Convention," *Weekly Underwriter*, vol. 99 (December 7, 1918): 846; quoted in Beito, *From Mutual Aid to the Welfare State*, p. 157.

15. See, for example, "Compulsory Sickness Insurance," *National Civic Federation Review*, April 1, 1920, pp. 6–8.

16. "Revolutionary Forces in Our Midst," *National Civic Federation Review*, April 1, 1920, pp. 10–11. A subsequent issue (July 10, 1920, p. 5) announced the decision of the NFC leadership to form several committees to "study and combat revolutionary radicalism." Clearly,

Gompers was forced into a balancing act between the demands of labor activists and the threat of red-baiters.

17. Skocpol, *Protecting Soldiers and Mothers*, p. 234; B. Hoffman, *Wages of Sickness*, p. 4.

18. "United in Attack on Health Insurance," *New York Times*, March 20, 1919, p. 5; emphasis added. Labor representatives are portrayed here as lobbying in support of the Davenport-Donohue compulsory insurance bill, further evidence that labor was deeply divided over social insurance.

19. Walter Basye, *History and Operation of Fraternal Insurance* (Rochester, N.Y.: Fraternal Monitor, 1919), p. 131.

20. Ibid.

21. The single exception to this observation is David Beito's *From Mutual Aid to Welfare State* (chap. 8, "It Substitutes Paternalism for Fraternalism"), which ironically addresses the issue from the opposite perspective as mine. Beito emphasizes fraternal efforts to defeat compulsory health insurance as an example of the danger government growth poses to mutual aid organizations. I couldn't disagree more, though I commend Beito for being one of the first contemporary historians to touch on the role of fraternal organizations in the fight against compulsory insurance.

22. "If Not Compulsory Insurance?"

23. "Compulsory Insurance Opposed by Women's Benefit Societies," *National Civic Federation Review*, July 10, 1920, p. 14. Fraternal lobbyists were also present at a March 19, 1919, hearing of the New York Senate Judiciary Committee meeting; see "United in Attack on Health Insurance."

24. Beito, *From Mutual Aid to the Welfare State*, p. 2.

25. "Why That Exemption?" *New York Times*, March 24, 1915, p. 10; also "May Tax Property Worth $300,095,575," *New York Times*, March 22, 1915, p. 4.

26. "Sees Era of Peace Ahead: Texas Senator Believes Fraternal Spirit Will Put End to War," *New York Times*, June 26, 1916, p. 7.

27. See, for example, Skocpol, *Protecting Soldiers and Mothers*, pp. 480–524; see also B. Hoffman, *Wages of Sickness*.

28. Alvin J. Schmidt, *Fraternal Organizations* (Westport, Conn.: Greenwood, 1980), p. 354.

29. John Sullivan, "Social Insurance: An Address Delivered by John Sullivan . . . of the Modern Woodmen of America before the National Fraternal Congress of America," Philadelphia, Pennsylvania, August 28, 1918 (no bibliographic data given), p. 17.

30. Ibid.; emphasis added.

31. Ibid., pp. 23–24. For a similar attacks on German health insurance, see Frederick L. Hoffman, "Autocracy and Paternalism vs. Democracy and Liberty," An address delivered at the Annual Meeting of the International Association of Casualty and Surety Underwriters, New York City, December 4, 1918; Edgar Taylor Wheelock, *The Declaration of Fraternalism* (Chicago: Eidson [sic] Publishing, 1919).

32. "Menace of Social Insurance," p. 7.

33. Basye, *History and Operation of Fraternal Insurance*, pp. 113, 116.

34. Ibid., p. 116; see also Nathan Smith Boynton, "Fraternal Co-Operation: Can It Survive the Assaults Without and the Pressure Within," paper read at the Meeting of the National Fraternal Congress, Baltimore, Md., November 15–18, 1898 (Port Huron, Mich.: Riverside Printing, 1898).

35. Beito, *From Mutual Aid to the Welfare State*, p. 143.

36. Sullivan, "Social Insurance," p. 1.

37. Beito, *From Mutual Aid to the Welfare State*, p. 154.

38. Ibid., p. 155.

39. *San Francisco Chronicle*, January 17, 1917. David Beito (*From Mutual Aid to the Welfare State*, pp. 157–158) refers to this "story" as a paid advertisement; in my poorly microfilmed copy, it looks virtually indistinguishable from an actual story in the *Chronicle*, but I take Beito's observation on good faith. Such are the ways and means of twentieth-century interest-group lobbies.

40. John B. Andrews, April 19, 1917, reel 17, American Association for Labor Legislation papers; quoted in Beito, *From Mutual Aid to the Welfare State*, p. 158.

41. George Emery and J. C. Herbert Emery. *A Young Man's Benefit: The Independent Order of Odd Fellows and Sickness Insurance in the United States and Canada, 1860–1929* (Montreal: McGill-Queen's University Press, 1999), p. 16; Robert Whaples and David Buffum, "Fraternalism, Paternalism, the Family, and the Market: Insurance a Century Ago," *Social Science History*, vol. 15, no. 1 (Spring 1991): 97–122.

42. Lizbeth Cohen, *Making A New Deal: Industrial Workers in Chicago, 1919–1939* (Cambridge: Cambridge University Press, 1990), p. 64.

43. This phrase comes from the third stanza of Sir Edwin Arnold's poem "Armageddon: A War Song for the Future," published in *Edwin Arnold's Poetical Works*, vol. 2 (Boston: Roberts Brothers, 1892).

44. Lubove, *Struggle for Social Security*, pp. 137–138; Skocpol, *Protecting Soldiers and Mothers*, pp. 202, 234, 242, 430–432. Explaining why the Fraternal Order of Eagles (FOE) went against the grain of fraternal opposition to state-run social welfare programs is a question I have not endeavored to answer, though it would surely make a nice, manageable thesis or dissertation. According to Alvin J. Schmidt's *Fraternal Organizations* (p. 95), the FOE was founded in Seattle, Washington, in 1898 by "a small group of theater owners [who] met to form a fun organization. They called it the 'Seattle Order of Good Things.' A few years after its inception, the order chose the eagle as its symbol, calling itself the Fraternal Order of Eagles." Though the FOE did eventually turn from "fun things" to serious matters like providing insurance for members, Schmidt's account seems to indicate a rather casual approach to the business of fraternalism. "'The emphasis has shifted from solely recreation to a more balanced program of fun and fraternal activities of wide scope,'" says one (uncited) FOE publication. "The change in the Eagles' objectives from fun to more of a service posture also showed itself in the order's offering its members life insurance," Schmidt adds. "In 1927, however, it was decided not to sell regular life insurance any longer, but rather to make available sick and funeral benefits for those who desired to pay somewhat higher membership fees. As a result, the FOE has two categories of memberships, beneficial and nonbeneficial." Thus it would appear that the FOE had less to lose in supporting modest social welfare initiatives than other fraternities. It should be added, however, that even the FOE appears not to have lobbied in support of health insurance legislation, though it did support old-age and mothers' pensions.

45. Juvenile insurance, or "whole family protection," was originated by for-profit, industrial life insurance companies. According to fraternal historian Walter Basye, "Fraternal societies have been prevented from writing juvenile insurance from the beginning, not because of any positive objection, but because *the founders of fraternal insurance failed to conceive that child protection should be a part of their service to humanity*. Therefore several million children of fraternalists have gone without insurance and a million or more of the others were forced to take the policies of industrial companies." In April 1918, however, after almost three years of opposition, New York State Governor Charles Seymour Whitman signed a bill to allow "fraternal benefit societies the privilege to issue policies on the life of children between 2 and 8 years of age," further evidence of the rising political power and

financial desperation of fraternal benefit programs in the 1910s and 1920s. See Basye, *History and Operation of Fraternal Insurance*, pp. 203–204; and "Signs Insurance Bill: Fraternal Societies Privileged to Extend Policies to Children," *New York Times*, April 9, 1918, p. 8.

46. Basye, *History and Operation of Fraternal Insurance*, p. 50.

47. Boychuk, *Making and Meaning of Hospital Policy*; Michael B. Katz, *In the Shadow of the Poorhouse: A Social History of Welfare in America* (New York: Basic Books, 1986).

48. Chinese Hospital Association, *1st Annual Report* (Brooklyn, N.Y.: n.p., 1892) p. 2; quoted in David Rosner, *A Once Charitable Enterprise: Hospitals and Health Care in Brooklyn and New York, 1885–1915* (Princeton, N.J.: Princeton University Press, 1982), pp. 17, 19.

49. Beito, *From Mutual Aid to the Welfare State*, pp. 109–129; Starr, *Social Transformation of American Medicine*, pp. 206–209.

50. Charles E. Rosenberg, *The Care of Strangers: The Rise of America's Hospital System* (New York: Basic Books, 1987); Rosner, *A Once Charitable Enterprise*.

Chapter 8

1. David T. Beito, From *Mutual Aid to the Welfare State: Fraternal Societies and Social Services, 1890–1967* (Chapel Hill: University of North Carolina Press, 2000); Seymour Martin Lipset, *American Exceptionalism: A Double-Edged Sword* (New York: Norton, 1996); Marvin Olasky, *The Tragedy of American Compassion* (Wheaton, Ill.: Crossway Books, 1992); Robert D. Putnam, *Bowling Alone: The Collapse and Revival of American Community* (New York: Simon & Schuster, 2000); Theda Skocpol, "The Tocqueville Problem: Civic Engagement in American Democracy," *Social Science History*, vol. 21, no. 4 (Winter 1997): 455–479; Sidney Verba, Kay Lehman Schlozman, and Henry E. Brady, *Voice and Equality: Civic Voluntarism in American Politics* (Cambridge, Mass.: Harvard University Press, 1995).

2. James Curtis, Edward Grabb, and Douglas Baer, "Voluntary Association Membership in Fifteen Countries: A Comparative Analysis," *American Sociological Review*, vol. 57 (1992): 139–152; Bruce Western, *Between Class and Market: Postwar Unionization in the Capitalist Democracies* (Princeton, N.J. : Princeton University Press, 1997).

3. Skocpol, "Tocqueville Problem."

4. Putnam, *Bowling Alone*.

5. T. R. Fehrenbach, quoted in Alvin J. Schmidt, *Fraternal Organizations* (Westport, Conn.: Greenwood, 1980), p. 102; also Beito, *From Mutual Aid to the Welfare State*, p. 217; Lynn Dumenil, *Freemasonry and American Culture, 1880–1930* (Princeton, N.J.: Princeton University Press, 1984), p. xiv; and Clifford Putney, "Service Over Secrecy: How Lodge-Style Fraternalism Yielded Popularity to Men's Service Clubs," *Journal of Popular Culture*, vol. 27 (Summer 1993): 185.

6. Putney, "Service Over Secrecy," p. 185.

7. Robert S. Lynd and Helen M. Lynd, *Middletown: A Study in American Culture* (New York: Harcourt, Brace, & World, 1956), p. 306.

8. Sinclair Lewis, *Babbitt* (New York: Harcourt, Brace, 1922), p. 257.

9. Ibid.

10. George Emery and J. C. Herbert Emery, *A Young Man's Benefit: The Independent Order of Odd Fellows and Sickness Insurance in the United States and Canada, 1860–1929* (Montreal: McGill-Queen's University Press, 1999), p. 23. Emery and Emery compiled their data from annual reports issued by the Supreme Grand Lodge of the IOOF. My estimates of members per lodge are based simply on the quotient of total membership divided by the total number of lodges and are therefore only a rough approximation of actual membership size per lodge per year. Emery and Emery also provide data on IOOF encampments, which

are more exclusive than lodges, but I have omitted them here for simplicity's sake. The IOOF encampments generally tended to be smaller than the lodges, though the trends over time were virtually identical across the two.

11. Though the data do not permit us to assume that this was in fact the beginning of a downward trend, qualitative evidence would support the idea that this was the beginning of the end for the IOOF in the United States and Canada.

12. Quoted in Emery and Emery, *Young Man's Benefit*, p. 102.

13. The life insurance data given here come from two sources: J. Owen Stalson, *Marketing Life Insurance: Its History in America* (Cambridge, Mass.: Harvard University Press, 1942), app. 25, pp. 816–819; and Francis De Raismes Kip, *Fraternal Life Insurance in America* (Philadelphia: College Offset Press, 1953), pp. 12–18. There are some minor discrepancies in the aggregate statistics given by the two, though nothing that would lead one to believe that the trends illustrated here are not accurate.

14. Stalson, *Marketing Life Insurance*, p. 461.

15. So-called industrial life insurance was also available to less affluent families at low cost at this time; but as shown in figure 8.4, it made up a relatively small portion of the commercial insurance market before the early 1920s, when it surpassed fraternal insurance policies in terms of total dollars of insurance in force.

16. "You Don't Have to Die to Win," printed broadside, Baltimore, Md., October 20, 1884, in *An American Time Capsule: Three Centuries of Broadsides and Other Printed Ephemera* (online): //hdl.loc.gov/loc.rbc/rbpe.03103100 (May 10, 2001).

17. Roger L. Ransom and Richard Sutch, "Tontine Insurance and the Armstrong Investigation: A Case of Stifled Innovation, 1868–1905," *Journal of Economic History*, vol. 47, no. 2 (June 1987): 380.

18. Stalson, *Marketing Life Insurance*, p. 576.

19. Ibid., pp. 578–579.

20. See, for example, James R. Beniger, *The Control Revolution: Technological and Economic Origins of the Information Society* (Cambridge, Mass.: Harvard University Press, 1986); William Leach, *Land of Desire: Merchants, Power, and the Rise of a New American Culture* (New York: Vintage Books, 1993).

21. Stalson, *Marketing Life Insurance*, p. 579.

22. Ibid., pp. 585–586.

23. Kip, *Fraternal Life Insurance*; also Emery and Emery, *Young Man's Benefit*.

24. Walter Basye, *History and Operation of Fraternal Insurance* (Rochester, N.Y.: Fraternal Monitor, 1919), p. 222.

25. Beito, *From Mutual Aid to the Welfare State*, pp. 134, 142, 153, 172; Emery and Emery, *Young Man's Benefit*, pp. 86–101; Putney, "Service Over Secrecy," pp. 183–189.

26. Cf. Putnam, *Bowling Alone*.

27. Daniel Czitrom, *Media and the American Mind: From Morse to McLuhan* (Chapel Hill: University of North Carolina Press, 1982).

28. Henry N. Pringle, *The Lawless Clubs of the United States* (Washington, D.C.: International Reform Federation, 1927), p. 3.

29. Ibid.

30. Richard D. Alba, *Ethnic Identity: The Transformation of White America* (New Haven, Conn.: Yale University Press, 1990); Lizabeth Cohen, *Making a New Deal: Industrial Workers in Chicago, 1919–1939* (Cambridge: Cambridge University Press, 1990), pp. 53–97; Matthew Frye Jacobson, *Whiteness of a Different Color: European Immigrants and the Alchemy of Race* (Cambridge, Mass.: Harvard University Press, 1998), pp. 91–135; Stanley Lieberson, *A Piece of the Pie: Blacks and White Immigrants since 1880* (Berkeley: University

of California Press, 1980); Ivan H. Light, *Ethnic Enterprise in America: Business and Welfare Among Chinese, Japanese, and Blacks* (Berkeley: University of California Press, 1972), p. 176; Stephen J. Shaw, *The Catholic Parish as a Way-Station of Ethnicity and Americanization: Chicago's Germans and Italians, 1903–1939* (New York: Carlson, 1991), pp. 131–141; Mary C. Waters, *Ethnic Options: Choosing Identities in America* (Berkeley: University of California Press, 1990).

31. Orlando Patterson, *Ethnic Chauvinism: The Reactionary Impulse* (New York: Stein & Day, 1977), p. 15; emphasis added.

32. Debra C. Minkoff, *Organizing for Equality: The Evolution of Women's and Racial-Ethnic Organizations in America, 1955–1985* (New Brunswick, N.J.: Rutgers University Press, 1995).

33. Beito, *From Mutual Aid to the Welfare State*, p. 180.

34. Frank Dobbin, "The Origins of Private Social Insurance: Public Policy and Fringe Benefits in America, 1920–1950," *American Journal of Sociology*, vol. 97, no. 2 (1992): 1416–1450; Heather A. Haveman and Hayagreeva Rao, "Structuring a Theory of Moral Sentiments: Institutional and Organizational Coevolution in the Early Thrift Industry," *American Journal of Sociology*, vol. 102, no. 6 (1997): 1606–1651; Viviana A. Rotman Zelizer, *Morals and Markets: The Development of Life Insurance in the United States* (New York: Columbia University Press, 1979).

35. Robert Putnam makes a similar generational argument in *Bowling Alone* but gives short shrift to its ethnic dimensions.

36. Jennifer Lee, "Entrepreneurship and Business Development Among African Americans, Koreans, and Jews: Exploring Some Structural Differences," in Héctor R. Cordero-Guzmán, Ramón Grosfoguel, and Robert Smith, eds., *Transnational Communities and the Political Economy of New York City in the 1990s* (Philadelphia: Temple University Press, forthcoming); Ivan H. Light and Edna Bonacich, *Immigrant Entrepreneurs: Koreans in Los Angeles, 1965–1982* (Berkeley: University of California Press, 1988); Minkoff, *Organizing For Equality*, pp. 69–70. There is not a large literature on the relative prevalence of voluntary organizations in new immigrant communities, though informal conversations with several contemporary experts on American immigration have confirmed my sense that they are much less prevalent than they were at the turn of the last century. However, a recent article in the *New York Times* speaks of the frequency with which new immigrants are being swindled into investing in fly-by-night financial schemes by coethnic con-artists: "That type of swindle has become so prevalent . . . that the regulators have given it a name—*affinity fraud.*" Susan Sachs, "Immigrants Are Targets of Investment Schemes," *New York Times*, May 15, 2001 (online).

Chapter 9

1. Christopher J. Kauffman, *Faith and Fraternalism: The History of the Knights of Columbus*, rev. ed. (New York: Simon & Schuster, 1992), p. xxvi; emphasis added.

2. Ibid., pp. xxviii–xxix.

3. Edna Bonacich and John Modell, *The Economic Basis of Ethnic Solidarity: Small Business in the Japanese American Community* (Berkeley: University of California Press, 1980), p. 1; Orlando Patterson, *Ethnic Chauvinism: The Reactionary Impulse* (New York: Stein & Day, 1977), p. 10.

4. For a theoretical elaboration of the dynamics of high- and low-exit organizations, I highly recommend Albert O. Hirschman, *Exit, Voice, and Loyalty: Responses to Decline in Firms, Organizations, and States* (Cambridge, Mass.: Harvard University Press, 1970). See also chapter 3 in this text.

5. See, for example, Bonacich and Modell, *Economic Basis of Ethnic Solidarity*; John Modell, *The Economics and Politics of Racial Accommodation: The Japanese of Los Angeles, 1900–1942* (Urbana: University of Illinois Press, 1977).

6. Stanford Morris Lyman, *Chinatown and Little Tokyo: Power, Conflict, and Community Among Chinese and Japanese Immigrants in America* (Millwood, N.Y.: Associated Faculty Press, 1986), p. 72; emphasis added.

7. Pamela Oliver, "Rewards and Punishments as Selective Incentives for Collective Action: Theoretical Investigations," *American Journal of Sociology*, vol. 85, no. 6 (1980): 1356–1375.

8. Ivan H. Light, *Ethnic Enterprise in America: Business and Welfare Among Chinese, Japanese, and Blacks* (Berkeley: University of California Press, 1972), p. 74.

9. Ibid., pp. 75–76; see also Bonachich and Modell, *Economic Basis of Ethnic Solidarity*; Modell, *Economics and Politics of Racial Accommodation*.

10. Light, *Ethnic Enterprise in America*, p. 79.

11. Modell, *Economics and Politics of Racial Accommodation*, pp. 92–93.

12. Lyman, *Chinatown and Little Tokyo*, p. 72.

13. Light, *Ethnic Enterprise in America*, p. 46. See also John Silbey Butler, *Entrepreneurship and Self-Help Among Black Americans: A Reconsideration of Race and Economics* (Albany: SUNY Press, 1991); St. Clair Drake and Horace R. Cayton, *Black Metropolis: A Study of Negro Life in a Northern City*, rev. ed. (New York: Harper & Row, [1945] 1962); W. E. B. Du Bois, *The Philadelphia Negro* (Millwood, N.Y.: Kraus-Thomson, [1899] 1973); Booker T. Washington, *The Negro in Business* (Chicago: Afro-Am Press, [1907] 1969).

14. Abram L. Harris, *The Negro as Capitalist: A Study of Banking and Business Among American Negroes* (College Park, Md.: McGrath, [1936] 1968). Harris introduces the concept of racial protectionism on p. 178, where he notes that "with the penetration of the chain stores and some of the better organized independents into Negro neighborhoods, racial protectionism collapsed."

15. Ibid., p. 167.

16. Ibid., p. 49.

17. Du Bois, *Philadelphia Negro*, p. 123.

18. Light, *Ethnic Entrepreneurship*, p. 82; emphasis added.

19. Ibid., pp. 83–86.

20. Ibid., pp. 92–93; see also Min Zhou, *Chinatown: The Socioeconomic Potential of an Urban Enclave* (Philadelphia: Temple University Press, 1979).

21. Light, *Ethnic Entrepreneurship*, p. 95.

22. Ibid., pp. 175–176.

23. Robert D. Putnam, with Robert Leonardi and Raffaella Y. Nanetti, *Making Democracy Work: Civic Traditions of Modern Italy* (Princeton, N.J.: Princeton University Press, 1993), p. 167.

24. On the vagaries of social capital theory, I recommend the short article by Alejandro Portes and Patricia Landholt, "The Downside of Social Capital," *Journal of Democracy*, vol. 26 (May–June 1996): 18–21. See also Bob Edwards, Michael W. Foley, and Mario Diani, eds., *Beyond Tocqueville: Civil Society and Social Capital in Comparative Perspective* (Hanover, N.H.: University Press of New England, 2001).

25. Light, *Ethnic Entrepreneurship*, pp. 184–185; emphasis added.

26. Arthur Cecil Bining and Thomas C. Cochran. *The Rise of American Economic Life*, 4th ed. (New York: Scribner, 1964), pp. 674–682.

27. Mancur Olson, *The Logic of Collective Action* (Cambridge, Mass.: Harvard University Press, 1965).

28. Hirschman, *Exit, Voice, and Loyalty*; Oliver, "Rewards and Punishments."

29. Here again I refer you to Hirschman's brilliant *Exit, Voice, and Loyalty*. Though somewhat dated by now in its discussion of "American Ideology and Practice" (chapter 8), Hirschman's observations are no less trenchant today: "The novelty of the black power movement on the American scene consists in the rejection of this traditional pattern of upward social mobility" (p. 109). "Significantly, it combines scorn for individual penetration of a few selected blacks into white society with a strong commitment to 'collective stimulation' of blacks as a group and to the improvement of the black ghetto as a place to live."

30. Jason Kaufman and Steven J. Tepper, "Groups or Gatherings? Sources of Political Engagement in 19th Century American Cities," *Voluntas: International Journal of Voluntary and Nonprofit Organizations*, vol. 10, no. 4 (1999): 299–322; Portes and Landholt. "Downside of Social Capital"; Charles Tilly, *Durable Inequality* (Berkeley: University of California Press, 1999).

31. Orlando Patterson, *The Ordeal of Integration: Progress and Resentment in America's "Racial" Crisis* (Washington, D.C.: Civitas, 1997), p. 201.

32. Mary Waters, *Ethnic Options: Choosing Identities in America* (Berkeley: University of California Press, 1990).

33. Herbert Gans, "Symbolic Ethnicity: The Future of Ethnic Groups and Cultures in America," *Ethnic and Racial Studies*, vol. 2, no. 1 (1979): 9–17.

34. I have borrowed the concept of ethnic options from Mary Waters, *Ethnic Options*. On this subject, I also recommend Richard D. Alba, *Ethnic Identity: The Transformation of White America* (New Haven, Conn.: Yale University Press, 1990).

35. Raymond Breton, "Institutional Completeness of Ethnic Communities and the Personal Relations of Immigrants," *American Journal of Sociology*, vol. 70, no. 2 (September 1964): 193–205.

36. Most of my information about Boston's Brazilian and Portuguese communities comes from Irene Bloemraad, a graduate student in the Sociology Department at Harvard University who is working on a dissertation that compares the integrationist and isolationist tendencies of new immigrants in two different national contexts, the United States and Canada. She has interviewed Portuguese and Brazilian immigrants in the Somerville-Boston area and testifies to the lack of identity affiliation between the two groups.

37. Waters, *Ethnic Options*. Waters interviewed white, Catholic Americans about both their genealogy and their self-ascribed ethnic identity, thus allowing her to compare the relative impact of both on their sense of social location in the contemporary United States.

Conclusion

1. William James, *The Varieties of Religious Experience* (New York: Penguin, [1902] 1982), p. 47.

2. William H. McNeill, *Keeping Together in Time: Dance and Drill in Human History* (Cambridge, Mass.: Harvard University Press, 1995), p. 2; also Peter L. Berger and Thomas Luckmann, *The Social Construction of Reality: A Treatise on the Sociology of Knowledge* (New York: Anchor Books, 1966), pp. 53–67.

3. Jon M. Kingsdale, "The 'Poor Man's Club': Social Functions of the Urban Working-Class Saloon," *American Quarterly*, vol. 25, no. 4 (1973): 472–478; Roy Rosenzweig, *Eight Hours for What We Will: Workers and Leisure in An Industrial City, 1870–1920* (Cambridge: Cambridge University Press, 1983). Admittedly, nineteenth-century saloons were predominately an all-male affair, though this seems to have been changing in the decades just before Prohibition.

4. Robert Wuthnow, *Sharing the Journey: Support Groups and America's New Quest for Community* (New York: Free Press, 1994), pp. 4, 342.

5. Ibid., especially pp. 349–352.

6. *Oxford English Dictionary*, 3rd ed. (online), entry: "lodge." Variants of *lodge*, such as *aerie, court, encampment,* and *camp* seem to bear similar connotations in the Anglo-American context—that is, protection.

7. On the associational origins of the ideal-typical European city, see Max Weber, "The Occidental City," Guenther Roth and Claus Wittich, eds., *Economy and Society* (Berkeley: University of California Press, 1978); and Charles Tilly, *Coercion, Capital, and European States, A.D. 990–1990* (Cambridge: Blackwell, 1990). London is an exemplary example in this regard; membership in the city's corporate council was traditionally excluded to all except those belonging to the ancient city guilds; see Roy Porter, *London: A Social History* (London: Hamish Hamilton, 1994), especially pp. 244–247. On America's laggard cultural development, see Stuart M. Blumin, *The Emergence of the Middle Class: Social Experience in the American City, 1760–1900* (Cambridge: Cambridge University Press, 1989); Daniel J. Boorstin, *The Americans: The National Experience* (New York: Vintage, 1965); Peter Dobkin Hall, *The Organization of American Culture, 1700–1900: Private Institutions, Elites, and the Origins of American Nationality* (New York: New York University Press, 1982); Russel Blaine Nye, *The Cultural Life of the New Nation, 1776–1830* (New York: Harper & Brothers, 1960).

8. Edna Bonachich and John Modell, *The Economic Basis of Ethnic Solidarity: Small Business in the Japanese American Community* (Berkeley: University of California Press, 1980); Walter Licht, *Getting Work: Philadelphia, 1840–1950* (Cambridge, Mass.: Harvard University Press, 1992); Roger Waldinger, Howard Aldrich, and Robin Ward, eds., *Ethnic Entrepreneurs: Immigrant Business in Industrial Societies* (Newbury Park, Cal.: Sage, 1990); Min Zhou, *Chinatown: The Socioeconomic Potential of an Urban Enclave* (Philadelphia: Temple University Press, 1992).

9. Ira Katznelson, *City Trenches: Urban Politics and the Patterning of Class in the United States* (Chicago: University of Chicago Press, 1982); Ira Katznelson and Aristide R. Zolberg, eds., *Working-Class Formation: Nineteenth-Century Patterns in Western Europe and the United States* (Princeton, N.J.: Princeton University Press, 1986); Gary Marks, *Unions in Politics: Britain, Germany, and the United States in the Nineteenth and Early Twentieth Centuries* (Princeton, N.J.: Princeton University Press, 1989); Daniel T. Rodgers, *Atlantic Crossings: Social Politics in a Progressive Age* (Cambridge: Belknap, 1998); Theda Skocpol, *Protecting Soldiers and Mothers: The Political Origins of Social Policy in the United States* (Cambridge: Belknap, 1992).

10. William H. Sewell, Jr., *Work and Revolution in France: The Language of Labor from the Old Regime to 1848* (Cambridge: Cambridge University Press, 1980); George Steinmetz, *Regulating the Social: The Welfare State and Local Politics in Imperial Germany* (Princeton, N.J.: Princeton University Press, 1993).

11. P. H. J. H. Gosden, *The Friendly Societies in England, 1815–1875* (Manchester: Manchester University Press, 1961); Neil Smelser, *Social Change in the Industrial Revolution: An Application of Theory to the British Cotton Industry* (Chicago: University of Chicago Press, 1959); E. P. Thompson, *The Making of the English Working Class* (London: Victor Gollancz, 1963).

12. Roy Lubove, *The Struggle for Social Security, 1900–1935* (Pittsburgh: University of Pittsburgh Press, 1986); Skocpol, *Protecting Soldiers and Mothers*.

BIBLIOGRAPHY

Abanes, Richard. *American Militias*. Downers Grove, Ill.: InterVarsity Press, 1996.

Abbott, Andrew. *The System of Professions: An Essay on the Division of Expert Labor*. Chicago: University of Chicago Press, 1988.

Alba, Richard D. *Italian Americans: Into the Twilight of Ethnicity*. Upper Saddle River, N.J.: Prentice Hall, 1985.

———. *Ethnic Identity: The Transformation of White America*. New Haven, Conn.: Yale University Press, 1990.

The Albany Directory for the Year 1880. Albany, N.Y.: Sampson, Davenport, 1880.

Alford, Robert R. "Class Voting in the Anglo-American Political Systems." In Seymour Martin Lipset and Stein Rokkan, eds. *Party Systems and Voter Alignments: Cross-National Perspectives*. New York: Free Press, 1967.

Almond, Gabriel A., and Sidney Verba. *The Civic Culture: Political Attitudes and Democracy in Five Nations*. Princeton, N.J.: Princeton University Press, 1963.

Allswang, John M. *Bosses, Machines, and Urban Voters*. Baltimore: Johns Hopkins University Press, [1977] 1986.

Amenta, Edwin, Bruce G. Carruthers, and Yvonne Zylan. "A Hero for the Aged? The Townsend Movement, the Political Mediation Model, and U.S. Old-Age Policy, 1934–1950." *American Journal of Sociology*, vol. 98, no. 2 (September 1992): 308–339.

Amenta, Edwin, and Theda Skocpol. "Taking Exception: Explaining the Distinctiveness of American Public Policies in the Last Century." In Francis G. Castles, ed. *The Comparative History of Public Policy*. Oxford: Polity Press 1989.

American Federation of Labor. *Proceedings, 1887* Bloomington, Ind.: AFL, 1887.

"American Hebrew vs. Hebrew American." *Hebrew American*, March 30, 1894.

Aminzade, Ronald. *Class, Politics, and Early Industrial Capitalism: A Study of Mid-Nineteenth Century Toulouse, France*. Albany: SUNY Press, 1981.

Antenucci, Joseph, Christopher Hugh Ripman, and Kurt Zumwalt. *Armory, First Corps of Cadets, 1887–1973, at the Corner of Arlington Street and Columbus Avenue, Boston, Massachusetts*. Boston: Veteran Association of the First Corps of Cadets, 1973.

Ariel, Yaakov. *Evangelizing the Chosen People: Missions to the Jews in America, 1880–2000*. Chapel Hill: University of North Carolina Press, 2000.

Arnold, Sir Edwin. "Armageddon: A War Song for the Future." In *Edwin Arnold's Poetical Works*, vol. 2. Boston: Roberts Brothers, 1892.

Arnold, Joseph L. "The Neighborhood and City Hall: The Origin of Neighborhood Associations in Baltimore, 1880–1911." *Journal of Urban History*, vol. 6, no. 1 (November 1979): 3–30.

Atherton, Lewis. *Mainstreet on the Middle Border*. Bloomington: Indiana University Press, 1954.

Baernreither, Josef Maria. *English Associations of Working Men*, English ed. London: S. Sonnenschein, 1889.

Baird, Mary MacEachern. Editorial Comment, *Ladies Review*, vol. 25 (March 1919).

"Baltimore German Pythians in Revolt," *New York Times*, December 26, 1894.

Baltzell, E. Digby. *The Protestant Establishment: Aristocracy and Caste in America*. New York: Random House, 1964.

Banfield, Edward C. *The Moral Basis of a Backward Society*. Glencoe, Ill.: Free Press, 1958.

Barber, Benjamin R. "An American Civic Forum: Civil Society Between Market Individuals and the Political Community." *Social Philosophy and Policy*, vol. 13, no. 1 (1996): 269–283.

———. *A Place for Us: How to Make Society Civil and Democracy Strong*. New York: Hill & Wang, 1998.

Barney, Robert Knight. "Knights of Cause and Exercise: German Forty-eighters and Turnvereine in the United States During the Antebellum Period." *Canadian Journal of the History of Sport*, vol. 2 (1982): 62–79.

———. "German-American Turnvereins and Socio-Politico-Economic Realities in the Antebellum and Civil War Upper and Lower South." *Stadion*, vol. 10 (1984): 135–181.

Barr, Andrew. *Drink: A Social History of America*. Carroll & Graf, 1999.

Barton, Josef J. *Peasants and Strangers: Italians, Rumanians, and Slovaks in an American City, 1890–1950*. Cambridge, Mass.: Harvard University Press, 1975.

Basye, Walter. *History and Operation of Fraternal Insurance*. Rochester, N.Y.: Fraternal Monitor, 1919.

Beard, Charles A., and Mary Beard. *The Rise of American Civilization*. New York: Macmillan, 1927.

de Beaumont, Gustave. *Marie, Or Slavery in the United States: A Novel of Jacksonian America*. Barbara Chapman, trans. Stanford, Cal.: Stanford University Press, [1835] 1958.

Beckert, Sven. *The Monied Metropolis: New York City and the Consolidation of the American Bourgeoisie, 1850–1896*. New York: Cambridge University Press, 2001.

Beisel, Nicola. "Class, Culture, and Campaigns Against Vice in Three American Cities, 1872–1892." *American Sociological Review*, vol. 55 (February 1990): 44–62.

Beito, David T. *From Mutual Aid to the Welfare State: Fraternal Societies and Social Services, 1890–1967*. Chapel Hill: University of North Carolina Press, 2000.

Bell, Daniel. *The End of Ideology: On the Exhaustion of Political Ideas in the Fifties*. Glencoe, Ill.: Free Press, 1960.

Bellesiles, Michael A. "The Origins of American Gun Culture in the United States, 1760–1865." *Journal of American History*, vol. 83, no. 2 (September 1996): 425–455.

———. *Arming America: The Origins of a National Gun Culture*. New York: Knopf, 2000.

Bemis, Edward W., ed. *Municipal Monopolies: A Collection of Papers by American Economists and Specialists*. New York: Crowell, 1899.

Beniger, James R. *The Control Revolution: Technological and Economic Origins of the Information Society*. Cambridge, Mass.: Harvard University Press, 1986.

Bennett, Frank P., Jr. *The Story of Mutual Savings Banks*. Boston: Frank P. Bennett, 1924.

Bensel, Richard Franklin. *Sectionalism and American Political Development, 1880–1980*. Madison: University of Wisconsin Press, 1984.

———. *Yankee Leviathan: The Origins of Central State Authority in America, 1859–1877*. Cambridge: Cambridge University Press, 1990.

Benson, Lee. "Group Cohesion and Social and Ideological Conflict." *American Behavioral Scientist*, vol. 16 (1973): 741–767.

Berger, Peter L., and Thomas Luckmann. *The Social Construction of Reality: A Treatise on the Sociology of Knowledge.* New York: Anchor Books, 1966.

Berger, Peter L., and Richard John Neuhaus. *To Empower People: From State to Civil Society,* 20th anniversary ed. Michael Novak, ed. Washington, D.C.: AEI Press, [1977] 1996.

Berkowitz, Edward, and Kim McQuaid. *Creating the Welfare State: The Political Economy of Twentieth Century Reform.* New York: Praeger, 1980.

Bernard, Richard M. *The Melting Pot and the Altar: Marital Assimilation in Early Twentieth-Century Wisconsin.* Minneapolis: University of Minnesota Press, 1980.

Bernstein, Nina. *The Lost Children of Wilder: The Epic Struggle to Change Foster Care.* New York: Pantheon, 2001.

Bining, Arthur Cecil, and Thomas C. Cochran. *The Rise of American Economic Life,* 4th ed. New York: Scribner, 1964.

Blau, Peter M. *Inequality and Heterogeneity: A Primitive Theory of Social Structure.* New York: Free Press, 1977.

Blumin, Stuart M. *The Emergence of the Middle Class: Social Experience in the American City, 1760–1900.* Cambridge: Cambridge University Press, 1989.

Bodfish, H. Morton, ed. *History of Building and Loan in the United States.* Chicago: United States Building and Loan League, 1931.

Bodnar, John. *The Transplanted: A History of Immigrants in Urban America.* Bloomington: University of Indiana Press, 1985.

Bonacich, Edna, and John Modell. *The Economic Basis of Ethnic Solidarity: Small Business in the Japanese American Community.* Berkeley: University of California Press, 1980.

Bonnett, Clarence E. *Employers' Associations in the United States: A Study of Typical Associations.* New York: Macmillan, 1922.

Boorstin, Daniel J. *The Americans: The National Experience.* New York: Vintage, 1965.

Boston Directory Containing the City Record, A Directory of the Citizens, Business Directory, and Street Directory, with Map, No. XCVI, for the Year Commencing July 1, 1900. Boston: Sampson, Murdock, 1900.

Boston Directory . . . for the Year Commencing July 1, 1920. Boston: Sampson & Murdock, 1920.

Boychuk, Terry. *The Making and Meaning of Hospital Policy in the United States and Canada.* Ann Arbor: University of Michigan Press, 1999.

Boyd's Directory of the District of Columbia. Washington, D.C.: William H. Boyd, 1890.

Boyd's Paterson Directory, 1890–1891. N.p.: George S. Boudinot, 1890.

Boyer, Paul S. *Urban Masses and Moral Order in American, 1820–1920.* Cambridge, Mass.: Harvard University Press, 1978.

Boynton, Nathan Smith. "Fraternal Co-Operation: Can It Survive the Assaults Without and the Pressure Within." Paper read at the Meeting of the National Fraternal Congress, Held in Baltimore, Md., *November 15–18, 1898.* Port Huron, Mich.: Riverside Printing, 1898.

Breton, Raymond. "Institutional Completeness of Ethnic Communities and the Personal Relations of Immigrants." *American Journal of Sociology,* vol. 70, no. 2 (September 1964): 193–205.

Bridges, Amy. *A City in the Republic: Antebellum New York and the Origins of Machine Politics.* Cambridge: Cambridge University Press, 1984.

———. *Morning Glories: Municipal Reform in the Southwest.* Princeton, N.J.: Princeton University Press, 1997.

Bridges, Amy, and Richard Kronick. "Writing the Rules to Win the Game: The Middle-Class Regimes of Municipal Reformers." *Urban Affairs Review,* vol. 34, no. 5 (May 1999): 691–706.

Brown, Dorothy M., and Elizabeth McKeown. *The Poor Belong to Us: Catholic Charities and American Welfare.* Cambridge, Mass.: Harvard University Press, 1997.

Brown, M. Craig, and Charles N. Halaby. "Bosses, Reform, and the Socioeconomic Bases of Urban Expenditure, 1890–1940." In Terrence J. McDonald and Sally K. Ward, eds., *The Politics of Urban Fiscal Policy.* Beverly Hills, Cal.: Sage, 1984.

————. "Machine Politics in America, 1870–1945." *Journal of Interdisciplinary History,* vol. 17, no. 3 (Winter 1987): 587–612.

Browne, Henry J. *The Catholic Church and the Knights of Labor.* Washington, D.C.: Catholic University of America Press, 1949.

Brubaker, Rogers. *Citizenship and Nationhood in France and Germany.* Cambridge, Mass.: Harvard University Press, 1992.

Brucker, Gene. "Civic Traditions in Premodern Italy." *Journal of Interdisciplinary History,* vol. 29, no. 3 (1999): 357–377.

Bryce, James. *The American Commonwealth.* London: Macmillan, 1888.

Butler, John Silbey. *Entrepreneurship and Self-Help Among Black Americans: A Reconsideration of Race and Economics.* Albany: SUNY Press, 1991.

Calhoun, George Miller. *Athenian Clubs in Politics and Litigation.* Austin: University of Texas, 1913.

Carnes, Mark C. *Secret Ritual and Manhood in Victorian America.* New Haven, Conn.: Yale University Press, 1989.

Carroll, Glenn R. "Organizational Ecology." *Annual Review of Sociology, vol.* 10 (1984): 71–93.

Castles, Francis G., ed. *The Comparative History of Public Policy.* Cambridge: Polity Press, 1989.

"Casualty and Surety Convention," *Weekly Underwriter,* vol. 99 (December 7, 1918): 846.

Chambers, Marcia. "Female Golfers Shunned After Winning Case." *New York Times,* April 4, 2001 (online ed.).

Chandler, Alfred D., Jr. *Strategy and Structure: Chapters in the History of the Industrial Enterprise.* Cambridge, Mass.: MIT Press, 1962.

Chinese Hospital Association. *1st Annual Report.* Brooklyn, N.Y.: n.p., 1892.

Chronicle of the Union League of Philadelphia, 1862–1902. Philadelphia: Wm. F. Fell, 1902.

Chung, Chi-nien. "Networks and Governance in Trade Associations: AEIC and NELA in the Development of the American Electricity Industry, 1885–1910." *International Journal of Sociology and Social Policy,* vol. 17 (1997): 57–110.

Chung, Chi-nien, and Mark Granovetter. "Trade Associations as an Organizational Form: NELA and the Development of the Early American Electricity Industry." Paper presented at the 1999 Annual Meeting of the American Sociological Association, Chicago, August 6–10, 1999.

Cinel, Dino. *From Italy to San Francisco: The Immigrant Experience.* Stanford, Cal.: Stanford University Press, 1982.

Clark, Terry Nichols, and Lorna Crowley Ferguson. *City Money: Political Processes, Fiscal Strain, and Retrenchment.* New York: Columbia University Press, 1983.

Clawson, Mary Ann. *Constructing Brotherhood: Class, Gender, and Fraternalism.* Princeton, N.J.: Princeton University Press, 1989.

Clemens, Elisabeth S. "Organizational Repertoires and Institutional Change: Women's Groups and the Transformation of U.S. Politics, 1890–1920." *American Journal of Sociology,* vol. 98, no. 4 (January 1993): 755–798.

————. *The People's Lobby: Organizational Innovation and the Rise of Interest Group Politics in the United States, 1890–1925.* Chicago: University of Chicago Press, 1997.

Cohen, Jean L., and Andrew Arato. *Civil Society and Political Theory.* Cambridge, Mass.: MIT Press, 1994.

Cohen, Lizabeth. *Making a New Deal: Industrial Workers in Chicago, 1919–1939* (Cambridge: Cambridge University Press, 1990).

Coleman, James S. "Social Capital in the Creation of Human Capital." *American Journal of Sociology*, vol. 94 (1988): S95–S120.

Commissioner of Labor. *Sixteenth Annual Report of the Commissioner of Labor: Strikes and Lockouts.* Washington, D.C.: Government Printing Office 1901.

"Compulsory Insurance Opposed by Women's Benefit Societies." *National Civic Federation Review*, July 10, 1920.

"Compulsory Sickness Insurance." *National Civic Federation Review*, April 1, 1920.

Conzen, Kathleen Neils. *Immigrant Milwaukee, 1836–1860: Accommodation and Community in a Frontier City.* Cambridge, Mass.: Harvard University Press, 1976.

———. "Germans." In Stephen Thernstrom, ed., *Harvard Encyclopedia of American Ethnic Groups.* Cambridge, Mass.: Harvard University Press, 1980.

Cooper, Jerry. *The Rise of the National Guard: The Evolution of the American Militia, 1865–1920.* Lincoln: University of Nebraska Press, 1997.

Cornelius v. Benevolent Protective Order of the Elks, 382 F. Supp. 1182 (1974).

Coyle, Henry, Theodore Mayhew, and Frank S. Hickey, eds. *Our Church, Her Children and Institutions*, vol. 3. Boston: Angel Guardian Press, 1908.

Cress, Lawrence Delbert. *Citizens in Arms: The Army and the Militia in American Society to the War of 1812.* Chapel Hill: University of North Carolina Press, 1982.

———. "An Armed Community: The Origins and Meaning of the Right to Bear Arms." *Journal of American History*, vol. 71, issue 1 (June 1984): 22–42.

Crompton, Rosemary, ed. *Restructuring Gender Relations and Employment: The Decline of the Male Breadwinner.* Oxford: Oxford University Press, 1999.

Cummings, Scott, ed. *Self-Help in Urban America: Patterns of Minority Economic Development.* Port Washington, N.Y.: Kennikat Press, 1980.

Cunningham, Robert, and Robert M. Cunningham, Jr. *The Blues: A History of the Blue Cross and Blue Shield System.* Dekalb: Northern Illinois University Press, 1997.

Curtis, James, Edward Grabb, and Douglas Baer. "Voluntary Association Membership in Fifteen Countries: A Comparative Analysis," *American Sociological Review*, vol. 57 (1992): 139–152.

Czitrom, Daniel. *Media and the American Mind: From Morse to McLuhan.* Chapel Hill: University of North Carolina Press, 1982.

Dannenbaum, Jed. *Drink and Disorder: Temperance Reform in Cincinnati from the Washingtonian Revival to the WCTU.* Urbana: University of Illinois Press, 1984.

David, Henry. *The History of the Haymarket Affair: A Study in the American Socio-Revolutionary and Labor Movements.* New York: Farrar & Rinehart, 1936.

Davis, Lance E., and Douglass C. North. *Institutional Change and American Economic Growth.* Cambridge: Cambridge University Press, 1971.

Dawkins, Marvin P., and Graham C. Kinloch. *African American Golfers During the Jim Crow Era.* Westport, Conn.: Praeger, 2000.

Derthick, Martha. *The National Guard in Politics.* Cambridge, Mass.: Harvard University Press, 1965.

DiMaggio, Paul J., and Walter W. Powell. "The Iron Cage Revisited: Institutional Isomorphism and Collective Rationality in Organizational Fields." *American Sociological Review*, vol. 48 (1983): 147–160.

Diner, Hasia R. *A Time for Gathering: The Second Migration, 1820–1880.* Baltimore: Johns Hopkins University Press, 1992.

Dinnerstein, Leonard, and David M. Reiners. *Ethnic Americans: A History of Immigration and Assimilation.* New York: Harper & Row, 1982.

Dobbert, Guido Andre. *The Disintegration of an Immigrant Community: The Cincinnati Germans, 1870–1920*. New York: Arno [1965] 1980.

Dobbin, Frank. "The Origins of Private Social Insurance: Public Policy and Fringe Benefits in America, 1920–1950," *American Journal of Sociology*, vol. 97, no. 2 (1992): 1416–1450.

———. *Forging Industrial Policy: The United States, France, and Britain in the Railway Age*. New York: Cambridge University Press, 1994.

Doyle, Don H. "The Social Functions of Voluntary Associations in a Nineteenth-Century American Town." *Social Science History*, vol. 1, no. 3 (Spring 1977): 333–355.

Drake, St. Clair, and Horace R. Cayton. *Black Metropolis: A Study of Negro Life in a Northern City*, rev. ed. New York: Harper & Row, [1945] 1962.

Du Bois, W. E. B. *The Philadelphia Negro*. Millwood, N.Y.: Kraus-Thomson, [1899] 1973.

Duis, Perry. *The Saloon: Public Drinking in Chicago and Boston, 1880–1920*. Urbana: University of Illinois Press, 1983.

Dumenil, Lynn. *Freemasonry and American Culture, 1880–1939*. Princeton, N.J.: Princeton University Press, 1984.

Edmands, Col. Thomas F. "Memorial or Protest to Congress by First Corps Cadets, on the Effect of the Bill Known as 'H.R. 11654, 57th Congress, 1st Session.'" Set A315, Boston University Mugar Library, Department of Special Collections.

Edwards, Bob, Michael W. Foley, and Mario Diani, eds. *Beyond Tocqueville: Civil Society and Social Capital in Comparative Perspective*. Hanover, N.H.: University Press of New England, 2001.

Elfenbein, Jessica I. *Civics, Commerce, and Community: The History of the Greater Washington Board of Trade, 1889–1989*. Dubuque, Iowa: Kendall/Hunt, 1989.

Ellis, Charles Edward. *An Authentic History of the Benevolent and Protective Order of Elks*. Chicago: self-published, 1910.

Emery, George, and J. C. Herbert Emery. *A Young Man's Benefit: The Independent Order of Odd Fellows and Sickness Insurance in the United States and Canada, 1860–1929*. Montreal: McGill-Queen's University Press, 1999.

"Encampment of Pythians." *New York Times*, August 28, 1894.

Ethington, Philip J. *The Public City: The Political Construction of Urban Life in San Francisco, 1850–1900*. Cambridge: Cambridge University Press, 1994.

Etzioni, Amitai, ed. *Rights and the Common Good: The Communitarian Perspective*. New York: St. Martin, 1995.

———, ed. *The Essential Communitarian Reader*. Lanham, Md.: Rowman & Littlefied, 1998.

Fairfield, Francis Gerry. *The Clubs of New York*. New York: Arno, [1873] 1975.

Farrell, James J. *Inventing the American Way of Death, 1830–1920*. Philadelphia: Temple University Press, 1980.

Faust, Albert Bernhardt. *The German Element in the United States*, vol. 2. New York: Steuben Society of America, 1927.

Feldberg, Michael. *The Philadelphia Riots of 1844: A Study of Ethnic Conflict*. Westport, Conn.: Greenwood, 1975.

Ferguson, Charles W. *Fifty Million Brothers: A Panorama of American Lodges and Clubs*. New York: Farrar & Rinehart, 1937.

Finegold, Kenneth. *Experts and Politicians: Reform Challenges to Machine Politics in New York, Cleveland, and Chicago*. Princeton, N.J.: Princeton University Press, 1995.

Fink, Leon. *Workingmen's Democracy: The Knights of Labor and American Politics*. Urbana: University of Illinois Press, 1983.

Finke, Roger, and Rodney Stark. *The Churching of America: Winners and Losers in our Religious Economy.* New Brunswick, N.J.: Rutgers University Press, 1992.

Fischer, Claude S. "The Subcultural Theory of Urbanism: A Twentieth-Year Assessment." *American Journal of Sociology,* vol. 101, no. 3 (1995): 543–577.

Fishman, Joshua A. *Language Loyalty in the United States.* New York: Arno, [1966] 1978.

Flora, Peter, and Arnold J. Heidenheimer, eds. *The Development of Welfare States in Europe and America.* New Brunswick, N.J.: Transaction Books, 1981.

Floud, Roderick. "Britain, 1860–1914: A Survey." In Roderick Floud and Donald McCloskey, eds., *The Economic History of Britain Since 1700, Part 2. 1860 to the 1970s.* Cambridge: Cambridge University Press, 1981.

Fogelson, Robert M. *America's Armories: Architecture, Society, and Public Order.* Cambridge, Mass.: Harvard University Press, 1989.

Foner, Philip S. *History of the Labor Movement in the United States,* vol. 2. New York: International Publishers, 1947.

Forbes, Francis B. "Notes on the Fraternal Beneficiary Corporations Doing Business in Massachusetts." *Publications of the American Statistical Association,* vol. 8, issue 57 (March 1902): 1–29.

Fraternal Monitor, November 1, 1919, pp. 21–23.

Freeman, John, and Michael T. Hannan. "Growth and Decline Processes in Organizations." *American Sociological Review,* vol. 40 (1975): 215–228.

———. "Niche Width and the Dynamics of Organizational Populations." *American Journal of Sociology,* vol. 88 (1983): 1116–1145.

Friedman, Lawrence M. *A History of American Law,* 2nd ed. New York: Simon & Schuster, 1985.

Galambos, Louis. *Competition & Cooperation: The Emergence of a National Trade Association.* Baltimore: Johns Hopkins University Press, 1966.

———. "The Emerging Organizational Synthesis in American History." *Business History Review,* vol. 44 (1970): 279–290.

"Galveston's Government," *Tradesman,* June 15, 1906: 50.

Gamm, Gerald. *Urban Exodus: Why the Jews Left Boston and the Catholics Stayed.* Cambridge, Mass.: Harvard University Press, 1999.

Gamm, Gerald, and Robert D. Putnam. "The Growth of Voluntary Associations in America, 1840–1940." *Journal of Interdisciplinary History,* vol. 29, no. 3 (Winter 1999): 511–557.

Gans, Herbert. *The Urban Villagers: Group and Class in the Life of Italian-Americans.* New York: Free Press, 1962.

———. "Symbolic Ethnicity: The Future of Ethnic Groups and Cultures in America." *Ethnic and Racial Studies,* vol. 2, no. 1 (1979): 9–17.

Garlock, Jonathan. *Guide to the Local Assemblies of the Knights of Labor.* Westport, Conn.: Greenwood, 1982.

Geer's Hartford City Directory and Hartford Illustrated; for the Year Commencing July, 1880. Hartford, Conn.: Elihu Geer, 1880.

Gerteis, Joseph H. "Class and the Color Line: The Sources and Limits of Interracial Class Coalition, 1880–1896." Ph.D. dissertation, Department of Sociology, University of North Carolina, Chapel Hill, 2000.

Gerth, H. H., and C. Wright Mills, eds. *From Max Weber: Essays in Sociology.* New York: Oxford University Press, 1946.

Glazer, Nathan, and Daniel P. Moynihan. *Beyond the Melting Pot,* 2nd ed. Cambridge, Mass.: MIT Press, 1963.

Glazier, Captain Willard. *Peculiarities of American Cities.* Philadelphia: Hubbard Brothers, 1884.

Goldstein, Robert J. *Political Repression in 19th Century Europe.* Totowa, N.J.: Barnes & Noble, 1983.

Gompers, Samuel. *Seventy Years of Life and Labor: An Autobiography of Samuel Gompers.* Nick Salvatore, ed. Ithaca, N.Y.: ILR Press, [1925] 1984.

Gordon, Linda. "Social Insurance and Public Assistance: The Influence of Gender in Welfare Thought in the United States, 1890–1935." *American Historical Review,* vol. 97, no. 1 (1992): 19–54.

Gosden, P. H. J. H. *The Friendly Societies in England, 1815–1875.* Manchester: Manchester University Press, 1961.

Gosnell, Harold F. *Boss Platt and His New York Machine.* Chicago: University of Chicago Press, 1924.

Gould, Roger V. *Insurgent identities: Class, Community, and Protest in Paris from 1848 to the Commune.* Chicago: University of Chicago Press, 1995.

Granovetter, Mark. "Economic Action and Social Structure: The Problem of Embeddedness." *American Journal of Sociology,* vol. 91 (1985): 481–510.

Granovetter, Mark, and Patrick McGuire. "The Making of an Industry: Electricity in the United States." In Michel Callon, ed., *The Law of Markets.* Oxford: Blackwell, 1998, pp. 147–173.

Greenawalt, Kent. "Freedom of Association and Religious Association." In Amy Gutmann, ed., *Freedom of Association.* Princeton, N.J.: Princeton University Press, 1998.

Greene, Victor. *For God and Country: The Rise of Polish and Lithuanian Ethnic Consciousness in America, 1860–1910.* Madison: State Historical Society of Wisconsin, 1975.

Grew, Raymond. "Finding Social Capital: The French Revolution in Italy." *Journal of Interdisciplinary History,* vol. 29, no. 3 (1999): 407–433.

Griffith, Ernest S. *A History of American City Government: The Progressive Years and their Aftermath, 1900–1920.* New York: Praeger, 1974.

Grob, Gerald N. *Workers and Utopia: A Study of Ideological Conflict in the American Labor Movement, 1865–1700.* Chicago: Quadrangle Books 1969.

Gunn, Steven H. "Second Amendment Symposium: A Lawyer's Guide to the Second Amendment." *Brigham Young University Law Review,* vol. 35 (1998): 34–46.

Gusfield, Joseph R. *Symbolic Crusade: Status Politics and the American Temperance Movement.* Urbana: University of Illinois Press, 1963.

Gutmann, Amy, ed. *Freedom of Association.* Princeton: Princeton University Press, 1998.

Gutmann, Amy, and Dennis Thompson. *Democracy and Disagreement.* Cambridge: Belknap, 1996.

Hall, Peter Dobkin. *The Organization of American Culture, 1700–1900: Private Institutions, Elites, and the Origins of American Nationality.* New York: New York University Press, 1982.

———. "A Historical Overview of the Private Nonprofit Sector." In Walter W. Powell, ed., *The Nonprofit Sector: A Research Handbook.* New Haven, Conn.: Yale University Press, 1987.

Halpern, Thomas, and Brian Levin. *The Limits of Dissent: The Constitutional Status of Armed Civilian Militias.* Amherst, Mass.: Aletheia Press, 1996.

Hammack, David C. *Power and Society: Greater New York at the Turn of the Century.* New York: Russell Sage Foundation, 1982.

Hanagan, Michael P. *Nascent Proletarians: Class Formation in Post-Revolutionary France.* New York: Oxford University Press, 1989.

Handlin, Oscar. *The Uprooted.* Boston: Little, Brown, 1951.

Handlin, Oscar, and Mary F. Handlin. "The Origins of the American Business Corporation." *Journal of Economic History,* vol. 5 (1945): 1–23.

————. *Commonwealth: A Study of the Role of Government in the American Economy: Massachusetts, 1774–1861.* New York: New York University Press, 1947.

Hankins, F. H. "Fraternal Orders." *Encyclopedia of the Social Sciences*, vol. 6 (New York: Macmillan, 1935), pp. 424–425.

Hannan, Michael T., and John Freeman. "The Population Ecology of Organizations." *American Journal of Sociology*, vol. 82 (1977): 929–964.

————. *Organizational Ecology.* Cambridge, Mass.: Harvard University Press, 1989.

Hansmann, Henry. *The Ownership of Enterprise.* Cambridge: Belknap, 1996.

Harris, Abram L. *The Negro as Capitalist: A Study of Banking and Business Among American Negroes.* College Park, Md.: McGrath, [1936] 1968.

Hartog, Hendrik. *Public Property and Private Power: The Corporation of the City of New York in American Law, 1730–1870.* Ithaca, N.Y.: Cornell University Press, [1983] 1989.

Hartz, Louis. *Economic Policy and Democratic Thought: Pennsylvania, 1776–1860.* Cambridge, Mass.: Harvard University Press, 1948.

————. *The Liberal Tradition in America: An Interpretation of American Political Thought Since the Revolution.* New York: Harcourt, Brace & World, 1955.

Harwood, W. S. "Secret Societies in America." *North American Review*, vol. 164, no. 486 (May 1897): 617–624.

Hattam, Victoria. "Economic Visions and Political Strategies: American Labor and the State, 1865–1896." *Studies in American Political Development*, vol. 4 (1990): 82–129.

————. *Labor Visions and State Power: The Origins of Business Unionism in the United States.* Princeton, N.J.: Princeton University Press, 1993.

Haveman, Heather A., and Hayagreeva Rao. "Structuring a Theory of Moral Sentiments: Institutional and Organizational Coevolution in the Early Thrift Industry." *American Journal of Sociology*, vol. 102, no. 6 (1997): 1606–1651.

Haven, Charles T., and Frank A. Belden. *A History of the Colt Revolver and Other Arms Made by Colt's Patent Fire Arms Manufacturing Company from 1836 to 1940.* New York: William Morrow, 1940.

Hawthorn, Geoffrey. *Plausible Worlds: Possibility and Understanding in History and the Social Sciences.* Cambridge: Cambridge University Press, 1991.

Hays, Samuel P. *The Response to Industrialism, 1885–1914.* Chicago: University of Chicago Press, 1957.

————. "The Changing Political Structure of the City in Industrial America." *Journal of Urban History*, vol. 1, no. 1 (1974): 6–38.

Hebrew-American, vol. I, no. 1 (March 16, 1894).

Hechter, Michael. "Group Formation and the Cultural Division of Labor." *American Journal of Sociology*, vol. 84, no. 2 (September 1978): 293–318.

————. *Containing Nationalism.* New York: Oxford University Press, 2000.

Heinz, John P., Edward O. Laumann, Robert L. Nelson, and Robert H. Salisbury. *The Hollow Core: Private Interests in National Policy Making.* Cambridge, Mass.: Harvard University Press, 1993.

Henrotin, Ellen M. "The Attitude of Women's Clubs and Associations Toward Social Economics." *Bulletin of the Department of Labor*, no. 23 (July 1899): 501–545.

Herberg, Will. *Protestant—Catholic—Jew: An Essay in American Religious Sociology.* Garden City, N.Y.: Doubleday, 1955.

Hernandez, Jose Amaro. *Mutual Aid for Survival: The Case of the Mexican American.* Malabar, Fla.: Krieger, 1983.

Hickey, Dave. *Air Guitar: Essays on Art and Democracy.* Los Angeles: Art Issues, 1997.

Higham, John. *Strangers in the Land: Patterns of American Nativism, 1860–1925*. New Brunswick, N.J.: Rutgers University Press, 1955.

———. *Send These to Me: Jews and Other Immigrants in American History*. Baltimore: Johns Hopkins University Press, 1984.

Hirschman, Albert O. *Exit, Voice, and Loyalty : Responses to Decline in Firms, Organizations, and States*. Cambridge, Mass.: Harvard University Press, 1970.

———. *Shifting Involvements: Private Interest and Public Action*. Princeton, N.J.: Princeton University Press, 1982.

Hobsbawm, Eric J. *Primitive Rebels: Studies in Archaic Forms of Social Movement in the 19th and 20th Centuries*. New York: Norton, 1959.

Hoffman, Beatrix. *The Wages of Sickness: The Politics of Health Insurance in Progressive America*. Chapel Hill: University of North Carolina Press, 2001.

Hoffman, Frederick L. *Race Traits and Tendencies of the American Negro*. New York: Publications of the American Economic Association, 1896.

———. "Fifty Years of American Life Insurance Progress." *Publications of the American Statistical Association*, vol. 12, issue 95 (September 1911): 667–712.

———. "Autocracy and Paternalism vs. Democracy and Liberty." An address delivered at the Annual Meeting of the International Association of Casualty and Surety Underwriters, New York City, December 4, 1918.

Hofmann, Annette R. "The Turners' Loyality for Their New Home Country: Their Engagement in the American Civil War." *International Journal of the History of Sport*, vol. 12, no. 3 (December 1995): 153–168.

Hofstadter, Richard. *The Age of Reform: From Bryan to F.D.R.* New York: Knopf, 1955.

———. *The Paranoid Style in American Politics and Other Essays*. New York: Vintage Books, 1967.

Hofstadter, Richard, and Seymour Martin Lipset, eds. *Turner and the Sociology of the Frontier*. New York: Basic Books, 1968.

Holbrook's Newark City and Business Directory for the Year Ending April 1, 1883, vol. 48. Newark, N.J.: Holbrooks' Steam Press, 1882.

Hollingsworth, J. Rogers. "The United States." In Raymond Grew, ed., *Crises of Political Development in Europe and the United States*. (Princeton, N.J.: Princeton University Press, 1978).

Horowitz, Donald L., and Gérard Noirel. *Immigrants in Two Democracies: French and American Experience*. New York: New York University Press, 1992.

Horowitz, Morton J. *The Transformation of American Law, 1870–1960: The Crisis of Legal Orthodoxy*. New York: Oxford University Press, 1992.

Hunt, Lynn, and George Sheridan. "Corporatism, Association, and the Language of Labor in France, 1750–1850." *Journal of Modern History*, vol. 58, no. 4 (December 1986): 813–844.

Huntington, Samuel P. *Political Order in Changing Societies* (New Haven, Conn.: Yale University Press, 1968.

"If Not Compulsory Insurance—What?" *National Civic Federation Review*, vol. 14, no. 15 (June 5, 1919).

Ignatiev, Noel. *How the Irish Became White*. New York: Routledge, 1995.

Independent Company of Cadets. *Roll of the Independent Company of Cadets—1814*. Boston: n.p., 1814.

Irving, R. E. M. *The Christian Democratic Parties of Western Europe*. London: Allen & Unwin, 1979.

Jackson, Kenneth T. *The Ku Klux Klan in the City, 1915–1930*. New York: Oxford University Press, 1967.

Jacobson, Matthew Frye. *Whiteness of a Different Color: European Immigrants and the Alchemy of Race.* Cambridge, Mass.: Harvard University Press, 1998.

James, William. *The Varieties of Religious Experience.* Martin E. Marty, ed. New York: Penguin, [1902] 1982.

Jenney, Charles A. *Report on Insurance Business in the United States at the Eleventh Census: 1890, Part II. Life Insurance.* Washington, D.C.: U.S. Government Printing Office, 1895.

Joyce, Michael S., and William A. Schambra. "A New Civic Life." In Michael Novak, ed., *To Empower People: From State to Civil Society,* 2nd ed. Washington, D.C.: AEI Press, 1996.

Karel, Judge John C. "New Blood for a Fraternal Society." *Fraternal Monitor,* November 1, 1919, p. 22.

Katz, Michael B. *In the Shadow of the Poorhouse: A Social History of Welfare in America.* New York: Basic Books, 1986.

Katznelson, Ira. *City Trenches: Urban Politics and the Patterning of Class in the United States.* Chicago: University of Chicago Press, 1982.

Katznelson, Ira, and Aristide R. Zolberg, eds. *Working-Class Formation: Nineteenth-Century Patterns in Western Europe and the United States.* Princeton, N.J.: Princeton University Press, 1986.

Kauffman, Christopher J. *Faith and Fraternalism: The History of the Knights of Columbus,* rev. ed. New York: Simon & Schuster, 1992.

Kaufman, Jason. "Conflicting Conceptions of Individualism in Contemporary American AIDS Policy: A Re-examination of Neo-Institutionalist Analysis." *Theory and Society,* vol. 27, no. 5 (October 1998): 635–669.

Kaufman, Jason. "Three Views of Associationalism in 19th Century America: An Empirical Examination." *American Journal of Sociology,* vol. 104, no. 5 (March 1999): 34–83.

———. "'Americans and Their Guns': Civilian Military Organizations and the Destabilization of American National Security." *Studies in American Political Development,* 15 (Spring 2001): 88–102.

———. "Economic Associations and Interest-Group Formation in American Political Development, 1865–1900." Unpublished paper, Department of Sociology, Harvard University, Cambridge, Mass., Spring 2001.

———. "Rise and Fall of a Nation of Joiners: The Knights of Labor Revisited." *Journal of Interdisciplinary History,* vol. 31, no. 4 (Spring 2001): 553–579.

———. "The Political Economy of Inter-Denominational Competition in Late 19th Century American Cities." *Journal of Urban History* (2002).

Kaufman, Jason, and Steven J. Tepper. "Groups or Gatherings? Sources of Political Engagement in 19th Century American Cities." *Voluntas: International Journal of Voluntary and Nonprofit Organizations,* vol. 10, no. 4 (1999): 299–322.

Kaufman, Jason, and David Weintraub. "The Spatial Distribution of Sectarian Civic Associations: New Evidence on the Geographical Loci of Civic Associational Activity." *Mobilization* (forthcoming).

Keller, Morton. *The Life Insurance Enterprise, 1885–1910: A Study in the Limits of Corporate Power.* Cambridge: Belknap, 1963.

Kerber, Linda K. *No Constitutional Right to Be Ladies: Women and the Obligations of Citizenship.* New York: Hill & Wang, 1998.

Kerr, K. Austin. *Organized for Prohibition: A New History of the Anti-Saloon League.* New Haven, Conn.: Yale University Press, 1985.

Ketcham, Ralph, ed. *The Anti-Federalist Papers and the Constitutional Convention Debates.* New York: Penguin, 1986.

Kindleberger, Charles P. *Manias, Panics, and Crashes: A History of Financial Crises*. New York: Basic Books, 1989.

Kingsdale, Jon M. "The 'Poor Man's Club': Social Functions of the Urban Working-Class Saloon." *American Quarterly*, vol. 25, no. 4 (1973): 472–478.

Kip, Francis De Raismes. *Fraternal Life Insurance in America*. Philadelphia: College Offset Press, 1953.

Kirschbaum, Erik. *The Eradication of German Culture in the United States, 1917–1918*. Stuttgart: Verlag Hans-Deiter Heinz, 1986.

Kleppner, Paul. "From Ethnoreligious Conflict to 'Social Harmony': Coalitional and Party Transformations in the 1890s." In Seymour Martin Lipset, ed., *Emerging Coalitions in American Politics*. San Francisco: Institute for Contemporary Studies, 1978.

———, ed. *The Evolution of American Electoral Systems*. Westport, Conn.: Greenwood, 1981.

Kloss, Heinz. "German-American Language Maintenance Efforts." In Joshua A. Fishman, ed., *Language Loyalty in the United States*. New York: Arno, [1966] 1978.

Knight, Charles Kelley. "The History of Life Insurance in the United States to 1870." Ph.D. dissertation, University of Pennsylvania, Philadelphia, 1920.

Knoke, David. "The Spread of Municipal Reform: Temporal, Spatial, and Social Dynamics." *American Journal of Sociology*, vol. 87, no. 6 (1982): 1314–1339.

Kolko, Gabriel. *The Triumph of Conservatism: A Reinterpretation of American History, 1900–1916*. New York: Free Press of Glencoe, 1963.

Krooss, Herman E., and Martin R. Blyn. *A History of Financial Intermediaries*. New York: Random House, 1971.

The Lakeside Annual Directory of the City of Chicago, 1880. Chicago: Chicago Directory Co., 1880.

Lamont, Michele. *Money, Morals, and Manners: The Culture of the French and American Upper-Middle Class*. Chicago: University of Chicago Press, 1992.

———. *The Dignity of Working Men: Morality and the Boundaries of Race, Class, and Immigration*. Cambridge, Mass.: Harvard University Press, 2000.

Landa, Janet Tai. *Trust, Ethnicity, and Identity: Beyond the New Institutional Economics of Ethnic Trading Networks, Contract Law, and Gift-Exchange*. Ann Arbor: University of Michigan Press, 1994.

Langley's San Francisco Directory for the Year Commencing April, 1880. San Francisco: Francis, Valentine, 1880.

Langley's San Francisco Directory for the Year Commencing May, 1890. San Francisco: Francis, Valentine, 1890.

Lapides, Kenneth, ed. *Marx and Engels on the Trade Unions*. New York: Praeger, 1987.

Larson, Magali Sarfatti. *The Rise of Professionalism*. Berkeley: University of California Press, 1977.

Laslett, John M., and Seymour Martin Lipset, eds. *Failure of a Dream: Essays in the History of American Socialism*. Garden City, N.Y.: Anchor Press, 1974.

Leach, William. *Land of Desire: Merchants, Power, and the Rise of a New American Culture*. New York: Vintage Books, 1993.

Lee, Jennifer. "Entrepreneurship and Business Development Among African Americans, Koreans, and Jews: Exploring Some Structural Differences." In Héctor R. Cordero-Guzmán, Ramón Grosfoguel, and Robert Smith, eds., *Transnational Communities and the Political Economy of New York City in the 1990s*. Philadelphia: Temple University Press, forthcoming.

Lender, Mark Edward, and James Kirby Martin. *Drinking in America: A History*. New York: Free Press, 1982.

Levine, Lawrence W. *Highbrow/Lowbrow: The Emergence of Cultural Hierarchy in America.* Cambridge, Mass.: Harvard University Press, 1988.

Lewis, Sinclair. *Babbitt.* New York: Harcourt, Brace, 1922.

Licht, Walter. *Getting Work: Philadelphia, 1840–1950.* Cambridge, Mass.: Harvard University Press, 1992.

Lichtman, Allan J. "Political Realignment and 'Ethnocultural' Voting in Late Nineteenth Century America." *Journal of Social History,* vol. 16 (1983): 55–83.

Lieberson, Stanley. *A Piece of the Pie: Blacks and White Immigrants Since 1880.* Berkeley: University of California Press, 1980.

———. *A Matter of Taste: How Names, Fashions, and Culture Change.* New Haven, Conn.: Yale University Press, 2000.

Lieberson, Stanley, and Mary C. Waters. *From Many Strands: Ethnic and Racial Groups in Contemporary America.* New York: Russell Sage Foundation, 1988.

Light, Ivan H. *Ethnic Enterprise in America: Business and Welfare among Chinese, Japanese, and Blacks.* Berkeley: University of California Press, 1972.

Light, Ivan H., and Edna Bonacich. *Immigrant Entrepreneurs: Koreans in Los Angeles, 1965–1982.* Berkeley: University of California Press, 1988.

Linder, Douglas O. "Comment: Freedom of Association After *Roberts v. United States Jaycees.*" *Michigan Law Review,* vol. 82 (1984): 1878–1903.

Lineberry, Robert L., and Edmund P. Fowler. "Reformism and Public Policies in American Cities." *American Political Science Review,* vol. 61, no. 3 (September 1967): 701–716.

Linenthal, Arthur J. *First a Dream: The History of Boston's Jewish Hospitals, 1896 to 1928.* Boston: Beth Israel Hospital, 1990.

Lintner, John. *Mutual Savings Banks in the Savings and Mortgage Markets.* Boston: Andover Press, 1948.

Lipset, Seymour Martin. *Political Man: The Social Bases of Politics.* New York: Anchor Books, 1963.

———. *Continental Divide: The Values and Institutions of the United States and Canada.* New York: Routledge, 1990.

———. *American Exceptionalism: A Double-Edged Sword.* New York: Norton, 1996.

Lipset, Seymour Martin and Gary Marks. *It Didn't Happen Here: Why Socialism Failed in the United States.* New York: Norton, 2000.

Lipset, Seymour Martin and Stein Rokkan, eds. *Party Systems and Voter Alignments: Cross-National Perspectives.* New York: Free Press, 1967.

"Liquor Dealers Ruled Out." *Buffalo Evening News,* September 1, 1894.

London, Lena. "The Militia Fine, 1830–1860," *Military Affairs,* vol. 15 (Fall 1951): 133–144.

Lorwin, Lewis L. *The American Federation of Labor: History, Policies, Prospects.* Washington, D.C.: Brookings Institution, 1933.

Lowi, Theodore. *At the Pleasure of the Mayor: Patronage and Power in New York City, 1898–1958.* London: Free Press of Glencoe, Collier-MacMillan, 1964.

Lubove, Roy. *The Professional Altruist: The Emergence of Social Work as a Career, 1880–1930.* Cambridge, Mass.: Harvard University Press, 1965.

———. *The Struggle for Social Security, 1900–1935.* Pittsburgh: University of Pittsburgh Press, 1986.

Lustig, R. Jeffrey. *Corporate Liberalism: The Origins of Modern American Political Theory, 1890–1920.* Berkeley: University of California Press, 1982.

Lyman, Stanford Morris. *Chinatown and Little Tokyo: Power, Conflict, and Community Among Chinese and Japanese Immigrants in America.* Millwood, N.Y.: Associated Faculty Press, 1986.

Lynd, Robert S., and Helen M. Lynd. *Middletown: A Study in American Culture*. New York: Harcourt, Brace, 1956.

Madison, James. "Federalist Paper No. 10." *The Federalist Papers*. Clinton Rossiter, ed. New York: Mentor, [1788] 1961.

Madison Schützenverein. *Constitution, Neben-Gesetz und Regeln des Madison Schuetzenverein*. Madison: Wisconsin Staats-Zeitung, 1895.

Mandelbaum, Seymour. *Boss Tweed's New York*. New York: Wiley, 1965.

Mansbridge, Jane J. *Beyond Adversary Democracy*. Chicago: University of Chicago Press, 1980.

Manza, Jeff, and Clem Brooks. *Social Cleavages and Political Change: Voter Alignments and U.S. Party Coalitions*. New York: Oxford University Press, 1999.

Mark, Noah. "Beyond Individual Differences: Social Differentiation from First Principles." *American Sociological Review*, vol. 63 (1998): 309–330.

Marks, Gary. *Unions in Politics: Britain, Germany, and the United States in the Nineteenth and Early Twentieth Centuries*. Princeton, N.J.: Princeton University Press, 1989.

Massachusetts, First Corps of Cadets. *The One Hundred and Fiftieth Anniversary of the Foundation of the First Corps Cadets, Massachusetts Volunteer Militia, October 19, 1891*. Boston: N. Sawyer, 1892.

Massachusetts Militia, First Division, Independent Company of Cadets. *The Constitution of the Independent Company of Cadets, Attached to the First Division, Mass. Volunteer Militia*. Boston: Franklin Printing House, 1857.

"May Tax Property Worth $300,095,575." *New York Times*, March 22, 1915.

McAdam, Doug. *Political Process and the Development of Black Insurgency, 1930–1970*. Chicago: University of Chicago Press, 1994.

McCormick, Richard L. "Ethno-Cultural Interpretations of Nineteenth Century American Voting Behavior." *Political Science Quarterly*, vol. 89 (1974): 351–377.

McDonald, Terrence J. "San Francisco: Socioeconomic Change, Political Culture, and Fiscal Politics, 1870–1906." In Terrence J. McDonald and Sally K. Ward, eds., *The Politics of Urban Fiscal Policy*. Beverly Hills, Cal.: Sage, 1984.

McGerr, Michael. *The Decline of Popular Politics: The American North, 1865–1928*. New York: Oxford University Press, 1986.

McKeown, Thomas. *The Role of Medicine: Dream, Mirage, or Nemesis?* Princeton, N.J.: Princeton University Press, 1979.

McNeill, William H. *Keeping Together in Time: Dance and Drill in Human History*. Cambridge, Mass.: Harvard University Press, 1995.

McPherson, J. Miller, and James R. Ranger-Moore. "Evolution on a Dancing Landscape: Organizations and Networks in Dynamic Blau Space." *Social Forces*, vol. 70, no. 1 (1991): 19–42.

McSeveney, Samuel T. *The Politics of Depression: Political Behavior in the Northeast, 1893–1896*. New York: Oxford University Press, 1972.

Melendy, Royal L. "The Saloon in Chicago, Part II." *American Journal of Sociology*, vol. 6, no. 4 (1901): 433–464.

"A Menace." *Chicago Tribune*, April 21, 1879.

"Menace of Social Insurance." *Fraternal Monitor*, vol. 30 (November 1, 1919).

Menes, Rebecca. "Public Goods and Private Favors: Patronage Politics in American Cities During the Progressive Era, 1900–1920." PhD. dissertation, Harvard University, Cambridge, Mass., 1996.

Merton, Robert K. "The Latent Functions of the Machine." In *Social Theory and Social Structure*. New York: Free Press, 1968.

Metzner, Henry. *A Brief History of the American Turnerbund.* Theodore Stempfel, Jr., trans. Pittsburgh: National Executive Committee of the American Turnerbund, 1924.

Meyer, B. H. "Fraternal Beneficiary Societies in the United States." *American Journal of Sociology,* vol. 6, no. 5 (March 1901): 646–661.

Meyer, John, and Bryan Rowan. "Institutionalized Organizations: Formal Structure as Myth and Ceremony." *American Journal of Sociology,* vol. 83 (1977): 340–363

"Military Despotism." *Socialist,* March 1, 1879.

Mink, Gwendolyn. *Old Labor and New Immigrants in American Political Development: Union, Party, and State, 1875–1920.* Ithaca, N.Y.: Cornell University Press, 1986.

Minkoff, Debra C. *Organizing for Equality: The Evolution of Women's and Racial-Ethnic Organizations in America, 1955–1985.* New Brunswick, N.J.: Rutgers University Press, 1995.

Misra, Joya, and Alexander Hicks. "Catholicism and Unionization in Affluent Postwar Democracies: Catholicism, Culture, Party, and Unionization." *American Sociological Review,* vol. 59 (1994): 304–326.

Mitchell, B. R. *International Historical Statistics: The Americas and Australasia.* Detroit: Gale Research, 1983.

Modell, John. *The Economics and Politics of Racial Accommodation: The Japanese of Los Angeles, 1900–1942.* Urbana: University of Illinois Press, 1977.

Moehring, Eugene P. *Public Works and the Patterns of Urban Real Estate Growth in Manhattan, 1835–1894.* New York: Arno, 1981.

Mohr, John W. "Soldiers, Mothers, Tramps and Others: Discourse Roles in the 1907 New York City Charity Directory." *Poetics,* vol. 22 (1994): 327–357.

Monkkonen, Eric H. *Police in Urban America, 1860–1920.* Cambridge: Cambridge University Press, 1981.

———. *America Becomes Urban: The Development of U.S. Cities and Towns, 1780–1980.* Berkeley: University of California Press, 1988.

———. *The Local State: Public Money and American Cities.* Stanford, Cal.: Stanford University Press, 1995.

Moore, Deborah Dash. *B'nai B'rith and the Challenge of Ethnic Leadership.* Albany: SUNY Press, 1981.

Moore, R. Laurence. *Religious Outsiders and the Making of Americans.* New York: Oxford University Press, 1986.

———. *Selling God: American Religion in the Marketplace of Culture.* New York: Oxford University Press, 1994.

Moose Lodge No. 107 v. Irvis, 407 U.S. 163 (1972).

Morawska, Eva. *Insecure Prosperity: Small-Town Jews in Industrial America, 1890–1940.* Princeton, N.J.: Princeton University Press, 1996.

Muir, Edward. "The Sources of Civil Society in Italy." *Journal of Interdisciplinary History,* vol. 29, no. 3 (1999): 379–406.

Munro, William Bennett. *The Government of American Cities.* New York: Macmillan, 1916.

Muraskin, William. *Middle-Class Blacks in a White Society: Prince Hall Freemasonry in America.* Berkeley: University of California Press, 1975.

National Golf Foundation (online): <http: www.ngf.org.faq> (August 2000).

Nettl, J. P. "The State as a Conceptual Variable." *World Politics,* 1967–1968, pp. 559–592.

Newman, T. S. *The Story of Friendly Societies and Social Security: Past, Present, Future.* London: Hearts of Oak Benefit Society, 1945.

New York State Club Assn. v. City of New York, 487 U.S. 1 (1988).

Noirel, Gérald. "Difficulties in French Historical Research on Immigration." In Donald L. Horowitz and Gérard Noirel, eds., *Immigrants in Two Democracies: French and American Experience.* New York: New York University Press, 1992.

North, Douglass C. "Capital Accumulation in Life Insurance Between the Civil War and the Investigation of 1905." In William Miller, ed., *Men in Business: Essays on the Historical Role of the Entrepreneur.* Cambridge, Mass.: Harvard University Press, 1952.

————. "The Growth of Government in the United States: An Economic Historian's Perspective." *Journal of Public Economics,* vol. 28 (1985): 383–399.

Numbers, Ronald L. *Almost Persuaded: American Physicians and Compulsory Health Insurance, 1912–1920.* Baltimore: Johns Hopkins University Pres, 1978.

Nye, Russel Blaine. *The Cultural Life of the New Nation, 1776–1830.* New York: Harper & Brothers, 1960.

Ober, Josiah. *Mass and Elite in Democratic Athens: Rhetoric, Ideology, and the Power of the People.* Princeton, N.J.: Princeton University Press, 1989.

O'Connor, Julia S., Ann Shola Orloff, and Sheila Shaver, eds. *States, Markets, Families: Gender, Liberalism, and Social Policy in Australia, Canada, Great Britain, and the United States.* New York: Cambridge University Press, 1999.

O'Dea, John. *History of the Ancient Order of Hibernians and Ladies' Auxiliary.* Notre Dame, Ind.: University of Notre Dame Press, 1995.

Oestreicher, Richard. "Urban Working-Class Political Behavior and Theories of American Electoral Politics, 1870–1940." *Journal of American History,* vol. 74 (1988): 1257–1286.

Olasky, Marvin. *The Tragedy of American Compassion.* Wheaton, Ill.: Crossway Books, 1992.

Oliver, Pamela. "Rewards and Punishments as Selective Incentives for Collective Action: Theoretical Investigations." *American Journal of Sociology,* vol. 85, no. 6 (1980): 1356–1375.

Olson, Mancur. *The Logic of Collective Action.* Cambridge, Mass.: Harvard University Press, 1965.

Olzak, Susan. *The Dynamics of Ethnic Competition and Conflict.* Stanford, Cal.: Stanford University Press, 1992.

Orloff, Ann Shola. "The Political Origins of America's Belated Welfare State." In Margaret Weir, Ann Shola Orloff, and Theda Skocpol, eds., *Politics of Social Policy in the United States.* Princeton, N.J.: Princeton University Press, 1988.

————. *The Politics of Pensions: A Comparative Analysis of Britain, Canada, and the United States, 1880–1940.* Madison: University of Wisconsin Press, 1993.

Palfrey, John Gorham. "A Plea for the Militia System in a Discourse Delivered Before the Ancient and Honorable Artillery Company, on its CXCVIIth anniversary, June 1, 1835." Boston: Dutton & Wentworth, 1835.

Palmer, Edward Nelson. "Negro Secret Societies." *Social Forces,* vol. 23, no. 2 (December 1944): 207–212.

Palmore, Erdman B. "Ethnophaulisms and Ethnocentrism." *American Journal of* Sociology, vol. 67, no. 4. (January 1962): 442–445.

Park, Robert E., and Herbert A. Miller. *Old World Traits Transplanted.* New York: Harper & Brothers, 1921.

Patterson, Orlando. *Ethnic Chauvinism: The Reactionary Impulse.* New York: Stein & Day, 1977.

————. *The Ordeal of Integration: Progress and Resentment in America's "Racial" Crisis.* Washington, D.C.: Civitas, 1997.

Pedersen, Susan. *Family, Dependence, and the Origins of the Welfare State: Britain and France, 1914–1945.* Cambridge: Cambridge University Press, 1993.

Perlman, Selig. "Upheaval and Reorganization (Since 1876)." In John R. Commons, ed., *History of Labour in the United States,* vol. 2. New York: Macmillan, 1926.

Perrow, Charles. "A Society of Organizations." *Theory and Society*, vol. 20 (1991): 725–762.

Peterson, H. C., and Gilbert C. Fite. *Opponents of War, 1917–1918*. Madison: University of Wisconsin Press, 1957.

Peterson, Paul E. *City Limits*. Chicago: University of Chicago Press, 1981.

Pierre Larousse Grand Dictionaire Universel du XIXth Siecle, Vol. I, Deuxieme Partie. Geneve: Slatkine, [1866–1879] 1982.

Pitcavage, Mark. "Ropes of Sand: Territorial Militias, 1801–1812." *Journal of the Early Republic*, vol. 13 (Winter 1993): 481–500.

Popielarz, Pamela A., and J. Miller McPherson. "On the Edge or in Between: Niche Position, Niche Overlap, and the Duration of Voluntary Association Memberships." *American Journal of Sociology*, vol. 101, no. 3 (1995): 698–720.

Porter, Robert P. *Compendium of the 11th Census: 1890*. Washington, D.C.: Government Printing Office 1892.

Porter, Roy. *London: A Social History*. London: Hamish Hamilton, 1994.

Portes, Alejandro, and Patricia Landholt. "The Downside of Social Capital." *American Prospect*, vol. 26 (May–June, 1996): 18–21.

Porzelt, Paul. *The Metropolitan Club of New York*. New York: Rizzoli, 1982.

Post, Louis F., and Fred C. Leubuscher. *Henry George's 1886 Campaign: An Account of the George-Hewitt Campaign in the New York Municipal Election of 1886*. Westport, Conn.: Greenwood, [1887] 1961.

Powderly, Terence V. *Thirty Years of Labor*. New York: A. M. Kelley [1890] 1967.

Powell, Michael. *From Patrician to Professional Elite: The Transformation of the New York City Bar Association*. New York: Russell Sage Foundation, 1988.

Press, Eyal. "Faith-Based Discrimination: The Case of Alicia Pedreira." *New York Times*, April 1, 2001.

Presser v. Illinois, 116 U.S. 2552 (1886).

Pringle, Henry N. *The Lawless Clubs of the United States*. Washington, D.C.: International Reform Federation, 1927.

Putnam, Robert D., with Robert Leonardi and Raffaella Y. Nanetti. *Making Democracy Work: Civic Traditions of Modern Italy*. Princeton, N.J.: Princeton University Press, 1993.

———. "Bowling Alone: America's Declining Social Capital." *Journal of Democracy*, vol. 6 (1995): 65–78.

———. *Bowling Alone: The Collapse and Revival of American Community*. New York: Simon & Schuster, 2000.

Putney, Clifford. "Service Over Secrecy: How Lodge-Style Fraternalism Yielded Popularity to Men's Service Clubs." *Journal of Popular Culture*, vol. 27, no. 1 (Summer 1993): 179–190.

"Pythians Opposed to Liquor Dealers." *New York Times*, September 6, 1894.

"Pythian Supreme Lodge." *Buffalo Evening News*, September 5, 1894.

Ransom, Roger L. *Conflict and Compromise: The Political Economy of Slavery, Emancipation and the American Civil War*. New York: Cambridge University Press, 1989.

Ransom, Roger L., and Richard Sutch. "Tontine Insurance and the Armstrong Investigation: A Case of Stifled Innovation, 1868–1905." *Journal of Economic History*, vol. 47, no. 2 (June 1987): 379–390.

"Revolutionary Forces in Our Midst: Peace with Bolshevist Regime Would Aid Efforts Toward World Revolution—Red Propaganda Active In America—Bolshevism and Socialism Identical." *National Civic Federation Review*, April 1, 1920.

Riker, William H. *Soldiers of the States: The Role of the National Guard in American Democracy*. Washington, D.C.: Public Affairs Press, 1957.

Rueschemeyer, Dietrich, and Theda Skocpol, eds. *States, Social Knowledge, and the Origins of Modern Social Policies.* Princeton, N.J.: Princeton University Press, 1996.

Rice, Bradley Robert. *Progressive Cities: The Commission Government Movement in America, 1901–1920.* Austin: University of Texas Press, 1977.

Rippley, La Vern J. *The German-Americans.* Boston: Twayne Publishers, 1976.

Roberts, Allen E. *Key To Freemasonry's Growth.* Richmond, Va.: Macoy Publishing and Masonic Supply Company, 1969.

Roberts v. Jaycees, 468 U.S. 609 (1984).

Rodgers, Daniel T. *Atlantic Crossings: Social Politics in a Progressive Age.* Cambridge: Belknap, 1998.

Rorabaugh, W. J. *The Alcoholic Republic: An American Tradition.* New York: Oxford University Press, 1979.

Rose, Kenneth D. *American Women and the Repeal of Prohibition.* New York: New York University Press, 1996.

Rosenberg, Charles E. *The Cholera Years: The United States in 1832, 1849, and 1866.* Chicago: University of Chicago Press, 1962.

———. *The Care of Strangers: The Rise of America's Hospital System.* New York: Basic Books, 1987.

Rosenblum, Nancy L. "Compelled Association: Public Standing, Self-Respect, and the Dynamic of Exclusion." In Amy Gutmann, ed., *Freedom of Association.* Princeton, N.J.: Princeton University Press, 1998.

———. *Membership and Morals: The Personal Uses of Pluralism in America.* Princeton, N.J.: Princeton University Press, 1998.

Rosenzweig, Roy. *Eight Hours for What We Will: Workers and Leisure in An Industrial City, 1870–1920.* Cambridge: Cambridge University Press, 1983.

Rosner, David. *A Once Charitable Enterprise: Hospitals and Health Care in Brooklyn and New York, 1885–1915.* Princeton, N.J.: Princeton University Press, 1982.

Rotary International v. Rotary Club of Duarte, 481 U.S. 537 (1987).

Roth, Guenther and Claus Wittich, eds. *Economy and Society.* Berkeley: University of California Press, 1978.

Roy, William G. *Socializing Capital: The Rise of the Large Industrial Corporation in America.* Princeton, N.J.: Princeton University Press, 1997.

Rubinow, I. M. "20,000 Miles Over the Land: A Survey of the Spreading Health Insurance Movement." *Survey,* vol. 37 (March 3, 1917): 631–635.

———. *The Quest for Security.* New York: Holt, 1934.

Rueschmeyer, Dietrich and Theda Skocpol, eds. *States, Social Knowledge, and the Origins of Modern Social Policies.* Princeton, N.J.: Princeton University Press, 1996.

Ryan, Mary P. *Civic Wars: Democracy and Public Life in the American City During the Nineteenth Century.* Berkeley: University of California Press, 1997.

Sachs, Susan. "Immigrants Are Targets of Investment Schemes." *New York Times,* May 15, 2001 (online).

Salamon, Lester M. "Partners in Public Service: The Scope and Theory of Government-Nonprofit Relations." In Walter W. Powell, ed., *The Nonprofit Sector: A Research Handbook.* New Haven, Conn.: Yale University Press, 1987.

Salisbury, Robert H. "An Exchange Theory of Interest Groups." *Midwest Journal of Political Science,* vol. 13, no. 1 (1969): 1–32.

Sanders, Elizabeth. *Roots of Reform: Farmers, Workers, and the American State, 1877–1917.* Chicago: University of Chicago Press, 1999.

Sante, Luc. *Low Life: Lures and Snares of Old New York.* New York: Vintage, 1991.

Sass, Steven A. *The Promise of Private Pensions.* Cambridge, Mass.: Harvard University Press, 1997.

Schiesl, Martin J. *The Politics of Efficiency: Municipal Administration and Reform in America, 1800–1920.* Berkeley: University of California Press, 1977.

Schlesinger, Arthur M. *The Rise of the City, 1878–1898.* New York: Macmillan, 1933.

———. "Biography of a Nation of Joiners." *American Historical Review,* vol. 50, no. 1 (October 1944): 1–25.

———. *The Age of Jackson.* Boston: Little, Brown, 1945.

Schmidt, Alvin J. *Fraternal Organizations.* Westport, Conn.: Greenwood, 1980.

Schneider, Dorothee. *Trade Unions and Community: The German Working Class in New York City, 1870–1900.* Urbana: University of Illinois Press, 1994.

Schneirov, Richard. *Labor and Urban Politics: Class Conflict and the Origins of Modern Liberalism in Chicago, 1864–1897.* Urbana: University of Illinois Press, 1998.

Schudson, Michael. *The Good Citizen: A History of American Civic Life.* New York: Free Press, 1998.

Seavoy, Ronald E. *The Origins of the American Business Corporation, 1784–1855: Broadening the Concept of Public Service During Industrialization.* Westport, Conn.: Greenwood, 1982.

"Sees Era of Peace Ahead: Texas Senator Believes Fraternal Spirit Will Put End to War." *New York Times,* June 26, 1916.

Sennett, Richard. *The Fall of Public Man.* New York: Norton, 1974.

Sewell, Richard H. *Ballots for Freedom: Antislavery Politics in the United States, 1837–1860.* New York: Norton, 1976.

Sewell, William H., Jr. *Work and Revolution in France: The Language of Labor from the Old Regime to 1848.* Cambridge: Cambridge University Press, 1980.

Shalev, Michael, and Walter Korpi. "Working Class Mobilization and American Exceptionalism." *Economic and Industrial Democracy,* vol. 1 (1980): 31–61.

Sharpe, Philip B. *The Rifle in America.* New York: William Morrow, 1938.

Shaw, Stephen J. *The Catholic Parish as a Way-Station of Ethnicity and Americanization: Chicago's Germans and Italians, 1903–1939.* New York: Carlson, 1991.

Shea, John Gilmary. "Puritanism in New England." *American Catholic Quarterly Review,* vol. 9 (January 1884).

Shefter, Martin. "Party and Patronage." *Politics and Society,* vol. 7 (1977): 404–451.

———. "Party, Bureaucracy and Political Change in the United States." In Louis Maisel and Joseph Cooper, eds., *Political Parties: Development and Decay.* Beverly Hills, Cal.: Sage, 1978.

———. "Trade Unions and Political Machines: The Organization and Disorganization of the American Working Class in the Late Nineteenth Century." In Ira Katznelson and Aristide R. Zolberg, eds., *Working-Class Formation: Nineteenth-Century Patterns in Western Europe and the United States.* Princeton, N.J.: Princeton University Press, 1986.

Sholes Directory of the City of Charleston, November 15, 1879. Charleston, S.C.: Walker, Evans & Cogswell, 1879.

"Signs Insurance Bill: Fraternal Societies Privileged to Extend Policies to Children." *New York Times,* April 9, 1918.

Silbey, Joel. *The Transformation of American Politics, 1840–1860.* Englewood Cliffs, N.J.: Prentice Hall, 1967.

Simmel, Georg. "The Secret Society." In *The Sociology of Georg Simmel.* Kurt H. Wolff, trans. New York: Free Press, 1950.

Simon, Linda. *Genuine Reality: A Life of William James.* New York: Harcourt Brace, 1998.

Singh, Jitendra V., and Charles Lumsden. "Theory and Research in Organizational Ecology." *Annual Review of Sociology*, vol. 16 (1990): 161–195.

Sirianni, Carmen, and Lewis Friedland. *Civic Innovation in America: Community Empowerment, Public Policy, and the Movement for Civic Renewal.* Berkeley: University of California Press, 2001.

Skocpol, Theda. *States and Social Revolutions.* Cambridge: Cambridge University Press, 1979.

———. *Protecting Soldiers and Mothers: The Political Origins of Social Policy in the United States.* Cambridge: Belknap, 1992.

———. "The Tocqueville Problem: Civic Engagement in American Democracy." *Social Science History*, vol. 21, no. 4 (Winter 1997): 455–479.

Skocpol, Theda, Marshall Ganz, and Ziad Munson. "A Nation of Organizers: The Institutional Origins of Civic Voluntarism in the United States." *American Political Science Review*, vol. 94, no. 3 (September 2000): 527–546.

Skocpol, Theda, Christopher Howard, Susan Goodrich Lehmann, and Marjorie Abend-Wein. "Women's Associations and the Enactment of Mothers' Pensions in the United States." *American Political Science Review*, vol. 87 (1993): 686–699.

Skowronek, Stephen. *Building a New American State: The Expansion of National Administrative Capacities, 1877–1920.* Cambridge: Cambridge University Press, 1982.

Sloane, David Charles. *The Last Great Necessity: Cemeteries in American History.* Baltimore: Johns Hopkins University Press, 1991.

Smelser, Neil J. *Social Change in the Industrial Revolution: An Application of Theory to the British Cotton Industry.* Chicago: University of Chicago Press, 1959.

Smith, Timothy L. "Religion and Ethnicity in America." *American Historical Review*, vol. 83, no. 5 (1978): 1155–1185.

Sombart, Werner. *Why Is There No Socialism in the United States?* White Plains, N.Y.: M. E. Sharpe, 1976.

Soyer, Daniel. *Jewish Immigrant Associations and American Identity in New York, 1880–1939.* Cambridge, Mass.: Harvard University Press, 1997.

Sparks, Cheryl Logan, and Peter R. Walniuk. "The Enactment of Mothers' Pensions: Civic Mobilization and Agenda Setting or Benefits of the Ballot?" *American Political Science Review*, vol. 89 (1995): 710–720.

Stalson, J. Owen. *Marketing Life Insurance: Its History in America.* Cambridge, Mass.: Harvard University Press, 1942.

Starr, Paul. *The Social Transformation of American Medicine.* New York: Basic Books, 1982.

———. "The Meaning of Privatization." *Yale Law and Policy Review*, vol. 6, no. 6 (1988): 6–41.

Steinmetz, George. *Regulating the Social: The Welfare State and Local Politics in Imperial Germany.* Princeton, N.J.: Princeton University Press, 1993.

Stern, Kenneth S., *A Force Upon the Plain: The American Militia Movement and the Politics of Hate.* New York: Simon & Schuster, 1996.

Stevens, Albert C. *The Cyclopedia of Fraternities.* New York: E. B. Treat, 1907.

Stinchcombe, Arthur L. "Social Structure and Organizations." In James March, ed., *Handbook of Organizations.* New York: Rand McNally, 1965.

———. "The Conditions of Fruitfulness of Theorizing About Mechanisms in Social Science." *Philosophy of the Social Sciences*, vol. 21, no. 3 (September 1991): 385–386.

Stone, I. F. *The Trial of Socrates.* Boston: Little, Brown, 1988.

Suhay, Lisa. "Moose and Elk: Endangered Species?" *New York Times*, N.J. ed., August 29, 1999, sec. 14.

Sullivan, John. "Social Insurance: An Address Delivered by John Sullivan . . . of the Modern Woodmen of America Before the National Fraternal Congress of America, Philadelphia, Pennsylvania, August 28, 1918" (no bibliographic data).

Suttles, Gerald D. *The Social Construction of Communities.* Chicago: University of Chicago Press, 1972.

Tarrow, Sidney. *Power in Movement: Social Movements, Collective Action and Politics.* New York: Cambridge University Press, 1994.

———. "'The Very Excess of Democracy': State Building and Contentious Politics in America." In Anne N. Costain and Andrew S. McFarland, eds., *Social Movements and American Political Institutions.* Lanham, Md.: Rowman & Littlefield, 1998.

Thernstrom, Stephan. *The Other Bostonians: Poverty and Progress in the American Metropolis, 1880–1970.* Cambridge, Mass.: Harvard University Press, 1973.

Thompson, E. P. *The Making of the English Working Class.* London: Victor Gollancz, 1963.

Thompson, Margaret Susan. "Corruption—or Confusion? Lobbying and Congressional Government in the Early Gilded Age." *Congress and the Presidency,* vol. 10, no. 2 (Autumn 1983): 169–193.

Tiebout, Charles M. "A Pure Theory of Local Expenditures." *Journal of Political Economy,* vol. 64 (1956): 416–424.

Tilly, Charles. *From Mobilization to Revolution.* Reading, Pa.: Addison-Wesley, 1978.

———. *Big Structures, Large Processes, Huge Comparisons.* New York: Russell Sage Foundation, 1984.

———. "War Making and State Making as Organized Crime." In Peter B. Evans, Dietrich Rueschemeyer, and Theda Skocpol, eds., *Bringing the State Back In.* Cambridge: Cambridge University Press, 1985.

———. *The Contentious French.* Cambridge, Mass.: Harvard University Press, 1986.

———. *Coercion, Capital, and European States, A.D. 990–1990.* Cambridge: Blackwell, 1990.

———. "Transplanted Networks." In Virginia Yans-McLaughlin, ed., *Immigration Reconsidered: History, Sociology, Politics.* New York: Oxford University Press, 1990, pp. 79–95.

———. "Macrosociology, Past and Future." In Charles Tilly, Jeff Goodwin, and Mustafa Emirbayer, "The Relational Turn in Macrosociology: A Symposium," New School for Social Research Working Paper No. 215 (July 1995), pp. 1–3.

———. *Durable Inequality.* Berkeley: University of California Press, 1998.

de Tocqueville, Alexis. *Democracy in America.* George Lawrence, trans. New York: Harper & Row, [1966] 1988.

Tone, Andrea. *The Business of Benevolence: Industrial Paternalism in Progressive America.* (Ithaca, N.Y.: Cornell University Press, 1997.

Trefethen, James B., and James E. Serven. *Americans and Their Guns: The National Rifle Association Story Through Nearly a Century of Service to the Nation.* Harrisburg, Pa.: Stackpole, 1967.

Trent, W. J., Jr. "Development of Negro Life Insurance Enterprises." Master's thesis, University of Pennsylvania, Philadelphia, 1932.

Trommler, Frank, and Joseph McVeigh, eds. *America and the Germans: An Assessment of a Three-Hundred-Year History, vol. 1, Immigration, Language, Ethnicity.* Philadelphia: University of Pennsylvania Press, 1985.

Truant, Cynthia Maria. *The Rites of Labor: Brothers of Compagnonnage in Old and New Regime France.* Ithaca, N.Y.: Cornell University Press, 1994).

Truman, David B. *The Governmental Process: Political Interests and Public Opinion.* New York: Knopf, 1951.

Turner, Frederick Jackson. *The Frontier in American History.* New York: H. Holt, 1920.

Turner, George Kibbe. "Galveston: A Business Corporation." *McClure's Magazine*, vol. 27, no. 6 (October 1906): 610–620.

Ueberhorst, Horst. "Die Nordamericanischen Turner und Ihr Jahnbild." *Stadion*, vol. 4, no. 1(1978): 358–364.

Ulman, Lloyd. *The Rise of the National Trade Union.* Cambridge, Mass.: Harvard University Press, 1955.

"United in Attack on Health Insurance," *New York Times*, March 20, 1919.

Verba, Sidney, Kay Lehman Schlozman, and Henry E. Brady. *Voice and Equality: Civic Voluntarism in American Politics.* Cambridge, Mass.: Harvard University Press, 1995.

Vichniac, Judith Eisenberg. *The Management of Labor: The British and French Iron and Steel Industries, 1860–1918.* Greenwich, Conn.: JAI Press, 1990.

Vogel, Morris. *The Invention of the Modern Hospital: Boston, 1870–1930.* Chicago: University of Chicago Press, 1980.

The Volunteer, vol. 1, no. 2 (May 1889).

von Hoffman, Alexander. *Local Attachments: The Making of an American Urban Neighborhood, 1850 to 1920.* Baltimore: Johns Hopkins University Press, 1994.

Voss, Kim. "Labor Organization and Class Alliance: Industries, Communities, and the Knights of Labor." *Theory & Society*, vol. 17, no. 3 (May 1988): 329–364.

———. *The Making of American Exceptionalism: The Knights of Labor and Class Formation in the Nineteenth Century.* Ithaca, N.Y.: Cornell University Press, 1994.

———. "The Collapse of a Social Movement: The Interplay of Mobilizing Structures, Framing, and Political Opportunities in the Knights of Labor." In Doug McAdam, John D. McCarthy, and Mayer N. Zald, eds., *Comparative Perspectives on Social Movements: Political Opportunities, Mobilizing Structures and Cultural Framings.* New York: Cambridge University Press, 1996.

Waldinger, Roger. *Still the Promised City? African-Americans and New Immigrants in Postindustrial New York.* Cambridge, Mass.: Harvard University Press, 1996.

Waldinger, Roger, Howard Aldrich, and Robin Ward, eds. *Ethnic Entrepreneurs: Immigrant Business in Industrial Societies.* Newbury Park, Cal.: Sage, 1990.

Walzer, Michael. "On Voluntary Association." In Amy Gutmann, ed., *Freedom of Association.* Princeton, N.J.: Princeton University Press, 1998.

Ware, Norman J. *The Labor Movement in the United States, 1860–1895: A Study in Democracy.* New York: D. Appleton, 1929.

Warner, R. Stephen. "Work in Progress Toward a New Paradigm for the Sociological Study of Religion in the United States." *American Journal of Sociology*, vol. 98, issue 5 (March 1993): 1044–1093.

Warren, Mark E. *Democracy and Association.* Princeton, N.J.: Princeton University Press, 2001.

Washington, Booker T. *The Negro in Business.* Chicago: Afro-Am Press, [1907] 1969.

Waters, Mary C. *Ethnic Options: Choosing Identities in America.* Berkeley: University of California Press, 1990.

———. *Black Identities: West Indian Immigrant Dreams and American Realities.* Cambridge, Mass.: Harvard University Press, 1999.

Weber, Eugen. *Peasants Into Frenchmen: The Modernization of Rural France, 1870–1914.* Stanford, Cal.: Stanford University Press, 1976.

Weber, Max. "Class, Status, and Party." In H. H. Gerth and C. Wright Mills, eds., *From Max Weber: Essays in Sociology.* New York: Oxford University Press, 1946.

———. "The Protestant Sects and the Spirit of Capitalism." In H. H. Gerth and C. Wright

Mills, eds., *From Max Weber: Essays in Sociology*. New York: Oxford University Press, 1946.

———. *Economy and Society*. Guenther Roth and Claus Wittich, eds. Berkeley: University of California Press, 1978.

Weinstein, James. "Organized Business and the City Commission and Manager Movements." *Journal of Southern History*, vol. 29 (February–November 1962): 166–182.

———. *The Corporate Ideal in the Liberal State, 1900–1918*. Boston: Beacon, 1968.

Weir, Margaret, Ann Shola Orloff, and Theda Skocpol, eds. *The Politics of Social Policy in the United States*. Princeton, N.J.: Princeton University Press, 1988.

Weir, Robert E. *Beyond Labor's Veil: The Culture of the Knights of Labor*. University Park: Pennsylvania State University Press, 1988.

Weisser, Michael R. *A Brotherhood of Memory: Jewish Landsmanshaftn in the New World*. New York: Basic Books, 1985.

Weld, Louis Dwight Harvell. "Social and Economic Survey of a Community in the Red River Valley." University of Minnesota, Current Problems No. 4 (January 1915): 74–75.

West, Darrell M., and Burdett A. Loomis. *The Sound of Money: How Political Interests Get What They Want*. New York: Norton, 1999.

Western, Bruce. *Between Class and Market: Postwar Unionization in the Capitalist Democracies*. Princeton, N.J.: Princeton University Press, 1997.

Whaples, Robert, and David Buffum. "Fraternalism, Paternalism, the Family, and the Market: Insurance a Century Ago." *Social Science History*, vol. 15, no. 1 (Spring 1991): 97–122.

Wheelock, Edgar Taylor. *The Declaration of Fraternalism*. Chicago: Eidson [sic] Publishing, 1919.

White, Harrison C. *Identity and Control: A Structural Theory of Social Action*. Princeton, N.J.: Princeton University Press, 1992.

"Why That Exemption?" *New York Times*, March 24, 1915.

Wiebe, Robert H. *The Search for Order, 1877–1920*. New York: Hill & Wang, 1967.

Wilentz, Sean. *Chants Democratic: New York City and the Rise of the American Working Class, 1788–1850*. New York: Oxford University Press, 1984.

———. "Against Exceptionalism: Class Consciousness and the American Labor Movement, 1790–1920." *International Labor and Working Class History*, vol. 26 (1984): 1–24.

Williams, C. Arthur. "Governing Cities by Commission," *World To-Day*, vol. 11 (September 1906): 945.

Williamson, Oliver E. *The Economic Institutions of Capitalism: Firms, Markets, and Relational Contracting*. New York: Free Press, 1985.

Wilmshurst, Walter Leslie. *The Meaning of Masonry*. London: W. Rider & Son, 1922.

Wilson, James Q. "The Rise of the Bureaucratic State." *Public Interest*, vol. 41 (Fall 1975): 88–89.

Winston, Diane. *Red-Hot and Righteous: The Urban Religion of the Salvation Army*. Cambridge, Mass.: Harvard University Press, 1999.

Woloch, Isser. *The New Regime: Transformations of the French Civic Order, 1789–1820s*. New York: Norton, 1994.

Woodward, C. Vann. *The Strange Career of Jim Crow*, 3rd rev. ed. New York: Oxford University Press, 1974.

Wright, James E. "The Ethnocultural Model of Voting: A Behavioral and Historial Critique." *American Behavioral Scientist*, vol. 16 (1973): 653–674.

Wuthnow, Robert. "The Voluntary Sector: Legacy of the Past, Hope for the Future?" In Robert Wuthnow, ed., *Between States and Markets: The Voluntary Sector in Comparative Perspective*. Princeton, N.J.: Princeton University Press, 1991.

————. *Sharing the Journey: Support Groups and America's New Quest for Community*. New York: Free Press, 1994.

Yans-McLaughlin, Virginia, ed. *Immigration Reconsidered: History, Sociology, and Politics*. New York: Oxford University Press, 1990.

Yearley, C. K. *The Money Machines: The Breakdown and Reform of Governmental and Party Finance in the North, 1860–1920*. Albany: SUNY Press, 1970.

"You Don't Have to Die to Win." Printed broadside, Baltimore, Md., October 20, 1884. In *An American Time Capsule: Three Centuries of Broadsides and Other Printed Ephemera* (online): HTTP://hdl.loc.gov/loc.rbc/rbpe.03103100 (May 10, 2001).

Young, Michael P. "Confessional Protest: The Evangelical Origins of Social Movements in the United States, 1800–1840." PhD. dissertation, Department of Sociology, New York University, New York, 2000.

Zieber, Eugene, ed. *Ancestry: The Objects of the Hereditary Societies and Military and Naval Orders of the United States*. Philadelphia: Bailey, Banks & Biddle, 1895.

Zelizer, Viviana A. Rotman. *Morals and Markets: The Development of Life Insurance in the United States*. New York: Columbia University Press, 1979.

Zhou, Min. *Chinatown: The Socioeconomic Potential of an Urban Enclave*. Philadelphia: Temple University Press, 1992.

Zunz, Oliver. *The Changing Face of Inequality: Urbanization, Industrial Development, and Immigrants in Detroit, 1880–1920*. Chicago: University of Chicago Press, 1982.

INDEX

weakening of labor movement as, 10,
97, 101–19, 122, 142, 163
Populism, 34, 88, 118, 126, 142, 197
Powderly, Terence, 109–13, 118
Presser v. Illinois, 134–36
Prince Hall Masonry, 27, 79
private police forces, 134, 136
professional organizations, 23, 38, 86,
93–94, 148, 156, 198
Professional Organizations in Boston,
1850–1940 (Figure 4.2), 94
Prohibition, 174–75, 194
Putnam, Robert, 4, 43, 75, 78, 163

Race Segregation in Boston Fraternal
Lodges, 1900 (Figure 1.1), 19
Racial Protectionism. *See* self-
segregation
Relationship between Occupational
and Fraternal Organizations and
Social Welfare Policy Outcomes,
Circa 1890–1930 (Table 7.1),
147
Religious Associations in Boston, 1850–
1940 (Figure 3.3), 71
Republican Party, 92, 113, 132, 142,
234n30
Resolutions Adopted by the National
Fraternal Congress of America at
Philadelphia, August 28, 1918,
Opposing Social Insurance (Figure
7.1), 155
rituals of associationalism, 9, 46–47,
104, 109–11, 113, 121, 133, 175,
189
Rotary International, 18, 164
Royal Templars of Temperance, 58

Schlesinger, Arthur M., 3–4, 6, 9
Second Amendment, 23, 122–24, 135–
36
sectarianism, 8–9, 28–29, 58–82, 107,
158–59, 175–77, 178–92
elite groups and, 83, 91–93, 98–99,
102, 133–34, 142, 147, 154
exclusion and, 9, 27–28, 58–59, 73,
106, 127, 176, 195–96

Factors Shaping the Ascription and
Adoption of Sectarian Social
Identities in Late Nineteenth-
Century American Cities (Table
3.1), 66
race and gender exclusion and, 9, 18,
27–28, 69, 78, 152, 176, 183–85,
188
self-segregation and, 8, 18, 24, 28–29,
58–59, 73–78, 80, 158, 161, 178–80,
183–86, 194–96
Security Benefit Association, 174–76
self-segregation, 8, 18, 24, 29, 58–59, 73–
78, 80, 158, 161, 178–80, 183–86
194–96
separatism. *See* sectarianism
service or luncheon clubs, 21, 164–65
Sex Segregation in Boston Fraternal
Lodges, 1900 (Figure 1.2), 19
Sheppard, Morris, 151–52
Sheppard-Towner Infancy and
Maternity Protection Act, 152
Six Companies. *See* Chinese
Consolidated Benevolent
Association
Skocpol, Theda, 4, 12, 78, 88, 98, 146–48
social capital, 4–5, 163, 180, 186–88,
192, 194
social identity construction, 67, 70, 161,
175, 177, 178–81, 190–92, 194,
213n34, 219n43
Factors Shaping the Ascription and
Adoption of Sectarian Social
Identities in Late Nineteenth-
Century American Cities (Table
3.1), 66
social insurance, 29, 84, 97, 144–60,
161–77, 194
vs. commercial insurance, 38, 48–50,
144, 148, 156, 161–77
compulsory insurance and, 144–60,
197
employer benefit plans and, 148, 174
European policies for, 8, 53–54, 145,
153–55, 197
as maternalism, 82, 95, 146, 152, 163
Social Security, 47